The Correspondence of Pope Julius I

THE LIBRARY OF EARLY CHRISTIANITY

An imaginary portrait of Julius I from Bartolomeo Platina's *Delle Vite de' Pontefici* (Venice, 1666), woodcut, p. 74. Reproduced courtesy of Rare Books and Special Collections, The Catholic University of America.

THE LIBRARY OF EARLY CHRISTIANITY

VOLUME 3

The Correspondence of Pope Julius I

Greek and Latin text and
English translation with introduction
and commentary by

GLEN L. THOMPSON

The Catholic University of America Press
Washington, D.C.

The paper used in this publication meets the minimum requirements of American National Standards for Information Science—Permanence of Paper for Printed Library Materials, ANSI Z39.48–1984.
∞
Designed and typeset by Kachergis Book Design;
Printed by Sheridan Books

Library of Congress Cataloging-in-Publication Data
Catholic Church. Pope (337–352 : Julius I)
[Correspondence. Selections. English]
The correspondence of Pope Julius I : Greek and Latin text and English translation / with introduction and commentary by Glen L. Thompson.
pages cm. — (The library of early Christianity ; Volume III)
Includes bibliographical references and index.
ISBN 978-0-8132-2707-8 (cloth : alk. paper)
1. Julius I, Pope, –352—Correspondence. I. Julius I, Pope, –352. II. Thompson, Glen L., translator. III. Title.
BX1036.A4 2015
282.092—dc23 2014035019

CONTENTS

Contents

ACKNOWLEDGMENTS

John F. Petruccione, Editorial Director of the Library of Early Christianity

I am very grateful to Professor Glen L. Thompson for choosing the LEC for his edition and translation of the correspondence of Pope Julius I. Due to the scarcity of time and resources, the process of editing has lasted several years, during which Prof. Thompson has demonstrated the patience of Job. I can only hope that the accuracy of the contents and the printing will show that the long wait has not been time wasted. During two academic years (2008–09 and 2009–10), my principal research assistant, Mr. Brent Gilbert, verified all the citations of primary and secondary sources. In consulting sources in Armenian and Syriac, he received the assistance of Dr. Monica Blanchard, Librarian of the Institute for Christian Oriental Research of the Catholic University of America. Midway through the editing, Mr. Stephen Beck helped proofread the volume and organized the manuscript for review by Prof. Thompson. In preparation for copy-editing, Mr. Gilbert proofread the entire volume and adjusted the layout. His philological acumen, historical knowledge, and attention to the details of orthography and usage have very much improved every aspect of this volume. Our copy-editor, Dr. Joel Kalvesmaki, has much improved the consistency of our usage, but more importantly, he has saved us from many errors that had escaped our re-readings. We have been fortunate to be able to avail ourselves of the services of such a careful and sharpsighted scholar/editor.

The LEC owes its existence to a challenge grant from the National Endowment for the Humanities. Many generous patrons, individuals and foundations, contributed toward the matching funds. I wish once more to express my particular gratitude to my professional colleagues, the members of the North American Patristic Society who supported the series from concept to realization. I hope they will continue to regard the LEC as a venture in which they have a personal stake.

Glen L. Thompson

I began work on the early papal correspondence in 1986 as a doctoral candidate under the direction of Professor Roger Bagnall at Columbia University. The completed dissertation, accepted in 1990, contained manuscript lists and sample texts. It also included historical accounts of all the fourth-century Roman bishops from Julius through Anastasius. Thus, it represented the first step toward the completion of this volume and of those that will contain the correspondence of Julius' successors.

In the intervening years, I have accumulated debts to various scholars, institutions, and libraries. While I cannot remember all who have assisted me, I must give thanks to some. I am grateful to Prof. Bagnall for his patient help and encouragement. Robert Somerville, Roger Reynolds, and the late Hubert Mordek deserve special mention for instructing me in the intricacies of medieval canon law manuscripts. Mark Clark, John Roth, Jean-Jacques Aubert, and Brian Matz assisted in reviewing the Latin and Greek texts and translations. Richard Balge, Paul Prange, Adam Gawel, Aaron West, Aaron Jensen, and Jacob Behnken reviewed parts of the manuscript at various stages. The late Leonard Boyle and many other librarians allowed me access to their manuscripts and other resources. The librarians of the Vatican Microfilm Collection at St. Louis University, the Hill Museum and Manuscript Library at St. John's University (Collegeville, Minn.), and the Marquette University Library were ever helpful and cheerful in accommodating my many needs. I am especially grateful to the Wisconsin Lutheran College

Library. The administrators and my colleagues at Michigan Lutheran Seminary, Martin Luther College, Wisconsin Lutheran College, and Asia Lutheran Seminary supported and encouraged me during this long project. Support from The Fischer Family Foundation enabled me to put the final touches on the manuscript. My wife, Beth, also deserves special mention for being the widow-tourist while I sat in dozens of European libraries. *Soli Deo Gloria!*

ABBREVIATIONS

BIBLICAL BOOKS

OT	Old Testament
Gn	Genesis
Ex	Exodus
Lv	Leviticus
Nm	Numbers
Dt	Deuteronomy
Jos	Joshua
Jgs	Judges
Ru	Ruth
1–2Sm	The first and second books of Samuel
1–2Kgs	The first and second books of Kings
1–2Chr	The first and second books of Chronicles
Ezr	Ezra
Neh	Nehemiah
Tb	Tobit
Est	Esther
Jdt	Judith
1–2Mc	The first and second books of Maccabees
Jb	Job
Ps(s)	Psalms
Prv	Proverbs
Eccl	Ecclesiastes
Song	Canticle of Canticles, Song of Songs
Wis	Wisdom of Solomon
Sir	Wisdom of Jesus ben Sirach, Ecclesiasticus

Abbreviations

Is	Isaiah
Jer	Jeremiah
Lam	Lamentations
Bar	Baruch
Ezek	Ezekiel
Dn	Daniel
Hos	Hosea
Jl	Joel
Am	Amos
Ob	Obadiah
Jon	Jonah
Mi	Micah
Na	Nahum
Hab	Habakkuk
Zep	Zephaniah
Hag	Haggai
Zec	Zechariah
Mal	Malachi
NT	New Testament
Mt	Matthew
Mk	Mark
Lk	Luke
Jn	John
Acts	Acts
Rom	The Epistle to the Romans
1–2Cor	The first and second Epistles to the Corinthians
Gal	The Epistle to the Galatians
Eph	The Epistle to the Ephesians
Phil	The Epistle to the Philippians
Col	The Epistle to the Colossians
1–2Thes	The first and second Epistles to the Thessalonians
1–2Tm	The first and second Epistles to Timothy

Abbreviations

Ti	The Epistle to Titus
Phlm	The Epistle to Philemon
Heb	The Epistle to the Hebrews
Jas	The Epistle of St. James
1–2Pt	The first and second Epistles of St. Peter
1–3Jn	The first through third Epistles of St. John
Jude	The Epistle of St. Jude
Rv	Apocalypse, Revelation

ANCIENT AUTHORS AND WORKS

Ad ath.	Iuln., *epistula ad athenienses*
Ad don.	Aug., *Ad donatistas post collationem* (*CPL* #338)
Adu. apol. Iul.	Seu. ant., *Aduersus apologiam Iuliani* (in Syriac; *CPG* #7030)
Alex.	Alexander alexandrinus
Amm.	Ammianus Marcellinus
Anac.	Epiph., *Anacephalaeoses*
Anast. S.	Anastasius Sinaita
Anc.	Epiph., *Ancoratus*
Apol. Const.	Ath., *Apologia ad Constantium*
Apol. xii cap.	Cyr., *Apologia xii capitulorum contra orientales* or *De recta fide ad reginas* (*CPG* #5221)
Apoll.	Leont. Byz., *Aduersus fraudes apollinaristarum* (*CPG* #6817)
Apol. phil.	Seu. ant., *Apologia philalethis* (in Syriac; *CPG* #7031)
Apol. sec.	Ath., *Apologia secunda* or *Apologia contra arianos*
Ar. 1–3	Ath., *Orationes III contra arianos*
Arcad.	Cyr., *De recta fide ad Arcadiam et Marinam*
Aster.	Marcell., *Contra Asterium*
Ast. Soph.	Asterius Sophista
Ath.	Athanasius alexandrinus
Att.	Cic., *epistulae ad Atticum*

Abbreviations

Aug.	Augustinus hipponensis
Auel. coll.	*Auellana collectio*
Bap.	Aug., *Liber de unico baptismo*
Bas.	Basilius caesariensis Cappadociae
Bibl.	Phot. constan., *Bibliotheca*
Breu. coll. don.	Aug., *Breuiculus collationis cum donatistis* (*CPL* #337)
Cass.	Cassiodorus Senator
Cassian.	Iohannes Cassianus
Cens.	Seu. ant., *Censura tomi Iuliani* (in Syriac; *CPG* #7027)
Chron.	Hier., *Chronicon* and Mich. Syr., *Chronicle*
Chrys.	Iohannes Chrysostomus
Cic.	Marcus Tullius Cicero
C. nic.	*Concilium nicaenum*
Cod. theod.	*Codex theodosianus*
Conc. antioch.	*Concilium antiochenum* (*ca.* 324)
Constan.	Tim. II al., *epistula ad constantinopolitanum* (*CPG* #5476)
Const. apost.	*Constitutiones apostolicae*
Contra eos	Tim. II al., *Contra eos qui dicunt duas naturas* (in Armenian; *CPG* #5475)
Cypr.	Cyprianus carthaginiensis
Cyr.	Cyrillus alexandrinus
Decr.	Ath., *De decretis nicaenae synodi*
Dion.	Ath., *De sententia Dionysii*
Disc. eccl.	Reg. Prum., *Libri duo de synodalibus causis et disciplinis ecclesiasticis*
Doct. patr.	Anast. S. (?), *De doctrina patrum* (*CPG* #7781)
Eccl. off.	Isid., *De ecclesiasticis officiis*
ep. ad Hom.	Tim. ber., *epistula ad Homonium episcopum* (*CPG* #3723)
ep. Aeg. Lib.	Ath., *epistula ad episcopos Aegypti et Libyae* (*CPG* #2092)

Abbreviations

ep. Alex.	Arius, *epistula ad Alexandrum alexandrinum*
ep. encycl.	*epistula encyclica*
Epiph.	Epiphanius constantiensis (Epiphanius of Salamis)
ep. mort. Ar.	Ath., *epistula ad Serapionem de morte Arii*
ep(p).	*epistula(e)*
epp. festt.	Ath., *epistulae festales* (in Syriac; *CPG* #2102)
ep. syn.	Conc. antioch., *epistula synodica* (in Syriac; *CPG* #8509)
E. th.	Eus., *De ecclesiastica theologia*
Etym.	Isid., *Etymologiarum libri xx*
Euag. Schol.	Euagrius Scholasticus
Eus.	Eusebius caesariensis
Exp. fid.	Epiph., *Expositio fidei*
frag(g).	*fragmentum* (*-ta*)
fragg. histt.	Hil., *Ex opere historico fragmenta*
Fug.	Ath., *Apologia de fuga sua*
Gennad.	Gennadius Presbyter
Gram.	Seu. ant., *Liber contra impium grammaticum* (in Syriac; *CPG* #7024)
Gr. naz.	Gregorius nazianzenus
Haer.	Epiph., *Panarion* or *Aduersus lxxx haereses*
Haer. com.	Thdt., *Haereticarum fabularum compendium*
H. ar.	Ath., *Historia arianorum ad monachos*
H. e.	*Historia ecclesiastica*
Hier.	Hieronymus Presbyter (Jerome)
Hil.	Hilarius pictauiensis (Hilary of Poitiers)
Hist. aceph.	*Historia acephala*
Hist. trip.	Cass., *Historia ecclesiastica tripartita*
Hom. in Heb.	Chrys., *Homiliae in epistulam ad hebraeos*
Hom. in Ioh.	Chrys., *Homiliae in Iohannem*
Incarn.	Cassian., *De incarnatione Domini contra Nestorium, libri VII*

Abbreviations

in Gal.	Hier., *Commentarii in epistulam Pauli apostoli ad Galatas*
Io. nic.	Iohannes nicaenus
Isid.	Isidorus hispalensis (Isidore of Seville)
Itin. Ant.	*Itinerarium prouinciarum Antonini augusti*
Iul.	Iulius romanus (Pope Julius I)
Iuln.	Iulianus Imperator (Julian)
Iustn.	Iustinianus Imperator (Justinian)
Leont. Byz.	Leontius Byzantinus
Leont. H.	Leontius Hierosolymitanus (Leontius of Jerusalem)
Lib.	Libanius
Lib. Con.	Sev. Ibn al-Muqaffaʿ, *Liber Conciliorum Refutation of Saʿīd Ibn-Batriq* (*Eutyches*)
L. P.	*Liber pontificalis*
M. Agap.	*Martyrium Agapae, Irenae, et Chionae*
Marcell.	Marcellus ancyranus
Marcell.	Eus., *Contra Marcellum*
Mens.	Epiph., *De mensuris et ponderibus*
Mich. Syr.	Michael Syrus
Monach.	Philox., *epistula ad monachos in Senum*
Monoph.	Iustn., *Tractatus contra monophysitas* and Leont. H., *Contra monophysitas*
M. P.	Eus., *De martyribus Palestinae*
Natiu.	Ioh. nic., *De natiuitate domini*
Nephal.	Seu. ant., *Orationes ad Nephalium* (in Syriac; *CPG* #7022)
Niceph.	Nicephorus Callistus Xanthopulus
Optat.	Optatus mileuitanus
or(*r*).	*oratio* (*-iones*)
Or. syn. serd.	*Oratio synodi serdicensis ad Constantium imperatorem*
Parm.	Optat., *Contra Parmenianum donatistam*
Petil.	Aug., *Contra litteras Petiliani libri tres*

Abbreviations

Philost.	Philostorgius
Philox.	Philoxenus hierapolitanus (Philoxenus of Mabbug)
Phot. constan.	Photius constantinopolitanus
praef.	*praefatio*
Priscill.	Priscillianus abilensis (Priscillian of Ávila)
Ref. syn.	Tim. II al., *Refutatio synodi chalcedonensis et tomi Leonis* (in Syriac; *CPG* #5482)
Reg. Prum.	Regino Prumiensis
Ruf.	Rufinus
Ruf.	Hier., *Aduersus Rufinum libri III*
Serg. gram.	Seu. ant., *ep. ad Sergium grammaticum* (in Syriac: *CPG* #7025)
Seu. ant.	Seuerus antiochenus
Sev. Ibn al-Muqaffaʿ	Severus Ibn al-Muqaffaʿ
Socr.	Socrates Scholasticus
Soz.	Sozomenus
Symb. nic. (325)	*Symbolum synodi nicaenae*
Symb. rom.	*Symbolum romanum*
Syn.	Ath., *epistula de synodis Arimini et Seleuciae* and Hil., *De synodis*
Syn. uet.	*Synodicon uetus*
Tab. peut.	*Tabula peutingeriana*
Thdt.	Theodoretus cyrrhensis
Tim. ber.	Timotheus berytensis
Tim. II al.	Timotheos II alexandrinus (Timothy Aelurus)
Tom.	Ath., *Tomus ad antiochenos*
tract.	*tractatus*
V. C.	Eus., *De uita Constantini*
Vir. ill.	*De uiris illustribus*
Zach. Mit.	Zacharias Mitylenensis Rhetor

Abbreviations

MODERN EDITIONS, SERIES, PERIODICALS, AND REFERENCE WORKS

ABAW.PPH	*Abhandlungen der (k.) bayerischen Akademie der Wissenschaften, Philosophisch-philologische und historische Klasse*
ABla	*Analekta Blatadon*
ACO	Schwartz, E., *Acta conciliorum oecumenicorum*
ACW	Ancient Christian Writers
ADB	*Allgemeine deutsche Biographie*
AGWG.PH	*Abhandlungen der Gesellschaft der Wissenschaften zu Göttingen, philologisch-historische Klasse, ns*
AKG	Arbeiten zur Kirchengeschichte
Ant.	*Antiquitas*
Apoll.	*Apollinaris. Commentarius juris canonici*
Arte	*L'arte, Rivista di storia dell'arte*
AST	*Analecta sacra tarraconensia*
BAB	*Bulletin de l'Académie royale de Belgique, Classe des lettres et des sciences morales et politiques*
BEFAR	*Bibliothèque des écoles françaises d'Athènes et de Rome*
BGDS(H)	*Beiträge zur Geschichte der deutschen Sprache und Literatur* (Halle)
BNP.A	*Brill's New Pauly, Antiquity*
BVP	Bibliotheca veterum patrum antiquorum scriptorum ecclesiasticorum
Byz.	*Byzantion*
ByzZ	*Byzantinische Zeitschrift*
CCaHi	Colección canónica hispana
CCEH	Collectio canonum ecclesiae hispanae
CChr.SL	Corpus Christianorum: Series latina
CE	*The Catholic Encyclopedia* (New York 1907–12)
CFHB.W	Corpus fontium historiae Byzantinae, Series washingtoniensis

Abbreviations

CHaer	*Corpus haereseologicum*
CLA	*Codices latini antiquiores,* ed. E.A. Lowe
CLA, Sup.	"Selected Supplementary Bibliography for C.L.A., I–XI" in *CLA, Supplement*
Clavis	Fowler-Magerl, L., *Clavis canonum*
CLCIC	Commentarium lovaniense in codicem iuris canonici
Comm. hum. Litt.	*Commentationes humanarum Litterarum*
Coustant	Coustant, P., *Epistolae romanorum pontificum,* vol. 1
CPG	*Clavis patrum graecorum*
CPL	*Clavis patrum latinorum*
CSCO	Corpus scriptorum christianorum orientalium
CSEL	Corpus scriptorum ecclesiasticorum latinorum
DACL	*Dictionnaire d'archéologie chrétienne et de liturgie*
DGMFT	*Dissertationes ad gradum magistri in facultate theologica vel in facultate iuris canonici consequendum conscriptae, Universitas catholica lovaniensis*
DHGE	*Dictionnaire d'histoire et de géographie ecclésiastiques*
DThC	*Dictionnaire de théologie catholique*
EEC	*Encyclopedia of the Early Church*
EHR	*English Historical Review*
EOMIA	*Ecclesiae occidentalis monumenta iuris antiquissima: Canonum et conciliorum graecorum interpretationes latinae* (Oxford 1899–1939)
Ferrua	Ferrua, A., *Epigrammata damasiana*
GCS	Die griechischen christlichen Schriftsteller der ersten drei Jahrhunderte
Hahn	Hahn, A., G.L. Hahn, and A. Harnack, *Bibliothek der Symbole und Glaubensregeln der alten Kirche,* 3rd ed. (Wroclaw 1897; rpt. Hildesheim 1962)
HThR	*Harvard Theological Review*
ICUR	*Inscriptiones christianae urbis romae*

Abbreviations

IPM	*Instrumenta patristica et mediaevalia*
JK	Jaffé, P., and F. Kaltenbrunner, *Regesta pontificum romanorum*, 2nd ed. (1885)
JThS	*Journal of Theological Studies*
JThS ns	*Journal of Theological Studies*, new series
KStT	*Kanonistische Studien und Texte*
LEC	The Library of Early Christianity
Lietzmann	Lietzmann, H., *Apollinaris von Laodicea und seine Schule*
LSJ	Liddell, H.G., R. Scott, H.S. Jones, and R. McKenzie, *A Greek-English Lexicon*, 9th ed.
MAH	*Mélanges d'archéologie et d'histoire*
Mansi	Mansi, J.D., *Sacrorum conciliorum nova et amplissima collectio*
MBTh	*Münsterische Beiträge zur Theologie*
MEFR	*Mélanges de l'École française de Rome*
MGH.AA	Monumenta Germaniae historica, Auctores antiquissimi
MGH.Cap	Monumenta Germaniae historica, Leges, sectio 2: Capitularia regum francorum
MGH.Conc	Monumenta Germaniae historica, Concilia
MGH.H	Monumenta Germaniae historica, Hilfsmittel
MGH.LNG	Monumenta Germaniae historica, Leges nationum germanicarum
MHS.C	Monumenta Hispaniae sacra, serie canónica
MIC.C	Monumenta iuris canonici, series B, Corpus collectionum
MIC.S	Monumenta iuris canonici, series C, Subsidia
NA	*Neues Archiv der Gesellschaft für ältere deutsche Geschichtskunde*
NBAC	*Nuovo bullettino di archeologia cristiana*
NGWG.PH	*Nachrichten der Gesellschaft der Wissenschaften Göttingen, philologisch-historische Klasse*
NHS	Nag Hammadi and Manichaean Studies

Abbreviations

NPNF	A Select Library of Nicene and Post-Nicene Fathers of the Christian Church
OCP	*Orientalia christiana periodica*
ODB	*The Oxford Dictionary of Byzantium*
ODCC	*The Oxford Dictionary of the Christian Church,* 3rd ed.
OECT	Oxford Early Christian Texts
OLA	*Orientalia lovaniensia analecta*
OLD	*The Oxford Latin Dictionary*
OTM	*Oxford Theological Monographs*
PG	Patrologia graeca
PL	Patrologia latina
PO	Patrologia orientalis
PTS	Patristische Texte und Studien
RAC	*Reallexikon für Antike und Christentum*
RDC	*Revue de droit canonique*
RHE	*Revue d'histoire ecclésiastique*
RQ	*Römische Quartalschrift für christliche Altertumskunde und Kirchengeschichte*
RThAM	*Recherches de théologie ancienne et médiévale*
SAWW.PH	*Sitzungsberichte der Akademie der Wissenschaften in Wien, philosophisch-historische Klasse*
SBAW.PH	*Sitzungsberichte der bayerischen Akademie der Wissenschaften in München, philosophisch-historische Abteilung*
SC	Sources chrétiennes
Scr	*Scriptorium*
Script. vet.	Mai, A., Scriptorum veterum nova collectio
SE	*Sacris erudiri*
SÖAW.PH	*Sitzungsberichte der österreichischen Akademie der Wissenschaften in Wien, philosophisch-historische Klasse*
Spic.	Mai, A., Spicilegium romanum
SSAC	*Sussidi allo studio delle antichità cristiane*

Abbreviations

StD	Studies and Documents
StPatr	*Studia patristica*
STPIMS	*Studies and Texts. Pontifical Institute of Mediaeval Studies*
StT	*Studi e testi*
StudMed	*Studi medievali*
SupVigChr	Supplements to *Vigiliae christianae*
TaS	*Texts and Studies (Cambridge)*
TLG	*Thesaurus linguae grecae* (stephanus.tlg.uci.edu)
TTK	*Tidsskrift for teologi og kirke*
TU	*Texte und Untersuchungen zur Geschichte der altchristlichen Literatur*
ZKG	*Zeitschrift für Kirchengeschichte*
ZKTh	*Zeitschrift für katholische Theologie*
ZNTW	*Zeitschrift für die neutestamentliche Wissenschaft*
ZSRG.K	*Zeitschrift der Savigny-Stiftung für Rechtsgeschichte, kanonistische Abteilung*

ABBREVIATIONS USED IN MANUSCRIPT SHELF-MARKS

add.	*additional*
Ambros.	Ambrosiana
arab.	*arabicus*
Baroc.	*Barocci*
BAV	Biblioteca Apostolica Vaticana
Bayer.	Bayerische
Bibl.	Biblioteca, Bibliothèque, Bibliothek
BN	Bibliothèque Nationale
Bodl.	Bodleian
Brit.	British
Cap.	Capitolare
Clm	*Codices latini monacenses*
Com.	Comunale

Abbreviations

Conv. soppr.	*Conventi soppressi*
eth.	*ethiopicus*
fol(l).	*folio(s)*
gr.	*graecus*
lat.	*latinus*
Laud.	*Laudensis*
Laur.	Laurenziana
Libr.	Library
Marc.	Marciana
Med.	Medicea
Mun.	Municipale
Naz.	Nazionale
nouv. acq.	*nouvelle acquisition*
Öster. Nationalbibl.	Österreichische Nationalbibliothek
Pal.	*Palatinus*
plut.	*pluteus* (shelf)
reg.	*reginensis*
Staatsbibl.	Staatsbibliothek
syr.	*syriacus*
Univ.	University, Uniuersitas (-tatis)
Vallicell.	Vallicelliana
Vat.	*vaticanus*
Voss.	*Vossius*

OTHER

ad loc.	*ad locum* = the aforementioned passage
ap. crit.	*apparatus criticus* = the critical notes to the Greek or Latin text
ap. font.	*apparatus fontium* = the listing of ancient sources
App.	Appendix
c.	century
ca.	*circa* = approximately

Abbreviations

cf.	*confer* = compare
c. n.	critical note (*i.e.*, a note of the *ap. crit.*)
col(l).	column(s)
e.g.	*exempli gratia* = for example
fasc.	fascicle
fol(l).	folio(s)
gr.	*graecus*
i.e.	*id est* = that is
lat.	*latinus*
LXX	Septuagint
MT	Masoretic Text
n.	note
p(p).	page(s)
rpt.	reprint(ed)
sec(c).	section(s)
u. l.	*uaria lectio* = variant reading
v.	*uide* = see

INTRODUCTION TO THE LIFE AND WORKS OF POPE JULIUS I

1. The Development of the Roman Episcopal Archives

From earliest times, letter writing was one of the principal means by which the scattered members and congregations of the Christian Church maintained contact. All but six of the New Testament writings are letters; and two of those, the Acts of the Apostles and the Revelation of St. John, contain letters within them. Among the other earliest Christian writings are letters authored by Clement of Rome (*1Clement* to the Corinthians) and Ignatius of Antioch.

As Rome grew into a spiritual and administrative center for the new religion, it was only natural that the bishop of Rome frequently engaged in correspondence with churches and individual Christians. Only bits and pieces of this correspondence have survived from the period prior to the Constantinian settlement of the early fourth century. We have mentioned *1Clement.* In addition, Eusebius describes an exchange between Dionysius of Corinth and Soter of Rome (bishop from *ca.* 166 to *ca.* 174) regarding the date of Easter and preserves extracts from Dionysius' letter; a quarter century later, Polycrates of Ephesus and Victor of Rome (189–98) exchanged letters on the same subject (*H. e.* 4.23 and 5.24). In that period, the correspondence emanating from the church of Rome was undoubtedly typical of that sent from all the major centers of the Church; like the vast majority of such early letters, this Roman correspondence has been lost.

The first extant collection of letters larger than those of St. Paul and St. Ignatius dates only to the mid-third century. This is the correspondence of Cyprian of Carthage, which contains more than eighty items. Besides Cyprian's letters to a wide range of recipients, these include more than a dozen letters addressed to Cyprian himself. Two are from Cornelius of Rome (251–53). In addition, twelve are directed to Cornelius and his successors, Lucius (253–54) and Stephen (254–57). These exchanges deal mainly with the terms on which Christians who had lapsed during persecution could be readmitted to the Church.[1]

It would have been only natural for bishops to keep copies of official exchanges between congregations. Nonetheless, in the periodic disruptions caused by outbreaks of hostilities against the Christians most such dossiers were lost. Cornelius' surviving correspondence has been preserved exclusively by Cyprian and Eusebius; no trace has survived from Rome itself. Indirect preservation remains the rule for almost another full century: only an occasional letter or fragment from Rome is preserved in the works of Eusebius, Athanasius, or other eastern writers.[2] The authentic pieces are preserved in Greek, Syriac, and Armenian, none in Latin. And the majority are letters written to the bishop of Rome, not by him.

The situation improves, but only gradually, in the fourth century. We have a letter from Constantine to Miltiades (311–14), quoted by Eusebius in Greek (*H. e.* 10.5.18–20), and one or two Latin letters from the Council of Arles (314) to Silvester I (314–35), preserved in

1. The letters to and from the Roman bishops are 44f., 47–52, 57, 59–61, 68, 72. For the Latin text *v.* that of Diercks in the CChr.SL; for an English translation, that of Clarke in the ACW. Eusebius preserves two additional letters of Cornelius in *H. e.* 6.43 and 46.

2. Besides the previously mentioned letters preserved in the Cyprianic corpus, the following letters to or from Roman bishops are extant: 1) Another letter to Stephen, *v.* Eus., *H. e.* 7.5.1f.; 2) three letters to Sixtus (257–58), *v.* Eus., *H. e.* 7.5.4–6 and 7.9; 3) two letters from Dionysius of Alexandria to Dionysius of Rome (259–68), *v.* Eus., *H. e.* 7.8 and Ath., *Dion.* 13–15; 4) a letter of reply from Dionysius of Rome to Dionysius of Alexandria, *v.* Ath., *Decr.* 26. *V.* the "Checklist of the Earliest Papal Correspondence (to 401)," in Thompson, "The Earliest Papal Correspondence," pp. 22–55.

early canonical collections.[3] Then there are the six letters either addressed to, or written by, Julius (337–52), which are the subject of this volume. The extant correspondence of his successors Liberius (352–66), Damasus (366–84), Siricius (384–99), and Anastasius (399–401) consists of *corpora* of fourteen, seventeen, seven, and four letters.[4] More of these letters are written and preserved in Latin, and more are letters written by the bishops of Rome.

Nevertheless, only a few of the extant letters seem to have been copied from exemplars in the Roman archives. Evidently, there was a major disruption in the maintenance of the collections. We have many more letters of fifth-century popes, and our earliest copies of many of these seem to derive from the Roman episcopal archives. Thus this disruption probably took place in the early fifth century. Yet this would have been just one among the numerous reasons for the loss of the earliest letters. For example, in the early fourth century, Eusebius was able to find the letter of Victor of Rome to Polycrates of Ephesus (*H. e.* 5.23.2), while, in the last decade of the century, Jerome could say only that "the memory of this exchange remains even to our day."[5]

It is clear, however, that, already in the fourth century, there was an episcopal archive in Rome. In 353 Liberius claimed to be in possession of a letter written to Silvester of Rome, and a few years later he was able to produce a letter addressed to his immediate predecessor, Julius (*ep.* 6).[6] Later, Siricius could refer to encyclicals (*generalia*

3. There are either two letters from the synod to Silvester or two quite different recensions of a single letter. The *incipits* are *Communi copula caritatis* and *Primo in loco*. The former is preserved in the canonical collections of Cologne and Novara and in Paris, BN, *lat. 1711*, the latter in the canonical collections of Albi, St. Amand, Cologne (twice), Corbie, Diessen, Lorsch, Lyon, St. Maur, Novara, Rheims, the Dionysio-Hadriana, and the Hispana, and in Carpentras, Bibl. mun., *74*. For information on these manuscripts and collections and for the best editions of *Communi copula caritatis* and *Primo in loco, v.* Munier, *Concilia,* pp. 3–6. Munier does not, however, discuss the relationship between the two versions.

4. On the letters from Liberius through Anastasius, *v.* Thompson, pp. 40–55.

5. *quarum memoria ad nos usque perdurat* (*Chron., sub anno* 196).

6. The first of these is mentioned in sec. 4 of Liberius' letter *Obsecro tranquil-*

decreta) sent out by Liberius.[7] Jerome assisted Damasus with his ecclesiastical records (*chartis ecclesiasticis, ep.* 123.9) and claimed that a quotation attributed to Anastasius I (399–401) could be checked in the Roman episcopal archives (*in Romanae ecclesiae chartario, Ruf.* 3.20). The *Liber Pontificalis* quotes from a letter of Siricius.[8] Yet only the two letters of Damasus to Paulinus of Antioch and three or four letters of Siricius, all of which circulated widely, found their way into the early Latin collections of councils and decretals. Thus, the evidence points to an episcopal archive that was functioning in the fourth century but later lost most, perhaps all, of its pre-fifth-century contents.

2. The Life of Julius

Our knowledge of Julius is derived from a few scattered references in ancient sources, one incomplete inscription,[9] the six genuine letters of his correspondence, and the brief notices in the *Liberian Catalogue* and the *Liber Pontificalis*. The so-called *Liberian Catalogue*, which dates to shortly after Julius' death, provides the

---

lissime (#212 in the catalogue of JK; for the relevant passage, *v.* Coustant, col. 426), the second in Sozomen, *H. e.* 4.11.

7. *V.* his *Directa ad decessorem* 1 (JK #255).

8. *L. P.* 40. An inscription composed by Damasus (Ferrua, #57) and said to have been discovered at the entrance to the church of San Lorenzo in Damaso has been taken to imply the building of "a new house for the archives" (*archiuis*). But this would not have been the appropriate location for the episcopal archives, and Scalia has argued (pp. 42–52) convincingly that *arcibus his* should be read in place of *archiuis*.

9. Wilpert, who published the inscription in 1903, says (pp. 316f.) that it was found in the cemetery of "Santi Marco-Marcelliano e Damaso," part of the catacomb of San Callisto on the Via Appia. Only the left part has survived, and he reconstructed it to read: SVB IVLIO A<B ALEXAN> / DRO FOSSO<RE> / PERCVSS<OR>. Leclercq (coll. 288f.) suggests the first line might read SVB IVLIO A<NTISTITE>, "under the episcopate of Julius." Ferrua prints (*ICUR*, ns, vol. 4, #11751) the third line as "PER CVSS[IUM]" I believe it would be better read as SVB IVLIO A<B ALEXAN> / DRO FOSSO<RE HAEC> / PERCVSS<A EST> or SVB IVLIO A<B ALEXAN> / DRO FOSSO<RE EST> / PERCVSS<A>: "This (*i.e., fossa* = catacomb tunnel) has been dug by Alexander the Digger during the episcopate of Julius."

following entry:[10] "Julius was bishop for fifteen years, one month, and eleven days in the time of Constantine, from February 6 in the consulship of Felicianus and Titianus[11] until April 12 in the year of the fifth consulship of Constantius (II) and (the first) of Constantius (Gallus) Caesar.[12] Among the many new churches he built were the basilica at the third mile on the Via Portuensis,[13] the basilica of Valentinus at the second mile of the Via Flaminia,[14] the basilica Iulia in region seven near the forum of the deified Trajan,[15] the basilica across the Tiber in region fourteen near Callistus,[16] and the basilica at the third mile on the Via Aurelia at Callistus."[17]

The entry on Julius in the original, sixth-century, recension of

10. *Iulius annos XV mensem I dies XI. fuit temporibus Constantini, a consulatu Feliciani et Titiani ex die VIII idibus Februariis in diem pridie idus Aprilis Constancio V et Constancio Caesare. hic multas fabricas fecit: basilicam in via Portese miliario III; basilicam in via Flaminia miliario II quae appelatur Valentini; basilicam Iuliam, quae est regione VII iuxta forum divi Traiani; basilicam trans Tiberim regione XIIII iuxta Callistum; basilicam in via Aurelia miliario III ad Callistum*; *v.* MGH.AA, vol. 9 (*Chronica minora, saec.* IV. V. VI. VII), *Chronographus anni CCCLIIII*, part 13: *Episcopi romani*. I have modified Mommsen's text by expanding the abbreviations.

11. Felicianus and Titianus were the ordinary consuls of 337, the year of Julius' accession; *v.* Bagnall *et al.*, pp. 208f.

12. For the consuls of 352, Constantius II and Gallus Caesar, *v. ibid.*, pp. 238f.

13. This basilica, later known as St. Felix in Pincis, was mentioned in several of the medieval pilgrim itineraries; it is no longer in existence. *V.* Huelsen, p. 252, and Armellini, vol. 2, p. 1292.

14. This basilica was later known as St. Valentinus outside the Gate. It was much frequented by pilgrims in the earlier middle ages but had fallen into ruins by the fourteenth century. *V.* Marucchi, *Il cimitero e la basilica di S. Valentino*; Armellini, vol. 2, pp. 1044–49; and Huelsen, pp. 496f.

15. This was either on or near the site of the current church of Santi Apostoli; *v.* Brandenburg, p. 112; Geertman, pp. 24–31.

16. The "Basilica Julia" bore the name of Julius I, an indication that he was viewed as the founder. The phrase *iuxta Callistum* is unclear; perhaps it was meant to indicate that the basilica was built on the site of an earlier building associated with Callistus I (217–22). It is uncertain whether the ancient Basilica Julia was on the spot of or within the immediate vicinity of the present-day church of Santa Maria in Trastevere; *v.* Brandenburg, p. 112; Huelsen, pp. 234, 371; Armellini, vol. 2, pp. 783–85 and 796f.; and Guerrini, pp. 379f.

17. Here, "Callistus" refers to the cemetery where Callistus I was buried and where Julius himself would be buried; Armellini, vol. 2, p. 1189. On this cemeterial and subterranean basilica, *v.* the study by Verrando, esp. pp. 1039–61.

the *Liber Pontificalis* (ch. 36) is in general agreement with that of the *Liberian Catalogue.* Though it omits information about his building projects, it contains additional mention of ordinations he performed and the site where he was buried:[18] "Julius, a Roman by birth, son of Rusticus, was bishop for fifteen years, two months, and seven days. This was in the time of Constantine, beginning in the consulship of Felicianus and Maximinus.[19] He established that no clergyman was to bring a case to the public courts.[20] He performed three December ordinations, at which he ordained eighteen priests and four deacons as well as nine bishops for various places. He was buried on the Via Aurelia in the cemetery of Calipodius at the third milestone on April 12. The bishopric was then vacant for twenty-five days."

Since the notice regarding ordinations has no historical foundation,[21] this account adds little to that of the *Liberian Catalog.* Together, they are quite uninformative; we learn the dates of Julius' episcopate and that he expanded the recent tradition of episcopal construction of basilicas and cemeteries. Nonetheless, we can infer that Julius felt a special affinity for Callistus, his predecessor of a century, for he expanded churches that Callistus had built, and he chose to be buried near him. This association with Callistus may have rested upon similarities in their views of penance and reconciliation: as Callistus had been charged with tolerating Sabellians and readmit-

18. The original version as reconstructed by Duchesne (*Le Liber Pontificalis,* vol. 1, p. 83) reads as follows: *IULIUS, natione Romanus, ex patre Rustico, sedit ann. XV, m. II, d. VII. Fuit autem temporibus Constantini et Feliciani et Maximini .... Hic constituit ut nullus clericus causam in publicam ageret. Hic fecit ordinationes III per mens. Decemb. presbiteros XVIII, diaconos IIII, episcopos per* [*diversa*] *loca VIIII.* [*Qui etiam*] *sepultus est via Aurelia in cimiterio Calipodi, milario III, prid. id. April.* [*Et*] *cessauit episcopatus dies XXV.*

19. As the *Liberian Catalog* indicates, the ordinary consuls for 337 were Felicianus and Titianus. The mention of Maximinus in the *L. P.* is an error.

20. The same regulation is ascribed to Silvester earlier in the *Liber Pontificalis.* Yet this entry may be accurate, for Julius may have found it necessary to affirm that, even under a government favorable to the Church, clergy were still not to make use of the secular courts.

21. The author of the *L. P.* provides an analogous list for all the bishops of Rome from Peter on!

ting adulterers into communion, Julius was attacked for readmitting into communion Marcellus of Ancyra, accused of Sabellianism, and Athanasius, the object of various charges of improper conduct.

3. The Six Genuine Letters

The remains of Julius' genuine correspondence comprise only six letters totaling fewer than 800 lines of text, two-thirds of which come from one letter (*ep.* 2). Of these, only two were written by Julius, the other four were addressed to him. Both of the letters he wrote, as well as one of those written to him, were composed in Greek;[22] the other three written to Julius appear to have been composed in Latin.[23] All six focus on the Arian controversy.

They fall into three pairs. The first two deal with the events of 341, when Rome was the site of a council that took up the cases of the bishops Athanasius of Alexandria and Marcellus of Ancyra, who had been deposed and exiled at the Council of Antioch (338/39). The first (Ἐπειδή τινες), written by Marcellus to Julius, is part of his defense against the charges that had been brought against him. It contains what appears to be the earliest extant text of the Roman baptismal creed. The second (Ἀνέγνων τὰ γράμματα) is addressed by Julius to seven eastern bishops "and to those with them who have written to us from Antioch," who had taken action against Marcellus and Athanasius. Though invited to send a delegation to a council in Rome, they had declined to do so. Julius' lengthy letter (518 lines) explains the decisions his own council had reached on these matters.

Epp. 3 and 4 are both addressed to Julius by the western participants in the Council of Sardica of 343. Following an already established custom, Julius did not attend in person, but sent several clerics as representatives of Rome. In *ep.* 3 (*Meminimus et tenemus*), the

22. *Ep.* 5, the second letter written by Julius, is also preserved in the Latin translation of the *Hist. trip.* 4.28, of Cassodorius/Epiphanius; *v.* App. C.

23. *Ep.* 6 is also extant in the Greek version of Athanasius. He included it in two of his works (*Apol. sec.* 54–56; *H. ar.* 23); *v.* App. D.

two leading westerners at the council, Hosius, the aged chaplain of the late emperor Constantine, and Protogenes, the host bishop, who must have chaired the council, inform Julius of the doctrinal issues under debate. Our only surviving copy is truncated. The letter states that the council has considered and condemned the false beliefs of Arius' more recent followers. *Ep.* 4 (*Quod semper credidimus*) is the official letter sent by the council upon completion of its work. Julius is informed of the council's decisions, including its confirmation of the decision of the Roman council in which Athanasius and Marcellus were cleared of all charges. In the conclusion (sec. 5), Julius is urged to pass on the news to "our brothers in Sicily, Sardinia, and Italy."

The last two, *epp.* 5f., dating to the second half of the 340s, complete the story of the involvement of the Roman see in the conflict between Athanasius and the eastern bishops. In the fifth (Συγχαίρω κἀγὼ ὑμῖν), Julius congratulates the church of Alexandria on the return of Athanasius from exile in 346. Part pastoral letter, part panegyric, it urges the Egyptian populace to unite again under Athanasius and prays that peace will once more prevail in the great and ancient see of Alexandria. In *ep.* 6 (*Quoniam constat nos*), Ursacius and Valens, two excommunicated bishops of Pannonia who had formerly supported the anti-Athanasian party, write to denounce Arius and his followers, to retract their accusations against Athanasius, and to seek renewed communion with Rome.

Thus, the correspondence of Julius begins with conflicts that followed the Council of Nicaea (325) and ends with a seeming victory for the Nicene and Athanasian parties. The correspondence of his successor Liberius will show that this was but a short-lived victory. Nonetheless, the Julian corpus gives us a picture of Julius and his episcopate much fuller than that of the *Liber Pontificalis*. Here we see no mere architect of basilicas, but a bishop playing a leading role in the most significant debates of his time. When he fails to resolve the controversies by mediation, he stands firmly with Athanasius and Marcellus against those he believes to be compromising the faith and ecclesiastical order.

In his list of famous ecclesiastical authors, Gennadius, a late fifth-century priest of Marseilles, devoted a paragraph to Julius: "Julius, bishop of the city of Rome, wrote to a certain Dionysius one letter about the incarnation of our Lord, which at the time seemed useful against those who were asserting that, through the incarnation, Christ had two persons, just as he had two natures; now, however, it is regarded as harmful, for it stokes the impious teachings of the Eutychians and Timotheans."[24] Thus, a century and a half after Julius' death, this western church leader remembered him for just a single letter, and a forgery at that! Julius' correspondence was so tightly connected to the Arian controversy that when the Nicene position finally prevailed late in the fourth century there was little need for further reference to his correspondence.

4. The Pseudo-Julian Corpus[25]

Apocryphal writings, gospels, acts, and letters, circulated inside and outside the Church from its earliest times. Often the purpose of such documents was to claim the authority of well-known Church leaders for condemned teachings or to associate them with historical events in which they had not participated. Because of the pres-

24. Gennad., *Vir. ill.* 2: *Iulius, urbis Romae episcopus, scripsit ad Dionysium quendam de incarnatione Domini epistulam unam, quae illo quidem tempore utilis uisa est aduersus eos qui ita duas per incarnationem asserebant in Christo personas, sicut et naturas, nunc autem perniciosa probatur: fomento enim est Eutychianae et Timotheanae impietatis.* Gennadius was probably referring to the letter Θαυμάζω πυνθανόμενος/*Miror audiens* (JK †190; *CPG* #3669); *v.* item C in App. B below and n. 2 in App. B below. The Eutychians, named after a mid-fifth-century archimandrite of Constantinople, and the Timotheans, named after Timothy Aelurus, patriarch of Alexandria in the third quarter of the fifth century (d. 477), held views on the union of the divinity and humanity of Christ that were rejected as heretical by those who adhered to the formulation of the Council of Chalcedon (451); *v.* Gregory, "Timotheos Ailouros."

25. In App. B, I provide a complete list of letters falsely attributed to Julius, with information on the manuscripts in which these are preserved and on editions in which they have been published. There I collect as well citations from these letters in the works of other ancient authors.

tige and importance of the bishops of Rome, it was only natural that Julius' name would be used in such forgeries. Though the name of Julius has been falsely attached to over two dozen documents, with very few exceptions, these fall within just three brief periods; each group was produced within a clearly defined context. The first (App. B, A–J) consists of documents written in the late fourth and early fifth centuries by supporters of the Apollinarian heresy and circulated under the name of Julius. The second (K–N) was composed in the mid-ninth century for insertion in a canonical collection that is now known as the *Decretals of Pseudo-Isidore*. They figure among a group of letters, almost all of which are forgeries, attributed mainly to the thirty-three popes from Silvester I (314–35) to Gregory II (715–31).[26] The final group (O–Y) is made up of passages attributed to Julius that have been incorporated into the canon law compilations of the eleventh and twelfth centuries. None of these is authentic, but, in this group, the attribution to Julius is sometimes due to scribal error rather than deliberate falsification.

In later times, the memory of Julius' support of Athanasius and Nicene theology commended his name to sectarians who were seeking to gain acceptance for suspect or condemned teachings by attributing their works to fathers of recognized orthodoxy. The letters and fragments listed as A–J in Appendix B are mostly Apollinarian documents. Distinguishing between "soul," the life force of the body, and "mind," the rational and volitive faculty, Apollinaris (d. 392) taught that the *Logos* had become man in an incomplete fashion: with a human body and soul, but without a human mind, whose place was supplied by the divine nature. In 381, the Council of Constantinople (*v.* canon 1) condemned his doctrine, and, by 388, Theodosius I had issued legal sanctions against his followers (*Cod. Theod.* 16.5.14.15). These then adopted the stratagem of placing the names of Athanasius and his one-time defender, Julius, on copies of works in which they expounded their theology. They were so successful that Cyril of Alexandria, among others, was deceived by

26. *V.* Saltet, esp. p. 773.

their falsifications. Though only a few letters fraudulently attributed to Julius have been preserved in their entirety, the unknown author of a Greek work written *ca.* 600 says that, in his day, seven letters by Apollinaris were circulating under Julius' name.[27] It is clear that they spread widely under this attribution, for bits have been transmitted in six languages: in Greek, the language of composition, and in Latin, Syriac, Arabic, Ethiopic, and Armenian translations.[28] As later sources often cite several letters in the same passage, it appears that letters at times circulated in groups.

Three of these letters (A–C) are probably works of Apollinaris himself. A) *De unione*, sometimes titled *The Fifth Letter* of Julius (JK †191; *CPG* #3646), survives entire in both Greek and Syriac; in addition, it has been cited in works composed or preserved in Syriac, Arabic, and Armenian. Apollinaris' disciple Timothy of Beirut names Apollinaris as the author.[29] B) *De fide et incarnatione* (JK †193; *CPG* #3647) survives entire only in Syriac. The original Greek (often with the *incipit* Μηδεὶς) and the Latin version, in some manuscripts entitled *Contra aduersarios diuinae incarnationis,* lack the first two sections. Chapters 8f. were sometimes copied separately under the title *The Second Letter* of Julius. In the *Doctrina patrum*, attributed to Anastasius of Sinai, the author identifes (41.46) Apollinaris as the author of a quotation from ch. 6, and Lietzmann argues that the whole letter should be assigned to Apollinaris.[30] This letter was cited also by Timothy Aelurus, Severus of Antioch, and Philox-

27. Gallandi's sixteenth-century edition of *De sectis* has been reprinted in PG, vol. 86.1, coll. 1193–1268; for the letters attributed to Julius, *v. actio* 8.3 (coll. 1253–56).

28. On the circulation of Apollinarian documents under the name of orthodox figures, *v.* also Lietzmann, pp. 82f.

29. *V. ibid.*, pp. 133f. Timothy, bishop of Beirut in the last decades of the fourth century, was one of the main supporters of Apollinaris and his teachings; *v.* Cavalcanti, "Timothy the Apollinarist." In the *Ep. ad Hom.*, preserved by Leont. Byz. in *Apoll.* (Lietzmann, pp. 277f.), Timothy attributes to Apollinaris excerpts from secc. 2 and 8 of A. The twelfth-century chronicler Michael the Syrian cites parts of A but disputes its attribution to Apollinaris; he asserts that even those who identify the author as Apollinaris admit that it is found everywhere under the name of Julius; *v.* Chabot, vol. 4, p. 234 (text) and vol. 2, p. 116 (French translation).

30. Lietzmann, pp. 136f.

enus of Mabbug.[31] It is also quoted in Greek, Syriac, Latin, Arabic, and Armenian florilegia. C) The *epistula ad Dionysium* (JK †190; *CPG* #3669) purports to be a letter from Julius to Dionysius, priest of Corinth.[32] It has survived in the original Greek, incorporated in full into the unpublished Greek christological miscellanies in BAV, *Vat. gr. 1481,* and in Syriac in a translation of Timothy Aelurus' polemical treatise *Against Those Who Assert the Two Natures* (*Contra eos qui dicunt duas naturas*).[33] Portions are extant in Latin, Armenian, and Arabic. We learn that Apollinaris is the author of this letter from the Apollinarian Valentinus' *capita apologiae,* from which Leontius of Byzantium excerpted for his *Apoll.*[34]

Lietzmann assigns a fourth letter, the *epistula ad Prosdocium* (D; JK †189; *CPG* #3726), to Timothy of Beirut, one of Apollinaris' closest disciples. In 429, Cyril of Alexandria, believing this a work of Julius, quoted from it in his collection of patristic christological citations, the *Apologia xii capitulorum contra orientales*, and this section of his work was read into the acts of the Council of Ephesus (431).[35] Translated into Latin, that section has also been incorporated into the *Vatican Collection* and the *Collection of St. Maur,* two western canonical collections. In 448, the monophysite Eutyches included

31. On Timothy Aelurus, *v.* n. 24 above. Severus was the monophysite patriarch of Antioch from 512–18. Another leading monophysite theologian, Philoxenus, was bishop of Mabbug (Hierapolis) in northern Syria from 485–518 or 519. Exiled by emperor Justin I, he died in 523. On Severus, *v.* the monograph of Allen and Hayward, on Philoxenus, the thesis by de Halleux. *V.* also the brief notices by Gregory, "Severos" and "Philoxenos of Mabbug."

32. For Gennadius' attribution of this letter to Julius, *v.* n. 24 above.

33. Tim. II al., *Contra eos* is preserved in full in Armenian (*v.* App. B below) and in a shortened version in Syriac preserved in Brit. Libr. *add. 12156,* from which Fleming and Lietzmann printed our C (*v.* App. B below).

34. Valentinus attributes to Apollinaris the opening words of sec. 1 and the first half of sec. 10, the fourth and fifth proof texts in Leont. Byz., *Apoll.* bk. 1. For this passage of *Apoll., v.* Mai, Spic., vol. 10.2, pp. 129f. (rpt. PG, vol. 86.2, coll.1949f.); *v.* also Lietzmann, pp. 103–08, 148. Muratori's discussion of Apollinaris' authorship (*v.* his letter to Antonius Maria Salvinius on pp. 347–65 of *Anecdota graeca*) is reproduced by Migne in PL, vol. 8, coll. 938–52.

35. *V.* n. 29.1 in App. B below. Cyril used the citation in his response to the fourth anathema; *v.* Lietzmann, p. 91 and McGuckin, pp. 85f.

the entire letter in a florilegium that he sent to Rome as part of his defense against the charge of heresy; Eutyches' work has survived in a rather free Latin translation preserved in a single manuscript (Novara, Bibl. Cap. di Santa Maria, *30*). Timothy Aelurus cited the entire letter in his *Contra eos,* which was translated into both Syriac and Armenian.[36] Severus of Antioch cites from this letter,[37] and it is quoted also in Syriac florilegia.

A fragment of a fifth letter (E; *CPG* #3705), consisting of several brief sentences followed by five anathemas, deals with the incarnation. In 430, Cyril of Alexandria had been able to attribute this to its real author,[38] Vitalis of Antioch, a disciple of Apollinaris and, in the late fourth century, one of the competing claimants to the patriarchal see of Antioch. Several decades later, Timothy Aelurus quoted E in his anti-Chalcedonian *Contra eos* and apparently identified Vitalis as the author, since that attribution stands in an abridged translation of Timothy's work into Syriac and in the Armenian translation. Yet in the church history of Zacharias Rhetor (first half of sixth century), which survives only in a Syriac epitome, E is attributed to Julius (*H. e.* 4.12). As Zacharias drew directly from the *Contra eos,* it may have have been the Syriac translator who first ascribed E to the bishop of Rome. Recognizing that Vitalis was not bishop of Rome, he would have chosen the name of the Roman bishop Julius because of the other Apollinarian writings (A–D) circulating under Julius' name. Of course, he should rather have kept the attribution to Vitalis and corrected the name of the see from Rome to Antioch. In any case, this attribution is probably due to error rather than to deliberate falsification on the part of the Apollinarians. In fact, E seems to be part of the exposition of faith that Vitalis submitted to Damasus of Rome.[39]

36. *V.* nn. 25f. in App. B below.
37. *V.* n. 29.2 in App. B below.
38. *V.* n. 30 in App. B below.
39. *V.* Gr. naz., *ep.* 102.6; Lietzmann, p. 152; and Diekamp, "Das Glaubensbekenntnis."

There are three more letters of which substantial portions have survived (F–H), and which are clearly Apollinarian, though their author has not been identified. F) The first, entitled *Encyclion* (JK †192; *CPG* #3735), or *Little Encyclical*, is a brief work addressed to "the bishops of the catholic Church everywhere." In the manuscripts it always follows the *epistula ad Dionysium* (C); it has been preserved also in Syriac and Latin translations and has been quoted in works transmitted in Armenian and Arabic. G) The original Greek text of *The Third Letter* (*CPG* #3739) has been lost. The piece is given this name in two manuscripts of the British Library,[40] in which it is copied after our B (Μηδεὶς) divided into two sections (chh. 3–7 and 8f.) regarded as separate letters; sections 8f. of B are entitled *The Second Letter* and G, *The Third*. It is preserved in Syriac, Arabic, and Armenian translations. H) *De fide* (*CPG* #3740), dealing with the natures of Christ, survives only partially in a Syriac translation preserved in one manuscript.[41] Lietzmann dates the extant recension to the time of Cyril of Alexandria (mid-fifth century). This, he theorizes, is derived from an earlier form that, like the other Apollinarian material, was originally composed in the late fourth century.[42]

In addition to these eight documents, there are six fragments surviving in Arabic translation (I–J), which also deal with christology and probably belong to the same Apollinarian corpus. They are too small to permit the reconstruction of the letters from which they were excerpted.

It is surprising that, already in the late fourth century, a mere half century after Julius' death, the Apollinarians were able to pass off their documents under his name. Perhaps this practice received added impetus when the Roman episcopal archive was destroyed in the early fifth century. The Apollinarians may have reckoned that it would be difficult to disprove their attributions. At any rate, their strategy was very successful. While, by the sixth century, some fa-

40. These are *add. 14608* (7th c.) and *17183* (10th c.).
41. This is Brit. Libr. *add. 14555*; *v.* App. B below.
42. *V.* pp. 161f.

thers had recognized that these documents were forgeries, they continued to circulate under the name of Julius for centuries to come.

There was no further fraudulent use of Julius' name until the mid-ninth century, when the author of the Pseudo-Isidorian Decretals ascribed to Julius four of his own compositions (K to N). To three of these (K, L, N) he attached dates in the same consular year; the names of the consuls are fictitious. The first (K), an encyclical introducing the Nicene Creed as the accepted *fides* of the Church, is attributed to a Roman council of 160 bishops meeting under Julius. This is followed by a lengthy letter of Julius to the eastern bishops (L), which serves as a cover letter for item K. The third (M) is a reply from the easterners, and the fourth (N) a lengthy rejoinder from Julius.[43] The author was aware that Julius had been a defender of the Nicene position and may have been acquainted with Julius' letter to the bishops at Antioch (*ep.* 2). Clearly, his main source of information was the *Historia tripartita* of Cassiodorus.[44] Julius does not seem to have been of especial interest to the forger, for he attributes similar exchanges of correspondence with easterners to both Mark and Liberius, Julius' predecessor and successor.

In the eleventh and twelfth centuries, the compilers of systematic canon law collections assigned to Julius at least seventeen quotations from works he did not write (O–X; JK †197–†206 = 10 items; Y = 7 items). Some falsely attributed to Julius their own forgeries or, more frequently, brief excerpts from works they knew to be by others. In the latter case, the attribution to Julius was an attempt to associate with a pope an idea or policy enunciated by a figure of lesser stature. The principal falsifier was Burchard of Worms. In his *Decretum* (1008–12), Burchard passed off seven citations—three from penitential works (P, W, and sentence four from X), one from a Carolingian

43. For the texts, which date between 835 and 850, *v.* Hinschius, pp. 454–74. I list these in the order in which they are found in the manuscripts. L is dated to the kalends of October, and K and N to the kalends of November, and M is left undated. This confusing and compressed chronology hardly supports the fiction of an exchange of correspondence. For a critique of Hinschius' text and an introduction to the decretals, *v.* Fuhrmann in Jasper and Fuhrmann, esp. pp. 153–77.

44. *V.* Davenport, p. 61 and nn. 15f.

capitulary (O), one from a conciliar canon (U), one from the Code of Justinian (R), and one from a work of Isidore of Seville (V)—as excerpts from the works of Julius. As Cushing has noted, "Burchard deliberately falsified inscriptions in an effort to give greater authority to canons from regional councils, or to capitulary texts which had not been sanctioned by Rome."[45]

In their attributions of materials to Julius, the compilers of several other collections seem to have made simple errors rather than deliberate falsifications. These include 1) either the author of the *Collection in Three Books* or the contemporary author of the *Collection of Polycarp* (Q);[46] 2) the compiler of the *Collectio casinensis* (the first three sentences of X); 3) Gratian in the first recension (*ca.* 1150) of his *Decretum* (S); 4) a copyist of Gratian's *Decretum* (T). As later collectors copied into their own works the misattributions of their sources, many of these passed on to subsequent collections. Indeed, sections of items O, P, Q, R, S, U, W, and X appear under Julius' name in the *Decretum*.[47] There were also some few misattributed passages that were never passed on to further collections (Y). More false quotations of Julius may still lie unnoticed in the many unstudied and unpublished penitential and canonical collections.

There is as well one document that does not fit into any of the three categories just enumerated of works or excerpts from works falsely claiming to have been written by Julius. This (Z) is a letter that purports to be addressed to him by a patriarch of Jerusalem. It is extant in two recensions; in one the patriarch is identified as Cyril, in the other as Juvenal. The letter discusses the proper dates for the commemoration of Christ's birth and baptism. The author and date of composition are unknown, as is the motivation for making Julius the recipient. It is probably ahistorical.

45. Cushing, pp. 68f.

46. Both collections, published around 1125, include and attribute to Julius *Si quis desponsauerit; v.* the fuller discussion in App. B.

47. In the present state of research on the early systematic collections and their inter-relationships, it is impossible to identify with certainty the source of each misattribution. What is presented here and in App. B is provisional.

5. The Transmission and Preservation of the Genuine Letters

Clearly, many letters sent to and from Julius have not survived. In *ep.* 2 alone, we learn of seven more for which we lack even excerpts.[48] As we have argued above (sec. 1), the episcopal archive was probably destroyed at some time in the early fifth century. Thus, it is improbable that the copies that stood at the head of the transmission that leads to our printed editions were those of the Roman episcopal archive.

Most likely, we possess the six genuine letters only because they were incorporated into other ancient works. A generation after the Synod of Rome, Epiphanius, Bishop of Salamis on Cyprus, included a copy of Marcellus' letter to Julius in his *Panarion* (72.2f.), a compendium detailing all the Christian heresies from the earliest times down to his own day.[49] Athanasius reproduced Julius' *ep.* 2 (to the bishops at Antioch), a part of *ep.* 5 (to the Church of Alexandria), and a Greek translation of *ep.* 6 in his *Apologia secunda,* also known as the *Apologia contra arianos,* which he wrote after his return to Alexandria (*ca.* 357) from his second exile.[50] As Socrates Scholasticus, one of the fifth-century church historians, quoted letter five in its entirety (*H. e.* 2.23.15–32), he must have had a source independent of Athanasius' treatise. What we have of the incomplete *ep.* 3 (to Julius from Hosius and Protogenes) was preserved in a canonical collection that seems to have been assembled in Carthage in the early fifth century. This is now known by the name of Theodosius the Deacon, a copyist, and perhaps the collector, of the canonical documents. In the mid-fourth century, Hilary, Bishop of Poitiers incorporated *epp.* 4 (to Julius from the Synod of Sardica) and 6 (to Julius from Valens and Ursacius) into his historical work on the Arian struggle, from

48. *V.* the Chronological Table (p. 28).

49. Quasten, p. 388.

50. For the quotation of *ep.* 2, *v.* chh. 20–35, for the excerpt from *ep.* 5, *v.* chh. 52f., and for the translation of *ep.* 6, *v.* ch. 58.2–4.

which we retain only excerpts (*fragmenta historica*).[51] The subsequent history of Julius' correspondence is, thus, largely that of historical and doctrinal works in which they were quoted.

6. The Printed Editions of Julius' Correspondence

Epiphanius' *Panarion*, which contains *ep.* 1 (Marcellus of Ancyra's letter to Julius), first appeared in a Latin translation by Cornarius (Basel 1543). The *editio princeps* of the Greek text by Oporinus (Herbst) followed a year later (Basel 1544).[52] In the following century, Petauius (Petau) produced a slightly revised edition (Paris 1622). In 1861, the study of the text of *ep.* 1 was much advanced in two new editions of the *Panarion:* in W. Dindorf's edition of the complete works of Epiphanius (Leipzig) and Öhler's edition of the *Panarion* in the *Corpus haereseologicum* (vol. 2, pt. 3, Berlin). These editions of Epiphanius were superseded by that of Holl for the *GCS* (Leipzig 1933).[53]

In addition, *ep.* 1 has been printed in part or *in toto* in works dealing with Marcellus himself. Rettberg discussed this letter in his dissertation, *Marcelliana, etc.* (Göttingen 1794); while he did not print the entire text, he suggested some plausible emendations. Klostermann published the fragments of Marcellus as an appendix to his edition of two works of Eusebius of Caesarea, the *Contra Marcellum* (*CPG* #3477) and the *De ecclesiastica theologia* (*CPG* #3478), in

51. Feder has edited the *fragg. histt.* under the title *Collectanea antiariana parisina;* for *ep.* 4, *v.* B.2.2f. This letter has been preserved also within four collections of canon law: the collections of St. Blaise (early sixth century), St. Maur (later sixth century), Diessen (mid-seventh century), and the Expanded Dionysiana (later eighth century). None of these collections has ever been completely published, and no edition of *ep.* 4 has ever been published from these sources. For these collections and their manuscripts, *v.* App. A.

52. The family name is attested also in the form "Herbster"; Oporinos is the Greek equivalent of Herbst = Autumn; *v.* "Oporinos, Johannes O.," *ADB,* vol. 24: *van Noort-Overbeck* (Leipzig 1887), p. 382.

53. Dummer re-edited Holl's *Epiphanius* (Berlin 1985) but made no changes in either the text or critical apparatus of *ep.* 1.

which Eusebius cites passages from Marcellus' writings and attacks his teaching. The reader will find much useful information in the notes to *ep.* 1 (frag. 129), both those providing biblical and patristic parallels and those dealing with textual issues. Klostermann's edition has been revised by Hansen (Berlin 1991). Vinzent has edited the letter of Marcellus in *Markell von Ankyra: Die Fragmente und der Brief an Julius von Rom* (Leiden 1997). Finally an edition with German translation has recently appeared in *Documente zur Geschichte des arianischen Streites* produced by Brennecke and a team of co-workers. Thus, for the reconstruction of *ep.* 1, the modern historian has at his disposal the manuscripts and editions of Epiphanius and the editions of Eusebius and Marcellus.

Athanasius' *Apol. sec.*, into which he had copied *ep.* 2 (from Julius to the bishops at Antioch) and an abridgement of *ep.* 5 (from Julius to the church of Alexandria), was published in numerous Latin translations in the late fifteenth and sixteenth centuries. There was no printed edition of the original Greek until 1600, when it was published at Heidelberg by Commelinus (Commelin) as part of the complete works of Athanasius; the editing of the ancient text was undertaken by the otherwise unknown Peter Felckmann.[54] Commelin's edition of Athanasius was reprinted during the following century and finally superseded by the complete edition of the works of Athanasius prepared by the Maurist de Montfaucon (Paris 1698). It was not until 1938 that Opitz published the first truly critical text of *ep.* 2 as part of his edition of the collected works of Athanasius (Berlin/Leipzig).

The complete text of *ep.* 5 (from Julius to the Church of Alexandria), thanks to its preservation by Socrates Scholasticus (*H. e.* 2.23.15–32), received early printed editions in several contexts. Socrates' own church history was first edited (Paris 1544) by R. Stephanus (Estienne). A century later (Paris 1668), it was re-edited by Valesius (de Valois), who, on the commission of the French clergy, edited all the major Greek church historians.[55] The nineteenth-

54. V. Opitz, *Untersuchungen*, p. 2.
55. Lejay, p. 264.

century editions by Hussey (Oxford 1853) and Bright (Oxford 1893) provided improved texts, but the first completely critical edition is that of Hansen (Berlin 1995).

In addition, the original Greek as well as a Latin translation were preserved within two works dependent on the church history of Socrates. The fourteenth-century monk Nicephorus Callistus Xanthopulus had copied *ep.* 5 from Socrates into his own ecclesiastical history (9.22). The *editio princeps* of Nicephorus' work (Paris 1630), indeed the only printed edition, was prepared by the Jesuit scholar Ducaeus (du Duc).[56] Socrates' work was also the source for the Latin version, made by the Greek scholar Epiphanius Scholasticus, which Cassiodorus incorporated into his *Tripartite History* (4.28). This received its *editio princeps* (Basel 1523) from the German humanist Beatus Rhenanus (Bilde von Rheinau). Of subsequent early modern editions the most important was that by the Maurist Garetius (Garet) (Rouen 1679). The first completely critical edition of the *Tripartite History* is that of Jacob and Hanslik (Vienna 1952) prepared for the CSEL. Thus, for the reconstruction of letter five, the principal sources are now Athanasius and Socrates. For the reconstitution of the text of the letter as transmitted by Socrates, we have not only his own church history but also the witness of Nicephorus and Cassiodorus/Epiphanius.

The collection of canonical material of the deacon Theodosius, within which the fragmentary *ep.* 3 (to Julius from Hosius and Protogenes) was transmitted, has never received a complete edition. The letter was first published by the brothers P. and G. Ballerini as an appendix to their edition of the works of Leo the Great (Venice 1757).[57] In the twentieth century, the letter was reedited by Opitz (1939) and Tetz (1985).[58]

Epp. 4 (to Julius from the Synod of Sardica) and 6 (to Julius from

56. Along with the Greek text, Ducaeus printed an annotated Latin translation first published by Johann Lange in 1553. Text and translation were reprinted in PG, vol. 146; *v.* Gentz, p. 3.

57. *V.* vol. 3, pp. 597f. The Ballerini edition was reprinted in *PL*, vol. 56; for *ep.* 3, *v.* coll. 839f.

58. Opitz edited this letter in Turner's *EOMIA*, vol. 1.2.3, p. 644; for Tetz' edi-

Valens and Ursacius), preserved among the fragments of a work (or works) by Hilary of Poitiers on the Arian struggle, were printed first by Baronius (*ep.* 4 under the year 347 and *ep.* 6 under the year 350) in his annalistic history of the Church (Rome 1593).[59] Five years later, they were published by Faber (Lefèvre) in his edition of Hilary (Paris 1598). A century later, the Maurist Coustant re-edited the *fragg. histt.* within the context of his ground-breaking edition of the collected works of Hilary (Paris 1693). These were republished in PL, vol. 10 (coll. 619–724).[60] It was only in the early twentieth century that Feder prepared for the CSEL the first truly critical edition based on a complete survey of the manuscript tradition (Vienna 1916).[61]

Ep. 6 (to Julius from Valens and Ursacius) is also transmitted in a Greek translation made by Athanasius, who included it in both the *Apol. sec.* (58.1–4) and the *H. ar.* (26.3). Sozomen, a contemporary of Socrates Scholasticus, transcribed Athanasius' translation into his church history (*H. e.* 3.23.2–5). This, like the history of Socrates, was first edited by R. Estienne in the mid-sixteenth century (Paris 1544) and then re-edited (Paris 1668) by de Valois. The first fully critical edition of Sozomen was that which Bidez and Hansen prepared for the GCS (Berlin 1960). Hansen has subsequently produced a revised edition (Berlin 1995). Nicephorus, who had transcribed *ep.* 5 from Socrates, took (9.27) Athanasius' translation of *ep.* 6 from the text of Sozomen. For the reconstruction of *ep.* 6, the modern editor can check the Latin transmitted within the *fragg. histt.* of Hilary against the Greek translation preserved by Athanasius, Sozomen, and Nicephorus.

---

tion, *v.* "Ante omnia," pp. 247–49. For studies of this canonical collection and the manuscript in which it is preserved, *v.* Schwartz, "Die Sammlung des Theodosius Diaconus" and "Über die Sammlung des Codex Veronensis LX"; Telfer, "The Codex Verona LX (58)"; and Field's monograph.

59. Under the year 347, Baronius printed two recensions of *ep.* 4. For the first, he cited a text from a *Collectio crescentiana* preserved in a manuscript of Monte Cassino (*ex collectionis Crescentianae codice Cassinate peruetusto,* coll. 732f.). I have not been able to identify the manuscript used by Baronius.

60. For *ep.* 4, *v.* coll. 639–42; for *ep.* 6, coll. 647f.

61. For *ep.* 4, *v.* B.2.2; for *ep.* 6, B.2.6.

This edition is the first dedicated solely to the correspondence of Julius I. There have, however, been previous attempts to collect some or all of the relevant pieces. The sixteenth-century church historian Baronius printed something from all the genuine letters except *ep.* 3: his own Latin translations of selections from *epp.* 1f., two recensions of *ep.* 4,[62] a Latin translation of Athanasius' abridged version of *ep.* 5, and *ep.* 6. The great Benedictine historian and philologist Pierre Coustant (1654–1721) was the first to try to produce a complete collection of the correspondence of Julius within the context of his ambitious project to edit all the papal correspondence from Clement I to Innocent III (67–1216). In the first volume, the only one ever completed by Coustant and his Maurist confrères, he published the materials available through the year 440. Coustant much advanced the study of Julius by discussing and rejecting many of the inauthentic letters that circulated under his name. Yet, as he did not know about *ep.* 3, his treatment of Julius was incomplete. Furthermore, the usefulness of Coustant's edition is limited by the faults common to the scholarship of his day: he did not provide clear designations of all the manuscripts he was using; he cited few variants; he did not always make it clear to the reader where the text was based on the manuscript evidence or on emendation, either his own or that of previous editors.[63]

7. The Roman Episcopate in the Time of Julius[64]

Upon his election in early 337, Julius inherited a see vastly different from that of only a quarter-century earlier. Although still a minority in the ancient capital, the Christians were no longer a persecuted sect, but the beneficiaries of imperial benefactions. Now

62. *V.* n. 59 above.

63. *V.* Ott's brief account of Coustant's life and work.

64. In this section, the dates assigned to the early bishops follow the chronology of Duchesne.

enjoying legal recognition, the Church could openly organize and systematize its ministry. The bishop of Rome was no longer only a spiritual leader but also the overseer of ever more impressive buildings and land holdings.

By the early fourth century, the Church was firmly rooted within Rome itself. Originally, the Roman church consisted predominantly of Greek-speaking immigrants, and this predominance diminished only gradually. While Victor, bishop toward the end of the second century, may have been native born, it was not until the second half of the third century that men of Roman stock predominated in that office. Likewise, the shift from Greek to Latin as the language of worship and ministry was a gradual process; Latin had become standard only by the fourth century. While Julius was able to compose letters in Greek, he may well have been the last bishop of Rome to write to the Christian leaders of the East in their own language. The Roman episcopacy was now truly Roman.

For some time already it had been recognized that the Roman church had canonical jurisdiction over the other churches of Italy. The sixth canon of the Council of Nicaea (325) referred to this as an example of good church order that should be imitated elsewhere.[65]

65. *V.* The Latin translation (known as that of Atticus) of the sixth canon: (*EOMIA*, vol. 1.1.2, pp. 120–23): *Antiqui mores obtineant qui apud Aegyptum sunt et Libiam et Penthapolim ut Alexandriae episcopus omnium habeat sollicitudinem quia et urbis Romae episcopo similis mos est. similiter autem et circa Antiochiam et in ceteris prouinciis priuilegia propria reseruentur metropolitanis aecclesiis. omnino autem manifestum est illud quia, si quis praeter consilium metropolitani factus fuerit episcopus, talem concilium magnum definiuit non debere esse episcopum. si uero communi omnium decreto rationabili et secundum canonem aecclesiasticum duo aut tres propter proprias inimicitias contradixerint, optineat sententia plurimorum.* "Let the ancient customs prevail that the bishop of Alexandria should have the care of those in Egypt, Libya, and the Pentapolis, because the same custom obtains for the bishop of Rome. Likewise with Antioch and other provinces, seniority ought to be reserved for the metropolitan churches. Furthermore, the following is entirely clear: that if any be ordained bishop without the consent of the metropolitan, the great council has established that such a man ought not to be bishop. And therefore, if a common decision reached with general support in accordance with reason and church order be opposed by two or three motivated by personal enmity, let the choice of the majority prevail" (my translation). Atticus, the patriarch of

Unfortunately, we have little evidence regarding the development and the full implications of this custom. It was normal for Julius and his successors to preside over regional councils of bishops and clergy; he could speak for "all the bishops of Italy and the surrounding regions" (*ep.* 2.6). The Council of Sardica expected Julius to forward the conciliar decisions to the brothers "in Sicily, Sardinia, and Italy" (*ep.* 4.5). It is unclear how widely this oversight extended beyond the Italian mainland and the surrounding islands.

By this time, the Roman church had become the leading church in the western Latin-speaking half of the empire. In previous centuries, Carthage had exerted great influence; the prolific theologian Tertullian and the outstanding bishop Cyprian were as well known in the wider Church as the Roman bishops who were their contemporaries. These two had helped shape the vocabulary of Latin Christianity. But by now, the influence of Carthage was waning, in part due to the Donatist struggle that would continue to convulse northern Africa for several more centuries. In fact, shortly after taking possession of Rome, Constantine had appointed the bishop Miltiades to chair a council to hear complaints of mistreatment raised by the Donatists (Eus., *H. e.* 10.5.18–20).

The Roman church had experienced periodic setbacks. It had weathered schism in the time of Novatian (251–58). The bishop Marcellinus (296–304) may even have committed apostasy.[66] The

Constantinople (406–25) sent to the Council of Carthage of 419 a Latin translation of the canons of Nicaea; this, one of four ancient Latin translations, is now known by his name (*v.* "Atticus," *ODCC*, pp. 124f.). For the Greek text of canon 6, *v.* Chadwick, p. 180. Chadwick points out that this canon was not intended to regulate affairs at Rome; it cites the case of Rome only as precedent (pp. 187–90). He cites Rufinus' reference to "suburbicarian" churches (*H. e.* 10.6) as evidence that Rome exercised a long-established oversight of the ten provinces comprising central and southern Italy, Sicily, and Sardinia (p. 188).

66. In the early fifth century, the Donatist bishop Petilianus alleged in controversy with Augustine 1) that Marcellinus had complied with an edict of persecution, presumably that of Diocletian in 303, according to which copies of the Scriptures were to be relinquished to the civil authorities for burning (*Petil.* 2.202) and 2) that he had offered incense to the pagan gods (*Bap.* 27). Indeed, his name is omitted in the list of Roman bishops, the *Depositio* of 336 and its augmented

decade following his death was tumultuous: the episcopal seat was vacant for more than three years, and his successors Marcellus and Eusebius (died 310) both died in exile.[67] The Novatians continued in schism into the fourth century, but, unlike the Donatists of North Africa and the Melitians of Egypt, who constituted large and powerful rival churches, they remained a small sect.[68] The particularly able Miltiades (311–14) and his successor Silvester (314–35) availed themselves of the newly instituted policy of official toleration of the Christian Church to foster unity within the community of Rome; unity in Rome strengthened the leadership of the Roman church in the west. After all the vicissitudes of recent history, the church of Rome could still boast of its double apostolic foundation by both Peter and Paul, a claim that no other church in East or West could match.

Within the city of Rome, the new policy of extending legal recognition to the Christian religion, usually referred to as "the peace of Constantine," really began shortly after the accession of Maxentius, perhaps as early as 306 (Optat., *Parm.* 1.18; Eus. *H. e.* 8.14.1). Restitution of confiscated church buildings, however, did not begin until shortly after the accession of Miltiades in 311 (Aug., *Breu. coll. don.* 3.18.34 and *Ad don.* 13.17). After Constantine defeated Maxenti-

second edition of 354, and in subsequent lists of the fifth and sixth centuries. In the *L. P.* (ch. 30) Marcellinus is said to have offered incense, but to have repented soon after and suffered martyrdom. For discussion of the documents relative to his alleged apostasy, *v.* Duchesne, pp. lxxiiif. and xcix.

67. For a brief account of the doubtful chronology of these two episcopacies, *v.* Kelly, pp. 25f.

68. The Novatianists, Donatists, and Melitians, though founded at different times and places, shared a rigorist approach to those who had compromised in some way—*e.g.*, by offering incense or handing over copies of the Scriptures—during persecution. Each, in its own provisions of discipline and ordination, insisted that the Church must be seen to be the church of the saints, rather than that of saints and sinners. Novatian, the rival of Cornelius of Rome (251), and Donatus, the rival of Caecilian of Carthage (*ca.* 311), were consecrated bishops by their sectaries. Melitius, the bishop of Lycopolis, was excommunicated by Peter of Alexandria (*ca.* 306), whose policies toward the lapsed Melitius had rejected as overly lax. All three schisms persisted for centuries; *v.* the articles "Novatianism" (p. 1165), "Donatism," (pp. 499f.), and "Melitian Schisms" (pp. 1067f.) in the *ODCC.*

us in late October, 312, he had the process of restitution accelerated (Eus., *H. e.* 10.5.15–17). During his short stay in Rome, Constantine donated land and funding for the Lateran basilica.[69] By early 313, the emperor had declared the Roman clergy immune from all public liturgies and personal taxes (Eus., *H. e.* 10.7.1f.). By the end of Miltiades' episcopacy, Constantine had become a major benefactor of the Christian Church and of the Roman church in particular.

Constantine's gifts to the church of Rome are described in great detail, and probably substantial accuracy, in the extensive entry for Silvester I in the *L. P.* (ch. 34).[70] The *L. P.* records that Constantine supported the building, furnishing, and endowing of the "Constantinian Basilica" (*i.e.*, the Lateran Basilica) and its baptistery. It also credits him with building a basilica in the Sessorian Palace (now Santa Croce in Gerusalemme); this project, however, may owe its conception and execution to Helena, Constantine's mother. Outside the walls of the city, the emperor had basilicas constructed near the burial sites of the martyrs Laurence and Sts. Marcellinus and Peter. The imperial family sponsored construction of other churches at the graves of St. Agnes on the Via Nomentana, of St. Peter on the Vatican hill, and of St. Paul on the Via Ostiense. Agnes' church was almost certainly built under the patronage of Constantine's daughter Constantia, those of Peter and Paul appear to have been principally due to his son Constans.[71] This activity of building and endowment extended beyond Rome to Ostia, Albano, Capua, and Naples. In addition, the emperor gave furnishings and endowments to the parish church (now San Martino ai Monti) built by Silvester himself. Thus,

69. On the timing of this donation and the interaction between civil and ecclesiastical authorities required for this project, *v.* Krautheimer, "The Ecclesiastical Building Policy of Constantine."

70. *V.* the *L. P.* ch. 34, pp. 74–81 and the translation of Davis, pp. 14–27. Due to the detailed catalogue of imperial benefactions, the entry on Silvester I is nearly as long as those of all his predecessors combined.

71. The entry of the *L. P.* for Silvester credits all these basilicas to Constantine; Logan ("Constantine," *etc.*), however, argues convincingly that other members of the imperial family played a part in this work of construction.

the emperor and his family made their beliefs clear to the citizenry of Rome through their patronage of places of worship and commemoration scattered throughout the city and its surroundings.

At this period, however, the church of Rome must still have been in the process of moving from its dozens of smaller and less public meeting places to the larger and more public basilicas. Already in the mid-third century, bishop Cornelius (251–53) had presided over forty-six priests, seven deacons, seven sub-deacons, forty-two acolytes, fifty-two exorcists, readers and doorkeepers. In addition, the church supported more than 1,500 widows and indigents (Eus., *H. e.* 6.43.11). The numbers of clergy would seem to indicate a church that already had as many as forty to fifty groupings equivalent to parishes and a total of at least 10,000 adherents. By Julius' day, the total of church members must have been much larger, and the church had the legal right to own property and build public spaces of worship. By the third quarter of the fourth century, there were some forty basilicas in Rome. Not everyone approved of their wealth and beauty.[72]

Although the imperial family sponsored impressive basilicas, they were not responsible for the construction of most of the ecclesiastical facilities of Rome. Wealthy Christians were doubtless instrumental in the donation of land and the construction of churches. And the bishops of Rome played a central role. If the *L. P.* (ch. 27) is correct in stating that Felix (269–74) constructed a church on the Via Aurelia, this was probably a cemeterial basilica. Yet the church that Silvester built on the estate of one of his priests was a parish church in the city proper. Another church, perhaps begun during Mark's brief episcopate (336), was named for Mark, Silvester's successor. The *L. P.* tells us (ch. 36) that Julius completed this and constructed many buildings (*multas fabricas fecit*); these included two basilicas within the city and three suburban cemeterial churches. Thus, through the efforts of Julius, his immediate predecessors, and

72. For the number of churches, *v.* Optat., *Parm.* 2.4; for the disapproving remark of the Luciferians Faustinus and Marcellus, *v.* Auel. coll., *ep.* 2.121. *V.* also, Thompson, "The Pax Constantiniana."

successors, the older parish infrastructure quickly became visible throughout the fourteen ecclesiastical regions of the city.

The social status and family backgrounds of the fourth-century bishops are largely unknown. Organizational ability must soon have become an important prerequisite for the office. As the list of Cornelius' clergy indicates, well before the fourth century, the bishop directed an organizational structure equivalent to the households of the wealthiest senators. By Julius' day, the bishops, though still not from the highest strata of society, must have been men of some formal education who had gained experience in overseeing property and people while rising through the ranks of the clergy. By the later fourth century, the bishop of Rome had become one of the grandees of the imperial city. In church affairs, both doctrine and discipline, the leaders of the Roman church gradually acquired a predominant influence throughout Italy and the West.

8. The Early Years of Julius' Episcopate

Julius was elected Bishop of Rome on February 6, 337. Fifteen weeks later, on May 22, Constantine died. Constantine had named his three sons, Constantine II, Constans, and Constantius II, among those who were to divide the rule of the Empire. But it was only on September 9, after three tense months during which many other heirs were executed by the army, that the sons met and formally took the purple.[73]

Their father Constantine had been preoccupied by divisions within the Church. His initial concerns regarding the Donatist and Melitian schisms were soon overshadowed by the controversy that had arisen in Egypt over the preaching of Arius. In an attempt to settle

73. Constantine had also designated some of his uncles and nephews to share in the division of power; these were all victims of the purge. The extent of the role of the army in the transfer of power is unclear (*v.* Eus., *V. C.* 4.68). Constantius, who enjoyed the advantage of being the first of the brothers to reach Constantinople, may have ordered further executions (Iuln., *Or.* 1.12–15 and, esp., *Ad ath.* 3).

the growing dissensions, the emperor had tried to assemble the leadership of the entire Church at the Council of Nicaea in 325. The ecumenical council, where, in fact, eastern delegates far outnumbered those from the West, was almost unanimous in its condemnation of Arius. Yet almost immediately afterward, a group of eastern bishops began efforts to rehabilitate him and his main supporters. By 335, a council at Tyre, convened under the presidency of Flacillus, the bishop of Antioch, had not only confirmed Arius' orthodoxy, but had voted to depose and excommunicate Athanasius of Alexandria, one of Arius' most vocal opponents and the occupant of the only eastern see that could rival the power of Antioch. Although various charges, including that of murder, were brought against him, Athanasius' stance against Arius was certainly one of the principal factors motivating those who wished to depose him. Like the apostle Paul (Acts 25.11), he took his case directly to the emperor. Though not convinced of Athanasius' guilt, Constantine was concerned to keep the peace and ordered Athanasius to Trier for further investigation at the court of the western caesar, Constantine II.[74] He was still at Trier when the elder Constantine died.

Within weeks of the emperor's death, Constantine II, with the grudging approval of his brothers, issued a decree allowing Athanasius and other exiled bishops to return to their sees. To remove all doubt regarding the legitimacy of his return, the younger Constantine even provided Athanasius with a letter to the Alexandrian church. Leaving immediately, Athanasius interrupted his return voyage for an audience with Constantius at Viminacium in Upper Moesia (now Kostolac in Serbia). He re-entered Alexandria on November 23, 337 (Ath., *Apol. sec.* 87.4–7; *H. ar.* 8; Socr., *H. e.* 2.3.1–4; Thdt., *H. e.* 2.2.1–4).[75]

74. Barnes notes the extraordinary nature of the emperor's action. Though sending Athanasius to Gaul, he also vetoed the replacement chosen by the Council of Tyre, and the see of Alexandria remained vacant; *v. Athanasius and Constantius*, pp. 24f.

75. Barnard ("Two Notes," pp. 337f.) and Nordberg (p. 33), argue that, prior to his recognition as emperor, Constantine II could not have concerned himself with

This amnesty and the return of Athanasius were major setbacks for the eastern bishops, for Athanasius' permanent removal was a prerequisite to the fulfillment of their theological objectives. Yet they soon had new hopes for success. Constantius II had no love for the outspoken Alexandrian bishop and his friends. His main concern was to maintain peace and unity in the Church.[76] When, in 337, at the death of Bishop Alexander, the see of Constantinople fell vacant, he personally intervened to set aside Paul, who had been elected and consecrated by the Nicene Christians, and secured the transfer to the capital of Eusebius, bishop of Nicomedia, who had baptized his father Constantine during his final illness (Socr., *H. e.* 2.7).[77] Eusebius, a determined supporter of Arius and opponent of the Nicene definition of faith, would remain the leader of the anti-Athanasian party until his death, in 341.[78] Now, with Eusebius in Constantinople and Flacillus in Antioch, the anti-Athanasian party held all the key bishoprics of the East, except for Alexandria.

Eusebius and his supporters (the Eusebians) now devised a three-pronged counter-offensive. First they redoubled their efforts to win

Athanasius; both date his letter and Athanasius' return to the following year (338). Nonetheless, the circumstances are best understood if the unlikely did occur. In addition, note that Constantine II refers to himself as "Caesar" (Ath., *Apol. sec.* 87.4).

76. Klein argues that, from the beginning of his reign, Constantius was motivated solely by a concern for the unity of the Church. He eventually concluded that this could be achieved only by the deposition of Athanasius and the adoption of a compromise creed. He thought that the necessary creed had been produced in 359 by the Councils of Seleucia and Ariminum; *v.* pp. 157–59 for his summary.

77. Paul's election had been hastily managed to pre-empt the chances of his Arian rival Macedonius. Constantius' objections to the consecration of Paul may have been procedural, political, or both. On the early career of Paul of Constantinople, *v.* Barnes, *Athanasius and Constantius*, pp. 212–17 (App. 8). While the translation from Nicomedia to Constantinople much increased Eusebius' influence, it also opened him to criticism. Such transfers had been condemned by numerous councils, including that of Nicaea (canon 15). In their attacks on the Eusebians, the Athanasian party would soon emphasize this irregularity.

78. Eusebius and Arius had been fellow pupils in the school of Lucian of Antioch, a renowned biblical scholar and martyr (317) of the Great Persecution; *v.* Baldwin, "Lucian of Antioch" and Baldwin and Talbot, "Eusebios of Nikomedeia."

acceptance for Pistus, an Arian whom they had chosen to replace Athanasius as bishop of Alexandria.[79] Then they sent a delegation to Constantine II and the other emperors to charge the returned Athanasius with acts of criminal violence (Ath., *Apol. sec.* 3.5–7). Finally, in the hope of winning his support against Athanasius, they sent a delegation with a letter (E^2)[80] to Julius, the new bishop of Rome (*H. ar.* 9).[81] This delegation, headed by the presbyter Macarius and the deacons Martyrius and Hesychius must have arrived during the spring of 338 (Iul., *ep.* 2.2, 4, and 6). Athanasius also sent a delegation of Egyptian clergy, who brought to Rome a letter from a recent Egyptian council that would serve as a defense of their bishop (A^1; Ath., *Apol. sec.* 3–19).[82]

The eastern bishops opposed to Athanasius claimed that the large and canonically convened regional council of Tyre had already conducted a proper investigation and determined that Athanasius was guilty of violent and immoral conduct unbecoming a clergyman (*Apol. sec.* 8.4). Excommunication and removal from office were the obvious and proper penalties. His Egyptian supporters claimed that Athanasius was being removed by outsiders who had no authority to judge someone else's shepherd, and that these outsiders were motivated by their Arian theology rather than a true concern for the well-being of the Church. Neither side regarded Rome as a final

79. On Pistus, *v.* Iul., *ep.* 2.4 below. Parvis argues (pp. 154f.) that the Eusebian party may have already selected Pistus at Tyre in 335, though his election had never been ratified by Constantine.

80. For the *sigla* used to designate letters exchanged between easterners and Rome during the controversy surrounding Athanasius, *v.* the Chronological Table (p. 28). In 335, the Council of Tyre undoubtedly sent a synodal letter announcing their decisions (E^1), but we know nothing about this letter's arrival or reception in Rome. We have more information about the letter (E^2) that arrived at Rome in 338.

81. *V.* Pietri, "La question," pp. 96f. This move was a grave miscalculation. The bishop of Rome had not yet taken part in the post-Nicene Arian quarrels and might have continued to ignore them. But once his intervention had been requested by one of the parties, he became irrevocably involved.

82. Barnes argues that the letter was composed by Athanasius himself; *v. Athanasius and Constantius*, pp. 39f.

court of appeal. Both sought the support of the most important and prestigious western see, just as they sought the support of the three emperors.

Julius wished to heal this growing rift between Antioch and Alexandria, the two most important sees of eastern Christianity. He was also troubled by inconsistencies in the accusations against Athanasius and by the conduct of the legates from the eastern bishops. After consulting his own clergy, he decided that a formal meeting of the two sides was the only way to reach a solution. Some time later in 338, he sent letters (R^1) to the East and to Athanasius urging both sides to meet at Rome (Ath., *H. ar.* 9).[83]

As both sides had failed to secure the unequivocal support of the bishop of Rome, neither responded enthusiastically. The Eusebians, concluding they had little hope for a favorable verdict in Rome, convoked their own council at Antioch in the winter of 338/39. Eusebius chaired the assemblage, and Constantius attended at times. Some ninety bishops joined in condemning Athanasius and, in their synodal letter (E^3), promulgated a new confession of faith. In addition, since Pistus had not been successful in rallying support in Alexandria, they elected a new bishop for Alexandria, Gregory, a Cappadocian (Socr., *H. e.* 2.10).[84]

83. In 340, Julius dispatched a second call for the easterners to send a delegation (R^2); this repeated invitation is mentioned by Athanasius (*Apol. sec.* 20) and is implied in many parts of *ep.* 2. Sozomen confuses the chronology in his condensed account (*H. e.* 3.8.3) of the events of 338–341. When he reports that Julius, rebuking the easterners for their unjust condemnation of Athanasius and Marcellus of Ancyra "and for abandoning the Nicene doctrines, … summoned a few among them to appear," Sozomen conflates one or both of Julius' earlier letters with the extant *ep.* 2 (R^3). Julius himself says that the eastern envoys were the first to request a council (Ath., *Apol. sec.* 22). Athanasius, perhaps unreliably, adds that the eastern bishops also proposed that Julius himself judge between the parties (*ibid.*, 20). Elsewhere Athanasius says that Julius proposed that a council "be held wherever we should desire" (*H. ar.* 9). Pietri (*Roma Christiana*, pp. 199f.) accepts this latter assertion and points out that Julius would have followed Roman civil law by allowing Athanasius, the accused, to choose the site of the hearing.

84. Socrates' chronology is also (*v.* the previous note) inaccurate. Among other mistakes, he conflates several Antiochene synods of 339 and 341; *v.* 2.10.

Constantius' backing of the Council of Antioch became even more overt, when shortly thereafter, imperial troops escorted Gregory into Alexandria.[85] Another Cappadocian, Philagrius, recently appointed prefect of Egypt, was instructed to oversee the arrival and installation of the new bishop. Now an Egyptian council sent letters in support of Athanasius to Rome (A^2) and to all three emperors, but to no avail. On March 17, 339, Athanasius went into hiding; on March 22, the new bishop arrived, and, on April 16, Athanasius fled Egypt. Because the eastern emperor clearly supported his removal, the exile was forced to seek refuge in the western empire. Almost a year had passed since Julius had invited him to a council; Athanasius took the road to Rome only when he had nowhere else to turn. There he would make friends among members of the imperial family and with another exiled bishop, Marcellus of Ancyra (Ath., *Apol. Const.* 6).[86]

9. This Edition

A century ago, Eduard Schwartz declared that the story of the early development of the papacy could not yet be told since scholars were still lacking "das Fundament," a reliable edition of the episcopal correspondence.[87] This volume is the first of several that will cover the correspondence of the fourth-century Roman bishops. Together they will help lay that foundation.

As we have indicated (secc. 5f. above), each letter has its own history of transmission and publication. It has, therefore, been necessary to provide separate discussions of the sources for their reconstruction. The reader will find each discussion at the end of the historical introduction to the relevant letter. Appendix A provides

85. Athanasius (*H. ar.* 9.3–10.1) mentions letters of Constantius in support of the decision of the council; both Socrates (*H. e.* 2.11.1) and Sozomen (*H. e.* 3.6.9) speak of Gregory's large military escort.

86. *Cf.* also Barnes, *Athanasius and Constantius*, pp. 52f.

87. Schwartz, "Die Kanonessammlungen," pp. 20f., n. 1.

additional information on the medieval manuscripts of the patristic works and canonical collections within which the letters were preserved until their first printing.

The correspondence of Julius and his fourth-century successors survived the middle ages within the works of at least thirty authors and collections that are preserved in over 200 manuscripts. In an effort to minimize the number of manuscript *sigla* and to ensure their consistent use in this and successive volumes, I have adopted the following practices: 1) I assign its own *siglum* to each canonical collection or ancient work in which a letter has been preserved. "A" indicates Athanasius' *Apologia secunda,* "C" Cassiodorus' *Historia ecclesiastica tripartita,* and "M" the *Collection of St. Maur.* 2) A number designating each manuscript of that collection or ancient work is appended to the *siglum.* Thus, the five manuscripts of Ath. *Apol. sec.* are designated A^1 through A^5. 3a) Readings shared by all the manuscripts of a given work are identified by the simple *siglum:* "A" indicates a reading common to all five manuscripts of Ath., *Apol. sec.* 3b) As a general rule, when the members of a class disagree among themselves, only those manuscripts that differ from the accepted reading will be listed in the apparatus. 3c) I have excluded from the notes most variants that are clearly wrong, isolated, meaningless, or merely orthographical.[88]

In general, I cite the previous editors only where they disagree with the reading adopted. In cases where I simply record a conjecture that has not been taken into the text, I give only the name(s) of the editor(s) who has (have) suggested or endorsed that conjecture. When I print a conjecture, I cite all the editors. Their names are always listed in chronological order according to the italicized abbreviations provided in the *Conspectus siglorum.*

88. Given considerations of space and the editorial policies of the LEC, the number of variants has had to be limited. Thus, in the apparatus of this volume, the reader will find fewer variants than in those of other editions, including that of *epp.* 1–4 in Brennecke, *Documente.* A more complete apparatus is available at http://www.fourthcentury.com.

The current edition is based on fresh collations of sixty manuscripts, in the case of most letters, all those extant. For the Latin translation of *ep.* 5, I have collated only sixteen of the 138 manuscripts of Cassiodorus' *Hist. trip.* I explain my choice of manuscripts in the introduction to the edition in Appendix C below. For each letter, I have studied as well the readings of the principal editions listed in sec. 6 above.

My editions, while much dependent on centuries-long traditions of palaeographical and text-critical work, make significant advances. First, in some cases, they rest on a wider foundation of manuscript evidence. This is partly the consequence of my aim to recover the text of each letter as it was written or received by Julius. Thus, while Opitz reconstructed *ep.* 5 as epitomized by Athanasius in his *Apologia secunda*, and Hansen reconstructed the text as it first appeared in the history of Socrates Scholasticus, I have consulted the entire medieval tradition: the manuscripts of Athanasius, Socrates, Nicephorus, and Cassiodorus. In addition, in constituting the text of the Latin translation of this letter, I have looked at previously unexploited manuscripts; as the reader will see, my collations have brought to light variants that improve the comprehensibility of this document.

Second, I have not infrequently preferred readings wrongly rejected by, or unknown to, other editors. In some cases where I have chosen a different manuscript variant, my choice has been guided by the consideration of masses of parallels derived from reference tools, such as the *Thesaurus linguae graecae*, that were not available to most of my predecessors. I have also had access to a store of conjectural emendations, *e.g.*, those of Scheidweiler on *ep.* 2, some of which I regard as very likely restorations of the truth and have, therefore, introduced into the text. At the end of the introduction to each letter, I list the readings in which I differ from my most recent predecessor. I do not, however, mention mere orthographical variations. As a general rule, I have followed the classicising orthography of the learned men of late antiquity, even when the manuscripts presented medieval usage; *v.*, *e.g.*, the end of the introduction to *ep.* 4, where I explain my spellings of the names of the deposed bishops and their sees. Where the variety of possibile readings would result in substantially different meanings, I have provided alternative translations, so that even readers unschooled in the ancient languages can form an idea of what is at stake.

Finally, I have repunctuated all the letters. In some cases (*e.g.*, the last sentence of *ep.* 2.19), the new punctuation has restored the coherent development of ideas to passages that had been misunderstood. Perhaps most importantly, the new punctuation provides a consistency of usage that was not there to guide those who had to read these letters in the different contexts in which each had been preserved.

The ancient text has one set of call-outs, the translation two. In both text and translation, quotations and allusions are signaled by superscript lowercase letters that direct the reader to the *apparatus fontium,* the catalogue of sources listing references to the Bible and other ancient works that stands beneath the textual notes at the bottom of the lefthand page. When the author is clearly quoting, the citation in the text is italicized; in the translation, these quotations stand within quotation marks. In the text, allusions to ancient sources are not italicized; in both text and translation, they are identified, like quotations, with superscript lowercase letters. Where it seems impossible to determine if the author intends to quote or refer to a given text, perhaps because he intends to refer to a group of similar texts (*e.g.*, gospel parallels), or he is simply using similar phraseology, the entry in the *apparatus fontium* is set off by "*cf.*" = *confer* ("compare"). In the translation, superscript arabic numerals call attention to explanatory notes at the foot of the page.

The challenge of translation is to put the content of the letters into a form easily comprehensible to the modern reader. Several sorts of terms—those regarding church law and ecclesiastical community and the honorific forms of address—have proven problematic. In the fourth century, the Church made increasing use of local councils of priests and deacons and regional and trans-regional councils of bishops to address issues of faith and morals. In my translation, the English words "synod" and "council" are used without distinction. The decisions of these councils were recorded in summary statements, known as "canons," and shared with other congregations. Eventually, these canons would be collected; together with the decrees of the Roman pontiffs they were organized into a body of opinion and precedent that formed the basis for canon law in the western church. Our letters frequently use the noun κανών/*canon* and the adverb κανονικῶς (*ep.* 2.13, 14, 17) to speak of good order and just procedure.[89] To convey these ideas, I have usually translated the Greek and Latin nouns with expressions such as "church law." Thus, I have tried to avoid suggesting that the later concept of canon law was already in force at a time when it was still embryonic.

From early on, the Church had gathered like-minded believers but separated from itself those who followed other teachings, *i.e.*, heresies. Such separation was most apparent when the separated were excluded from the Eucharist. Fellowship, whether physical, spiritual, or ritual, was viewed as an integral whole. Thus, in early Christian literature, it is often difficult to determine whether the nouns κοινωνία/*communio* and their related verb forms refer to sharing the Eucharist or to some other formal or informal acknowledgement of unity. Consequently, I have rendered such terms with "communion" and left it to the reader to decide the particular emphasis of each passage.

In the late-antique church, the use of honorific forms of address, a borrowing from the practice of the imperial court, became widespread. To assist the reader in spotting honorifics, I have capitalized them in both the text and the translation. Frequently, they have no, even rough, equivalents in contemporary English. For example, in just one section (5) of *ep.* 4, the bishops assembled at Sardica address Julius as *Tua Excellens Prudentia, Sincera Caritas Tua,* and *Vnanim-*

89. *Cf.* the expression of simialr meaning, ἔννομον καὶ ἐκκλησιαστικὴν (*ep.* 2.11).

itas Tua. In such cases, I have tried only to convey the sense of the abstract nouns: "Your Surpassing Farsightedness," "your True Charity," "your Concord."

Four appendices follow the letters. Appendix A lists the ancient works or collections in which the letters were preserved and the manuscripts of those ancient works or collections. Appendix B provides more information about the transmission of each of the inauthentic items long attributed to Julius. Appendix C contains my edition of the ancient Latin translation of *ep.* 5, and Appendix D my edition of the Greek translation of *ep.* 6. As these can witness to the text from which they were translated, they are of some use to the textual critic.[90]

10. The Identification, Translation, and Presentation of Quotations and Allusions to Scripture (J.F.P.)

In his Greek letters, Julius used the Septuagint version of the Old Testament (LXX), which was made from a Hebrew text that differed in many places from that constituted in the early middle ages by the Jewish masoretic scholars (MT). The reader will find a full discussion of our previous use of the abbreviation "(LXX)" in section 11 of the first introduction to volume 1. In this volume, it is used only to indicate that the numeration of chapter and verse of the Septuagint depart from that of the Hebrew text.

We define quotations as verbal equivalencies with our authorities. For the LXX, these are agreements with the wording of the Göttingen Septuagint, where this is available, or with Rahlfs' edition of 1935 for those books still unpublished by the Göttingen Academy; for the Greek NT, agreements with the wording of the fourth edition of *The Greek New Testament* edited by B. Aland *et al.* Quotations of the

90. Unless otherwise indicated, quotations and references to ancient texts follow the critical editions listed in the bibliography; English versions follow the translations listed under each author.

Latin Bible present less difficulty than might be expected. As there are no direct quotations of Scripture in *epp.* 3f., there is no need to identify the strand(s) of the *Vetus latina* used by Julius and his correspondents. In the Latin translation of *ep.* 5, direct quotations follow the wording of the Vulgate.

In the ancient texts, we signal direct quotation by the use of italics, in the English translation, with quotation marks. We regard as direct quotation passages that agree with the wording of our authorities in two or more contiguous or nearly contiguous words or even in one especially significant or odd word. We also regard as quotations passages where differences between the text of the letters and that of our authorities are due to no more than changes imposed by the exigencies of the inflected languages. Throughout, we use points of suspension to note the omission in quotation of material appearing in our authorities. We do not pretend to know whether Julius and his correspondents were abbreviating their biblical text or quoting it in full.

We have tried to make the documentation as full as possible and have included numerous references in addition to direct quotations. We have not, however, attempted to list cross-references. Thus, if the wording of a quotation allows a secure identification of the source, we do not cite parallels for passages presented by more than one evangelist. If it seems clear that the reference is to a passage of the Pauline epistles containing a quotation from a prophet, we cite only the epistle.

BIBLIOGRAPHY

Bible: Ancient Texts, Versions, and Concordance

I. ANCIENT TEXTS AND VERSIONS

Septuagint (LXX)

Rahlfs, A., *Septuaginta: Id est Vetus Testamentum graece iuxta LXX interpretes* (Stuttgart 1935)

Wevers, J.W., *Genesis, Septuaginta,* vol. 1 (Göttingen 1974)

Wevers, J.W., and U. Quast, *Leviticus, Septuaginta,* vol. 2.2 (Göttingen 1986)

Wevers, J.W., and U. Quast, *Numeri, Septuaginta,* vol. 3.1 (Göttingen 1982)

Wevers, J.W., and U. Quast, *Deuteronomium, Septuaginta,* vol. 3.2 (Göttingen 1977)

Rahlfs, A., *Psalmi cum odis,* 3rd ed., *Septuaginta,* vol. 10 (Göttingen 1977)

Ziegler, J., *Duodecim prophetae, Septuaginta,* vol. 13 (Göttingen 1984)

Ziegler, J., *Jeremias, Baruch, Threni, Epistula Jeremiae,* 2nd ed., *Septuaginta,* vol. 15 (Göttingen 1976)

Ziegler, J., and D. Fraenkel, *Ezechiel,* 2nd ed., *Septuaginta,* vol. 16.1 (Göttingen 1977)

Ziegler, J., O. Munnich, and D. Fraenkel, *Susanna, Daniel, Bel et Draco,* 2nd ed., *Septuaginta,* vol. 16.2 (Göttingen 1999)

Vulgate

Weber, R., and R. Gryson, *Biblia sacra iuxta vulgatam versionem,* 4th ed. (Stuttgart 1994)

New Testament

Aland, B., *et al., The Greek New Testament,* 4th ed. (Stuttgart 1994)

II. CONCORDANCE

Hatch, E., and H.A. Redpath, *A Concordance to the Septuagint and the Other Greek Versions of the Old Testament,* 2 voll. (Oxford 1897)

Ancient and Medieval Authors and Works: Texts, Translations, and Commentaries

I. IULIUS ROMANUS, *EPISULARUM COMMERCIUM* (LETTERS WRITTEN BY OR TO JULIUS I)[1]

Baronius (Baronio), C., *Annales ecclesiastici* (Antwerp 1593)

Brennecke, H.C., U. Heil, A. von Stockhausen, and A. Wintjes, *Athanasius Werke,* vol. 3.1: *Dokumente zur Geschichte des arianischen Streites,* fasc. 3: *Bis zur Ekthesis Makrostichos* (Berlin/New York 2007)

Coustant, P., *Epistolae romanorum pontificum, et quae ad eos scriptae sunt, a S. Clemente I. usque ad Innocentium III. etc.,* vol. 1 (Paris 1721)

Mansi, J.D., *Sacrum conciliorum nova et amplissia collectio,* 31 voll. (Florence / Venice 1759–98)

Schönemann, K., *Pontificum Romanorum a S. Clemente usque ad S. Leonem M. epistolae genuinae … ex recensione et cum notis Petri Coustantii et fratrum Balleriniorum* (Göttingen 1796)

Thiel, A., *Epistulae Romanorum pontificum genuinae et quae ad eos scriptae sunt,* vol. 1: *a S. Hilaro usque ad Pelagium II.* (Braunsberg 1868)

Wendelstein, J., *Canones apostolorum; veterum conciliorum constitutiones; decreta pontificum antiquiora* (Mainz 1525)

Wurm, H., "Decretales selectae ex antiquissimis Romanorum Pontificum epistulis decretalibus," *Apoll.* 12 (1939), pp. 40–93

1. The following are the most recent editions of the letters included in this volume: *ep.* 1) M. Vinzent, *Markell von Ankyra,* pp. 124–28 and H.C. Brennecke *et al.,* vol. 3.1.3, pp. 152–56; *ep.* 2) H.-G. Opitz, *Athanasius Werke,* vol. 2, pp. 102–13 and H.C. Brennecke *et al.,* vol. 3.1.3, pp. 156–75; *ep.* 3) M. Tetz, "Ante omnia," pp. 247–49 and H.C. Brennecke *et al.,* vol. 3.1.3, pp. 231f.; *ep.* 4) A.L. Feder, *S. Hilarii pictaviensis opera,* part 4, pp. 126–30 and H.C. Brennecke *et al.,* vol. 3.1.3, pp. 222–27; *ep.* 5) H.-G. Opitz, *Athanasius Werke,* vol. 2, pp. 133f. (secc. 1, 3f.) and G.C. Hansen, *Sokrates Kirchengeschichte,* pp. 126–28 (sec. 2); *ep.* 6) A.L. Feder, *S. Hilarii pictaviensis opera,* part 4, pp. 133f.

II. OTHER ANCIENT AND MEDIEVAL AUTHORS AND WORKS[2]

Acta conciliorum oecumenicorum, *v.* Concilia (Canones, Epistulae), *Concilia oecumenica*

Alexander alexandrinus, *epistula encyclica*

Opitz, H.-G., *Athanasius Werke,* vol. 3.1: *Urkunden zur Geschichte des arianischen Streites 318–328* (Berlin 1934–35), #4b, pp. 6–11

Anonymi Liber poenitentialis ex scrinio romanae ecclesiae assumptus (two recensions)

Canisius (De Hondt), H., *Thesaurus monumentorum ecclesiasticorum et historicorum, sive Lectiones antiquae,* vol. 2.1 (rpt. Antwerp 1725), pp. 121–39; rpt. PL, vol. 105 (Paris 1864), coll. 693–730

Anastasius Sinaita, *Doctrina patrum*

Diekamp, F., and E. Chrysos, *Doctrina patrum de incarnatione verbi,* 2nd ed. (Münster 1982)

Ansegisus

Schmitz, G., *Die Kapitulariensammlung des Ansegis,* MGH.Cap, ns, vol. 1 (Hannover 1996), pp. 431–681

Apollinaris laodicensis

Graece (Works preserved in Greek)

Lietzmann, H., *Apollinaris von Laodicea und seine Schule: Texte und Untersuchungen* (Tübingen 1904)

Syriace (Works preserved in Syriac)

Flemming, J., and H. Lietzmann, *Apollinaristische Schriften Syrisch,* AGWG.PH, vol. 7.4 (Berlin 1904)

De fide et incarnatione

Mai, A., Script. vet., vol. 7 (Rome 1833), pp. 168f.; rpt. PL, vol. 8 (Paris 1844), coll. 876f.

2. In this section, editions of the text are listed alphabetically, translations after the editions.

De unione

Mai, A., Script. vet., vol. 7 (Rome 1833), pp. 165–68; rpt. PL, vol. 8 (Paris 1844), coll. 873–75

Encyclion

Mai, A., Script. vet., vol. 7 (Rome 1833), p. 163; rpt. PL, vol. 8 (Paris 1844), col. 876

Epistula ad Dionysium

Muratori, L.A., *Anecdota graeca* (Padua 1709), pp. 341–46

Arius, *epistula ad Alexandrum*

Opitz, H.-G., *Athanasius Werke,* vol. 3.1: *Urkunden zur Geschichte des arianischen Streites 318–328* (Berlin 1934–35), #6, pp. 12f.

Asterius Sophista

Vinzent, M., *Asterius von Kappadokien: Die theologischen Fragmente, SupVigChr,* vol. 20 (Leiden 1993)

Athanasius alexandrinus

Opera omnia

Brennecke, H.C., U. Heil, A. von Stockhausen, and A. Wintjes, *v.* **Iulius romanus, *Episularum commercium***

Commelinus, H. (Commelin, J.), *B. Athanasii archiepiscopi Alexandrini opera quae reperiuntur omnia,* vol. 1 (Heidelberg 1600)

Montfaucon, B. de, *Sancti patris nostri Athanasii archiep. Alexandrini opera omnia quae extant . . . ,* vol. 1 (Paris 1698)

Apologia ad Constantium, Apologia de fuga sua, Apologia secunda, De decretis nicaenae synodi, De sententia Dionysii, epistula ad Serapionem de morte Arii, epistula encyclica, Historia arianorum ad monachos, Orationes III contra arianos, epistula de synodis Arimini et Seleuciae

Opitz, H.-G., *Athanasius Werke,* vol. 2.1–7 (Berlin/Leipzig 1935–40)

Epistula ad episcopos Aegypti et Libyae

Metzler, K., D.U. Hansen, and K. Savvidis, *Athanasius Werke,* vol. 1.1: *Die dogmatischen Schriften* (Berlin/New York 1996), pp. 1–64

Bibliography

Epistulae festales

Cureton, W., *The Festal Letter of Athanasius Discovered in an Ancient Syriac Version* (London 1848)

Lefort, L.T.S., *Athanase, Lettres festales et pastorales en copte*, CSCO, vol. 150 (Coptic) and vol. 151 (French transl.) (Paris 1955)

Tomus ad antiochenos

Montfaucon, B. de, *Sancti patris nostri Athanasii archiep. Alexandrini opera omnia quae extant . . .*, vol. 1 (Paris 1698), pp. 769–77.

Robertson, A., *St. Athanasius: Select Works and Letters*, NPNF, ser. 2, vol. 4 (London 1891)

Auellana collectio

Guenther, O., *Epistulae imperatorum pontificum aliorum inde ab. a. CCCLXVII usque ad a. DLIII datae, Auellana quae dicitur collectio*, vol. 1, CSEL, vol. 35, part 1: *Prolegomena, Epistulae I–CIV* (Vienna, *etc.* 1895), pp. 5–44

Augustinus hipponensis

Ad donatistas post collationem, Breuiculus collationis cum donatistis, Liber de unico baptismo

Petschenig, M., *Sancti Aureli Augustini Scripta contra Donatistas*, part 3: *Liber de unico baptismo, Breuiculus collationis cum donatistis, Contra partem Donati post gesta, etc.*, CSEL, vol. 53 (Vienna/Leipzig 1910)

Contra litteras Petiliani libri tres

Petschenig, M., *Sancti Aureli Augustini Scripta contra Donatistas*, part 2: *Contra litteras Petiliani libri tres, etc.*, CSEL, vol. 52 (Vienna/Leipzig 1909)

Epistulae

Goldbacher, A., *S. Aureli Augustini hipponiensis episcopi epistulae*, CSEL, vol. 33 (Prague, *etc.* 1885)

Basilius caesariensis Cappadociae, *Epistulae*

Courtonne, Y., *Saint Basile, Lettres*, 3 voll. (Paris 1957–66)

Bibliography

Benedictus Leuita

Baluzius, S. (Baluze, É.), *Capitularia regum francorum* (Paris 1677)

Hartmann, W., and G. Schmitz, *Edition der falschen Kapitularien des Benedictus Levita,* http://www.benedictus.mgh.de/

Pertz, G.H., *Benedicti capitularia,* MGH.Leges, vol. 2.2: *Capitularia spuria, etc.* (Hannover 1837), pp. 17–158; rpt. PL, vol. 97 (Paris 1862), coll. 697–912

Bonitho sutrinus (Bonizo of Sutri)

Perels, E., *Bonizo, Liber de vita christiana* (Berlin 1930)

Burchard wormatensis (Burchard of Worms)

Questenburgh, B., *D. Burchardi di Wormaciensis ... Decretorum libri xx, etc.* (Cologne 1548); rpt. with additions by Fransen, G., and T. Kölzer, *Decretorum libri xx, etc.* (Aalen 1992)

Capitulare missorum Niumagae datum (Capitulare missorum of Nijmegen)

Boretius, A., *Capitulare missorum Niumagae datum,* MGH.Cap, vol. 1 (Hannover 1883), pp. 131–33

Cassiodorus Senator

Opera omnia

Garetius (Garet), J., *Magni Aurelii Cassiodori ... opera omnia, etc.*, 2 voll. (Rouen 1679)

Historia tripartita

Jacob, W., and R. Hanslik, *Cassiodori-Epiphanii Historia ecclesiastica tripartita,* CSEL, vol. 71 (Vienna 1952)

Rhenanus (von Rheinau), B., *Auctores historiae ecclesiasticae: Eusebii Pamphili caesariensis libri IX Rufino interprete ... ; item ex Theodorito ... , Sozomeno, et Socrate ... Libri XII versi ab Epiphanio Scholastico, adbreviati per Cassiodorum senatorem unde illis Tripartitae historiae vocabulum, etc.* (Basel 1523)

Chronographus anni CCCLIV (Chronographer of 354)

Mommsen, T., "Chronographus anni CCCLIIII," in MGH.AA, vol. 9: *Chronica minora saec. IV–VII,* vol. 1 (Berlin 1892), pp. 13–153

Chrysostomus, *v.* **Iohannes Chrysostomus**

Marcus Tullius Cicero, ***Epistulae ad Atticum***

Shackleton Bailey, D.R., *Cicero's Letters to Atticus,* vol. 6: *44 B.C., 355–426* (*Books XIV–XVI*) (Cambridge 1967)

Codex theodosianus

Mommsen, T., and P. Krueger, *Theodosiani libri XVI cum constitutionibus sirmondianis* (Berlin 1905)

Collectio canonum trium librorum

Motta, G., *Collectio canonum trium librorum,* vol. 1, MIC.C, vol. 8 (Vatican 2005)

Collectio diessensis

Amort, E., *Elementa iuris canonici veteris et moderni,* 2 voll. (Augsburg 1757)

Collectio II librorum

Bernhard, J., "La collection en deux livres (cod. *Vat. lat. 3832*)," *etc.*, *RDC,* vol. 12 (1962), pp. 1–601

Collectio hispana

González, F.A., CCEH, 2 voll. (Madrid 1808–12); rpt. PL, vol. 84 (Paris 1862), coll. 93–848

Collectio Theodosii diaconis, *v.* **Leo Magnus**

Concilia (Canones, Epistulae)

Labbeus (Labbe), P., and G. Cossartius (Cossart), *Sacrosancta concilia ad regiam editionem exacta,* 17 voll. (Paris 1671–72)

Concilia oecumenica

Schwartz, E., *ACO,* 4 voll. in 14 parts (Strassburg, *etc.* 1914–74)

Percival, H., *Seven Ecumenical Councils,* NPNF, ser. 2, vol. 14 (New York 1900; rpt. Grand Rapids, Mich. 1983)

Concilium antiochenum (ca. 324), epistula synodica

F. Nau, "Littérature canonique syriaque inédite," *ROC* 14 (1909), pp. 12–24

Concilium aralatense, canones

Munier, C., *Concilia Galliae, a. 314–a. 506*, CChr.SL, vol. 148 (Turnhout 1963), pp. 3–24

Concilium eliberritanum, canones

Martínez Díez, G., CCaHi, vol. 4: *Concilios galos, Concilios hispanos, primera parte*, MHS.C, vol. 4 (Madrid 1984), pp. 233–64

Concilium neocaesariense

Turner, C.H., *EOMIA*, vol. 2.1 (Oxford 1907), pp. 116–41

Concilium nicaenum, canones

Turner, C.H., *EOMIA*, vol. 1.1 (Oxford 1904), pp. 112–43, 178–243, 255–73

Concilium serdicense, canones

Hess, H., *The Canons of the Council of Sardica, A.D. 343* (Oxford 1958), pp. 211–55

Tetz, M., "Ante omnia de sancta fide et de integritate veritatis: Glaubensfragen auf der Synode von Serdika (342)," *ZNTW* 76 (1985), pp. 252–58

Concilium serdicense, Oratio synodi serdicensis ad Constantium imperatorem

Feder, A.L., *S. Hilarii pictaviensis opera*, part 4: … *Collectanea antiariana parisina (fragmenta historica), etc.*, CSEL, vol. 65 (Vienna / Leipzig 1916), pp. 181–84

Constitutiones apostolicae

Cotelerius (Cotelier), J.-B., *Sanctorum patrum qui temporibus apostolicis floruerunt … opera*, vol. 1 (Antwerp 1698), pp. 199–423; rpt. PL, vol. 1 (Paris 1886), coll. 555–1156

Creeds, *v.* Symbola

Cyprianus carthaginiensis

Opera omnia

Hartel, W., *S. Thasci Caecili Cypriani Opera omnia, CSEL*, vol. 3.2 (Vienna 1871)

Epistulae

Diercks, G.F., *Sancti Cypriani episcopi epistularium,* CChr.SL, vol. 3B–C (Turnhout 1994–96)

Clarke, G.W., *The Letters of St. Cyprian of Carthage,* voll. 1–4, ACW, voll. 43f., 46f. (New York/Ramsey, N.J. 1984–89)

Cyrillus alexandrinus

Apologia xii capitulorum contra orientales (De recta fide ad reginas)

Schwartz, E., *ACO,* vol. 1.1.7, pp. 33–65

De recta fide ad Arcadiam et Marinam

Schwartz, E., *ACO,* vol. 1.1.5, pp. 62–118

Epiphanius constantiensis (Epiphanius of Salamis)

Opera omnia

Cornarius, J., *D. Epiphanii episcopi Constantiae Cypri, Contra octaginta haereses opus, Panarium, etc.* (Basel 1543)

Dindorf, W., *Epiphanii episcopi Constantiae opera,* vol. 3, Bibliotheca Patrum Graecorum et Latinorum (Leipzig 1861)

Oporinus, J. (Herbst or Herbster), *D. Epiphanii episcopi Constantiae Cypri, Contra octoaginta haereses opus eximium, Panarium, etc.* (Basel 1544)

Petauius (Petau), D., *Sancti patris nostri Epiphanii Constantiae ... episcopi opera omnia,* vol. 1 (Paris 1622)

Panarion

Holl, K., *Epiphanius,* vol. 3: *Panarion haer. 65–80, etc.,* GCS, vol. 37 (Leipzig 1933)

Holl, K., and J. Dummer, *Epiphanius,* vol. 3: *Panarion haer. 65–80, etc.,* 2nd ed., GCS, vol. 37 (Berlin 1985)

Öhler, F., *Panaria eorumque anacephalaeosis,* vol. 2, *CHaer,* vol. 2, pt. 3 (Berlin 1861)

Williams, F., *The Panarion of Epiphanius of Salamis, Books II and III,* NHS, vol. 36 (Leiden 1994)

Bibliography

Eusebius caesariensis

Contra Marcellum, De ecclesiastica theologia

Klostermann, E., *Eusebius Werke*, vol. 4: *Gegen Marcell, Über die kirchliche Theologie, Die Fragmente Marcells*, GCS, vol. 14 (Leipzig 1906)

Klostermann, E., and G.C. Hansen, *Eusebius Werke*, vol. 4: *Gegen Marcell, Über die kirchliche Theologie, die Fragmente Marcells*, 3rd ed., GCS, vol. 14 (Leipzig 1991)

De uita Constantini

Heikel, I.A., and F. Winkelmann, *Eusebius Werke*, vol. 1.1: Über das Leben Constantins, *etc.*, 2nd ed., GCS, vol. 7 (Berlin 1989)

Richardson, E.C., *The Life of Constantine, etc.*, in NPNF, ser. 2, vol. 1: *Eusebius: Church History, Life of Constantine the Great, etc.* (London 1890)

Eutyches, *Florilegium*

Amelli, E., *Spicilegium casinense complectans analecta sacra et profana*, vol. 1 (Monte Cassino 1888)

Florilegium edessenum

Rucker, I., *Florilegium edessenum anonymum, SBAW.PH*, 1933.5 (Munich 1933)

Gennadius Presbyter, *De uiris illustribus*

Herding, W., *Hieronymi De viris inlustribus liber. accedit Gennadii catalogus virorum inlustrium* (Leipzig 1879)

Gratianus, *Decretum*

Friedberg, E., *Corpus Iuris Canonici*, vol. 1: *Decretum Magistri Gratiani*, 2nd ed. (Leipzig 1879)

Gregorius de Sancto Grisogono, *Polycarpus*

Erdmann, C., and U. Horst, *Die Sammlung "Polycarpus" des Kardinals Gregor von S. Crisogono.* http://www.mgh.de/datenbanken/kanonessammlung-polycarp

Gregorius nazianzenus, *Epistulae*

Gallay, P., *Grégoire de Nazianze, Lettres théologique* (= *epp.* 101f., 202), SC, vol. 208 (Paris 1974)

Halitgar cameracensis (Halitgar or Haltigar of Cambrai), *Liber paenitentialis*

Schmitz, H.J., *Die Bussbücher und die Bussdisciplin der Kirche, nach handschriftlichen Quellen dargestellt* (Mainz 1883), pp. 721–33

Hieronymus Presbyter (Jerome)

Aduersus Rufinum libri III

Lardet, P., *Contra Rufinum*, CChr.SL, vol. 79 (Turnhout 1982)

Chronicon

Helm, R., and U. Treu, *Eusebius Werke,* vol. 7: *Die Chronik des Hieronymus,* GCS, vol. 47 (Berlin 1984)

Commentarii in epistulam Pauli apostoli ad Galatas

Raspanti, G., *Commentarii in epistulam Pauli apostoli ad Galatas,* CChr.SL, vol. 77A (Turnhout 2006)

Epistulae

Labourt, J., *Saint Jérôme, Lettres,* 8 voll. (Paris 1949–63)

De uiris illustribus

Richardson, E.C., *Hieronymus, Liber de uiris inlustribus, etc., TU,* vol. 14.1 (Leipzig 1896)

Hilarius pictauiensis (Hilary of Poitiers)

Opera omnia

Coustant, P., *S. Hilarii Pictavorum episcopi opera ad manuscriptos codices Gallicanos, Romanos, Belgicos, necnon ad veteres editiones castigata* (Paris 1693)

Ex opere historico fragmenta

Faber (Lefèvre), N., *B. Hilarii pictavensis . . . ex opere historico fragmenta* (Paris 1598)

Feder, A.L., *S. Hilarii pictaviensis opera,* part 4: ... *Collectanea antiariana parisina (fragmenta historica), etc.*, CSEL, vol. 65 (Vienna/Leipzig 1916)

Wickham, L., *Hilary of Poitiers: Conflicts of Conscience and Law in the Fourth-century Church* (Liverpool 1997)

Hincmarus laudensis (Hincmar of Laon), *Pittaciolus*

Schieffer, R., *Die Streitschriften Hinkmars von Reims und Hinkmars von Laon 869–871,* MGH.Conc, vol. 4, Suppl. 2 (Hannover 2004), pp. 65–97

Hippolytus

Achelis, H., *Hippolytus Werke: Kleinere exegetische und homiletische Schriften,* GCS, vol. 1.2 (Leipzig 1897)

Historia acephala

Martin, A., and M. Albert, *Histoire "acéphale" et index syriaque des lettres festales d'Athanase d'Alexandrie,* SC, vol. 317 (Paris 1985)

Inscriptiones christianae urbis Romae

De Rossi, I., and A. Silvagni, *ICUR,* 8 voll. (Rome 1861–1983)

Iohannes Chrysostomus

Homiliae in epistulam ad hebracos

Montfaucon, B. de, *Sancti patris nostri Ioannis Chrysostomi opera omnia quae extant* ..., vol. 12 (Paris 1728), pp. 1–452; rpt. PG, vol. 63, coll. 9–236

Homiliae in Iohannem

Montfaucon, B. de, *Sancti patris nostri Ioannis Chrysostomi opera omnia quae extant* ..., vol. 8 (Paris 1735), pp. 1–603; rpt. PG, vol. 59 (Paris 1862), coll. 23–482

Iohannes nicaenus, *De natiuitate domini*

Combefisius (Combefis), F., *Bibliothecae graecorum patrum auctarium novissimum* ... *opuscula Flavii Josephi, S. Hipolyti* ... *et aliorum,* vol. 2 (Paris 1672), p. 302

Isidorus hispalensis (Isidore of Seville)

De ecclesiasticis officiis

Lawson, C.M., *Sancti Isidori episcopi hispalensis De ecclesiasticis officiis,* CChr.SL, vol. 113 (Turnhout 1989)

Etymologiarum libri xx

Lindsay, W.M., *Isidori hispalensis episcopi Etymologiarum siue originum libri xx,* vol. 1: *Libros I–X continens* (Oxford 1911)

Itineraria

Itinerarium Antonini Augusti

Cuntz, O., *Itineraria romana,* vol. 1: *Itineraria Antonini Augusti et Burdigalense* (Leipzig 1929)

Tabula peutingeriana

Miller, K., *Itineraria romana: Römische Reisewege an der Hand der Tabula peutingeriana* (Stuttgart 1916)

Iudicium poenitentis

Gerbertus (Gerbert), M., *Monumenta veteris liturgiae alemannicae,* part 2 (St. Blasien 1779), pp. 12–27; rpt. PL, vol. 138 (Paris 1853), coll. 959–87

Iulianus imperator

Oratio I

Bidez, J., *L'empereur Julien, Oeuvres complètes,* vol. 1.1 (Paris 1932), pp. 10–68

Epistula ad athenienses

Bidez, J., *L'empereur Julien, Oeuvres complètes,* vol. 1.1 (Paris 1932), pp. 213–35

Iuo carnotensis (Ivo of Chartres), ***Panormia***

Brant, S., *Liber Decretorum siue Panormia Iuonis* (Basel 1499)

Brasington, B., and M. Brett, provisional edition: http://wtfaculty.wtamu.edu/~bbrasington/panormia.html

de Vosmediano, M., *Panormia seu Decretum D. Iuonis carnothensis episcopi* (Louvain 1557); rpt. PL, vol. 161 (Paris 1855), coll. 1037–1344

Iustinianus

Codex iustinianus

Krüger, P., *Corpus Iuris Ciuilis,* vol. 2: *Codex iustinianus* (Berlin 1929)

Tractatus contra monophysitas

Schwartz, E., M. Amelotti, *et al., Drei dogmatische Schriften Iustinians,* 2nd ed. (Milan 1973)

Komitas, *Sigillum fidei*

Ter-Merkerttschian, K., *Sigillum fidei* (Echmiadzin, Armenia 1914); rpt. as *Komitas, Sceau de la foi* (Louvain 1974)

***Leges uisigothorum* (Visigothic Laws)**

Zeumer, K., *Leges visigothorum,* MGH.LNG, vol. 1 (Hannover/Leipzig 1902)

Leo Magnus (Leo the Great)

Ballerini, P., and G. Ballerini, *Sancti Leonis Magni opera,* vol. 3: *Appendix ad Sancti Leonis opera* (Venice 1757); rpt. PL, vol. 56 (Paris 1865)

Leontius Byzantinus

Aduersus fraudes apollinistarum

Mai, A., Spic., vol. 10.2 (Rome 1844), pp. 128–51; rpt. PG, vol. 86.2 (Paris 1865), coll. 1947–76

De sectis, v. **Ps.-Leontius Byzantinus**

Leontius Hierosolymitanus, *Contra monophysitas*

Gray, P.T.R., *Leontius of Jerusalem, Against the Monophysites: Testimonies of the Saints and Aporiae,* OECT (Oxford 2006)

Liber poenitentialis ex scrinio romanae ecclesiae, v. Anonymi liber poenitentialis, etc.

Liber pontificalis

Duchesne, L., *Le liber pontificalis,* vol. 1 (Paris 1886)

Vogel, C., *Le liber pontificalis,* vol. 3 (Paris 1957)

Davis, R., *The Book of Pontiffs* (*Liber pontificalis*): *The Ancient Biographies of the First Ninety Roman Bishops to AD 715* (Liverpool 2000)

Liber sacramentorum augustodunensis

Heiming, O., *Liber sacramentorum augustodunensis* (Turnhout 1984)

Libri poenitentiales, v. Anonymi liber poenitentialis ex scrinio romanae ecclesiae assumptus;* Halitgar cameracensis (Halitgar or Haltigar of Cambrai); *Iudicium poenitentis; Liber sacramentorum augustodunensis; Ps.-Cummeanus, Poenitentiale; Ps.-Theodorus cantuariensis* (Ps.-Theodore of Canterbury), *Poenitentiale

Marcellus ancyranus

De sancta ecclesia

Logan, A., "Marcellus of Ancyra (Pseudo-Anthimus), 'On the Holy Church': Text, Translation and Commentary," *JThS* ns 51 (2000), pp. 81–112

Fragmenta

Klostermann, E., and G.C. Hansen, *Eusebius Werke*, vol. 4: *Gegen Marcell, Über die kirchliche Theologie, die Fragmente Marcells*, 3rd ed., GCS, vol. 14 (Leipzig 1991)

Rettberg, C.H.G., *Marcelliana, etc.* (Göttingen 1794)

Vinzent, M., *Markell von Ankyra: Die Fragmente und der Brief an Julius von Rom, SupVigChr*, vol. 39 (Leiden 1997)

Martyrium Agapae, Irenae, et Chionae

Musurillo, H., *The Acts of the Christian Martyrs* (Oxford 1972), pp. 280–93

Michael Syrus, *Chronicon*

Chabot, J.-B., *Chronique de Michel le Syrien: Patriarche Jacobite d'Antioche* (*1166–99*), 4 voll. (Paris 1899–1924)

Nicaea, Canons of the Council of, *v.* Concilia (Canones, Epistulae), *Concilium nicaenum, etc.*

Nicephorus Callistus, *Historia ecclesiastica*

Ducaeus (du Duc), F., *Nicephori Callisti filii Xanthopuli ecclesiasticae historiae libri XVIII*, 2 voll. (Paris 1630); rpt. PG, voll. 145f. (Paris 1865)

Optatus mileuitanus, *Contra Parmenianum donatistam*

Ziwsa, C., *Optatus mileuitanus, Contra Parmenianum dontatistam,* CSEL, vol. 26 (Vienna/Leipzig 1893)

Oratio synodi serdicensis, v.* Concilia (Canones, Epistulae), *Concilium serdicense, etc.

Penitential books, *v.* Libri poenitentiales

Philostorgius, *Historia ecclesiastica*

Bidez, J., and F. Winkelmann, *Kirchengeschichte,* 3rd ed., GCS, vol. 21 (Berlin 1981)

Philoxenus hierapolitanus (Philoxenus of Mabbug), *Epistula ad monachos in Senun*

Halleux, A. de, *Philoxène de Mabbog, Lettre aux moines de Senoun,* CSCO, voll. 231 (Syriac) and 232 (French transl.) (Louvain 1963)

Photius constantinopolitanus, *Bibliotheca*

Henry, R., Photius, *Bibliothèque,* vol. 4: *Codices 223–229* (Paris 1965)

Ps.-Cummeanus, *Poenitentiale*

Wasserschleben, F.W.A., *Die Bußordnungen der abendländischen Kirche* (Halle 1851), pp. 460–93

Ps.-Isidorus Mercator (Ps.-Isidore), *Decretalium collectio*

Merlin, J., *Concilia generalia graeca et latina* (Cologne 1530; corrected ed. in PL, vol. 130, Paris, 1880, coll. v–1178)

Hinschius, P., *Decretales pseudo-isidorianae, et Capitula Angilramni* (Leipzig 1863)

Schon, K.-G., and K. Zechiel-Eckes, *Projekt Pseudoisidor,* http://www.pseudoisidor.mgh.de/html/text.html

Ps.-Iulius romanus

Anaphora

Raes, A., "Anaphora Iulii Papae," *Anaphorae syriacae,* vol. 3.1 (Rome 1981), pp. 73–101

Epistulae, v. App. B

Ps.-Leontius Byzantinus, *De sectis* (*CPG* #6823)

Gallandius (Gallandi), A., BVP, vol. 12 (Venice 1778), pp. 625-57; rpt. PG, vol. 86.1 (Paris 1860), coll. 1193–1268

Ps.-Theodorus cantuariensis (Ps.-Theodore of Canterbury), *Poenitentiale*

Wasserschleben, F.W.A., *Die Bußordnungen der abendländischen Kirche* (Halle 1851), pp. 145–219

McNeill, J.T., and H.M. Gamer, *Medieval Handbooks of Penance,* Records of Western Civilization (New York 1938), pp. 182–215

Regino Prumiensis, *Libri duo de synodalibus causis et disciplinis ecclesiasticis*

Wasserschleben, F.W.A., *Reginonis abbatis prumiensis libri duo de synodalibus causis et disciplinis ecclesiasticis* (Leipzig 1840); rpt. PL, vol. 132 (Paris 1880), coll. 187–370

Rufinus, *Historia ecclesiastica*

Schwartz, E., and T. Mommsen, *Eusebius Werke*, vol. 4.2: *Kirchengeschichte VI–X, Die lateinische Übersetzung des Rufinus,* GCS, vol. 9.2 (Leipzig 1908)

Seuerus antiochenus

Aduersus apologiam Iuliani

Hespel, R., *La polémique antijulianist*e, 2B, CSCO, voll. 301 (Syriac) and 302 (French transl.) (Louvain 1969)

Apologia philalethis

Hespel, R., *La polémique antijulianiste*, 3, CSCO, voll. 318 (Syriac) and 319 (French transl.) (Louvain 1971)

Censura tomi Iuliani

Hespel, R., *La polémique antijulianiste,* 1, CSCO, voll. 244 (Syriac) and 245 (French transl.) (Louvain 1964)

Epistula ad Sergium grammaticum

Lebon, J., *Severi antiocheni Orationes ad Nephalium eiusdem ac Sergii Grammatici epistulae mutuae*, CSCO, vol. 119, pp. 73–177 (Syriac) and vol. 120, pp. 53–136 (Latin transl.) (Paris 1929–38)

Liber contra impium grammaticum

Lebon, J., *Severi antiocheni liber contra impium grammaticum, Orationes III,* CSCO, voll. 93, 101, 111 (Syriac) and 94, 102, 112 (Latin transl.) (Paris 1929–38)

Orationes ad Nephalium

Lebon, J., *Orationes ad Nephalium,* CSCO, voll. 119, pp. 1–69 (Syriac) and 120, pp. 1–50 (Latin transl.) (Louvain 1949)

Severus Ibn al-Muqaffaʿ, *Refutation of Saʿīd Ibn-Batriq (Eutychius) (The Book of the Councils)*

Chébli, P., PO, vol. 3.2: *Réfutations d'Eutychius, par Sévère, évêque d'Aschmounaïn* (Paris 1909), pp. 121–242

***Sigillum fidei, v.* Komitas**

Socrates Scholasticus, *Historia ecclesiastica*

Bright, W., *Socrates' Ecclesiastical History* (Oxford 1878; 2nd ed., 1893)

Hansen, G.C., *Sokrates Kirchengeschichte,* GCS, neue Folge, vol. 1 (Berlin 1995)

Hussey, R., *Socratis Scholastici Ecclesiastica historia,* 3 voll. (Oxford 1853)

Stephanus (Estienne), R., *Ecclesiasticae historiae ... Socratis libri VII* (Paris 1544)

Valesius (de Valois), H., *Socratis Scholastici et Hermiae Sozomeni Historia ecclesiastica* (Paris 1668)

Zenos, A.C., *The Ecclesiastical History of Socrates Scholasticus,* NPNF, ser. 2, vol. 2, *Socrates, Sozomenus: Church Histories* (London 1890)

Sozomenus, *Historia ecclesiastica*

Bidez, J., and G.C. Hansen, *Sozomenus Kirchengeschichte,* GCS, vol. 50 (Berlin 1960)

Hansen, G.C., *Sozomenus Kirchengeschichte,* 2nd ed., GCS, neue Folge, vol. 4 (Berlin 1995)

Hussey, R., *Sozomeni Ecclesiastica historia,* 3 voll. (Oxford 1860)

Stephanus (Estienne), R., *Ecclesiasticae historiae ... Hermii Sozomeni libri IX* (Paris 1544)

Valesius (de Valois), H., *Socratis Scholastici et Hermiae Sozomeni Historia ecclesiastica* (Paris 1668)

Walford, E., *The Ecclesiastical History of Sozomen Comprising a History of the Church from 324 to A.D. 440, Translated from the Greek, etc.* (London 1855)

Symbola (Creeds)

Hahn, A., G.L. Hahn, and A. Harnack, *Bibliothek der Symbole und Glaubensregeln der alten Kirche,* 3rd ed. (Wroclaw 1897; rpt. Hildesheim 1962)

Symbolum nicaenum

Dossetti, G.L., *Il simbolo di Nicea e di Costantinopoli* (Rome 1967)

Opitz, H.-G., *Athanasius Werke,* vol. 3.1: *Urkunden zur Geschichte des arianischen Streites 318–328* (Berlin 1934–35), #24, pp. 51f.

Symbolum romanum

Hahn, A., G.L. Hahn, and A. Harnack, *Bibliothek der Symbole und Glaubensregeln der alten Kirche,* 3rd ed. (Wroclaw 1897; rpt. Hildesheim 1962), #19, pp. 24f.

Synodicon uetus

Duffy, J.M., and J. Parker, *The Synodicon vetus,* CFHB.W, vol. 15 (Washington, D.C. 1979)

Theodoretus cyrrhensis

Epistulae

Azéma, Y., *Théodoret de Cyr, Correpondance,* vol. 2f., SC, voll. 98 (*Epist. sirm. 1–95*) and 111 (*Epist. sirm. 96–147*) (Paris 1964–65)

Haereticarum fabularum compendium

Schulze, J.L., *Theodoreti cyrensis episcopi opera omnia,* vol. 4 (Halle 1772), pp. 285–481; rpt. PG, vol. 83 (Paris 1859), coll. 336–556

Historia ecclesiastica

Parmentier, L., F. Scheidweiler, and G.C. Hansen, *Theodoretus Cyri, Kirchengeschichte,* 3rd ed., GCS, vol. 19 (Berlin 1998)

Timotheos (apollinarista) berytensis, *Epistula ad Homonium episcopum*

Lietzmann, H., *Apollinaris von Laodicea und seine Schule: Texte und Untersuchungen* (Tübingen 1904), pp. 277f.

Mai, A., Spic., vol. 10.2 (Rome 1844), pp. 138–40; rpt. PG, vol. 86.2 (Paris 1865), col. 1961

Timotheos II alexandrinus (Timothy Aelurus)

Contra eos qui dicunt duas naturas

Ter-Merkerttschian, K., and E. Ter-Minassiantz, *Timotheus Älurus' des Patriarches von Alexandrien Widerlegung der auf der Synode zu Chalcedon festgesetzten Lehre: Armenischer Text mit deutschem und armenischem Vorwort* (Leipzig 1908)

Epistula ad constantinopolitanum

Ebied, R., and L. Wickham, "A Collection of Unpublished Syriac Letters of Timothy Aelurus," *JThS* 21 (1970), pp. 332f. and 351f.

Refutatio synodi chalcedonensis et tomi Leonis

Ebied, R., and L. Wickham, "Timothy Aelurus: Against Chalcedon," = pp. 115–66 in Laga, C., *et al., After Chalcedon: Studies in Theology and Church History Offered to Professor Albert van Roey for His Seventieth Birthday, OLA,* vol. 18 (Leuven 1985)

Nau, F., PO, vol. 13.2: *Texts monophysites, Extraits de Timothée Ælure* (Paris 1917), pp. 218–36

Visigothic Laws, *v.* ***Leges uisigothorum***

Zacharias Mitylenensis Rhetor (Zacharias Rhetor), ***Historia ecclesiastica (= The Syriac Chronicle)***

Brooks, E., *Historia ecclesiastica Zachariae Rhetori vulgo adscripta,* CSCO, voll. 83 (Syriac) and 87 (Latin transl.) (Louvain 1953)

Hamilton, F., and E. Brooks, *The Syriac Chronicle Known as That of Zachariah of Mitylene* (London 1899)

Secondary Works: Dictionaries, Monographs, Essays, Articles, *Etc.*

Achelis, H., *v.* **Hippolytus**

Allen, P., and C.T.R. Hayward, *Severus of Antioch* (London 2004)

Amelli, E., *v.* **Eutyches, *Florilegium***

Amman, E., "Jules I," *DThC,* vol. 8.2 (Paris 1925), coll. 1914–17

Amort, E., *v.* ***Collectio diessensis***

Bibliography

Andrieu, M., *Les ordines romani du haut moyen age*, vol. 1: *Les manuscrits* (Louvain 1931)

Armellini, M., *Le chiese di Roma dal secolo IV al XIX*, 2 voll. (Rome 1942)

Bagnall, R., *et al.*, *Consuls of the Later Roman Empire* (Atlanta 1987)

Baldwin, B., "Lucian of Antioch," *ODB*, pp. 1255f.

Baldwin, B., and A.-M. Talbot, "Eusebios of Nikomedeia," *ODB*, pp. 752f.

Barbour, R., *Greek Literary Hands, A.D. 400–1600* (Oxford 1981)

Bardy, G., "17. Athanase d'Alexandrie," *DHGE*, vol. 4: *Argaiz–Athaulf* (Paris 1930), coll. 1313–40

_______, *Recherches sur saint Lucien d'Antioche et son école* (Paris 1936)

_______, "The Eusebian Reaction and the Schism of Sardica," in *The Church in the Christian Roman Empire*, vol. 1, ed. J. Palanque (London 1949), pp. 110–56

Barnard, L.W., "Pope Julius, Marcellus of Ancyra, and the Council of Sardica: A Reconsideration," *RThAM* 38 (1971), pp. 69–79

_______, "Two Notes on Athanasius," in *Studies in Church History and Patristics, ABla* 26 (1978), pp. 329–40

_______, *Studies in Athanasius' Apologia Secunda* (Bern 1992)

Barnes, T.D., *Constantine and Eusebius* (Cambridge, Mass. 1981)

_______, *Athanasius and Constantius: Theology and Politics in the Constantinian Empire* (Cambridge, Mass. 1993)

Bernhard, J., *v.* ***Collectio II librorum***

Bidez, J., *La tradition manuscrite de Sozomène et la Tripartite de Théodore le Lecteur, TU*, vol. 59 (Leipzig 1908)

Bischoff, B., *Die Südostdeutschen Schreibschulen und Bibliotheken in der Karolingerzeit*, vol. 1: *Die bayrischen Diözesen*; vol. 2: *Die vorwiegend österreichische Diözesen* (Wiesbaden 1960)

_______, "Panorama der Handschriftenüberlieferung aus der Zeit Karl des Grossen," in *Karl der Grosse: Lebenswerk und Nachleben*, ed. W. Braunfels, vol. 2 (Düsseldorf 1965), pp. 233–54

_______, *Mittelalterliche Studien: Ausgewählte Aufsätze zur Schriftkunde und Literaturgeschichte*, 2 voll. (Stuttgart 1966–67)

_______, "Frühkarolingische Handschriften und ihre Heimat," *Scr* 22 (1968), pp. 306–14

Bibliography

Boretius, A., *v.* ***Capitulare missorum of Nijmegen***

Brandenburg, H., *Ancient Churches of Rome from the Fourth to the Seventh Century,* Bibliothèque de l'antiquité tardive, vol. 8 (Turnhout 2005)

Brennecke, H.C., *Hilarius von Poitiers und die Bischofsopposition gegen Konstantius II.: Untersuchungen zur dritten Phase des arianischen Streites* (337–361), *PTS,* vol. 26 (Berlin 1984)

Brennecke, H.C., U. Heil, A. von Stockhausen, and A. Wintjes, *Athanasius Werke, v.* **Iulius romanus, *Episularum commercium***

Brett, M., "Urban II and the Collections attributed to Ivo of Chartres," in *Proceedings of the Eighth International Congress of Medieval Canon Law,* ed. S. Chodorow (San Diego 1988) = MIC.S, vol. 9 (1992), pp. 27–46

Brightman, F., "Six Notes," *JThS* 29 (1928), pp. 158–65

Burian, J., "Itinerare, II. Imperium romanum," *BNP.A,* vol. 6: *Hat–Jus* (Leiden/Boston 2005), pp. 1023f.

Burn, A., *The Athanasian Creed and Its Early Commentaries, TaS,* vol. 4.1 (Cambridge 1895)

Camplani, A., *Le lettere festali di Atanasio di Alessandria: Studio storico-critico* (Rome 1989)

Canisius, H., *Antiquae lectiones,* vol. 4 (Ingolstadt 1603)

Caspar, E., *Geschichte des Papsttums,* vol. 1: *Römische Kirche und Imperium romanum* (Tübingen 1930)

Caspari, C.P., *Ungedruckte, unbeachtete und wenig beachtete Quellen zur Geschichte des Taufsymbols und der Glaubensregel,* vol. 3 (Oslo 1875)

Catalogus codicum graecorum qui in bibliotheca urbica vratislaviensi adservantur (Wroclaw 1889)

Cavalcanti, E., "Timothy the Apollinarist," *EEC,* vol. 2: *N–Z* (Cambridge 1992), pp. 841f.

Ceresi, M., *Catalogo dei manoscritti della Biblioteca casanatense,* vol. 4 (Rome 1961)

Chabot, P., "Les citations patristiques grecques du 'Sceau de la foi,'" *RHE* 25 (1929), pp. 5–32

Chadwick, H., "Faith and Order at the Council of Nicaea: A Note on the Background of the Sixth Canon," *HThR* 53.3 (1960), pp. 171–95

Chapman, J., *Studies on the Early Papacy* (London 1928)

Combefis, F., *v.* **Iohannes nicaenus**

Conybeare, F.C., "Newly Discovered Letters of Dionysius of Alexandria to the Popes Stephen and Xystus," *EHR* 25 (1910), pp. 111–14

Cross, F.L., and E.A. Livingstone, *ODCC*, 3rd ed. (Oxford 1997)

Cuntz, O., *v.* **Itineraria, *Itinerarium Antonini Augusti***

Cushing, K., *Papacy and Law in the Gregorian Revolution: The Canonistic Work of Anselm of Lucca* (Oxford 1998)

Davenport, E.H., *The False Decretals* (Oxford 1916)

de Andrés, G., *Catálogo de los códices griegos de la Real Biblioteca de El Escorial,* vol. 2: *Códices 179–420;* vol. 3: *Códices 421–649* (Madrid 1965, 1967)

De Clercq, V.C., *Ossius of Cordova: A Contribution to the History of the Constantinian Period* (Washington, D.C., 1954)

de Halleux, A., *Philoxène de Mabbog: Sa vie, ses écrits, sa théologie, DGMFT,* ser. 3, vol. 8 (Louvain 1963)

De León, E., *La "cognatio spiritualis" según Graciano,* Pontificio Ateneo della Santa Croce, Monografie Giuridiche, vol. 10 (Milan 1996)

Diekamp, F., "Das Glaubensbekenntnis des apollinaristischen Bischofs Vitalis von Antiochien," *ThQ* 86 (1904), pp. 497–511.

Diercks, G.F., *Sancti Cypriani episcopi epistularium: Prolegomena,* CChr.SL, vol. 3D (Turnhout 1999)

Dobiaš-Roždestvenskaja, O., *Les anciens manuscrits latins de la bibliothèque publique Saltykov-Ščedrin de Leningrad: VIIIe–début IXe siècle* (Paris 1991)

Dossetti, G., *v.* **Symbola (Creeds), *Symbolum nicaenum***

Duchesne, L., *Fastes épiscopaux de l'ancienne Gaule,* vol. 1, 2nd ed. (Paris 1907).

_______, *v.* ***Liber pontificalis***

Eltester, W., "Die Kirchen Antiochias im IV. Jahrhundert," *ZNTW* 36 (1937), pp. 251–86

Feder, A.L., *Studien zu Hilarius von Poitiers 1–3, SAWW.PH* 162.4 (1910), pp. 1–188; 166.5 (1910), pp. 1–133; 169.5 (1912), pp. 1–144

Ferrua, A., *Epigrammata damasiana, SSAC,* vol. 2 (Vatican 1942)

Field, L., *On the Communion of Damasus and Meletius: Fourth-Century Synodal Formulae in the Codex Veronensis LX, STPIMS,* vol. 145 (Toronto 2004)

Flemming, J., and H. Lietzmann, *v.* **Apollinaris laodicensis, *Syriace***

Fournier, P., and G. Le Bras, *Histoire des collections canoniques en occident depuis les fausses décrétales jusqu'au Décret de Gratien,* 2 voll., Bibliothèque d'Histoire du Droit, voll. 4f. (Paris 1931–32)

Fowler-Magerl, L., *Clavis canonum: Selected Canon Law Collections before 1140,* MGH.H, vol. 21 (Hannover 2005)

Gallandi, A., *v.* **Ps.-Leontius Byzantinus, *De sectis***

Geerard, M., *CPG,* vol. 2 (Turnhout 1974)

Geertman, H., *Hic fecit basilicam: Studi sul Liber pontificalis e gli edifici ecclesiastici di Roma da Silvestro a Silverio* (Leuven 2004)

Gentz, G., *Die Kirchengeschichte des Nicephorus Callistus Xanthopulus und ihre Quellen, TU,* vol. 98 (Berlin 1966)

Girardet, K., *Kaisergericht und Bischofsgericht, Ant.,* ser. 1, Abhandlungen zur alten Geschichte, vol. 21 (Bonn 1975)

Glare, P.G.W., *OLD* (Oxford 1982)

Graf, G., "Unechte Zeugnisse römischer Päpste für den Monophysitismus im arabischen 'Bekenntnis der Väter,'" *RQ* 36 (1928), pp. 197–233

_______, "Zwei dogmatische Florilegien der Kopten," *OCP* 3 (1937), pp. 49–77, 345–402

Gregory, T.E., "Philoxenos of Mabbug," *ODB,* p. 1664

_______, "Severos," *ODB,* pp. 1884f.

_______, "Timotheos Ailouros," *ODB,* pp. 2086f.

Griffith, S.H., "Michael I the Syrian," *ODB,* pp. 1362f.

Guerrini, P., "Le chiese e i monasteri del Trastevere" in *Ecclesiae Urbis: Atti del congresso internazionale di studi sulle chiese di Roma, (IV–X secolo) Roma, 4–10 settembre 2000,* 3 voll., ed. F. Guidobaldi and A.G. Guidobaldi, vol. 1 (Vatican City 2002), pp. 377–96

Gwynn, D.M., *The Eusebians: The Polemic of Athanasius of Alexandria and the Construction of the 'Arian Controversy,' OTM* (Oxford 2006)

Halfond, G., *Archaeology of Frankish Church Councils, AD 511–768* (Leiden/Boston 2010)

Hanson, R.P.C., "The Fate of Eustathius of Antioch," *ZKG* 95 (1984), pp. 171–79

_______, *The Search for the Christian Doctrine of God: The Arian Controversy 318–381* (Edinburgh 1988)

Heil, U., "Markell von Ancyra und das Romanum" in *Von Arius zum Athanasianum: Studien zur Edition der Athanasius Werke*, ed. H.C. Brennecke and A. von Stockhausen, *TU*, vol. 164 (Berlin 2010), pp. 85–103

Heiming, O., *v.* ***Liber sacramentorum augustodunensis***

Hess, H., *v.* **Concilia (Canones, Epistulae),** ***Concilium serdicense, canones***

Hinschius, P., *v.* **Ps.-Isidorus Mercator**

Hoffmann, H., and R. Pokorny, *Das Dekret des Bischofs Burchard von Worms: Textstufen—frühe Verbreitung—Vorlagen*, MGH.H, vol. 12 (Munich 1991)

Hofmann, J., "Altenglische und althochdeutsche Glossen aus Würzburg und dem weiteren angelsächsischen Missionsgebiet," *BGDS*(*H*) 85 (1963), pp. 27–131

Holl, K., *Die handschriftliche Überlieferung des Epiphanius—Ancoratus und Panarion*, *TU*, vol. 36.2 (Leipzig 1910)

_______, "Ein Bruchstück aus einem bisher unbekannten Brief des Epiphanius," *Gesammelte Aufsätze zur Kirchengeschichte*, vol. 2 (Tübingen 1928), pp. 204–24

Honigmann, E., "La liste originale des Pères de Nicée: à propos de l'évêché de 'Sodoma' en Arabie," *Byz.* 14 (1939), pp. 17–76

Huelsen, C., *Le chiese di Roma nel medio evo, cataloghi ed appunti* (Florence 1927)

Hunger, H., *Katalog der griechischen Handschriften der Österreichischen Nationalbibliothek*, part 1: *Codices historici; codices philosophici et philologici* (Vienna 1961)

Inguanez, M., *Codicum casinensium manuscriptorum catalogus*, vol. 2.2 (Monte Cassino 1934)

Jacob, W., and R. Hanslik, *Die handschriftliche Überlieferung der sogenannten Historia tripartita des Epiphanius-Cassiodor*, *TU*, vol. 59 (Berlin 1954)

Jaffé, P., and F. Kaltenbrunner, *Regesta pontificum romanorum ab condita ecclesia ad annum post Christum natum MCXCVIII*, vol. 1: *A S. Petro ad a. MCXLIII*, 2nd ed. (Leipzig 1885)

Jalland, T., *The Church and the Papacy* (London 1944)

Jasper, D., and H. Fuhrmann, *Papal Letters in the Early Middle Ages* (Washington, D.C., 2001)

Johns, J., "Latin Palaeography" in *Medieval Studies: An Introduction,* 2nd ed., J.M. Powell (Syracuse 1992), pp. 3–81

Kazhdan, A., *et al., ODB,* vol. 1: *Aaro–Eski;* vol. 2: *Esot–Nika;* vol. 3: *Nike–Zygo* (New York/Oxford 1991)

Kelly, J.N.D., *Early Christian Creeds,* 3rd ed. (London 1972)

Kéry, L., *Canonical Collections of the Early Middle Ages (c. 400–1140): A Bibliographical Guide to the Manuscripts and Literature* (Washington, D.C. 1999)

Kirsch, J.P., "Benedict Levita," *CE,* vol. 2: *Assize–Brown* (New York 1907), pp. 466f.

Klein, R., *Constantius II. und die christliche Kirche,* Impulse der Forschung, vol. 26 (Darmstadt 1977)

Kraus, H.P. (firm), *Choice Books and Manuscripts from Distinguished Private Library,* Catalogue 126 (New York 1971)

Krausmuller, D., "Leontius of Jerusalem, a Theologian of the Seventh Century," *JThS* ns 52 (2001), pp. 637–57

Krautheimer, R., "The Ecclesiastical Building Policy of Constantine," in *Costantino il Grande: Dall'antichità all'umanesimo, Colloquio sul cristianesimo nel mondo antico, Macerata, 18–20 dicembre 1990,* 2 voll., ed. G. Bonamente and F. Fusco (Rome 1993), vol. 2, pp. 509–52

Kuttner, S., and R. Elze, *A Catalogue of Canon and Roman Law Manuscripts in the Vatican Library,* vol. 1: *Codices vaticani latini 541–2299;* vol. 2: *Codices vaticani latini 2300–2746, StT,* voll. 322 and 328 (Vatican 1986–87)

Labbeus (Labbe), P., *v.* **Concilia (Canones, Epistulae)**

Landau, P., "Kanonistische Aktivität in Regensburg im frühen Mittelalter," in *U.R.: Schriftenreihe der Universität Regensburg,* vol. 1: *Zwei Jahrtausende Regensburg,* ed. D. Albrecht (Regensburg 1979), pp. 55–74

Leclercq, H., "Jules 1er," *DACL,* vol. 8.1 (Paris 1928), coll. 288f.

Lejay, P., "Valois, Henri," *CE,* vol. 15: *Tournon–Zwirner, Errata* (New York 1912), pp. 263f.

Lettenbauer, W., "Eine lateinische Kanonessammlung in Mähren im IX. Jh.," *OCP* 18 (1952), pp. 246–69

Levison, W., "Die Handschriften des Museums Meermanno-Westreenianum im Haag," *NA* 38 (1913), pp. 503–34

LSJ, 9th ed., *With a Supplement* (Oxford 1968)

Lienhard, J., "Did Athanasius Reject Marcellus?" in *Arianism after Arius: Essays on the Development of the Fourth-Century Trinitarian Conflicts,* ed. M. Barnes and D. Williams (Edinburgh 1993), pp. 65–80

_______, *Contra Marcellum: Marcellus of Ancyra and Fourth-Century Theology* (Washington, D.C., 1999)

Logan, A., "Marcellus of Ancyra and the Councils of AD 325: Antioch, Ancyra, and Nicaea," *JThS,* ns 43.2 (1992), pp. 428–46

_______, "Constantine, the Liber Pontificalis, and the Christian Basilicas of Rome," *StPatr* 50 (2011), pp. 31–53

Löhr, W., *Die Entstehung der homöischen und homöusianischen Kirchenparteien: Studien zur Synodalgeschichte des 4. Jahrhunderts* (Witterschlick / Bonn 1986)

Lowe, E.A., *Scriptura beneventana: Facsimiles of South Italian and Dalmatian Manuscripts from the Sixth to the Fourteenth Century,* 2 voll. (Oxford 1929)

_______, *CLA,* 11 voll. and *Supplement* (Oxford 1934–71)

Maassen, F., *Bibliotheca latina juris canonici manuscripta,* 1: "Italy" *SAWW.PH* 53 (1866), pp. 373–427; 2: "France" 54 (1866), pp. 157–288; 3: "Spain, England, Belgium, Switzerland," 56 (1867), pp. 157–212

_______, *Geschichte der Quellen und der Literatur des canonischen Rechts,* vol. 1: *Die Rechtssammlungen bis zur Mitte des 9. Jahrhunderts* (Graz 1870)

Mai, A., Script. vet., *v.* **Apollinaris laodicensis, *De fide et incarnatione, De unione, Encyclion***

_______, Spic., *v.* **Leontius Byzantinus**

Martínez Díez, G., *v.* **Concilia (Canones, Epistulae), *Concilium eliberritanum, canones***

Marucchi, O., *Il cimitero e la basilica di S. Valentino* (Roma 1890)

Massigli, R., "Sur l'origine de la collection canonique dite Hadriana augmentée," *MAH* 32 (1912), pp. 363–83

McGuckin, J., *Saint Cyril of Alexandria and the Christological Controversy, SupVigChr,* vol. 23 (Leiden 1997; rpt. Crestwood, NY 2004)

McNeill, J.T., and H.M. Gamer, *v.* **Ps.-Theodorus cantuariensis (Ps.-Theodore of Canterbury), *Poenitentiale***

Meslin, M., *Les ariens d'occident, 335–430* (Paris 1967)

Miller, K., *v.* **Itineraria, *Tabula peutingeriana***

Mordek, H., *Kirchenrecht und Reform in Frankreich: Die Collectio "Vetus gallica," die älteste systematische Kanonessammlung des fränkischen Gallien* (Berlin 1975)

Moschonas, T.D., *Κατάλογοι τῆς πατριαρχικῆς βιβλιοθήκης,* vol. 1, *Χειρόγραφα* (Alexandria 1945); rpt. as *Catalogue of MSS of the Patriarchal Library of Alexandria* in J. Geerlings, ed., *Studies and Documents* XXVI (Salt Lake City, Utah 1965)

Mösinger, G., *Monumenta syriaca ex romanis codicibus collecta,* vol. 2 (Innsbruck 1878)

Munby, A.N.L., *Phillipps Studies,* vol. 5 (Cambridge 1960)

Munier, C., "Cinq canons inédits du concile d'Hippone du 8 Octobre 393," *RDC* 18 (1968), pp. 16–29

_______, *v.* **Concilia (Canones, Epistulae),** ***Concilium aralatense, canones***

Muratori, L.A., *v.* **Apollinaris laodicensis,** ***Epistula ad Dionysium***

Muzzioli, G., "Il codice veronese LX (58) (+ Casan. 378) e il vescovo Raterio" in *Atti del congresso internazionale di diritto romano e di storia del diritto, Verona, 27–29 settembre 1948,* 4 voll., ed. G. Moschetti, vol. 1 (Milan 1951), pp. 215–31

Nordberg, H., *Athanasius and the Emperor, Comm. hum. Litt.*, vol. 30.3 (Helsinki 1963)

Norton, P., *Episcopal Elections 250–600: Hierarchy and Popular Will in Late Antiquity* (Oxford 2007)

Ohme, H., *Kanon ekklesiastikos: Die Bedeutung des altkirchliken Kanonbegriffs* (Berlin 1998)

Omont, H., *Inventaire sommaire des manuscrits grecs de la Bibliothèque Nationale,* vol. 1: *Ancien fonds grec, Theologie* (Paris 1886)

Opitz, H.-G., *Untersuchungen zur Überlieferung der Schriften des Athanasius,* AKG 23 (Berlin 1935)

_______, *v.* **Alexander alexandrinus,** ***epistula encyclica;*** **Arius,** ***epistula ad Alexandrum;*** **Athanasius alexandrinus,** ***Apologia ad Constantium, etc.;*** **Symbola (Creeds),** ***Symbolum nicaenum***

Ott, M., "Coustant, Pierre," *CE,* vol. 4: *Cland–Diocesan* (New York 1908), pp. 454f.

Parvis, S., *Marcellus of Ancyra and the Lost Years of the Arian Controversy 325–345* (Oxford 2006)

Percival, H., *v.* **Concilia (Canones, Epistulae),** ***Concilia oecumenica***

Perels, E., *v.* **Bonitho sutrinus**

Pietri, C., "La question d'Athanase vue de Rome (338–360)" in *Politique et théologie chez Athanase d'Alexandrie* (Actes du colloque de Chantilly 23–25 septembre 1973), ed. C. Kannengiesser (Paris 1974), pp. 93–126

_______, *Roma christiana,* 2 voll., *BEFAR,* vol. 224 (Rome 1976)

Pietri, C. and L. Pietri, *Prosopographie chrétienne du bas-empire,* vol. 2: *Prosopographie de l'Italie chrétienne (313–604),* part 2 (Rome 2000)

Pitra, J., *Analecta sacra spicilegio solesmensi parata,* 8 voll. (1876–91)

Plotzek, J., and A. von Euw, *Die Handschriften der Sammlung Ludwig,* vol. 4 (Cologne 1985)

Quasten, J., *Patrology,* vol. 3: *The Golden Age of Greek Patristic Literature from the Council of Nicaea to the Council of Chalcedon* (Utrecht 1950)

Quasten, J., and A. di Berardino, *Patrology,* vol. 4: *The Golden Age of Latin Patristic Literature from the Council of Nicaea to the Council of Chalcedon,* transl. P. Solari (Westminster, Md. 1986)

Raes, A., *v.* **Ps.-Iulius romanus**

Reifferscheid, A., *Bibliotheca patrum latinorum italica, SAWW.PH* 49 (1865), pp. 4–112; 50 (1865), pp. 737–72; 53 (1866), pp. 304–51; 56 (1867), pp. 441–556; 59 (1868), pp. 41–142; 63 (1870), pp. 567–749; 67 (1871), pp. 467–568; 68 (1871), pp. 471–638; 71 (1872), pp. 5–168; rpt. 2 voll. (Vienna 1872)

Renaudot, E., *Historia patriarcharum alexandrinorum jacobitarum* (Paris 1713)

Rist, J., "Dionysius [55] Exiguus," *BNP.A,* vol. 4: *Cyr–Epy* (Leiden /Boston 2004), p. 494

_______, "Eusebius, Bishop of Nicomedia," *BNP.A,* vol. 5: *Equ–Has* (Leiden/Boston 2004), pp. 226f.

Rius, J., "El Concilio de Nicea en la provincia eclesiástica tarraconense," *AST* 2 (1926), pp. 553–92

Rolker, C., *Canon Law and the Letters of Ivo of Chartres* (Cambridge 2010)

Rucker, I., *v.* ***Florilegium edessenum***

Saltet, L., "False Decretals," *CE,* vol. 5: *Diocese–Fathers* (New York 1901), pp. 773–80

Scalia, G., "Gli 'archiva' di papa Damaso e le biblioteche di papa Ilaro," *StudMed*, 3rd ser., 18 (1977), pp. 39–63

Schaefer, F.J., "Bonizo of Sutri," *CE*, vol. 2: *Assize–Brown* (New York 1907), p. 673

Scharnagl, A., "Die kanonistische Sammlung der Handschrift von Freising" in *Wissenschaftliche Festgabe zum zwölfhundertjährige Jubiläum des heilige Korbinian*, ed. J. Schlecht (Munich 1924), pp. 126–46

Scheidweiler, F., "Zur neuen Ausgabe des Athanasios," *ByzZ* 47 (1954), pp. 73–94

Schenkl, H., *Bibliotheca patrum latinorum britannica*, vol. 1, pt. 2: *Die Phillips'sche Bibliothek in Cheltenham* (Vienna 1892)

Schiaparelli, L., *Il codice 490 della Biblioteca capitolare di Lucca e la scuola scrittoria lucchese, StT* 36 (Rome 1924)

Schieffer, R., *v.* **Hincmarus laudensis (Hincmar of Laon)**

Schiktanz, M., *Die Hilarius-Fragmente* (Wroclaw 1905)

Schmitz, H., *v.* **Halitgar cameracensis (Halitgar or Haltigar of Cambrai)**

Schneemelcher, W., "Epiphanius," *RAC*, vol. 5 (Stuttgart 1962), coll. 909–27

Schwartz, E., "Die Sammlung des Theodosius Diaconus," *NGWG.PH*, 1904, pp. 357–91; rpt. in *Gesammelte Schriften*, vol. 3 (Berlin 1959), pp. 30–72

_______, "Von Konstantins Tod bis Sardika 342," *NGWG.PH*, 1911, pp. 469–522; rpt. in *Gesammelte Schriften*, vol. 3 (Berlin 1959), pp. 265–334

_______, *Codex vaticanus gr. 1431: Eine antichalkedonische Sammlung aus der Zeit Kaiser Zenos, ABAW.PPH*, vol. 32 (Munich 1927)

_______, "*Ecclesiae occidentalis monumenta iuris antiquissima canonum et conciliorum interpretationes latinae* ... edidit Cuthbertus Hamilton Turner, Tomus I fasciculus II pars III, *etc.*" *ZSRG.K* 20 (1931), pp. 590–607

_______, "Zur Kirchengeschichte des 4. Jahrhunderts," *ZNTW* 34 (1935), pp. 129–213; rpt. in *Gesammelte Schriften*, vol. 4 (Berlin 1960), pp. 1–110

_______, "Die Kanonessammlungen der alten Reichskirche," *ZSRG.K* 25 (1936), pp. 1–114; rpt. in *Gesammelte Schriften*, vol. 4 (Berlin 1960), pp. 159–275

_______, “Über die Sammlung des Codex veronensis LX,” *ZNTW* 35 (1936), pp. 1–23

Scudamore, W.E., *The Communion of the Laity* (London 1855)

Silva-Tarouca, K., “Beiträge zur Überlieferungsgeschichte der Papstbriefe des IV., V. und VI. Jahrhunderts,” *ZKTh* 43 (1919), pp. 467–81, 657–69

Skarsaune, O., “The Most Recent Debate on the Origin of the Apostles' Creed,” *TTK* 80 (2009), pp. 294–307

Smulders, P., *Hilary of Poitiers' Preface to His* Opus historicum, *SupVigChr*, vol. 29 (Leiden 1995)

Stählin, O., “*Athanasius Werke*, herausgegeben im Auftrage der Kirchenväter-Kommission der preußischen Akademie der Wissenschaften ... von Hans-Georg Opitz, *etc.*,” *ZKG* 58 (1939), pp. 586–89

Stevenson, J., *Creeds, Councils and Controversies, Documents Illustrative of the History of the Church A.D. 337–461* (London 1966)

Stickler, A.M., *Historia iuris canonici latini*, vol. 1: *Historia fontium* (Turin 1950)

Stürner, W., “Die Quellen der Fides Konstantins im Constitutum Constantini (§§3–5),” *ZSRG.K* 55 (1969), pp. 64–206

Telfer, W., “The Codex Verona LX (58),” *HThR* 36 (1943), pp. 169–246

Ter-Merkerttschian, K., *v.* **Komitas**

Ter-Merkerttschian, K., and E. Ter-Minassiantz, *v.* **Timotheos II alexandrinus (Timothy Aelurus), *Contra eos, etc.***

Tetz, M., “Zur Theologie des Markell von Ankyra III: Das pseudoathanasianische *epistula ad Liberium*, ein markellisches Bekenntnis,” *ZKG* 83 (1972), pp. 145–94

_______, “Zum altrömischen Bekenntnis: Ein Beitrag des Marcellus von Ancyra,” *ZNTW* 75 (1984), pp. 107–27

_______, “Ante omnia de sancta fide et de integritate veritatis: Glaubensfragen auf der Synode von Serdika (342),” *ZNTW* 76 (1985), pp. 243–69

_______, “Die Kirchweihsynode von Antiochien (341) und Marcellus von Ancyra: Zu der Glaubenserklärung des Theophronius von Tyana und ihren Folgen,” in *Oecumenica et Patristica: Festschrift Wilhelm Schneemelcher*, ed. D. Papandreou *et al.* (Chambésy/Geneva 1989), pp. 199–217

Toesca, P., "Il Liber canonum della Biblioteca Vallicelliana," *Arte* 5 (1902), pp. 229–39

Thompson, G.L., "The Earliest Papal Correspondence," (Ph.D. diss., Columbia University, New York 1990)

_______, "The *Pax Constantiniana* and the Roman Episcopate," in *The Bishop of Rome in Late Antiquity,* ed. G. Dunn (Farnham, Surrey 2015)

Turner, C.H., "Latin Lists of the Canonical Books, 3: From Pope Innocent's Epistle to Exsuperius of Toulouse," *JThS* 13 (1912), pp. 77–82

_______, "Arles and Rome: The First Development of Canon Law in Gaul," *JThS* 17 (1916), pp. 236–47

_______, "Chapters in the History of Latin Manuscripts, VI: b) The Chieti manuscript (I) now Vat. Reg. 1997," *JThS* 31 (1930), pp. 9–20; "VII: The Collection named after the MS of St. Maur (F), Paris lat. 1451," *JThS* 32 (1931), pp. 1–11

Twomey, V., *Apostolikos thronos,* MBTh, vol. 49 (Münster 1982)

Ulrich, J., *Die Anfänge der Abendländischen Rezeption des Nizänums, PTS,* vol. 39 (Berlin 1994)

Van der Speeten, J., "Le dossier de Nicée dans la Quesnelliana," *SE* 28 (1985), pp. 383–450

Van Hove, A., *Prolegomena,* 2nd ed., CLCIC, vol. 1.1 (Mecheln / Rome 1945)

Van Nuffelen, P., "Three Historical Problems in the *Apologia secunda* of Athanasius," *SE* 44 (2005), pp. 93–115

Verrando, G.N., "L'attività edilizia di Papa Giulio I e la basilica al III miglio della Via Aurelia ad Callistum," *MEFR* 97 (1985), pp. 1021–61

Vinzent, M., "Die Gegner im Schreiben Markells von Ankyra an Julius von Rome," *ZKG* 105 (1994), pp. 285–328

_______, "Die Entstehung des 'römischen Glaubensbekenntnisses'" in *Tauffragen und Bekenntnis,* ed. W. Kinzig *et al.* (Berlin 1999), pp. 185–409

von Dobschütz, E., *Das Decretum gelasianum de libris recipiendis et non recipiendis, TU,* ser. 3, vol. 8.4 (Leipzig 1912)

Wasserschleben, F.W.A., *v.* **Ps.-Cummeanus, *Poenitentiale;* Ps.-Theodorus cantuariensis (Ps.-Theodore of Canterbury); *Poenitentiale;* Regino Prumiensis**

Weber, N.A., "Cotelier," *CE*, vol. 4: *Cland–Diocesan* (New York 1908), p. 421

Weissengruber, F., *Epiphanius Scholasticus als Übersetzer, SÖAW.PH* 283 (Vienna 1972)

Wermelinger, O., "Marcus, I. Greek, 3, Bishop of Arethusa," *BNP.A*, vol. 8: "Lyd–Mine," (Leiden/Boston 2006), p. 323.

Westra, L., *The Apostles' Creed: Origin, History, and Some Early Commentaries, IPM*, vol. 43 (Turnhout 2002)

Williams, R., *Arius: Heresy and Tradition*, 2nd ed. (Grand Rapids, Mich. 2001)

Williams, S., *Codices pseudo-Isidoriani: A Palaeographico-Historical Study*, MIC.S, vol. 3 (New York 1971)

Wilpert, G., "Scavi nel cimitero dei santi Marco-Marcelliano e Damaso," *NBAC* 9 (1903), pp. 315–19

Winroth, A., *The Making of Gratian's Decretum* (Cambridge 2000)

Wright, W., *Catalogue of Syriac Manuscripts in the British Museum*, 3 voll. (London 1870–72)

Wurm, H., *Studien und Texte zur Dekretalensammlung des Dionysius Exiguus, KStT*, vol. 16 (Bonn 1939)

Wybrew, H., *The Orthodox Liturgy: The Development of the Eucharistic Liturgy in the Byzantine Rite* (Crestwood, N.Y. 1990)

Zangmeister, K., *Bericht über die im Auftrage der Kirchenväter-Commission unternommene Durchforschung der Bibliotheken Englands, SAWW.PH* 84 (1877), pp. 485–584

Zechiel-Eckes, K., "Ein Blick in Pseudoisidors Werkstatt: Studien zum Entstehungsprozess der Falschen Dekretalen," *Francia* 28.1 (2001), pp. 37–90

———, *Rebellische Kleriker? Eine unbekannte kanonistisch-patristische Polemik gegen Bischoff Hinkmar von Laon in Cod. Paris, BNF, nouv. acq. lat. 1746*, MGH, Studien und Texte, vol. 49 (Hannover 2009)

Zeumer, K., *v.* ***Leges visigothorum***

Zotenberg, H., *Catalogue des manuscrits éthiopiens de la Bibliothèque Nationale* (Paris 1877)

CONSPECTUS SIGLORUM

1. Manuscripts

N.B. The number(s) in parentheses following the heading for each group of manuscripts designate(s) the letter(s) contained in that work.

A Athanasius, *Apologia secunda* (2, 5, 6)

- A^1 Paris, Bibliothèque Nationale, *gr. 474* (11th c.)
- A^2 El Escorial, Real Biblioteca de San Lorenzo, *gr. Ω.III.15* (12th c.)
- A^3 Basel, Universitätsbibliothek, *A.III.4* (12th–13th c.)
- A^4 El Escorial, Real Biblioteca de San Lorenzo, *gr. X.II.11* (13th–14th c.)
- A^5 Athos, Μονὴ Βατοπαιδίου, *6* (14th c.)

B *Collectio sanblasiana* (4)

- B^1 St. Paul in Lavanttal, Stiftsbibliothek, *7/1* (8th c.)
- B^2 Paris, Bibliothèque Nationale, *lat. 3836* (late 8th c.)
- B^3 Cologne, Erzbischöfliche Diözesan- und Dombibliothek, *213* (early 8th c.)
- B^4 Lucca, Biblioteca Capitolare, *490* (*ca.* 800)
- B^7 Paris, Bibliothèque Nationale, *lat. 1455* (late 9th c.)

C Cassiodorus, *Historia ecclesiastica tripartita* (5)

C: Class Ia

- C^1 Paris, Bibliothèque Nationale, *nouv. acq. lat 1746* (10th c.)
- C^2 Naples, Biblioteca Nazionale Vittorio Emanuele III, *VI.D.18* (10th c.)
- C^3 Leiden, Universiteitsbibliotheek, *Voss. lat. fol. 62* (mid-10th c.)
- C^4 London, British Library, *Harley 3630* (13th c.)

C: Class Ib

- C^5 St. Petersburg, National Library (Saltykov-Shchedrin), *F.v.I.11* (early 9th c.)

C^6 Paris, Bibliothèque Nationale, *lat. 17581* (11th c.)
C^7 Angers, Bibliothèque Municipale, *676* (11th c.)
C^8 Vienna, Österreichische Nationalbibliothek, *3141* (1432)

C: Class Ic
C^9 Charleville-Mézières, Bibliothèque Municipale, *lat. 4* (12th c.)

C: Class Id
C^{10} Monte Cassino, Archivio dell'Abbazia, *302* (10th–12th c.)

C: Class Ie
C^{11} London, British Library, *add. 19961* (10th c.)

C: Class If
C^{12} Florence, Biblioteca Medicea Laurenziana, *San Marco 383* (10th c.)
C^{13} Chartres, Bibliothèque Municipale, *lat. 10* (10th c.)

C: Class III
C^{14} Vatican, Biblioteca Apostolica Vaticana, *Vat. lat. 1970* (10th c.)

C: Class IV
C^{15} Vatican, Biblioteca Apostolica Vaticana, *Pal. lat. 823* (10th c.)

C^{Ia} the agreement of manuscripts C^{1-4}
C^{Ib} the agreement of manuscripts C^{5-8}
C^{If} the agreement of manuscripts C^{12-13}

Di *Collectio diessensis* (4)
Di Munich, Bayerische Staatsbibliothek, *Clm 5508* (late 8th c.)

E *Collectio dionysiana aucta* (4)
E^2 Munich, Bayerische Staatsbibliothek, *Clm 14008* (latter 9th c.)
E^4 Vatican, Biblioteca Apostolica Vaticana, *Vat. lat. 5845* (915–34)

Ep Epiphanius, *Panarion* (1)
Ep^1 Jena, Universitätsbibliothek, *Bose 1* (1304)
Ep^2 Wroclaw, Biblioteka Uniwersytecka, *Rehdiger 240* (15th c.; now lost)

H Hilary of Poitiers, *fragmenta historica* (4, 6)

H[1] Paris, Bibliothèque de l'Arsenal, *483* (early 9th c.)

H[2] Rheims, Bibliotheca Sancti Remigii (12th c.; now lost)

H[3] *Cod. Pithoeanus* (15th c.; now lost)

H[4] Paris, Bibliothèque Nationale, *lat. 1700* (late 16th c.)

M *Collectio Sancti Mauri* (4)

M[1] The Hague, Museum Meermanno-Westreenianum, *10.B.4* (late 8th c.)

M[2] Paris, Bibliothèque Nationale, *lat. 1451* (early 9th c.)

M[3] Vatican, Biblioteca Apostolica Vaticana, *Reg. lat. 1127* (early 9th c.)

N Nicephorus Callistus, *Historia ecclesiastica* (5, 6)

N Vienna, Österreichische Nationalbibliothek, *hist. gr. 8* (early 14th c.)

P Ps.-Isidori Mercatoris, *Decretalium collectio* (the Latin translation of *ep.* 5)

P[1] Florence, Biblioteca Nazionale Centrale, *Conv. soppr. J.3.18* (10–11th c.)

P[2] Bernkastel-Kues, St. Nikolaus-Hospital/Cusanusstift, Bibliothek, *52* (12th c.)

Sc Socrates, *Historica ecclesiastica* (5)

Sc[1] Florence, Biblioteca Medicea Laurenziana, *plut. 69.5* (11th c.)

Sc[2] Florence, Biblioteca Medicea Laurenziana, *plut. 70.7* (10th c.)

Sc[3] Alexandria, Patriarchal Library, *Alex. 60* (13th c.)

Sc[4] Athos, Μονὴ Ξηροποτάμου, *226* (14th c.)

Sz Sozomen, *Historia ecclesiastica* (6)

Sz[1] Alexandria, Patriarchal Library, *Alex. 60* (13th c.)

Sz[3] Oxford, Bodleian Library, *Baroc. 142* (early 14th c.)

Sz[4] Vatican, Biblioteca Apostolica Vaticana, *Vat. gr. 976* (14th c.)

Td *Collectio Theodosii diaconis* (3)

Td Verona, Biblioteca Capitolare, *60* + Rome, Biblioteca casanatense, *378* (later 8th c.)

2. Editions and Emendations

Section A lists all previous editions of the letters. Most, but not all of these, are cited in the *apparatus criticus* to at least one letter. Those cited are preceded by an italicized abbreviation; those not cited have no abbreviation. Section B contains the names of those who have suggested emendations, and, where relevant, the work in which these have already been published. The number(s) in parentheses following each listing designate(s) the letter(s) edited or emended.

A. Editions

Bal.	P. and G. Ballerini, *Opera S. Leonis*, vol. 3 (3)
Bar.	C. Baronius (Baronio), *Annales ecclesiastici,* vol. 3 (1, 4)
	J. Bidez and G.C. Hansen, *Sozomenus Kirchengeschichte* (the Greek version of 6)
	W. Bright, *Socrates' Ecclesiastical History* (5)
Bre.	H.C. Brennecke *et al., Athanasius Werke,* vol. 3.1.3: *Dokumente zur Geschichte des arianischen Streites, Bis zur Ekthesis Makrostichos* (1, 2, 3, 4)
Com.	H. Commelinus (J. Commelin), *B. Athanasii … opera,* vol. 1 (2, 5, the Greek version of 6)
Cor.	J. Cornarius, *D. Epiphanii … Panarium* (1)
Cou.	P. Coustant, *Epistolae romanorum pontificum* (1, 2, 4, 5, 6)
Cou.[1]	P. Coustant, *S. Hilarii … opera* (4)
Cou.[2]	agreement of *Cou.* and *Cou.*[1] (4)
Din.	W. Dindorf, *Epiphanii … opera,* vol. 3 (1)
Duc.	F. Ducaeus (du Duc), *Nicephori Callisti Xanthopuli ecclesiasticae historiae libri* (5, the Greek version of 6)
Fab.	N. Faber (Lefèvre), *B. Hilarii … ex opere historico fragmenta* (4)
Fed.	A. Feder, *S. Hilarii … opera,* part 4: … *Collectanea antiariana parisina (fragmenta historica), etc.* (4)
Gar.	J. Garetius (Garet), *Magni Aurelii Cassiodori … opera,* vol. 1 (the Latin version of 5)
	G.C. Hansen, *Socrates Kirchengeschichte* (5)
Hans.[2]	G.C. Hansen, *Sozomenus Kirchengeschichte* (the Greek version of 6)
Hans.[3]	G.C. Hansen, *Eusebius Werke,* vol. 4: … *Die Fragmente Marcells* (1)

Hansl. W. Jacob and R. Hanslik, *Cassiodori-Epiphanii Historia ecclesiastica tripartita* (the Latin version of 5)

Holl K. Holl and J. Dummer, *Epiphanius*, vol. 3: *Panarion haer. 65–80* (1)

Hus.[1] R. Hussey, *Socratis Scholastici Ecclesiastica historia* (5)

Hus.[2] R. Hussey, *Sozomeni Ecclesiastica historia* (the Greek version of 6)

Klo. E. Klostermann, *Eusebius' Werke*, vol. 4: ... *Die Fragmente Marcells* (1)

Mon. B. de Montfaucon, *S.... Athanasii ... opera*, vol. 1 (2, the Greek version of 6)

Öh. F. Öhler, *Panaria eorumque anacephalaeosis* (1)

Op. H.-G. Opitz, *Athanasius Werke*, vol. 2 ... *Apologia secunda, etc.* (2, 5, the Greek version of 6)

EOMIA, vol. 1.2.4 (3)

Opo. J. Oporinus, *D. Epiphanii ... Panarium* (1)

Pet. D. Petauius (Petau), *Sancti ... Epiphanii ... opera*, vol. 1 (1)

Ret. C.H.G. Rettberg, *Marcelliana, etc.* (1)

Rhe. B. Rhenanus (Bilde von Rheinau), *Autores historiae ecclesiasticae ... adbreuiati per Cassiodorum Senatorem, unde illis Tripartitae historiae uocabulum, etc.* (the Latin version of 5)

M. Schiktanz, *Die Hilarius-Fragmente* (6)

Tetz M. Tetz, "Ante omnia de sancta fide et de integritate veritatis" (3)

Val.[1] H. Valesius, Socrates in *Socratis Scholastici et Hermiae Sozomeni Historia ecclesiastica* (5)

H. Valesius, Sozomen in *Socratis Scholastici et Hermiae Sozomeni Historia ecclesiastica* (the Greek version of 6)

Vin. M. Vinzcnt, *Murkell von Ankyra* (1)

B. Emendations

Eng. A. Engelbrecht; *v.* Feder, A.L., *S. Hilarii pictaviensis opera*, part 4, p. 2: *Index notarum* (4)

Gilb. B. Gilbert, Principal Editorial Assistant, LEC (2, 4)

J.P. J. Petruccione, Editorial Director, LEC (2, the Latin version of 5)

Schd. F. Scheidweiler, "Zur neuen Ausgabe des Athanasios" (2)

Schw. E. Schwartz, “Von Konstantins Tod” (2)

Stäh. O. Stählin, “*Athanasius Werke*” (2)

Thomp. G.L. Thompson (3, 4)

Wick. L. Wickham, *Hilary of Poitiers* (4)

3. Editorial Abbreviations

ac *ante correctionem*

coni. *coniecit* (*i.e.*, suggested an emendation but did not introduce it into the text)[1]

edd. *editores*

homotel. *homoteleuton*

om. *omisit,* omits

pc *post correctionem* (*i.e.*, by either the first or another hand)

scr. *scripsit, -erunt* (*i.e.*, emended a word [or words] passed down in the manuscript tradition)[2]

signif. *significauit*

suppl. *suppleuit* (*i.e.*, supplied a word or words not passed down in the manuscript tradition)

transp. *transposuit*

X^{-3} the concurrent reading of all mss. of class X with the exception of X^3

? perhaps

/ illegible letter

[ ] to be deleted

< > to be added

‡ textual corruption

1. In cases where more than one editor is named after *coni.*, the first is to be credited with the suggestion with which the following has/have concurred.

2. In cases where more than one editor is named after *scr.*, the first is to be credited with introducing the emendation into the text; the following has/have concurred.

The Correspondence of Pope Julius I

LETTER I

To Julius, Bishop of Rome,
from Marcellus of Ancyra
(Ἐπειδή τινες)

Introduction

Marcellus was a member of the generation that experienced the Great Persecution while in their teens and twenties. He must have proved himself both courageous and capable, for, when he was elected bishop of the Galatian metropolis Ancyra in 314, he could hardly have met the minimum canonical age of 30. He continued to play a role in ecclesiastical politics for another sixty years, until his death, about 374.[1] Marcellus claimed that, at the Council of Nicaea, he had defended orthodoxy (*ep.* 1.1), and this claim was confirmed by the priests who had represented the bishop of Rome (2.12).[2]

Though Arius and a few followers were condemned at Nicaea, within a decade modified versions of his teaching were being championed by a powerful group of eastern bishops led by Eusebius of Nicomedia. The heart of the Arian-Eusebian position was what Lienhard has called "*dyohypostatic* theology."[3] This view of divinity took as its point of departure the great chain of being of neo-Platonic speculation. God stood at the top of this life-chain, and the various created beings were each allotted distinct positions at lower levels. God the Father was the uncreated, unbegotten beginning of all, the first principle; his Son, the *Logos*, was begotten and had his source in the Father, hence he had to be at a somewhat lower level. Thus, while the Son/*Logos*/Christ was clearly a divine being of some sort and superior to other created beings, he still had to be

1. Perhaps, due to a shortage of candidates after the persecution, Marcellus was elected while under age. As Parvis notes (pp. 11f.), the synod of Neocaesarea soon afterwards insisted (canon 11; *v. EOMIA*, vol. 2.1.132f.) that there should be no exceptions made to the minimum age requirements. For the date of Marcellus' death, *v.* Epiph., *Haer.* 72.1.2. For the much reduced influence of the deposed Marcellus, *v.* Barnes, *Athanasius and Constantius*, pp. 92f.

2. Logan argues that Marcellus played an important role at Nicaea, whether publicly or behind the scenes, and that this fact was deliberately concealed after his orthodoxy had been called into question.

3. *V.* Lienhard, *Contra Marcellum*, pp. 35–46.

classed as something other than pure divinity. As he was not equal to the Father nor of the same being or *ousia,* he had to be an entity or *hypostasis* separate from the Father. Hence, as the name coined by Lienhard indicates, divinity was attributed to two distinct and different entities.[4]

In contrast, the viewpoint that prevailed at Nicaea was that the Son was "begotten, not made" (γεννηθέντα οὐ ποιηθέντα) and "of the same substance" (ὁμοούσιον = *homoousion*) with the Father. The Son, "begotten of the Father, his only-begotten" (γεννηθέντα ἐκ τοῦ πατρὸς μονογενῆ), possessed the same divine substance (*ousia*) as the Father. The council did not attempt to explain how a son could be equal to his father, or how the begotten could be eternal. It simply confessed that there was but one *ousia* or *hypostasis* of the Godhead, or as Lienhard's term "*miahypostatic* theology" indicates, there was just one divine substance.

In the decade after Nicaea, the conflicting representatives of these two viewpoints became more intransigent. Marcellus, a strong proponent of the *miahypostatic* position, composed his *Contra Asterium,* a refutation of the positions of the Arian rhetorician Asterius, a strong proponent of the *dyohypostatic* cause.[5] In 335, Marcellus had been present at the Council of Tyre but had refused to countenance the Eusebians' efforts to silence Athanasius by laying charges of misconduct in office. A few months later, when that synod reconvened in Jerusalem to take part in the dedication of the Church of the Holy Sepulcher, Marcellus again refused to participate. After returning to Tyre, the Eusebians threatened to condemn the still recalcitrant Marcellus for his attack on the *dyohypostatic* position in *Contra Asterium.*

4. The terms *ousia* (οὐσία) and *hypostasis* (ὑπόστασις) may both be translated by the English "being." In the anathema following the creedal declaration of the Council of Nicaea (ἐξ ἑτέρας ὑποστάσεως ἢ οὐσίας … φάσκοντας εἶναι … τὸν υἱὸν τοῦ θεοῦ) the two terms are used synonymously to refer to the basic stuff of which something is composed. Most easterners, however, including the Arians, reserved the term *hypostasis* to refer to an "individual existent" or "person"; *v.* Kelly, pp. 240–42.

5. Having sacrificed during the persecution of Diocletian, the brilliant Asterius was never admitted into the clergy (Ath., *Syn.* 18.2).

They alleged that Marcellus' teaching denied real distinctions within the godhead and thus revived the old modalist heresy of Sabellianism.

In response to this charge, Marcellus traveled to Constantinople to present his book to Emperor Constantine. The emperor, however, already under the influence of Eusebius of Nicomedia, turned the matter over to a hand-picked council of Eusebians, who met at Constantinople in 336.[6] The aged church historian Eusebius of Caesarea, another member of the *dyohypostatic* leadership, was chosen to lead the prosecution against Marcellus. For this he used the arguments he had recently assembled in a hastily composed tract *Contra Marcellum.*[7] As was to be expected, the council excommunicated and deposed Marcellus.

Upon the death of Constantine, Marcellus was among the bishops who were allowed by the new emperors to return from exile. But, after briefly regaining his see, he was again condemned and exiled by a council meeting at Antioch (338/39). Like Athanasius, he sought help in Rome and there joined the growing camp of refugee bishops.[8] In 341, his theology and episcopal record were cleared by a Roman council of some 50 bishops, which reaffirmed his communion with Rome. Marcellus composed *ep.* 1 to Julius to supplement his oral examination at this council; the letter was probably entered into the conciliar acts as a permanent testimony to his orthodoxy.[9]

6. This is Parvis' reconstruction of events (pp. 123–27). On the association of Eusebius of Nicomedia with the court of Licinius and the family of Constantine, *v.* Parvis, pp. 40f., esp. n. 12. In 337, the extent of Eusebius' influence was particularly apparent when he attended the emperor in his last days and baptized him on his deathbed.

7. Following Vinzent (*Markell von Ankyra*, p. xix), Parvis maintains (p. 129) that the *Contra Marcellum* was composed expressly in support of the council's prosecution of Marcellus. The following year, Eusebius wrote a more thorough refutation of Marcellus, the *De ecclesiastica theologia*. Except for a couple of brief passages in Epiphanius' *Panarion*, all the surviving fragments of Marcellus' *Aster.* are preserved as citations in these two works of Eusebius of Caesarea.

8. Barnes argues that Marcellus arrived in Rome in the spring of 340 and lists some of the other refugees who can be shown to have been there at that time; *v.* *Athanasius and Constantius*, pp. 57, 61.

9. The composition of this letter has been dated to 1) immediately before,

Letter I

The letter consists of six sections: an introduction, four theological sections, and a conclusion. In his introduction, Marcellus explains his predicament, recalls his defense of orthodoxy at Nicaea, and decries his opponents' attempt to shift the accusation of heresy from themselves to him. Their guilt is confirmed by their refusal to appear in Rome to bring accusations during the fifteen months he has been awaiting the opportunity to defend himself. Now he will present a written statement of his faith and contrast it with the erroneous formulations by which his opponents deceive the faithful. In the conclusion, he affirms that the teaching expounded in the body of the letter is what he proclaims in his ecclesiastical office. Insisting that he has learned this doctrine from Scripture and his parents, he forestalls the accusation that it is an innovation of his own. Finally, Marcellus asks Julius to include his confession in the letter he will send to the bishops so that all will see his innocence.

The body of the letter consists of sections two through five. Until recently, scholars have focused on section four, which seems to be an almost verbatim copy of the old Roman creed. They have analyzed the structure of Marcellus' confession as tripartite, consisting of sections three through five, with the old Roman creed in the middle.[10] This, however, obscures the correspondence between sections two and five. In the second, Marcellus sets out the beliefs of his opponents, and in the fifth provides a contrasting account of his own *miahypostatic* theology. These frame sections three and four,

---

2) during, or 3) immediately after the council of Rome. Vinzent (*Markell von Ankyra,* pp. lxxxiii–lxxxv) gives two cogent reasons for supporting the second option: First, after a stay of fifteen months (1.1), Marcellus would not have left Rome just when his case was going to be taken up. Second, as Julius writes (2.16), "When we went further and demanded that he [Marcellus] state his faith to us, he boldly gave answer himself," Marcellus must have attended the council. Since Marcellus concludes (1.6) with a request that Julius include his letter in a letter to the bishops, it is clear that the council had not yet come to an end.

10. Thus, Tetz ("Zum altrömischen Bekenntnis," pp. 113–16) and Vinzent ("Die Entstehung des 'römischen Glaubensbekenntnisses,'" pp. 379–81) both follow the lead of Caspari (pp. 31–34) in regarding Marcellus' confession as tripartite (secc. 3–5, with the Roman creed in the middle).

each introduced by the verb πιστεύω ("I believe"), in which Marcellus sets out his faith in a more biblical, less polemic fashion. Thus, as the introduction and conclusion stand in symmetrical balance, so the second section corresponds to the fifth, and the third to the fourth.[11]

Scholars have often viewed Marcellus' use of the Roman creed as a devious ploy to win absolution from the Roman council.[12] More recently, some scholars have denied that the creedal formulation of section four was that of Rome. In 1989, Tetz claimed that Marcellus copied the creed that Theophronius of Tyana had presented to the Council of Antioch in 341. Yet, this argument presupposes an unlikely chronology and can claim no explicit support in the ancient sources.[13] Ten years later, Vinzent argued that Marcellus had himself composed the creed, which won such favor among the Romans that they

11. Lienhard ("Did Athanasius Reject Marcellus?" p. 71) is the only recent commentator to note that the body of the letter consists of four sections.

12. Thus, Barnard declares that Marcellus was "an arch intriguer" and "an arch trimmer" who "duped Julius" by using the Roman creed ("Pope Julius," pp. 72, 74). Yet, Barnard is merely choosing the easterners' view of Marcellus, that of the Eusebians and later Epiphanius (*Haer.* 72), Basil (*epp.* 69, 125, 263, 265), Chrysostom (*Hom. in Ioh.* 7.2; *Hom in Heb.* 2.1), and Theodoret (*Haer. com.* 2.10), rather than the westerners', that of Julius and the western Council of Sardica. We lack sufficient evidence to decide the question of his orthodoxy. Lienhard has pointed out that Marcellus' theology underwent development. After the publication of the *Aster.*, his beliefs came "more and more in line with *miahypostatic* orthodoxy," perhaps under the influence of Athanasius; *v. Contra Marcellum*, p. 137, and "Did Athanasius Reject Marcellus?" pp. 70f. Marcellus must be viewed as a serious theologian and churchman. He changed his terminology and views when convinced that they were theologically problematic, and he stood firm against the Eusebians during many years of exile, even when extremely advanced in age. On his later life, *v.* Barnes, *Athanasius and Constantius*, pp. 92f.

13. Tetz ("Die Kirchweihsynode," p. 209) questions the general consensus that the Dedication Synod of Antioch opened in January of 341, and that Julius' synod began in spring or early summer. Yet, his chronology remains problematic even if Parvis is correct in her conclusion (pp. 192f.) that the Roman council ended by early April. Furthermore, Vinzent ("Die Gegner," pp. 293–323) has shown that neither the letter Marcellus wrote to Julius during the council nor that which Julius wrote to the Eusebians afterward reveals any sign of dependence on documents produced in Antioch in 341.

adopted it as their own,[14] but this reconstruction has found little support.[15] The traditional view, that Marcellus incorporated the Roman creed into his own defense, remains the most likely. Nonetheless, the more recent studies have shown that Marcellus acted in good conscience, for the Roman creed complements the other three sections of his theological defense.[16] Parvis, who has drawn attention to parallels of phraseology between *ep.* 1 and Athanasius' first *Oration against the Arians,* suggests "that Marcellus and Athanasius <may> have drawn up a list of propositions" on which they both agreed.[17]

In the *Contra Asterium,* Marcellus had singled out Eusebius of Caesarea, Eusebius of Nicomedia, Narcissus of Neronias, Paulinus of Tyre, and Asterius the sophist as his opponents. Though in his letter to Julius he never names his opponents, he is obviously still responding to this same Eusebian party. Vinzent has shown that, in the summary of his opponents' theology (sec. 2), Marcellus is directing his attack particularly against the teachings of Asterius: Christ was not the Word or Reason (*Logos*) intrinsic to God but a *Logos* brought into being by God; he was a being (*hypostasis*) distinct from the Father. Therefore, the Father pre-existed the Son, who was "from God" only in the same way that all things are from God. The Son was a creature who at one time did not exist, hence an entity separate from the Father (ll. 24–26).[18] Such views, Marcellus concludes, are foreign to Catholic faith.

Claiming the support of Holy Scripture, Marcellus lays out his own *miahypostatic* beliefs in section three, the first of the two introduced

14. Vinzent, "Die Entstehung," esp. pp. 407f.

15. *V.* Westra, pp. 30–46, for a critique of Vinzent's proposal.

16. *V.* Tetz, "Zum altrömischen Bekenntnis," pp. 118–20; Vinzent, "Die Entstehung," pp. 407f.; Lienhard, "Did Athanasius reject Marcellus?" p. 71. Heil has suggested (pp. 97–100) that the Roman synod of 341 was the first to adopt this creed, and that Marcellus reproduced it to prove his orthodoxy. This seems to me implausible.

17. Parvis, pp. 181–85, esp. p. 184. She also notes parallels with the letter Ἑνὸς σώματος (*CPG* #2000) written against Arius by Athanasius' predecessor, Alexander. Barnes finds additional evidence for the interaction of the two exiles in Rome; *v. Athanasius and Constantius,* p. 55.

18. *V.* Vinzent's analysis in "Die Gegner," pp. 294–323.

by the verb πιστεύω ("I believe"). God is one, and the *Logos* has coexisted with the Father from all eternity. In earlier works, Marcellus had spoken of a temporary kingdom of Christ that would continue only until all of God's enemies had been subdued, at which time it would be subsumed into the eternal kingdom of the Father (fragg. 113f.).[19] This doctrine seemed to deny the eternal subsistence of the Son and so to obviate any enduring distinctions within the godhead; it raised concerns on all sides and was the object of vehement attack by the Eusebians. Now Marcellus, saying nothing about this temporary kingdom, follows the apostolic testimony that Christ will reign with God the Father and that "his kingdom shall have no end."[20] Thus, as Jn 1.1–3 and Lk 1.2 state, Christ is the one and only *Logos*, indivisible from the Father. Jesus himself spoke of his unity with the Father, from whom he came and to whom he would return. Tetz points out that the Pauline expression "our Lord Jesus Christ," used twice in section 3, does not occur in the fragments of Marcellus' earlier works. This was used against him, and he now appropriates the phrase for his own purpose.[21] Also, Marcellus had previously reserved the title *Logos* for the period prior to the incarnation (fragg. 48f.), "Son" and "Jesus Christ" for that following (42f.). Here, abandoning such distinctions, he comes "more and more in line with *mia-hypostatic* orthodoxy."[22] As in section 2 Marcellus recalled false views with language drawn from the anathema of the Nicene Creed (ἦν ποτε ὅτε οὐκ ἦν = "there was a time when he did not exist"), here he cites correct teaching with a quotation from the creed itself (κατελθὼν διὰ τὴν ἡμετέραν σωτηρίαν = "he came down for our salvation").

Having shown that his understanding of the *Logos* is the reverse

19. The numbering of the fragments of Marcell., *Aster.* follows the edition of Klostermann and Hansen.

20. V. Lienhard, *Contra Marcellum*, pp. 64–66.

21. Tetz, "Zum altrömischen Bekenntnis," pp. 116f. and 121.

22. Lienhard, *Contra Marcellum*, p. 137. Epiphanius, our sole source for this text and an author unsympathetic toward Marcellus, stresses that, in his portrayal of the controversial theologian, he is adhering strictly to what he has been told. Thus, we can be assured that none of the theological accommodations are due to changes introduced by Epiphanius himself.

of his opponents' and enjoys the support of Scripture, Marcellus now draws the important consequence[23] that his beliefs are in perfect accord with those of Rome as expressed in her own creed. Though omitting the term "Father" (πατέρα) before "almighty" (παντοκράτορα),[24] he regards the rest of the creed as expressing his own beliefs. Thus, the Roman creed must be viewed as an important part—but, as Caspari has insisted, only a part—of Marcellus' own theological confession in *ep.* 1.[25]

In section five, the last of the four doctrinal sections, Marcellus offers his response to the Arian formulations quoted in section two. While the Arians divide the Son from the Father, Marcellus insists that "inseparable" (ἀδιαίρετον) is the proper term to describe their relationship. While the Arians claim that the Word begotten of the Father is not the Word intrinsic to divinity, Marcellus insists that the *Logos* is divine; in support he cites Jn 1.1. While the Arians hold that the Son is not the Wisdom and Power intrinsic to the divinity, Marcellus declares that the Son is the Power of the Father and indivisible (ἀδιαίρετος) and inseparable (ἀχώριστος) from him. In confirmation he quotes Jn 10.38, 30 and 14.9. Thus, Marcellus demonstrates that his own terminology, unlike that of the Arians, rests upon the sanction of Scripture.

Marcellus undoubtedly wrote *ep.* 1 in his native Greek. He surely kept a copy for himself, and, as we have seen, he urged Julius (sec. 6) to circulate it within the *acta* of the council. Copies would also have been read at the western Council of Sardica, which again examined and reaffirmed Marcellus' orthodoxy. Athanasius, though he nowhere cites this letter, may well have received a copy. Nevertheless, Epiphanius, who incorporated the entire text into the chapter of the *Panarion* dealing with Marcellus (72.2f.), is our sole source.

23. Note the οὖν at the beginning of sec. 4, the second introduced by the verb πιστεύω ("I believe").

24. *V.* Tetz, "Zur Theologie des Markell," pp. 178f. According to Vinzent ("Die Entstehung," pp. 263f.), Marcellus avoids the term because of Asterius' anthropomorphic understanding of Father and Son.

25. *V.* Caspari, p. 43.

Perhaps Epiphanius received his copy of *ep.* 1 from Marcellus himself. We know that there was some interaction between the two, since one of Epiphanius' few extant letters is addressed to a group of bishops including Marcellus.[26] As this letter dates between 367 and 373, and the *Panarion* was completed in 376/77,[27] there would have been time for Marcellus to provide his correspondent with a copy of his letter to Julius. This hypothesis gains some support from Epiphanius' claim that he is giving an exact transcription (ἀντίγραφον) of the letter. On the other hand, it is unlikely that his copy was made from one kept in the papal archives, for Epiphanius is not known to have visited Rome before 382, five years after he had completed the *Panarion*.

There are only two surviving manuscript copies of the later section of the *Panarion*, which contains Marcellus' letter. The earlier *Ep¹* is a book of the early fourteenth century. As the other, *Ep²*, is merely an apograph of *Ep¹*, the latter is the sole independent witness to the text of *ep.* 1.[28]

I cite as well the editors of Epiphanius' *Panarion* and the editors of some or all of the fragments of Marcellus. The former include Cornarius (*Cor.*; Latin translation only), Oporinus (*Opo.*), Petauius (*Pet.*), Dindorf (*Din.*), Öhler (*Öh.*), and Holl, the latter Coustant (*Cou.*), Rettberg (*Ret.*), Klostermann (*Klo.*), Hansen (*Hans.³*), Vinzent (*Vin.*), and Brennecke (*Bre.*). Finally, I have taken into account those portions of the text as printed and emended by Schwartz (*Schw.*) in the context of his article "Von Konstantins Tod bis Sardika 342."[29]

26. This letter, preserved only in part, is addressed to "Eusebius, Marcellus, Vivianus, Carpus, and the Egyptians." *V.* the edition of Holl, "Ein Bruchstück," pp. 205–07.

27. *V.* Schneemelcher, col. 916. The introduction to the letter contains a note stating that it was written by Marcellus "who was condemned by the council." As "the council" refers to the Council of Constantinople of 381, this note was likely inserted, either by Epiphanius or a later redactor, after the first publication of the *Panarion*.

28. For the shelf-marks of these manuscripts and further details, *v.* App. A, item Ep.

29. For information on the editors and their editions, *v.* sec. 6 of the Introduc-

Letter I

My edition differs from that of Vinzent at two places and from that of Brennecke in one. Unlike Vinzent, in sec. 2, I have followed Cornarius and a number of more recent editors in supplying a conjunction (καὶ) to join the two indirect statements dependent on ἀποφαίνονται. In sec. 3, I have followed Klostermann in printing πάντα τὰ γενόμενα instead of the manuscript reading with two articles. The form of πάντα / ἅπ- + article + participle is that offered by Mt 18.31 and 28.11 and in numerous passages of patristic authors; the manuscript reading printed by Vinzent and Brennecke is otherwise unattested in the *TLG*.

---

tion. For Schwartz' text, *v.* "Von Konstantins Tod," n. 1, p. 294; n. 1, pp. 303f.; n. 2, p. 304; and n. 1, p. 305.

I

Epistula Marcelli ancyrani ad Iulium, episcopum urbis Romae

Τῷ μακαριωτάτῳ συλλειτουργῷ Ἰουλίῳ Μάρκελλος ἐν Χριστῷ χαίρειν.

(1) Ἐπειδή τινες τῶν καταγνωσθέντων πρότερον ἐπὶ τῷ μὴ ὀρθῶς πιστεύειν, οὓς ἐγὼ ἐν τῇ κατὰ Νίκαιαν συνόδῳ διήλεγξα, κατ' ἐμοῦ γράψαι Τῇ Θεοσεβείᾳ Σου ἐτόλμησαν ὡς ἂν ἐμοῦ μὴ ὀρθῶς μηδὲ ἐκκλησιαστικῶς φρονοῦντος, τὸ ἑαυτῶν ἔγκλημα εἰς ἐμὲ μετατεθῆναι σπουδάζοντες, τούτου ἕνεκεν ἀναγκαῖον ἡγησάμην, ἀπαντήσας εἰς τὴν Ῥώμην, ὑπομνῆσαί σε ἵνα τοὺς κατ' ἐμοῦ γράψαντας μεταστείλῃ ὑπὲρ τοῦ ἀπαντήσαντας αὐτοὺς ἐπ' ἀμφοτέροις ἐλεγχθῆναι ὑπ' ἐμοῦ· ὅτι τε καὶ ἃ γεγράφασι κατ' ἐμοῦ ψευδῆ ὄντα τυγχάνει, καὶ ὅτι ἔτι καὶ νῦν ἐπιμένουσι τῇ ἑαυτῶν προτέρᾳ πλάνῃ καὶ δεινὰ κατά τε τῶν τοῦ θεοῦ ἐκκλησιῶν καὶ ἡμῶν τῶν προεστώτων αὐτῶν τετολμήκασιν. ἐπεὶ τοίνυν ἀπαντῆσαι οὐκ ἠβουλήθησαν, ἀποστείλαντός σου πρεσβυτέρους πρὸς αὐτούς, καὶ ταῦτα ἐμοῦ ἐνιαυτὸν καὶ τρεῖς ὅλους μῆνας ἐν τῇ Ῥώμῃ πεποιηκότος, ἀναγκαῖον ἡγησάμην, μέλλων ἐντεῦθεν ἐξιέναι, ἔγ-

l. 6 μηδὲ *scr. Din. Klo. Schw. Vin. Hans.*[3]: μήτε *Ep, Opo. Pet. Cou. Ret. Öh. Holl*
l. 9 ἀπαντήσαντας *scr. Cor.* (praesentes) *Cou. Ret. Öh. Din. Klo. Schw. Holl Hans.*[3] *Vin. Bre.* : -τος *Ep, Opo. Pet.*

I

To Julius, Bishop of Rome, from Marcellus of Ancyra

Marcellus[1] to my most blessed co-worker, Julius, greetings in Christ.

(1) Some of those previously condemned for their false beliefs and whom I had refuted at the Council of Nicaea have dared to lodge complaints against me with your Reverence. Claiming that my beliefs are incorrect and contrary to those of the Church, they have tried to turn against me the very accusations made against themselves.[2] I decided, therefore, that I had to present myself in Rome and call this to your attention, so that you would send for my critics, they would present themselves, and I could then refute them on two counts: that their complaints against me are simply false, and that they still persist in their previous errors and have made outrageous accusations against both the churches of God and against us who have been placed over them. But they chose not to present themselves, even after you sent your priests to them. So, since I have now spent all the last fifteen months in Rome and am about to leave, I decided it was imperative to write with my own hand and present

1. In the manuscript tradition of the *Panarion*, there is a heading preceding the opening address: Ἀντίγραφον ἐπιστολῆς Μαρκέλλου ὃν καθεῖλεν ἡ σύνοδος χάριν ἑτεροδοξίας ("A copy of a letter of Marcellus whom the council deposed for heresy"). Marcellus was explicitly condemned by councils at Constantinople (336, 338/39) and Antioch (341, 344); teachings associated with him were condemned at numerous subsequent councils.

2. His unnamed opponents include the late Eusebius of Caesarea, the author of two books against him, Eusebius of Nicomedia, the leader of those opposed to the Nicene position, and especially Asterius; *v.* Vinzent, "Die Gegner," pp. 293–323. As Brennecke observes (*Dokumente,* p. 152), Marcellus' use of the adverb ἐκκλησιαστικῶς probably indicates that he is confronting the charges of Eusebius of Caesarea, whose longer book against Marcellus was apparently known as τὰ συγγράμματα τῆς ἐκκλησιαστικῆς θεολογίας.

γραφόν σοι τὴν ἐμαυτοῦ πίστιν, μετὰ πάσης ἀληθείας τῇ ἐμαυτοῦ χειρὶ γράψας, ἐπιδοῦναι, ἣν ἔμαθον ἔκ τε τῶν θείων γραφῶν ἐδιδάχθην, καὶ τῶν κακῶς ὑπ' αὐτῶν λεγομένων ὑπομνῆσαί σε ἵνα γνῷς οἷς χρώμενοι πρὸς ἀπάτην τῶν ἀκουόντων λόγοις τὴν ἀλήθειαν κρύπτειν βούλονται.

(2) Φασὶ γὰρ μὴ ἴδιον καὶ ἀληθινὸν λόγον εἶναι τοῦ παντοκράτορος θεοῦ τὸν υἱόν, τὸν Κύριον ἡμῶν Ἰησοῦν Χριστόν, ἀλλ' ἕτερον αὐτοῦ λόγον εἶναι καὶ ἑτέραν σοφίαν καὶ δύναμιν· τοῦτον γενόμενον ὑπ' αὐτοῦ ὠνομάσθαι *λόγον* καὶ *σοφίαν* καὶ *δύναμιν*· καὶ διὰ τὸ οὕτως αὐτοὺς φρονεῖν, ἄλλην ὑπόστασιν, διεστῶσαν τοῦ πατρός, εἶναί φασιν. ἔτι μέντοι καὶ προϋπάρχειν τοῦ υἱοῦ τὸν πατέρα[a] δι' ὧν γράφουσιν ἀποφαίνονται, <καὶ> μὴ εἶναι αὐτὸν ἀληθῶς υἱὸν ἐκ τοῦ θεοῦ. ἀλλά, κἂν λέγωσιν *ἐκ τοῦ θεοῦ*, οὕτως λέγουσιν ὡς καὶ τὰ πάντα. ἔτι μὴν καὶ ὅτι *ἦν ποτε ὅτε οὐκ ἦν*[b] λέγειν τολμῶσι καὶ *κτίσμα* αὐτὸν καὶ *ποίημα* εἶναι,[c] διορίζοντες αὐτὸν ἀπὸ τοῦ πατρός. τοὺς οὖν ταῦτα λέγοντας ἀλλοτρίους τῆς καθολικῆς ἐκκλησίας εἶναι πεπίστευμαι.

(3) Πιστεύω δέ, ἑπόμενος ταῖς θείαις γραφαῖς, ὅτι εἷς θεὸς καὶ ὁ τούτου μονογενὴς υἱὸς λόγος, ὁ ἀεὶ συνυπάρχων τῷ πατρὶ καὶ μηδεπώποτε ἀρχὴν τοῦ εἶναι ἐσχηκώς, ἀληθῶς ἐκ τοῦ θεοῦ ὑπάρχων, οὐ κτισθείς, οὐ ποιηθείς, ἀλλὰ ἀεὶ ὤν, ἀεὶ συμβασιλεύων τῷ θεῷ καὶ πατρί, οὗ *τῆς βασιλείας*, κατὰ τὴν τοῦ ἀποστόλου μαρτυρίαν, *οὐκ ἔσται τέλος*.[d] οὗτος υἱός, οὗτος δύναμις, οὗτος σοφία,

l. 27 μέντοι : μέν *Ret.* : μὴν *coni. Klo. Hans.*[3] **l. 28** <καὶ> μὴ εἶναι *suppl. Cor.* (et non esse) *Öh. Klo. Holl Hans.*[3] *Bre.* : μὴ εἶναι *Ep, Opo. Pet. Cou. Ret. Din. Vin.* **l. 29** λέγωσιν *scr. Cor.* (dicant) *Ret. Din. Klo. Holl Hans.*[3] *Vin. Bre.* : -ουσιν *Ep, Opo. Pet. Cou. Öh.* **l. 30** καὶ τὰ πάντα *scr. Ret. Öh. Klo. Holl Hans.*[3] *Vin.* : κατὰ πάντα *Ep, Cor.* (per omnia) *Opo. Pet. Cou. Din.* = *"in the same way that all things are from God"*

a. Ast. Soph., frag. 14 b. *Symb. nic.* (325) c. Ast. Soph., frag. 63 d. Lk 1.33

you my own true confession of the faith,[3] which I have learned and which I have been taught from the holy Scriptures, and to remind you of the wrongheaded declarations of these men, so you will understand the terminology they employ to conceal the truth and deceive those who listen to them.

(2) They say that the Son, our Lord Jesus Christ, is not the proper and true *Logos* of the almighty God, but a *Logos* distinct from God, and a distinct Wisdom and Power, that, made by God, he was merely called "*Logos*" and "Wisdom" and "Power," and, since this is their view, they say that he is a second *hypostasis,* separate from the Father.[4] Furthermore, they declare in their writings that the Father existed before the Son,[a] and that he is not truly a Son from God. And, even when they say, he is "from God," they mean just as all things are from God. Furthermore, they even dare to say, "There was once a time when he did not exist,"[b] and that he is a "creature" and a "created being,"[c] and, thus, separate him from the Father.[5] I am convinced that those who say such things are no true citizens of the Catholic Church.

(3) But, in accord with holy Scripture, I believe that there is one God, and that the *Logos* is his only-begotten Son,[6] ever coëxisting with the Father and having no beginning of existence. He is truly from God, not created, not made, but existing from eternity, forever reigning with God, that is, the Father, "Whose kingdom," according to the testimony of the apostle, "will have no end." [7d] He is the Son,

3. By writing the letter himself, Marcellus provided a proof of authenticity and imitated the Apostle Paul (1Cor 16.21; Gal 6.11; Col 4.18; 2Thes 3.17; Phlm 19).

4. Asterius believed (frag. 52) in two *Logoi*, Wisdoms, and Powers and that the *Logos* that was Christ had a being (*hypostasis*) different from that of the Father.

5. *V.* Asterius, frag. 63: κτίσμα γάρ ἐστι καὶ ποίημα καὶ ἔργον.

6. *V.* Marcellus, Vinzent, frag. 109 (= Klostermann, frag. 121): νυνὶ δὲ πιστεύω ταῖς θείαις γραφαῖς, ὅτι εἷς θεὸς καὶ ὁ τούτου λόγος προῆλθεν … τοῦ πατρός.

7. Here the term "apostle" probably refers to the evangelist Luke. Though Vinzent (*Markell von Ankyra,* p. 127 and n. 185, p. 157) would identify the "apostle" as the angel Gabriel, who actually utters these words in Luke's Gospel, there is no biblical precedent for such a use of the term. Lienhard contends that Marcellus had been led "to clarify his own thought" and no longer held that the kingdom of Christ "would end, because it would be absorbed into the kingdom of God" (*Contra Marcellum,* pp. 142f.).

οὗτος ἴδιος καὶ ἀληθὴς τοῦ θεοῦ λόγος, ὁ Κύριος ἡμῶν Ἰησοῦς Χριστός, ἀδιαίρετος δύναμις τοῦ θεοῦ, δι᾽ οὗ πάντα τὰ γενόμενα γέγονε,[e] καθὼς τὸ εὐαγγέλιον μαρτυρεῖ λέγον, *Ἐν ἀρχῇ ἦν ὁ λόγος, καὶ ὁ λόγος ἦν πρὸς τὸν θεόν, καὶ θεὸς ἦν ὁ λόγος. … πάντα δι᾽ αὐτοῦ ἐγένετο, καὶ χωρὶς αὐτοῦ ἐγένετο οὐδὲ ἕν.*[f] οὗτός ἐστιν ὁ λόγος περὶ οὗ καὶ Λουκᾶς ὁ εὐαγγελιστὴς μαρτυρεῖ λέγων, *Καθὼς παρέδωκαν ἡμῖν οἱ ἀπ᾽ ἀρχῆς αὐτόπται καὶ ὑπηρέται γενόμενοι τοῦ λόγου.*[g] περὶ τούτου καὶ Δαυὶδ ἔφη, *Ἐξηρεύξατο ἡ καρδία μου λόγον ἀγαθόν.*[h] οὕτω καὶ ὁ Κύριος ἡμῶν Ἰησοῦς Χριστὸς ἡμᾶς διδάσκει διὰ τοῦ εὐαγγελίου λέγων, *Ἐγὼ … ἐκ τοῦ πατρὸς ἐξῆλθον καὶ ἥκω.*[i] οὗτος, *ἐπ᾽ ἐσχάτων τῶν ἡμερῶν*[j] κατελθὼν διὰ τὴν ἡμετέραν σωτηρίαν[k] καὶ ἐκ τῆς παρθένου Μαρίας γεννηθείς, τὸν ἄνθρωπον ἔλαβε.[l]

(4) *Πιστεύω* οὖν *εἰς θεὸν … παντοκράτορα καὶ εἰς Χριστὸν Ἰησοῦν, τὸν υἱὸν αὐτοῦ τὸν μονογενῆ, τὸν Κύριον ἡμῶν, τὸν γεννηθέντα ἐκ πνεύματος ἁγίου καὶ Μαρίας τῆς παρθένου, τὸν ἐπὶ Ποντίου Πιλάτου σταυρωθέντα καὶ ταφέντα, καὶ τῇ τρίτῃ ἡμέρᾳ ἀναστάντα ἐκ τῶν νεκρῶν, ἀναβάντα εἰς τοὺς οὐρανοὺς καὶ καθήμενον ἐν δεξιᾷ τοῦ πατρός, ὅθεν ἔρχεται κρίνειν ζῶντας καὶ νεκρούς, καὶ εἰς τὸ ἅγιον πνεῦμα, ἁγίαν ἐκκλησίαν, ἄφεσιν ἁμαρτιῶν, σαρκὸς ἀνάστασιν,*[m] ζωὴν αἰώνιον.

(5) Ἀδιαίρετον εἶναι τὴν θεότητα τοῦ πατρὸς καὶ τοῦ υἱοῦ[n] παρὰ τῶν θείων μεμαθήκαμεν γραφῶν. εἰ γάρ τις χωρίζει τὸν υἱόν,

l. 41 πάντα τὰ γενόμενα *scr. Klo. Schw. Hans.*[3] : τὰ π. τὰ γ. *Ep, Opo. Pet. Cou. Ret. Din. Öh. Holl Vin. Bre.* **l. 42** λέγον *Cor.* (Euangelium dicens) *Pet. Cou. Ret. Din. Öh. Klo. Holl Hans.*[3] *Vin. Bre.* : -ων *Ep, Opo.* **l. 52** ἔλαβε : ἀνέλαβε *coni. Klo. Hans.*[3]

e. Jn 1.3
f. Jn 1.1, 3
g. Lk 1.2
h. Ps 44.2 (LXX) = 45.1 (MT)
i. Jn 8.42; *cf.* Jn 16.28
j. *Cf.* Heb 1.2; Mi 4.1.
k. *Symb. nic.* (325)
l. *Cf.* Phil 2.7.
m. *Symb. rom.* (Hahn #19, pp. 24f.)
n. *Cf.* Jn 10.30; 17.11, 21; Col 2.9.

he the Power, he the Wisdom, he the proper and true *Logos* of God, our Lord Jesus Christ, the indivisible Power of God. Through him everything was made that has been made,[e] as the Gospel testifies when it says, "In the beginning was the *Logos*, and the *Logos* was with God, and the *Logos* was God; all things were made through him, and not one thing was made without him."[f] He is the *Logos* about whom Luke the evangelist also testifies, "Just as it was handed down to us by those who, from the beginning, were eyewitnesses and servants of the *Logos*."[g] It was of him that David said, "My heart poured forth a good *Logos*."[h] So also our Lord Jesus Christ teaches us through the gospel, when he says, "I have come from the Father and I am here."[i] He came down in the last days[8j] for our salvation,[9k] was born of the Virgin Mary, and became man.[l]

(4) Therefore, "I believe in God the almighty,[10] and in Christ Jesus his only-begotten Son, our Lord, born of the Holy Spirit and the Virgin Mary, crucified under Pontius Pilate, and buried, and on the third day risen from the dead, who ascended into the heavens and is seated at the right hand of the Father, whence he is coming to judge the living and the dead. And I believe in the Holy Spirit, the holy Church, the forgiveness of sins, the resurrection of the flesh, and life everlasting."[11m]

(5) We have learned from the holy Scriptures that the divinity of the Father and the Son is inseparable.[n] For if anyone divides the Son,

8. The phrase "in the last days" (ἐπ᾽ ἐσχάτων τῶν ἡμερῶν) may be a quotation of Heb 1.2 (so Vinzent, *Markell von Ankyra*, p. 128). While in Heb 1.2 most manuscripts read ἐσχάτου, the singular form of the substantival adjective = "the end of days," uncial Ψ and several minuscules read the plural attributive adjective ἐσχάτων = "the last days." The plural receives support also from several manuscripts of the *Vetus latina* that carry *novissimis temporibus* and *ultimis diebus*. Yet, according to Hatch and Redpath, the phrase "in the last days" occurs a dozen times in the LXX; for the form ἐπ᾽ ἐσχάτων τῶν ἡμερῶν *v.* also Gn 49.1; Jos 24.27; Jer 37.24; Ezek 38.16; Dn 2.28, 45; 10.14; Hos 3.5; Mi 4.1; for ἐπ᾽ ἐσχάτου τῶν ἡμερῶν, *v.* Nm 24.14; Jer 23.20; 25.19

9. The Nicene Creed reads διὰ τὴν ἡμετέραν σωτηρίαν κατελθόντα; *v.* Dossetti, pp. 226–41, esp. p. 232.

10. Marcellus, departing from the wording of the old Roman Creed, says "God the almighty," not "God the Father almighty."

11. Marcellus inserts into the old Roman Creed the words "life everlasting"; this is his only significant addition.

τουτέστι τὸν λόγον, τοῦ παντοκράτορος θεοῦ, ἀνάγκη αὐτὸν ἢ δύο θεοὺς εἶναι νομίζειν, ὅπερ ἀλλότριον τῆς θείας διδασκαλίας εἶναι νενόμισται, ἢ τὸν λόγον μὴ εἶναι θεὸν ὁμολογεῖν, ὅπερ καὶ αὐτὸ ἀλλότριον τῆς ὀρθῆς πίστεως εἶναι φαίνεται, τοῦ εὐαγγελιστοῦ λέγοντος, *Καὶ θεὸς ἦν ὁ λόγος.*[o] ἐγὼ δὲ ἀκριβῶς μεμάθηκα ὅτι ἀδιαίρετος καὶ ἀχώριστός ἐστιν ἡ δύναμις τοῦ πατρός, ὁ υἱός· αὐτὸς γὰρ ὁ σωτήρ, ὁ Κύριος ἡμῶν Ἰησοῦς Χριστός, φησίν, *Ἐν ἐμοὶ ὁ πατήρ, κἀγὼ ἐν τῷ πατρί,*[p] καί, *Ἐγὼ καὶ ὁ πατὴρ ἕν ἐσμεν,*[q] καί, *Ὁ ἐμὲ ἑωρακὼς ἑώρακε τὸν πατέρα.*[r]

(6) Ταύτην καὶ παρὰ τῶν θείων γραφῶν εἰληφὼς τὴν πίστιν καὶ παρὰ τῶν κατὰ θεὸν προγόνων διδαχθείς, ἔν τε τῇ τοῦ θεοῦ ἐκκλησίᾳ κηρύττω καὶ πρὸς σὲ νῦν γέγραφα, τὸ ἀντίγραφον τούτου παρ᾽ ἐμαυτῷ κατασχών. καὶ ἀξιῶ τὸ ἀντίτυπόν σε τούτου τῇ πρὸς τοὺς ἐπισκόπους ἐπιστολῇ ἐγγράψαι ἵνα μή τινες τῶν ἀκριβῶς μὴ εἰδότων ἡμᾶς κἀκείνους, τοῖς ὑπ᾽ αὐτῶν γραφεῖσι προσέχοντες, ἀπατηθῶσιν. ἔρρωσθε.

ll. 66f. τοῦ εὐαγγελιστοῦ : τοῦ εὐαγγελίου *Cou.* = "*since the gospel says*"
l. 68 ἡ : ᾗ *Ret. Klo. Hans.*[3] = "*inasmuch as he is the Power of the Father, the Son is*" **l. 77** κἀκείνους : κἀκείνοις *Ep*[2?], *Opo. Pet. Cou. Ret. Öh. Klo. Hans.*[3] = "*so that any who are not well acquainted with me will not be deceived by paying attention also to the complaints of my accusers*"

o. Jn 1.1
p. Jn 10.38
q. Jn 10.30
r. Jn 14.9

that is the *Logos*, from almighty God,[12] he must hold one of two positions: either that there are two Gods, a position regarded as foreign to divine teaching, or he must confess that the *Logos* is not God, which is also clearly foreign to the correct faith, since the evangelist says, "and the *Logos* was God."[o] But I have learned precisely this: that the Power of the Father, that is the Son, is indivisible and inseparable from him. For the Savior himself, our Lord Jesus Christ, says, "The Father is in me, and I am in the Father,"[p] and, "My Father and I are one,"[q] and, "He who has seen me has seen the Father."[r]

(6) This faith, which I received from the holy Scriptures and was taught by godly predecessors, I proclaim in the Church of God. Now I have also put it in writing for you and kept a copy for myself. I request that you include an exact copy in your letter to the bishops,[13] so that any who are not well acquainted with me or with my accusers will not be deceived by paying attention to their complaints. Farewell.

12. According to Marcellus, Asterius wrongly separates the Father from the Son; *v.* Ast. Soph., frag. 52: οὕτω τὸν υἱὸν τοῦ θεοῦ χωρίζων τοῦ πατρός.

13. This might be construed as evidence of a regular communication by the bishop of Rome, similar to the festal letters of Alexandrian bishops. More likely, however, it refers to the report that will be sent out at the conclusion of this council.

LETTER II

To the Bishops Assembled in Antioch
from Julius, Bishop of Rome
(Ἀνέγνων τὰ γράμματα)

INTRODUCTION

In 340, a quarrel between Constantine II and his younger brother Constans, the western heirs of Constantine, resulted in a major political change. The former, the ruler of Gaul, Britain, and Spain, invaded the realm of the latter, who had been allotted Italy, Africa, and Illyricum. This incursion ended on April 9 with the defeat and death of the invader at Aquileia, in northern Italy. Now Constans was ruler of the entire West. It has been argued that he visited Rome after his victory. If so, he may have met the two exiles, Marcellus and Athanasius, and taken up their cause.[1] Meanwhile, as no council representative of west as well as east had condemned Athanasius, Julius admitted the exiled bishop to the celebration of the holy days of the Easter season (Ath., *ep. fest.* 13).[2] Then, probably with the support of Constans, he sent two priests to the eastern bishops with a second letter (R^2; *v.* p. 28) pleading that they send a delegation to Rome to discuss the charges against Athanasius and Marcellus. In this letter, he apparently set a time limit for the Eusebian delegation to appear and accuse the exiled bishops face-to-face.[3]

1. On the possibility of a visit, *v.* Parvis, pp. 148 and 201, and Barnes, *Athanasius and Constantius,* pp. 225 and n. 47, p. 315. Barnes, however, postulates (*ibid.,* p. 52) that Athanasius had earlier appealed to Constantine II and, thus, compromised himself with Constans.

2. *V.* n. 16 below.

3. This table situates *ep.* 2 in the chronological sequence, stretching over six years, of exchanges of letters between Rome and the Eusebians and Rome and the Egyptian bishops. Preceding the issuance of *ep.* 2 (R^3), there had been four letters from the east to Rome (E^{1-4}), three from Alexandria to Rome (A^{1-3}), and the two others from Rome to the east (R^{1-2}). The letter dispatched in early 340, R^2, was that carried by Elpidius and Philoxenus (Ath., *Apol. sec.* 20). Schwartz, clearly sympathetic to the easterners, says that this letter must have been so arrogant and one-sided that it could not have received a favorable reply; *v.* "Von Konstantins Tod," p. 296. Yet, since the text of R^2 is no longer extant, this statement is only an expression of prejudice. Parvis assumes that, in his anger, Julius set too short a time limit for assembling, yet she admits that his letter went out in the "first half" of 340. Julius must have intended that the meeting take place in fall, not spring;

CHRONOLOGICAL TABLE: The Correspondence of Julius I and the Eastern Bishops

E = Letters sent by the Eusebian bishops A = Letters sent from Alexandria
R = Letters sent from Rome

Date	*Siglum*	Context / Summary
Fall, 335	E1	The Council of Tyre informs Julius and other bishops of its excommunication of Athanasius (Iul., *ep.* 2.9?; Soz., *H. e.* 2.25).
Spring, 338	E2	The Eusebian bishops send a letter confirming their excommunication of Athanasius and seeking recognition of Pistus as bishop of Alexandria. This, along with the report from the delegation sent to Mareotis, is brought to Rome by the priest Macarius and the deacons Martyrius and Hesychius (Iul., *ep.* 2.2, 4, 6f., 9?, 10).
Spring, 338	A1	An Alexandrian delegation brings a letter to Rome in support of Athanasius (Ath., *Apol. sec.* 1; Iul., *ep.* 2.4, 9?).
Summer/Fall, 338	R1	At the suggestion of the Eusebian delegation and after consulting his clergy, Julius invites the easterners and Athanasius to Rome (Iul., *ep.* 2.6, 13f.).
Spring, 339	E3	The Council of Antioch again reiterates the excommunication of Athanasius and now seeks recognition of Gregory as bishop of Alexandria (Iul., 2.9, 14).
Spring, 339	A2	The Alexandrians plead for help to prevent the exile of Athanasius.
Early 340	R2	Julius again summons both sides to a meeting at Rome (Iul., *ep.* 2.2, 6?, 8). This letter is carried to Antioch by Elpidius and Philoxenus (Iul., *ep.* 2.1), who return with E4.
340/41	A3	The Alexandrian church sends a delegation with a letter in support of Athanasius (Iul., *ep.* 2.9?, 18).
Jan., 341	E4	The Council of Antioch rejects Julius' proposal (Iul., *ep.* 2.1, 6, 9, 19f.).
Summer, 341	R3 = Iul., *ep.* 2	Julius informs the Eusebians of the acts of the Council of Rome.

The Eusebians received the invitation by late summer. From the tenor of the letter, and perhaps the testimony of the priests, they deduced that Julius' sympathies lay with the exiles. They petitioned Constantius to call a synod in the east that would be larger and more representative than the Council of Antioch of winter 338/39 and which would confirm the decisions taken there. The synod was scheduled to be held in Antioch when the emperor would be present at the dedication of the new Church of Holy Concord (Philost., *H. e.* 7.8). Rather than accept Julius' invitation or send an immediate answer, they detained his priests until they could draw up a formal response at this new synod.

The council, now known as the Dedication (Ἐγκαίνιον) Synod, may have begun in December but was certainly still meeting in early January of 341 (Socr., *H. e.* 2.12).[4] The Roman emissaries were finally allowed to leave with a letter (E^4) from the leading eastern bishops "and those with them." The letter appears to have been written before the completion of the council, since neither Julius' reply nor Marcellus' letter refers to any of the other official *acta*.[5] The letter clearly stated that the easterners saw no reason for Julius' proposed synod.[6] The priests bearing the letter arrived in Rome about mid-

this explains why he emphasizes the long detention of his priests and dismisses the easterners' complaints regarding the date as just another excuse. Parvis' position is based on Sozomen's description of R^2 and the response it provoked (*H. e.* 3.8.3–8). According to Sozomen, the tone of the letter was harsh, and it did set a deadline; he does not, however, imply that the deadline was unreasonable. Parvis has also postulated (pp. 148f., 158, 165–67), but without evidence, an earlier letter sent from Rome to the easterners in the spring of 339.

4. On the date established by Eltester (pp. 254f.), *v.* Brennecke, *Hilarius,* pp. 5–9, esp. n. 21; Van Nuffelen, pp. 106–09; and Parvis, pp. 160–77.

5. This is the view of Vinzent, based on his conclusion that the argumentation of Marcellus and Julius is directed, not against the neo-Arian theology of Eusebius, but against the older arguments of Asterius; *v.* his analysis of Marcellus' letter in "Die Gegner," esp. pp. 294–308. Parvis, however, thinks that the council had concluded and implies (pp. 165–67) that the letter to Julius was an official document of the synod, which concluded on January 6.

6. This letter (E^4) is summarized in Soz., *H. e.* 3.8.4–8, and is mentioned in Julius' letter (esp. 2.1). Schwartz ("Von Konstantins Tod," pp. 297–300) has assembled the fragments. Brennecke has suggested (*Hilarius,* pp. 4–9) that the so-called first

March, and, shortly afterward, Julius held his synod, with no eastern delegation present.[7] The approximately fifty bishops in attendance absolved Athanasius of wrongdoing and declared him the lawful bishop of Alexandria (Ath., *Apol. sec.* 1.2; *H. ar.* 15). The council also took up the case of Marcellus. He was examined, he presented a statement of faith (*ep.* 1 above), and the council reaffirmed their communion with him. In the lengthy *ep.* 2 (R^3), Julius relayed to the eastern bishops the decisions of his council (Ath., *Apol. sec.* 21–36). As Constans appointed one of his officials, Gabianus, to carry the letter to the east, Julius must have enjoyed the western emperor's support in this matter (*ibid.*, 20).

Julius addresses the letter to his "beloved brethren in the Lord": Dianius of Cappadocian Caesarea, Flacillus of Antioch, Narcissus of Neronias, Eusebius of Constantinople, Maris of Chalcedon, Macedonius of Mopsuestia, Theodore of Heraclea, and "those with them."[8] He begins by deploring the tone of their surly and unloving

creed of Antioch (Ath., *Syn.* 22, and Socr., *H. e.* 2.10) was the concluding segment of this letter, but neither Athanasius nor Socrates mentions Julius in connection with the letter containing the creed; *v.* also Parvis, pp. 165–67. The historian must exercise caution in using Sozomen to reconstruct the sequence of events, for his account of these letters contains many inaccuracies. He claims that, even before sending R^2, Julius had restored the exiles to their sees, and that Athanasius and Paul of Constantinople, not Julius, forwarded R^2 to the east.

7. Athanasius (*Apol. sec.* 20) says that it was held at the church of the priest Βίτων (Vito).

8. According to Sozomen (*H. e.* 3.5.2), ninety-seven bishops took part in the council of 341. Dianius (*v.* sec. 1, *ap. crit.*) was bishop of Caesarea in Cappadocia. His theological position can be judged from the fact, mentioned in the anonymous ninth-century *Syn. uet.* (#42), that he brought Asterius to this council; *v.* Hanson, *The Search*, pp. 284, 289. He signed the creed of the Council of Constantinople of 360 and died in 362 (Bas., *ep.* 51). Flacillus, bishop of Antioch (335?–342?) presided over the condemnation of Athanasius at the Council of Tyre in 335 and over the Dedication Council of Antioch in 341. He continued to support the Eusebian position until his death shortly after the sending of this letter (Hanson, *The Search*, p. 277 and n. 61, p. 292). Narcissus, bishop of Eirenopolis (also known as Neronias) in northeastern Cilicia, had supported Arius at Nicaea (*Marcell.* 1.4.39). He was one of three bishops who refused to sign the statement of faith presented at the council held in Antioch in 324 or 325 (*Conc. antioch., ep. syn.* 6), and he was a member of the delegation sent by the Dedication council (in January 342) to Constans at Trier (*v.* Hanson, *The Search*, pp. 146, 293). He was anathematized by the western

letter (E^4),[9] for "in matters concerning the Church, there is no place for displays of eloquence, but rather for apostolic canons (κανόνες ἀποστολικοί) and zeal 'not to offend one of the little ones' in the Church" (sec. 1). In re-examining decisions made by previous councils, the Roman church is not acting contrary to church law. If any such review is conducted justly, neither side need worry about the outcome; in fact, the Eusebian envoys (bearing E^2) had been the first to suggest a new hearing (sec. 2). Julius reminds the easterners that it was the teaching of Arius, not that of Athanasius or Marcellus, that was condemned by the Council of Nicaea (sec. 3). When it was discovered that Pistus, the claimant to the see of Alexandria

Synod of Sardica (Iul., *ep.* 4.5) but is known to have attended a subsequent council in Antioch in 351 (Soz., *H. e.* 4.8.4). Eusebius, usually known as "Eusebius of Nicomedia," was translated from his first bishopric in Beirut to Nicomedia in about 317. By mid-337, however, he had been translated yet again, this time to Constantinople, where he remained until his death in late 341. Julius and others often identified the anti-Nicene group as οἱ περὶ Εὐσέβιον, "Eusebius and his followers" (*e.g., ep.* 2.2, 8f.); *v.* Rist, "Eusebius, Bishop of Nicomedia," pp. 226f. Maris, bishop of Chalcedon, another early supporter of Arius, was pressured to accept the anti-Arian decision of Nicaea (*v.* #194, pp. 80f., in the list of the signatories to the council in *EOMIA,* vol. 1.1.1, as well as the shorter list presented by Honigmann, "La liste originale," #177, p. 48) but afterward reverted to his Arian sympathies. Also present at Tyre in 335, he was still an anti-Nicene leader at the Council of Constantinople in 360 (Socr., *H. e.* 2.41; Soz., *H. e.* 4.24; Bardy, "Recherches sur saint Lucien," pp. 214–16). Maris, together with the next two addressees, Macedonius and Theodore, was among the six men sent by the Council of Tyre to Egypt to investigate the charges against Athanasius (Iul., *ep.* 2.10; Hanson, *The Search,* pp. 259f.). Macedonius, bishop of Mopsuestia, signed the creed of Nicaea (*v.* #91, pp. 56f., in the list of the signatories to the council in *EOMIA,* vol. 1.1.1) but soon after became an open supporter of the Arian faction. He was a leader at Tyre in 335 and attended the Council of Sirmium in 351 (Hil., *fragg. histt.* B.7.9). Theodore, bishop of Heraclea in Thrace and a noted biblical exegete and commentator, was part of the Eusebian leadership from this time until his death about 355 (Soz., *H. e.* 4.8.4). Opitz (*Athanasius Werke,* vol. 2.1, n. to l. 13, p. 102) had referred to this group of bishops as a "standing committee" ("als ein Ausschuß der meisten orientalischen Bischöfe dauernd in Antiochien tagte"); Pietri ("La question d'Athanase," p. 101) used the very similar "le petit synode permanent de prélats." In contrast, Barnard prefers (*Studies,* pp. 70–72) to speak of a "semi-permanent group." Though they held only occasional meetings, they spent much of 338–341 in Antioch. They must have regarded these polemical issues as more important than the episcopal duties of their own sees.

9. It is often difficult to determine to which of the easterners' letters Julius is referring. Here, the mention of the envoys makes it clear that he is thinking of E^4.

supported by the easterners, was himself a condemned Arian, part of the eastern delegation had hurriedly left town (sec. 4).

Julius points out that the absolution of Athanasius and Marcellus has not depended on his decision alone but on that of "all the bishops throughout Italy and the surrounding regions" (sec. 8).[10] He enumerates the reasons for exonerating Athanasius: 1) the testimony against him was contradictory, some of it false (sec. 7); 2) the clergy of Egypt supported Athanasius, and the minutes (ὑπομνήματα) of the examinations conducted by the Egyptian clergy (included in A^1) cleared him of all wrongdoing (sec. 10); 3) Athanasius appeared at the council in Rome while his accusers did not (sec. 13). Thus, it is now apparent that it was not Athanasius, but Gregory, who was disrupting the peace of the Egyptian church (sec. 14). The arraignment of Athanasius' supporter, the presbyter Macarius, was irregular, for he was not permitted to face his accusers (sec. 15).[11] Marcellus has presented a full account of his teachings and faith, and this agrees with earlier reports of his orthodoxy. Hence, "we have received them in accordance with justice and canonical practice" (δικαίως καὶ κανονικῶς ἐδεξάμεθα, sec. 17).[12]

Like Athanasius and Marcellus, many other clergy have come to him at Rome with similar complaints of improper deposition (sec. 18).[13] Devoted to securing the peace of the Church and putting an end to divisive partisanship, the Roman council has reached its decisions fairly. If, at some future date, the easterners should present

10. Πάντων τῶν κατὰ τὴν Ἰταλίαν καὶ τῶν ἐν τούτοις τοῖς μέρεσιν ἐπισκόπων. As Julius continues, "though I alone am sending out this letter, you should know that its opinions are those of all the bishops," we may assume that the other bishops did not sign R^3.

11. At the Council of Tyre, Macarius was arraigned on the charge of disrupting Melitian communion services on Athanasius' orders (Ath., *Apol. sec.* 11 and 71–73).

12. Julius claims to base his judgment on the decisions of church councils (κανονικῶς) and Roman legal procedure (δικαίως). As he argues that it was his duty to remain in communion with Marcellus and Athanasius until they were proven to have been properly excommunicated, the verb "received" (ἐδεξάμεθα) probably refers to receiving them at the public celebration of the Eucharist.

13. *V.* n. 8 to the introduction to *ep.* 1.

themselves at Rome, any disagreements between them and the accused might still be settled face-to-face (sec. 21). According to custom, "we must be informed in writing before a just verdict can be determined.... I am setting forth for you the tradition we have received from the blessed apostle Peter." Julius concludes with a prayer for the good health of his "beloved and greatly missed brethren" (sec. 22).

The letter has been evaluated by some as a model of charity, by others as harsh though still conciliatory.[14] It does not, despite Julius' claims, present an impartial evaluation of the situation, nor does it demonstrate a complete grasp of the christological issues.[15] It does show that Julius and Rome have been drawn irrevocably into the interpersonal and theological conflicts of the east, where positions have already hardened.

Julius comes across not as a bishop grasping for power, but a churchman intent on healing a disastrous breach between the two most important sees of the eastern church. His intervention could be viewed, in the light of Mt 18.15–20, as an attempt to resolve a disagreement between two parties. In accord with 1Cor 6.1–6, he is concerned to avoid public scandal by keeping the matter within the Church. Julius wishes to be mediator rather than judge, but if a judge be required, he believes an impartial western-led council will furnish the most orderly solution. Admittedly, without access to his first two letters ($R^{1f.}$), we do not have a complete picture of his management of the dispute.

As the letter reveals, Julius was deeply concerned that a bad precedent could be set by the neglect of church law. His offer to mediate had already been ignored or rejected twice. In their meeting of 338, the easterners had increased tensions by making a third declaration of the deposition and excommunication of Athanasius and them-

14. For the positive assessment, *v.* Jalland, p. 214. Barnard believes that Julius, pressured by his colleagues, adopted a harsh tone but added a more conciliatory passage expressing his own views (secc. 19–21); v. "Pope Julius," pp. 70–72.

15. For a more detailed analysis, *v.* Girardet, pp. 87–95.

selves appointing a replacement. To assert the wrongfulness of their behavior and the correctness of his own, Julius cites tradition and custom (secc. 2, 14, 22) as well as Scripture (secc. 1, 3, 19).

As the Eusebians claimed for themselves the sanction of ecclesiastical precedent (secc. 2f., 5, 21), Julius insists also on long-established Roman legal procedures. The accused must be able to select the place of the hearing. As both Athanasius and Marcellus have come to Rome, their accusers are also bound to present themselves (*e.g.*, sec. 13). Accuser and accused must both be present and confront each other face-to-face (secc. 10, 21). Remaining in communion with Athanasius, he has treated as innocent his fellow bishop who has not yet been proven guilty of a crime.[16]

It is true that Julius was not sympathetic to the easterners. He had received most of his information on these disputes from Marcellus

16. It is not entirely clear when Athanasius was welcomed to partake in the eucharistic liturgy in Rome. When Julius became bishop in early 337, he must have followed the normal custom of sending a letter of communion to the bishop of Alexandria, just as Athanasius would have sent a letter to Silvester in 328. Athanasius was in Trier at the time of Julius' consecration, but he would have received the letter when he was recalled to Alexandria shortly afterward. As Julius reports (2.4), he had never accepted the letters of communion sent on behalf of Pistus (E^2) or Gregory (E^3), the men elected by the easterners to replace Athanasius. Thus, when Athanasius arrived in Rome, he and Julius were still in communion. In *ep. fest.* 13, written in 340 to fix the date of Easter for the following year, Athanasius declares (sec. 1) that he has written from Rome, where he celebrated the feast with his Roman brethren. Pietri (*Roma Christiana,* n. 4, p. 197) understands this letter to state that Athanasius had joined Julius and the Roman clergy in the public celebration of Easter 340. Elsewhere (*Apol. Const.* 4), Athanasius claims that he spent his time in Rome in public worship. One might argue that once he had welcomed Athanasius to the Eucharist, Julius could no longer be regarded as an impartial arbiter. If this occurred already in 340 shortly after Athanasius' arrival, one can understand the easterners' skepticism toward Julius' proposed council. It is conceivable that, if Julius reckoned it inexpedient to join in public worship with Athanasius until the canonical issues had been resolved, he might have allowed him to celebrate the Eucharist with his Egyptian party in a separate locale. In that case, the "brethren" mentioned in the festal letter would have been fellow Alexandrians. Julius might even have suggested this as a practical measure due to the difference in language. While we lack the evidence to resolve this question, I think it more likely that Athanasius and the other exiles were permitted to celebrate the Eucharist with their Roman brethren, pending the outcome of further investigations; *i.e.*, they were regarded as innocent until proven guilty.

and Athanasius and from other bishops exiled by the easterners. The original delegation from Antioch acquitted itself very poorly (secc. 2, 4). And the only other witnesses to the eastern position were the harsh letters from the synods of 339 and 341 (E^3 and E^4). In these circumstances, the decisions in favor of Athanasius and Marcellus were hardly surprising.

Indeed, since almost all the extant records come from Athanasius and his supporters, it is understandable that the easterners have incurred the odium of subsequent generations. Yet Parvis has persuasively argued the case that, from 327 on, the Eusebian party, despite some theological differences, were united in their opposition to Nicaea and its supporters, and that, with imperial support, they manipulated numerous councils to eliminate their opponents.[17] Thus, they merited the disapprobation with which they have been traditionally viewed.

Either Julius or a member of his staff composed the letter to the Eusebians in Greek. Perhaps Athanasius, Marcellus, and other exiled bishops assisted. Brightman argued that the presence of Latinisms indicates that the letter could not have been written "by any one who thought in Greek or habitually spoke it."[18] Yet Brightman could assemble fewer than a dozen of these unidiomatic usages in 519 lines of text. Thus, the composition appears to come from a nonnative user of Greek who was nonetheless quite competent in the language, a Roman who had become almost diglossic.

Given the importance of the letter to their own careers, Athanasius and Marcellus would have kept copies. Eight years later, Athanasius (A) transcribed his copy into chapters 21–35 of his *Apologia secunda* (also known as the *Apologia contra arianos*),[19] and it has been preserved in that context alone. There are five extant manu-

17. This is one of the principal arguments of her book on Marcellus and what she calls the "lost years of the Arian controversy."

18. *V.* Brightmann, p. 159.

19. Barnes makes a convincing case for dating this to 349; *v. Athanasius and Constantius,* pp. 99f.

scripts of this work, which, according to Opitz, all descend from a single archetype. He divided these into two subgroups, A^{1-2} and A^{3-5}. In the case of *ep.* 2, however, I would rather speak of three subgroups, for A^3 often stands apart from A^{4-5}.[20]

The principal editions of Athanasius are those of Commelin (*Com.*), de Mountfaucon (*Mont.*), and Opitz (*Op.*). I have cited as well Coustant's text from his edition of the early papal correspondence (*Cou.*) and Brennecke's from his *Dokumente* (*Bre.*). In addition, I mention emendations suggested by Scheidweiler (*Schd.*) and Stählin (*Stäh.*) in their review of Opitz' edition.[21] Throughout, I signal both the section divisions introduced into *ep.* 2 by Coustant and those traditionally observed by the editors of Athanasius, *Apol. sec.* Both sets of numbers stand within parentheses, but the numbers drawn from the editions of Athanasius are distinguished by the addition of a period and the italicising of the number and the parentheses within which it is enclosed.

My choices of readings differ from those of Opitz in eight places, from those of Brennecke in those same eight places and in two more where Opitz and I are in agreement against Brennecke. The two of greatest importance are at ll. 199 and 452. In the first (l. 199), I have restored the unanimous reading of A (εὔλογος), where Opitz and Brennecke print a conjecture of de Montfaucon. In this passage, Julius is not defending the reasonableness of his own behavior but pointing out the hypocrisy of the Eusebians. In the second (l. 452), following the witness of the majority of the manuscripts, I have chosen the subjunctive (σπουδάσητε) rather than the imperative (σπουδάσατε), since the sentence ἤκουσα γὰρ … αἴτιοι τυγχάνοντες is clearly a parenthesis dividing the two members of a compound purpose clause ἵνα … δυσωπήσητε … καὶ σπουδάσητε. This restores coherence to the conclusion of sec. 19. In three passag-

20. For the shelf-marks of these manuscripts, Opitz' discussion of their relationships, and further details, *v.* App. A, item A.

21. *V.* Scheidwieler, "Zur neuen Ausgabe des Athanasios" and Stählin, "Athanasius Werke."

es (ll. 287, 307, 452), I have preferred a different manuscript variant. With the printing of συνῆχθαι (l. 287), perhaps no more than a conjecture by the corrector of A^1, I free the text from the byzantine corruption σεσυνῆχθαι. In addition, I print a total of five conjectures, four of which were not adopted by Opitz or Brennecke. These four include one (l. 98) first found in the edition of Commelin and three more that have never before been printed: two (ll. 405f., 408) suggested by Scheidweiler and one (l. 479) by Petruccione. In contrast to Brennecke, I have adopted Opitz' deletion of a negative in l. 286 and rejected Scheidweiler's insertion of a τε and the concommitant reconfiguration of two sentences at ll. 53–56. Finally, I report five more conjectures: one by Scheidweiler (ll. 403f.) and one by Stählin (l. 507), both of which I regard as less likely, and three quite plausible suggestions by Gilbert (ll. 141, 306, 378).

II

Epistula Iulii, episcopi urbis Romae, ad episcopos Antiochiae congregatos

(21.) Ἰούλιος Διανίῳ καὶ Φλακίλλῳ, Ναρκίσσῳ, Εὐσεβίῳ, Μάρι, Μακεδονίῳ, Θεοδώρῳ, καὶ τοῖς σὺν αὐτοῖς, τοῖς ἀπὸ Ἀντιοχείας γράψασιν ἡμῖν, ἀγαπητοῖς ἀδελφοῖς, ἐν Κυρίῳ χαίρειν.

(1) Ἀνέγνων τὰ γράμματα τὰ διὰ τῶν πρεσβυτέρων μου Ἐλπιδίου καὶ Φιλοξένου ἀποκομισθέντα καὶ ἐθαύμασα πῶς ἡμεῖς μὲν ἀγάπῃ καὶ συνειδήσει ἀληθείας ἐγράψαμεν, ὑμεῖς δὲ μετὰ φιλονεικίας, καὶ οὐχ ὡς ἔπρεπεν, ἐπεστείλατε· ὑπεροψία γὰρ καὶ ἀλαζονεία τῶν γραψάντων διὰ τῆς ἐπιστολῆς ἐδείκνυτο. ταῦτα δὲ ἀλλότρια τῆς ἐν Χριστῷ πίστεώς ἐστιν· ἔδει γὰρ τὰ μετὰ ἀγάπης γραφέντα ἀμοιβῆς τῆς ἴσης μετὰ ἀγάπης τυχεῖν, καὶ μὴ μετὰ φιλονεικίας. ἢ οὐχὶ ἀγάπης ἐστὶ γνώρισμα πρεσβυτέρους ἀποστεῖλαι συμπαθεῖν τοῖς πάσχουσι, προτρέψασθαι τοὺς γράψαντας ἐλθεῖν ἵνα πάντα, θᾶττον λύσιν λαβόντα, διορθωθῆναι δυνηθῇ, καὶ μηκέτι μήτε οἱ ἀδελφοὶ ἡμῶν πάσχωσι, μήτε ὑμᾶς τινες διαβάλλωυιν; ἀλλ᾽ οὐκ οἶδα τί τὸ δόξαν οὕτως ὑμᾶς διατεθῆναι ὥστε καὶ ἡμᾶς ποιῆσαι λογίζεσθαι ὅτι, καὶ ἐν οἷς ἐδόξατε ῥήμασιν ἡμᾶς τιμᾶν, ταῦτα μετασχηματιζόμενοι,[a] μετὰ εἰρωνείας τινὸς εἰρήκατε. καὶ γὰρ καὶ οἱ πρεσβύτεροι οἱ ἀποσταλέντες, οὓς ἔδει μετὰ χαρᾶς ἐπανελθεῖν, τοὐναντίον λυπούμενοι ἐπανῆλθον ἐφ᾽ οἷς ἑωράκασιν ἐκεῖ γινομένοις. καὶ ἔγωγε, τοῖς γράμμασιν ἐντυχών, πολλὰ λογισάμενος, κατέσχον παρ᾽ ἐμαυτῷ τὴν ἐπιστολήν, νομίζων ὅμως ἥξειν τινάς, καὶ μὴ χρείαν εἶναι τῆς ἐπιστολῆς ἵνα μή, καὶ εἰς φανερὸν ἐλθοῦσα, πολλοὺς τῶν ἐνταῦθα λυπήσῃ.

l. 1 Διανίῳ *scr. Op. (cf. Soz., H. e. 3.5.10; Bas., ep. 51.1) Bre.* : Δαν- *A, Com. Cou. Mon.* : Διόγνιος *coni. Cou.* **l. 17** μετασχηματιζόμενοι : σχηματιζόμενοι *A*[1,2]

a. *Cf.* 2Cor 11.13–15.

II

To the Bishops assembled in Antioch from Julius, Bishop of Rome

(*21.*) Julius, to those who have written us from Antioch—Dianius, Flacillus, Narcissus, Eusebius, Maris, Macedonius, Theodore, and those with them—our beloved brethren; greetings in the Lord.

(1) When I read the letter brought back by my priests Elpidius and Philoxenus,[1] I was amazed! We had written in love and with a sincere conscience, but you sent a contentious and unfitting reply. Indeed, your letter exhibited the contempt and arrogance of its writers. These are attitudes alien to faith in Christ![2] What was written in love ought to have been repaid with an equally loving reply, not with contentiousness. Was it not a token of my love that I sent priests to show sympathy toward those who were suffering, and that I encouraged those who wrote me to come so we might find a swift solution, everything would be set right again, our brethren would suffer no longer, and no one would speak ill of you. Whatever your attitude may be, we are compelled to think that you have infused a note of sarcasm into the very words in which you pretend to honor us.[a] At any rate, the priests I sent, who should have returned with joy, returned just the opposite, grieving at what they saw happening there. I read your words, gave them serious consideration, and then kept the letter to myself, thinking some of you might still come, and there would be no need to produce the letter and cause grief to many people here when its contents were made public. But since no one

1. Elpidius and Philoxenus were the Roman priests who had carried Julius' *ep.* (R^2) to Antioch.

2. With the adjective "alien" (ἀλλότριος), Julius denies the Arians citizenship in Christ's kingdom. Marcellus applies the same adjective to his opponents (1.2) and their beliefs (1. 5).

ἐπειδὴ δέ, μηδενὸς ἐλθόντος, ἀνάγκη γέγονεν αὐτὴν προκομισθῆναι, ὁμολογῶ ὑμῖν, πάντες ἐθαύμασαν καὶ ἐγγὺς ἀπιστίας γεγόνασιν εἰ ὅλως παρ' ὑμῶν τοιαῦτα ἐγράφη· φιλονεικίας γὰρ μᾶλλον, καὶ οὐκ ἀγάπης, ἦν ἡ ἐπιστολή. εἰ μὲν οὖν φιλοτιμίας λόγων ἕνεκεν ὁ ὑπαγορεύσας ἔγραψεν, ἄλλων τὸ τοιοῦτον ἐπιτήδευμα. ἐν γὰρ τοῖς ἐκκλησιαστικοῖς οὐ λόγων ἐπίδειξίς ἐστιν, ἀλλὰ κανόνες ἀποστολικοὶ καὶ σπουδὴ τοῦ μὴ *σκανδαλίζειν ἕνα τῶν μικρῶν* τῶν ἐν τῇ ἐκκλησίᾳ. *Συμφέρει* γὰρ, κατὰ τὸν ἐκκλησιαστικὸν λόγον, *μύλον ὀνικὸν κρεμασθῆναι εἰς τὸν τράχηλον … καὶ καταποντισθῆναι* ἢ σκανδαλίσαι κἂν *ἕνα τῶν μικρῶν.*[b] εἰ δέ, ὥς τινων λελυπημένων διὰ τὴν πρὸς ἀλλήλους μικροψυχίαν· οὐ γὰρ ἂν εἴποιμι πάντων εἶναι ταύτην γνώμην· τοιαύτη γέγονεν ἡ ἐπιστολή, ἔπρεπε μὲν μηδὲ ὅλως λυπηθῆναι, μηδὲ ἐπιδῦναι τὸν ἥλιον ἐπὶ τῇ λύπῃ·[c] ἔδει δὲ ὅμως μὴ εἰς τοσοῦτον προαχθῆναι ὥστε καὶ ἔγγραφον αὐτὴν ἐπιδείξασθαι.

(2) *(22.)* Τί γὰρ καὶ γέγονεν ἄξιον λύπης, ἢ ἐν τίνι ἦν ἄξιον λυπηθῆναι ὑμᾶς οἷς καὶ ἐγράψαμεν; ἢ ὅτι προετρεψάμεθα εἰς σύνοδον ἀπαντῆσαι; ἀλλὰ τοῦτο μᾶλλον ἔδει μετὰ χαρᾶς δέξασθαι· οἱ γὰρ παρρησίαν ἔχοντες ἐφ' οἷς πεποιήκασι καί, ὡς αὐτοὶ λέγουσι, *κεκρίκασιν,* οὐκ ἀγανακτοῦσιν εἰ παρ' ἑτέρων ἐξετάζοιτο ἡ κρίσις, ἀλλὰ θαρροῦσιν ὅτι ἃ δικαίως ἔκριναν, ταῦτα ἄδικα οὐκ ἄν ποτε γένοιτο. διὰ τοῦτο καὶ οἱ ἐν τῇ κατὰ Νίκαιαν μεγάλῃ συνόδῳ συνελθόντες ἐπίσκοποι, οὐκ ἄνευ θεοῦ βουλήσεως, συνεχώρησαν ἐν ἑτέρᾳ συνόδῳ τὰ τῆς προτέρας ἐξετάζεσθαι ἵνα καὶ οἱ κρίνον-

l. 45 καὶ οἱ ἐν τῇ … συνόδῳ $A^{1,3}$ *(Cf. Mon., qui perperam dixit* καὶ *non nisi in* A^{1} *inueniri.)* : οἱ ἐν τῇ … συνόδῳ $A^{2,4,5}$, *Com. = "the bishops who gathered for the great council at Nicaea"*

b. Mt 18.6 c. Eph 4.26

appeared, it had to be made public, and, I assure you, everyone was amazed and could hardly believe that such a letter had actually been written by you. For the letter was contentious rather than loving. If the author composed it to display his eloquence, such a pursuit is for other arenas. In matters concerning the Church, there is no place for displays of eloquence, but rather for apostolic canons[3] and zeal "not to offend one of the little ones" in the Church. According to church teaching, "It would be better for a large millstone to be hung about one's neck, and that he be drowned in the sea rather than offend one of the little ones."[b] But if the tone of your letter is due to the fact that some (I would not say all) have conceived grievances arising from the mean-spiritedness with which they treat each other, it was not at all fitting to be overcome by a grievance, nor to "let the sun go down on a grievance";[c] nor should this grievance have been allowed to go so far as to be displayed in public in writing.

(2) (22.) What could have rightfully aroused resentment? Why should you, to whom we wrote, feel resentment? Was it that we urged you to present yourselves to a council? You should have gladly welcomed the suggestion! Those who have an opportunity to speak frankly about their actions and "decisions," as they say, are not angered if a decision is reëxamined by others. Rather they are confident that their own just verdicts can never turn out to be unjust. Therefore, even the bishops who gathered for the great council at Nicaea, following divine guidance, allowed for the acts of one council to be reviewed by a later council[4] so that those who were to pass

3. The term κανών originally denoted the clergy roster of a church, then the precepts and traditions of that church, and finally the decisions of a church council; on this development, *v.* Ohme, pp. 1–15. On the meaning of κανών in this passage, *v.* Jalland, p. 215, esp. n. 1. The word ἀποστολικοί implies a claim that those practices and procedures dating to the time of the apostles were normative. Because of their age, the churches of Rome, Antioch, and Alexandria should all have been especially cognizant of and attentive to these practices. On the translation of κανών and related terms, *v.* my remarks in sec. 9 of the Introduction.

4. The fifth canon of Nicaea allowed anyone who had been excommunicated by his bishop to appeal to a provincial synod. Julius argues by analogy that bishops deposed by provincial councils could appeal to a higher synod of some sort. The

τες, πρὸ ὀφθαλμῶν ἔχοντες τὴν ἐσομένην δευτέραν κρίσιν, μετὰ πάσης ἀσφαλείας ἐξετάζωσι, καὶ οἱ κρινόμενοι πιστεύωσι μὴ κατ' ἔχθραν τῶν προτέρων, ἀλλὰ κατὰ τὸ δίκαιον ἑαυτοὺς κρίνεσθαι. εἰ δὲ τὸ τοιοῦτον ἔθος, παλαιὸν τυγχάνον, μνημονευθὲν δὲ καὶ γραφὲν ἐν τῇ μεγάλῃ συνόδῳ, ὑμεῖς τοῦτο παρ' ὑμῖν ἰσχύειν οὐ θέλετε, ἀπρεπὴς μὲν ἡ τοιαύτη παραίτησις· τὸ γὰρ ἅπαξ συνήθειαν ἐσχηκὸς ἐν τῇ ἐκκλησίᾳ καὶ ὑπὸ συνόδων βεβαιωθὲν οὐκ εὔλογον ὑπὸ ὀλίγων παραλύεσθαι.

Ἄλλως τε οὐδὲ ἐν τούτῳ δικαίως ἂν φανεῖεν λυπηθέντες. οἱ γὰρ παρ' ὑμῶν, τῶν περὶ Εὐσέβιον, ἀποσταλέντες μετὰ γραμμάτων, λέγω δὴ Μακάριος ὁ πρεσβύτερος καὶ Μαρτύριος καὶ Ἡσύχιος οἱ διάκονοι, ἀπαντήσαντες ἐνταῦθα, ὡς οὐκ ἠδυνήθησαν πρὸς τοὺς ἐλθόντας Ἀθανασίου πρεσβυτέρους ἀντιστῆναι, ἀλλ' ἐν πᾶσι διετρέποντο καὶ διηλέγχοντο, τὸ τηνικαῦτα ἠξίωσαν ἡμᾶς ὥστε σύνοδον συγκροτῆσαι καὶ γράψαι καὶ Ἀθανασίῳ τῷ ἐπισκόπῳ εἰς Ἀλεξάνδρειαν, γράψαι δὲ καὶ τοῖς περὶ Εὐσέβιον ἵνα ἐπὶ παρουσίᾳ πάντων ἡ δικαία κρίσις ἐξενεχθῆναι δυνηθῇ. τότε γὰρ καὶ ἀποδεικνύναι πάντα τὰ κατὰ Ἀθανάσιον ἐπηγγείλαντο· κοινῇ γὰρ ὑφ' ἡμῶν διηλέγχθησαν οἱ περὶ Μαρτύριον καὶ Ἡσύχιον, καὶ οἱ Ἀθανασίου τοῦ ἐπισκόπου πρεσβύτεροι μετὰ πεποιθήσεως ἀνθίσταντο. οἱ δὲ περὶ Μαρτύριον, εἰ δεῖ τἀληθὲς εἰπεῖν, ἐν πᾶσι διετρέποντο, ὅθεν καὶ ἠξίωσαν σύνοδον γενέσθαι. εἰ τοίνυν, μηδὲ τῶν περὶ Μαρτύριον καὶ Ἡσύχιον ἀξιωσάντων γενέσθαι σύνοδον, προτρεψάμενος ἤμην ἐγὼ σκῦλαι τοὺς γράψαντας

ll. 53–56 *τὸ γὰρ … παραλύεσθαι. Ἄλλως τε … λυπηθέντες. : τὸ γὰρ … παραλύεσθαι· ἄλλως τε εἰ … λυπηθέντες. coni. Schd., scr. Bre. = "It would make no sense … and confirmed by councils, especially if their resentment were unjustified in that matter."* **l. 67** ἐπισκόπου : ἐ. τῆς Ἀλεξανδρείας $A^{1,2}$, *Cou. = "the priests of Bishop Athanasius of Alexandria"*

judgment would imagine the possibility of a future review, and thus deliberate with utmost caution, and those being judged could be confident that they were being judged fairly, not according to the ill will of the first set of judges. If it is your desire to be exempt from this old established practice, explicitly mentioned at the great council and entered into the acts, your request is out of order. It would make no sense for a few men to set aside a practice already established in the Church and confirmed by councils.[5]

Your resentment appears totally unjustified also in the following: You, the partisans of Eusebius, sent the priest Macarius and the deacons Martyrius and Hesychius with a letter,[6] but when they presented themselves, they could not hold their own against the priests who had come in support of Athanasius; they were routed and refuted on every point. It was they who at that moment requested us to assemble a council by writing to both Bishop Athanasius at Alexandria and to Eusebius and his party so a just settlement could be reached in the presence of all.[7] They also promised to prove all their charges against Athanasius at that time; for we publicly confuted the delegation of Martyrius and Hesychius, while the priests of Bishop Athanasius confidently stood up under questioning. To be perfectly candid, Martyrius and his companions were refuted on every point, and that is why they then requested the convocation of a council. But even if Martyrius and Hesychius and their delegation had not requested a council, and I had taken it upon myself to trouble the writers of

---

easterners had already taken this principle a step further. At the Synod of Nicomedia in 327/28, the decisions of the "great council" (*i.e.*, greater than a provincial council) of Nicaea were reviewed, and its depositions of bishops Theognis and Eusebius overturned; *v.* Barnes, *Athanasius and Constantius*, n. 24, p. 257. Julius, however, denies the validity of those actions.

5. Nicaea had been by far the largest and most diverse council of bishops held to date. Here the size and breadth of participation are used as an argument for the universal validity of the council's decisions; in contrast, the decisions of local or provincial councils (note the ὀλίγων in l. 55) were not regarded as universally binding. In l. 98, Nicaea is referred to as the council of "the three hundred."

6. This was E^2, the letter sent in 338.

7. Julius refers to R^1, the letter he wrote to the easterners in 338.

ἕνεκεν τῶν ἀδελφῶν ἡμῶν τῶν αἰτιωμένων ἀδικίαν πεπονθέναι, καὶ οὕτως εὔλογος ἦν καὶ δικαία ἡ προτροπή· ἔστι γὰρ ἐκκλησιαστικὴ καὶ θεῷ ἀρέσκουσα. ὅτε δὲ οὓς ὑμεῖς αὐτοί, οἱ περὶ Εὐσέβιον, ἀξιοπίστους ἡγήσασθε καὶ οὗτοι ἠξίωσαν ἡμᾶς συγκαλέσαι, ἀκόλουθον ἦν τοὺς κληθέντας μὴ λυπηθῆναι, ἀλλὰ μᾶλλον προθύμως ἀπαντῆσαι. οὐκοῦν ἡ μὲν δόξασα ἀγανάκτησις τῶν λυπηθέντων προπετής, ἡ δὲ παραίτησις τῶν μὴ θελησάντων ἀπαντῆσαι ἀπρεπὴς καὶ ὕποπτος ἐκ τούτων δείκνυται. αἰτιᾶταί τις ἃ πράττων αὐτὸς ἀποδέχεται εἰ παρ᾽ ἑτέρου γινόμενα βλέποι;

(3) Εἰ γάρ, ὡς γράφετε, *Ἀσάλευτον ἔχει τὴν ἰσχὺν ἑκάστη σύνοδος*, καί, *Ἀτιμάζεται ὁ κρίνας ἐὰν παρ᾽ ἑτέρων ἡ κρίσις ἐξετάζηται*, σκοπεῖτε, ἀγαπητοί, τίνες εἰσὶν οἱ σύνοδον ἀτιμάζοντες, καὶ τίνες τὰ τῶν φθασάντων κρῖναι διαλύουσι. καὶ ἵνα μή, τὰ καθ᾽ ἕκαστον νῦν ἐξετάζων, ἐπιβαρεῖν τινας δοκῶ, ἀλλὰ τό γε τελευταῖον γενόμενον, ἐφ᾽ ᾧ καὶ φρίξειεν ἄν τις ἀκούων, ἀρκεῖ πρὸς ἀπόδειξιν πάντων τῶν παραλειφθέντων. *(23.)* οἱ Ἀρειανοὶ οἱ ἀπὸ τοῦ τῆς μακαρίας μνήμης Ἀλεξάνδρου, τοῦ γενομένου ἐπισκόπου τῆς Ἀλεξανδρείας, ἐπὶ ἀσεβείᾳ ἐκβληθέντες οὐ μόνον ὑπὸ τῶν καθ᾽ ἑκάστην πόλιν ἀπεκηρύχθησαν, ἀλλὰ καὶ ὑπὸ πάντων τῶν κοινῇ συνελθόντων ἐν τῇ κατὰ Νίκαιαν μεγάλῃ συνόδῳ ἀνεθεματίσθησαν. οὐ γὰρ ἦν αὐτῶν τὸ τυχὸν πλημμέλημα, οὐδὲ εἰς ἄνθρωπον ἦσαν ἁμαρτήσαντες, ἀλλ᾽ εἰς αὐτὸν τὸν Κύριον ἡμῶν Ἰησοῦν *Χριστὸν τὸν υἱὸν τοῦ θεοῦ τοῦ ζῶντος*.[d] καὶ ὅμως οἱ ὑπὸ πάσης τῆς οἰκουμένης ἀποκηρυχθέντες καὶ κατὰ πᾶσαν ἐκκλησίαν στηλιτευθέντες νῦν λέγονται δεδέχθαι, ἐφ᾽ ᾧ καὶ ὑμᾶς ἀκούσαντας χαλεπαίνειν δίκαιον ἡγοῦμαι. τίνες οὖν εἰσιν οἱ σύνοδον ἀτιμάζοντες; οὐχὶ οἱ τῶν τριακοσίων τὰς ψήφους παρ᾽ οὐδὲν θέμενοι καὶ ἀσέβειαν εὐσεβείας προκρίναντες; ἡ μὲν γὰρ τῶν Ἀρειομανιτῶν αἵρεσις ὑπὸ πάντων τῶν ἁπανταχοῦ ἐπισκόπων κατεγνώ-

l. 80 βλέποι : -ει *A*[5] **l. 98** οὐχὶ *Com. Mon. Cou.* : οὐχ *A, Op. Bre.*

d. Mt 16.16

that letter due to complaints of injustice raised by our brethren, my exhortation would still have been sensible and just, as it is in accord with ecclesiastical practice and pleasing to God. But since it was the very men deemed trustworthy by you Eusebians who asked us to call together a council, it followed that those summoned, far from upset, would be eager to present themselves. So we conclude from this that the apparent indignation of those who have conceived a grievance is ill considered, and the refusal of those who decline to present themselves both inappropriate and suspicious. Should one person blame another for doing something he permits himself to do?

(3) If, as you write, "Each council has permanent force," and, "A judge is dishonored when his decision is reviewed by others," consider, beloved, who is actually doing dishonor to a council, and who is actually overturning previous decisions. To avoid the appearance of deliberately annoying anyone by listing each event, I go straight to the last. It will make anyone who hears it shudder and will be proof enough of everything I omit. (23.) When, at the insistence of Alexander of blessed memory, the former bishop of Alexandria, the Arians were expelled for impiety, they were not only publicly denounced in city after city, but declared anathema by the common consent of all those gathered at the great council of Nicaea. For theirs was no ordinary error, nor had they sinned against a man, but rather against our Lord Jesus Christ himself, "the Son of the living God."[d] Nevertheless, these same men who were publicly denounced by the entire world, and whose condemnation was posted in every church, are now said to have been readmitted.[8] I think you should also be indignant to hear this. So, who is it who is doing dishonor to a council? Is it not those who are setting aside the votes of the three hundred, and who prefer impiety to piety? The heresy of the Ariomaniacs has

8. At Nicaea, Arius and several of his allies were excommunicated for their beliefs. Three months later, Eusebius of Nicomedia and Theognis of Nicaea were removed from office for associating with Arian dissidents; *v.* Gwynn, pp. 117f. The council of Nicomedia (end of 327 or early 328) reinstated all three, and Arius was again rehabilitated in 335 by councils in Tyre and Jerusalem; *v.* Soz., *H. e.* 2.16, 27 and Barnes, *Athanasius and Constantius,* pp. 17, 56. Julius was addressing this letter to bishops who had attended those councils of 335.

σθη καὶ ἀπεκηρύχθη, Ἀθανάσιος δὲ καὶ Μάρκελλος οἱ ἐπίσκοποι πλείονας ἔχουσι τοὺς ὑπὲρ ἑαυτῶν λέγοντας καὶ γράφοντας. Μάρκελλος μὲν γὰρ ἐμαρτυρήθη ἡμῖν καὶ ἐν τῇ κατὰ Νίκαιαν συνόδῳ τοῖς τὰ Ἀρείου φρονοῦσιν ἀντειρηκώς, Ἀθανάσιος δὲ ἐμαρτυρήθη μηδὲ ἐν Τύρῳ καταγνωσθείς, ἐν δὲ τῷ Μαρεώτῃ μὴ παρεῖναι, ἔνθα τὰ ὑπομνήματα κατ᾽ αὐτοῦ γεγενῆσθαι λέγεται. οἴδατε δέ, ἀγαπητοί, ὅτι τὰ κατὰ μονομέρειαν ἰσχὺν οὐκ ἔχει, ἀλλ᾽ ὕποπτα τυγχάνει. καὶ ὅμως, τούτων ὄντων, ἡμεῖς, ὑπὲρ ἀκριβείας οὔτε ὑμῖν οὔτε τοῖς ὑπὲρ αὐτῶν γράψασι πρόκριμα ποιοῦντες, προετρεψάμεθα τοὺς γράψαντας ἐλθεῖν ἵν᾽, ἐπειδὴ πλείους εἰσὶν οἱ ὑπὲρ αὐτῶν γράψαντες, ἐπὶ συνόδου πάντα ἐξετασθῇ πρὸς τὸ μηδὲ τὸν ἀναίτιον κατακριθῆναι, μήτε τὸν ὑπεύθυνον ὡς καθαρὸν λογισθῆναι. οὐκοῦν οὐ παρ᾽ ἡμῶν ἀτιμάζεται σύνοδος, ἀλλὰ παρ᾽ ἐκείνων, τῶν, ἁπλῶς καὶ ὡς ἔτυχε, τοὺς παρὰ πάντων κατακριθέντας Ἀρειανοὺς καὶ παρὰ γνώμην τῶν κρινάντων δε-

been condemned and disavowed by all bishops everywhere,[9] while Bishops Athanasius and Marcellus have the majority speaking and writing on their behalf. We have heard testimony rendered in support of Marcellus for speaking out against the partisans of Arius at the Council of Nicaea, and in support of Athanasius, who was not found guilty at Tyre, nor was even present in the Mareotis, where minutes prejudicial to him were recorded.[10] As you know, beloved, one-sided proceedings have no force, but are regarded with suspicion. Nevertheless, in order to guarantee complete propriety, we have shown partiality neither to you nor to those who have written in defense of the other side, but have urged the writers to come,[11] so that, since those who write in support of the other side are more numerous, everything might be investigated in council, and the innocent not be condemned, nor the guilty declared innocent. Therefore, it is not we who do dishonor to a council, but rather those who, contrary to the decision of the judges of the case, simply and nonchalantly re-

9. The first known use of the term *Ariomaniac* is in a letter of Eustathius of Antioch dated to 328/29 (Thdt., *H. e.* 1.8.3); for the date, *v.* Hanson, "The Fate of Eustathius," pp. 173f. Constantine himself speaks of "Arius' mania" (Ἀρείου μανία) in a letter of *ca.* 333 (Ath., *Decr.* 40.18); the Alexandrian church refers to ἀρειομανῖται in a letter to the Council of Tyre (Ath., *Apol. sec.* 75) and employs both Ἀρείου μανία and ἀρειομανῖται in a synodal letter of 338 (*ibid.*, 6–8). Yet, Athanasius accounts for over half of the 120 uses of the various forms of ἀρειομανῖται recorded in the *TLG*. These include sixteen of the twenty-one prior to 341: twice in his *ep. mort. Ar.* of 337/38 (4.2; 5.1); five times in his *ep. encycl.* of 339 (2.3; 5.4; 7.1, 3, 5); and nine times in *Ar.* 1–3 (1.4.1; 2.17.1; 2.41.1; 2.70.3; 3.1.1; 3.15.3; 3.27.2; 3.44.5; 3.58.1), which Barnes dates as early as 340; *v. Athanasius and Constantius*, pp. 53–55 and n. 26. The use of ἀρειομανῖται in *ep.* 2 must reveal Athanasius' influence upon Julius. On this term, *v.* Logan, "Marcellus of Ancyra (Pseudo-Anthimus), *On the Holy Church*," pp. 104f.

10. In 335, Constantine had ordered a council to meet at Tyre to look into charges against Athanasius. The council sent a six-member investigative team, made up exclusively of opponents of Athanasius, to the scene of his alleged crimes in the Mareotis, a rural district close to Alexandria. The council then moved to Jerusalem, then back to Tyre. Athanasius, who had left Tyre before the team returned, was convicted and deposed in his absence. Julius may be saying that Athanasius was not convicted at the first session in Tyre. Rather than pleading that the investigative team was biased, he cites irregular procedure: the accused was not present to confront those testifying against him.

11. Julius argues that he was moved to issue his invitation to a council (R^1) by the letters sent from Antioch (E^2) and Egypt (A^1).

ξαμένων. οἱ γὰρ πλείονες, ἤδη ἀναλύσαντες, εἰσὶ *σὺν Χριστῷ*,[e] οἱ δὲ ἔτι καὶ νῦν ἐν τῷ βίῳ τούτῳ ἐξετάζονται ἀγανακτοῦντες ὅτι τὴν αὐτῶν κρίσιν ἔλυσάν τινες.

(4) *(24.)* Τοῦτο δὲ καὶ ἀπὸ τῶν γενομένων μὲν ἐν τῇ Ἀλεξανδρείᾳ ἔγνωμεν· καὶ γὰρ καὶ Καρπώνης τις, ἐκβληθεὶς ὑπὸ Ἀλεξάνδρου διὰ τὴν Ἀρείου αἵρεσιν, μετά τινων καὶ αὐτῶν ἐκβληθέντων διὰ τὴν αὐτὴν αἵρεσιν ἐληλύθασιν ἐνταῦθα, ἀποσταλέντες παρὰ Γρηγορίου τινός. ὅμως δὲ ἐμάθομεν καὶ παρὰ Μακαρίου τοῦ πρεσβυτέρου καὶ Μαρτυρίου καὶ Ἡσυχίου τῶν διακόνων. πρὸ τοῦ γὰρ ἀπαντῆσαι τοὺς Ἀθανασίου πρεσβυτέρους, προετρέποντο ἡμᾶς γράφειν ἐν Ἀλεξανδρείᾳ Πιστῷ τινι ἡνίκα καὶ Ἀθανάσιος ὁ ἐπίσκοπος ἐν Ἀλεξανδρείᾳ ἦν. τοῦτον δὲ τὸν Πιστὸν οἱ Ἀθανασίου τοῦ ἐπισκόπου πρεσβύτεροι παραγενόμενοι ἀπέδειξαν εἶναι Ἀρειανόν, ἐκβληθέντα μὲν ὑπὸ Ἀλεξάνδρου τοῦ ἐπισκόπου καὶ τῆς κατὰ Νίκαιαν συνόδου, κατασταθέντα δὲ ὑπὸ Σεκούνδου τινός, ὃν ἡ μεγάλη σύνοδος, Ἀρειανὸν ὄντα, ἐξέβαλε. τοῦτο δὲ οὐδὲ αὐτοὶ οἱ περὶ Μαρτύριον ἀντέλεγον οὐδὲ ἠρνοῦντο τὸν

e. Phil 1.23

admitted the Arians, whom everyone had condemned. For while the majority of these latter have already departed and are with Christ,[e] those who are still in this life are known to be indignant that their decision has been overturned by a few.

(4) (*24.*) We know this also from events that occurred at Alexandria. A man named Carpones,[12] who was expelled by Alexander for his Arian heresy, was sent here together with other exiled heretics by one Gregory.[13] And we learned about this also from the priest Macarius and the deacons Martyrius and Hesychius. Before the priests of Athanasius presented themselves, these others were urging us to exchange letters with a man named Pistus[14] in Alexandria, and that while Athanasius was still in Alexandria and bishop! But when the priests of Bishop Athanasius arrived, they made it clear that this Pistus was an Arian who had been expelled by Bishop Alexander and the Council of Nicaea but was later appointed bishop by a certain Secundus,[15] whom the great council had also expelled for being an Arian. Martyrius and his delegation neither refuted these claims nor de-

12. Carpones was an Alexandrian priest who was first a rival, but later a supporter of Arius. He was among those who subscribed to Arius' letter to bishop Alexander and among those excommunicated by the bishop; *v.* Epiph., *Haer.* 69.2, 7f.; Alex., *ep. encycl.* 6; and Arius, *ep. Alex.* Two decades later, Carpones was recruited by Gregory (*v.* the following note) who, shunned by the clergy loyal to Athanasius, was filling the ranks of the Alexandrian clergy with sympathetic Arians and Melitians. Gregory sent Carpones as his envoy to Julius.

13. After confirming the condemnation of Athanasius, the Council of Antioch (339) elected a Cappadocian named Gregory to take his place (Socr., *H. e.* 2.10.2). Gregory arrived in Alexandria in late March, 339 (*ibid.* 2.11, Ath., *ep. encycl.* 2–4). He was deposed by the Council of Sardica in 343 (Ath., *Apol. sec.* 39) but continued in office until his death in June, 345. Later, in secc. 14 and 18, Julius attacks Gregory's qualifications, the regularity of his appointment, and his conduct in office.

14. Pistus, a supporter of Arius, had been excommunicated by Alexander. Yet, in early 338, he was chosen by a council sitting in Antioch to replace the deposed Athanasius. The envoys sent to Rome had asked Julius to indicate, by an exchange of letters of communion, his acceptance of Pistus as the new bishop. It is unclear whether Pistus was ever consecrated in Alexandria; Gregory (*v.* the previous note) was soon sent to replace him; *v.* Ath., *Apol. sec.* 19 and Barnes, *Athanasius and Constantius,* pp. 36, 46, 48. On letters of communion (*litterae communicatoriae*), *v.* n. 10 to the translation of *ep.* 4 below.

15. Secundus of Ptolemais, one of the two bishops deposed for their support of

Πιστὸν ὑπὸ Σεκούνδου ἐσχηκέναι τὴν κατάστασιν. σκοπεῖτε τοίνυν καὶ ἐκ τούτων τίνες ἂν ὑπὸ μέμψιν δικαίως γένοιντο· οἱ μὴ πεισθέντες ἡμεῖς ὥστε Πιστῷ τῷ Ἀρειανῷ γράψαι, ἢ οἱ συμβουλεύοντες ἀτιμάσαι τὴν μεγάλην σύνοδον καὶ τοῖς ἀσεβέσιν ὡς εὐσεβέσι γράψαι; καὶ γὰρ καὶ Μακάριος ὁ πρεσβύτερος, ὁ παρὰ Εὐσεβίου μετὰ τῶν περὶ Μαρτύριον ἀποσταλείς, ὡς ἤκουσεν ἐπιστάντας τοὺς πρεσβυτέρους Ἀθανασίου, ἐκδεχομένων ἡμῶν τὴν παρουσίαν αὐτοῦ μετὰ τῶν περὶ Μαρτύριον καὶ Ἡσύχιον, ἀπεδήμησε νυκτός, καίτοι νοσῶν τῷ σώματι, ὡς ἐκ τούτου λοιπὸν ἡμᾶς ἀκολούθως στοχάζεσθαι ὅτι, αἰσχυνόμενος τὸν κατὰ Πιστοῦ ἔλεγχον, ἀνεχώρησεν. ἀδύνατον γὰρ τὴν κατάστασιν Σεκούνδου τοῦ Ἀρειανοῦ ἐν τῇ καθολικῇ ἐκκλησίᾳ ἰσχῦσαι· ἀτιμία γὰρ ἀληθῶς αὕτη κατὰ τῆς συνόδου καὶ τῶν ἐν αὐτῇ συνελθόντων ἐπισκόπων ἐὰν τὰ μετὰ τοσαύτης σπουδῆς καὶ εὐλαβείας, ὡς θεοῦ παρόντος, γενόμενα ἀντὶ μηδενὸς λυθῇ.

(5) *(25.)* Εἴπερ οὖν, ὡς γράφετε, *Ἐκ τοῦ κατὰ Νοβάτον καὶ τὸν Σαμοσατέα Παῦλον παραδείγματος τὰ τῶν συνόδων ἰσχύειν δόγματα χρή*, ἔδει μᾶλλον μὴ λυθῆναι τῶν τριακοσίων τὴν ψῆφον, ἔδει τὴν καθολικὴν σύνοδον ὑπὸ τῶν ὀλίγων μὴ ἀτιμασθῆναι· αἱρετικοὶ γὰρ οἱ Ἀρειανοί, ὥσπερ κἀκεῖνοι, καὶ ὅμοιαι αἱ κατὰ

l. 141 ὡς ἐκ τούτου : ὥστ᾽ ἐκ τούτου *coni. Gilb.*

nied that Pistus had received his appointment from Secundus.[16] On this basis, then, consider who deserves to be blamed: we, who would not be prevailed upon to correspond with Pistus the Arian, or those who advised us to do dishonor to the great council by writing to ungodly men as if they were godly? Furthermore, we were waiting for Macarius, the priest sent by Eusebius along with Martyrius and his delegation, to appear with Martyrius and Hesychius and their delegation. But when Macarius heard that Athanasius' priests were on hand, he decamped during the night, though ill. Of course, we surmised that he had left because he could not face the evidence against Pistus. Indeed, it is impossible to recognize the consecration of a bishop by the Arian Secundus as valid in the Catholic Church. It would be an act of disrespect toward Nicaea and the bishops who gathered there to set aside, as though entirely unimportant, decisions reached with such seriousness and care, in the belief that God himself was present.

(5) (25.) You write that "conciliar decisions must remain in force, according to the precedents regarding Novatian and Paul of Samosata."[17] If so, then all the more reason the decision of the three hundred ought not to have been set aside, nor a general council dishonored by a few men![18] After all, the Arians are heretics just like Novatian

---

Arius by the Council of Nicaea (*C. Nic. ep.* 5 = Socr., *H. e.* 1.9.4), was exiled with Arius to Illyricum (Philost., *H. e.* 1.9c). Nevertheless, he seems to have continued to play a role in Egyptian ecclesiastical politics; *v.* Ath., *Syn.* 12; *H. ar.* 65, 71. We learn from the fifth-century Arian historian Philostorgius (*H. e.* 3.19f.) that Secundus was a patron of Aëtius and Eunomius.

16. Julius rejects, as invalid, the consecration of Pistus by a heretic. It is unclear whether Secundus only ordained Pistus to the priesthood, or whether he also consecrated him bishop. Barnes (*Athanasius and Constantius*, pp. 40, 59, and n. 27, p. 251) supports the first alternative, Klein (pp. 68–71) the second.

17. In the mid-third century, Cornelius of Rome had condemned Novatian (*v.* n. 68 to the Introduction), and his decision had been accepted in the east. Two decades later, a council at Antioch had condemned the adoptionist christology of Paul of Samosata (*v.* "Paul of Samosata," *ODCC*, p. 1242), and the bishop of Rome had agreed with that decision. These were the precedents for the easterners' expectations that Julius would accept their condemnation of Athanasius and Marcellus. Julius rejoins that, if they wished to view conciliar judgments as inviolable precedents, the Eusebians should never have overturned the decision of Nicaea against Arius.

18. Julius argues that a trans-regional or more general council (καθολικὴ σύνοδος) possesses greater authority than a regional council.

τούτων ψῆφοι ταῖς κατ᾽ ἐκείνων. τούτων δὲ τολμηθέντων, τίνες εἰσὶν *οἱ φλόγα διχονοίας ἀνάψαντες;* ἡμᾶς γὰρ τοῦτο πεποιηκέναι γράψαντες ἐμέμψασθε. ἆρ᾽ οὖν ἡμεῖς διχονοίας εἰργασάμεθα, οἱ συναλγοῦντες τοῖς πάσχουσιν ἀδελφοῖς καὶ κατὰ κανόνα πάντα πεποιηκότες; ἢ οἱ φιλονείκως καὶ παρὰ κανόνα τῶν τριακοσίων τὴν ψῆφον λύσαντες καὶ κατὰ πάντα τὴν σύνοδον ἀτιμάσαντες; οὐ γὰρ μόνον οἱ Ἀρειανοὶ ἐδέχθησαν, ἀλλὰ καὶ ἀπὸ τόπου εἰς τόπον μεμελετήκασιν ἐπίσκοποι διαβαίνειν. εἰ οὖν ἀληθῶς ἴσην καὶ τὴν αὐτὴν ἡγεῖσθε τιμὴν τῶν ἐπισκόπων καὶ *μὴ ἐκ τοῦ μεγέθους τῶν πόλεων,* ὡς γράφετε, κρίνετε τοὺς ἐπισκόπους, ἔδει τὸν πεπιστευμένον μικρὰν μένειν ἐν τῇ πιστευθείσῃ καὶ μὴ ἐξουθενεῖν μὲν τὸ πεπιστευμένον, μεταβαίνειν δὲ εἰς τὴν μὴ ἐγχειρισθεῖσαν ἵνα τῆς μὲν παρὰ θεοῦ δοθείσης καταφρονῇ, τὴν δὲ τῶν ἀνθρώπων κενοδοξίαν ἀγαπήσῃ.

(6) Οὐκοῦν, ἀγαπητοί, ἔδει ἀπαντῆσαι καὶ μὴ παραιτήσασθαι ἵνα καὶ τέλος λάβῃ τὸ πρᾶγμα· τοῦτο γὰρ ὁ λόγος ἀπαιτεῖ. ἀλλ᾽ ἴσως ἡ προθεσμία ἐνεπόδισε· γράψαντες γὰρ ἐμέμψασθε ὅτι στενὴν τὴν προθεσμίαν τῆς συνόδου ὡρίσαμεν. ἀλλὰ καὶ τοῦτο, ἀγαπητοί, πρόφασίς ἐστιν. εἰ μὲν γὰρ ἐρχομένους τινὰς συνέκλεισεν ἡ ἡμέρα, στενὸν ἂν τὸ διάστημα τῆς προθεσμίας ἠλέγχθη, εἰ δὲ οἱ ἐλθεῖν μὴ βουλόμενοι κατεσχήκασι καὶ τοὺς πρεσβυτέρους ἕως αὐτοῦ τοῦ Ἰαννουαρίου μηνός, μὴ θαρρούντων ἐστὶν ἡ πρόφασις. ἦλθον γὰρ ἄν, ὡς προεῖπον, εἰ ἐθάρρουν, οὐ πρὸς τὸ διάστημα τῆς ὁδοῦ σκοποῦντες, οὐδὲ πρὸς τὴν προθεσμίαν ὁρῶντες, ἀλλ᾽ ἐπὶ τοῖς δικαίοις καὶ τοῖς εὐλόγοις παρρησιαζόμενοι.

l. 174 Ἰαννουαρίου : Ἰανουαρίου *Mon. Cou.*

and Paul of Samosata, and the decisions pronounced against the Arians are similar to those made against those two. Are not the people who dare to overturn these decisions the ones "fanning the flames of discord?" But in your letter you made that reproach against us! Are we the ones who have produced discord—we who have shown sympathy for our suffering brethren and have in everything acted in accord with church law? Or, is it they—they who have, contentiously and contrary to the canons, set aside the decision of the three hundred and done dishonor to the council in every step they have taken? Not only have the Arians been received back into communion, but bishops have made it a practice to move from one see to another.[19] Therefore, if you truly believe that "there is an equal and identical honor among all bishops" and, if, as you write, you do not judge bishops according to the size of their cities, one entrusted with a small city ought to remain where he has been given that trust; he should not despise it and, scorning what God has given him and loving the empty praise of men, move to a place that was not put in his care.

(6) Therefore, beloved, you should have presented yourselves and not refused the invitation, so that this matter might come to an end. Reason demands it. But perhaps the problem arose from the date we set. In your letter you complained that the interval of time we appointed before the council was too short.[20] But this, too, beloved, is just an excuse. If the appointed day had passed while some of you were still en route, the interval to the appointed day would have been proven too short; but if those who did not want to come detained our priests until January of this year, this is the excuse of mere cowards. As I said earlier, if they had had confidence, they would have come, not considering the length of the trip or worrying over the appointed time, but emboldened by the justice and reasonableness of their case.

19. Canons fifteen of Nicaea (325) and twenty-one of Antioch (*ca.* 328), had forbidden bishops to move from one see to another. The first provided that bishops guilty of this action be returned to their former sees. Julius is attacking Eusebius, bishop first of Beirut, then of Nicomedia (*ca.* 317), and finally of the eastern capital Constantinople (from 337).

20. In their most recent letter (E^4), the easterners had complained that they could not have reached Rome by the date Julius had set for the hearing (in R^2).

(7) Ἀλλ' ἴσως διὰ τὸν καιρὸν οὐκ ἀπήντησαν· τοῦτο γὰρ γράφοντες πάλιν ἐδηλώσατε ὡς ἄρα ἔδει ἡμᾶς, σκοπήσαντας τὸν ἐπὶ τῆς ἑῴας καιρόν, μὴ προτρέψασθαι ὑμᾶς ἀπαντῆσαι. εἰ μὲν οὖν διὰ τὸ τοιοῦτον εἶναι τὸν καιρὸν οὐκ ἀπηντήσατε, ὥς φατε, ἔδει προτέρους ὑμᾶς, τὸν καιρὸν τοῦτον σκοπήσαντας, μὴ αἰτίους σχίσματος, μηδὲ ὀλολυγῆς καὶ θρήνων, ἐν ταῖς ἐκκλησίαις γενέσθαι. νῦν δὲ οἱ ταῦτα πεποιηκότες ἔδειξαν μὴ τὸν καιρὸν αἴτιον, ἀλλὰ τὴν προαίρεσιν τῶν μὴ θελησάντων ἀπαντῆσαι.

(8) *(26.)* Θαυμάζω δὲ κἀκεῖνο τὸ μέρος τῆς ἐπιστολῆς, πῶς ὅλως κἂν ἐγράφη παρ' ὑμῶν ὅτι δὴ τοῖς περὶ Εὐσέβιον μόνοις, καὶ οὐ πᾶσιν ὑμῖν, μόνος ἔγραψα· εὐχέρειαν γὰρ τῶν μεμψαμένων μᾶλλον ἄν τις εὕροι ἤπερ ἀλήθειαν. ἐγὼ γάρ, οὐκ ἄλλοθεν λαβὼν κατὰ Ἀθανασίου γράμματα ἢ διὰ τῶν περὶ Μαρτύριον καὶ Ἡσύχιον, ἐκείνοις ἀνάγκῃ ἔγραψα τοῖς καὶ γράψασι κατ' αὐτοῦ. ἔδει τοίνυν ἢ τοὺς περὶ Εὐσέβιον μὴ μόνους χωρὶς πάντων ὑμῶν γράψαι, ἢ ὑμᾶς οἷς μὴ ἔγραψα μὴ λυπεῖσθαι εἰ ἐκείνοις ἐγράφη τοῖς καὶ γράψασιν. εἰ γὰρ ἐχρῆν καὶ πᾶσιν ὑμῖν ἐπιστεῖλαι, ἔδει καὶ ὑμᾶς σὺν ἐκείνοις γράψαι. νῦν δέ, τὸ ἀκόλουθον σκοποῦντες, ἐκείνοις ἐγράψαμεν τοῖς καὶ δηλώσασιν ἡμῖν καὶ τοῖς ἀποστείλασι πρὸς ἡμᾶς. εἰ δὲ καὶ τὸ μόνον ἐμὲ γεγραφέναι ἐκείνοις ἐκίνησεν ὑμᾶς, ἀκόλουθόν ἐστιν ὑμᾶς ἀγανακτεῖν, ὅτι καὶ μόνῳ ἐμοὶ ἔγραψαν. ἀλλὰ καὶ ἐν τούτῳ πιθανὴ μὲν καὶ οὐκ εὔλογος ἡ πρόφασις, ἀγαπητοί· ὅμως δὲ γνωρίσαι ὑμῖν ἀναγκαῖον ὅτι, εἰ καὶ μόνος ἔγραψα, ἀλλ' οὐκ ἐμοῦ μόνου ἐστὶν αὕτη ἡ γνώμη, ἀλλὰ καὶ πάντων τῶν κατὰ τὴν Ἰταλίαν καὶ τῶν ἐν τούτοις τοῖς μέρεσιν

l. 199 εὔλογος : ἄλ- *coni. Mon., scr. Op. Bre.* = *"But, beloved, even in this our motive was plausible and not unreasonable."*

(7) But perhaps they did not present themselves due to the critical times. Indeed, in your letter, you set out the objection that, making allowance for the critical situation in the east, we ought not to have urged you to present yourselves.[21] If, as you say, the crisis prevented you from coming, you ought to have thought about that crisis earlier and not caused divisions and uproar and lamentations in the Church. But those responsible for all this have now made it clear that the blame falls not on some crisis, but on the deliberate choice of those who refused to present themselves.[22]

(8) (*26.*) I was amazed by yet another part of your letter. There you actually wrote that it was only I who had written and that I had written only to Eusebius and his close associates and not to all of you.[23] This reveals, not the truthfulness, but the unscrupulousness of those who lay the blame! Since I had received a letter written against Athanasius only via the delegation led by Martyrius and Hesychius, I had to address my reply to those same men who had written against him. So either Eusebius and his colleagues should not have written alone without the rest of you, or those of you to whom I have not written should not be upset that my reply was to those who wrote the accusations. If it was incumbent on me to reply to all of you, you all should have written along with them. But, as it was, we tried to be consistent by writing only to those who explained the situation and sent us the delegation. Now, if you were angered by the fact that I was the only one who wrote, it follows that you should be equally annoyed that they wrote to me alone. But this, beloved, is just another plausible-sounding pretense that cannot stand up to analysis. Nonetheless, I must make clear to you that, even if I alone wrote, the content was not mine alone but that of all the bishops throughout Italy

21. The Eusebians had cited (in E^4) the ongoing war with Persia as another reason for not wishing to travel to Rome (Ath., *H. ar.* 11).

22. The Eusebians wanted any council to be held in the region controlled by the emperor Constantius, who favored their position (*v. H. ar.* 9). Thus, in 338, 339, and 340/41, the easterners chose to meet in the winter in Antioch when the imperial court was also in residence.

23. The Eusebians (in E^4) had raised two other objections to Julius' previous

ἐπισκόπων. καὶ ἔγωγε τοὺς πάντας οὐκ ἠθέλησα ποιῆσαι γράψαι ἵνα μὴ παρὰ πολλῶν τὸ βάρος ἔχωσιν. ἀμέλει καὶ νῦν τῇ ὁρισθείσῃ προθεσμίᾳ συνῆλθον ἐπίσκοποι καὶ ταύτης τῆς γνώμης γεγόνασιν ἣν πάλιν γράφων ὑμῖν σημαίνω, ὥστε, ἀγαπητοί, εἰ καὶ μόνος ἐπιστέλλω, ἀλλὰ πάντων γνώμην εἶναι ταύτην γινώσκετε. ταῦτα μὲν οὖν περὶ τοῦ μὴ εὐλόγως τινὰς ἐξ ὑμῶν προφάσεις, ἀλλὰ ἀδίκους καὶ ὑπόπτους, πορίσασθαι.

(9) *(27.)* Περὶ δὲ τοῦ μὴ εὐχερῶς μηδὲ ἀδίκως ἡμᾶς ὑποδεδέχθαι εἰς κοινωνίαν τοὺς συνεπισκόπους ἡμῶν Ἀθανάσιον καὶ Μάρκελλον, εἰ καὶ τὰ προλεχθέντα ἱκανά, ὅμως διὰ βραχέων εὔλογον ὑμῖν δεῖξαι. ἔγραψαν οἱ περὶ Εὐσέβιον πρότερον κατὰ τῶν περὶ Ἀθανάσιον, ἐγράψατε δὲ καὶ νῦν ὑμεῖς, ἔγραψαν δὲ καὶ πλεῖστοι ἐπίσκοποι ἀπὸ τῆς Αἰγύπτου καὶ ἐξ ἄλλων ἐπαρχιῶν ὑπὲρ Ἀθανασίου. πρῶτον μὲν οὖν τὰ κατ᾽ αὐτοῦ γράμματα παρ᾽ ὑμῶν μάχεται πρὸς ἑαυτά, καὶ οὐδεμίαν συμφωνίαν ἔχει τὰ δεύτερα πρὸς τὰ πρῶτα, ἀλλ᾽ ἐν πολλοῖς τὰ πρῶτα ὑπὸ τῶν δευτέρων λύεται, καὶ τὰ δεύτερα ὑπὸ τῶν πρώτων διαβάλλεται· ἀσυμφώνων δὲ ὄντων τῶν γραμμάτων, οὐδεμία πίστις περὶ τῶν λεγομένων ἐστίν. ἔπειτα, εἰ τοῖς παρ᾽ ὑμῶν γραφεῖσιν ἀξιοῦτε πιστεύειν, ἀκόλουθόν ἐστι καὶ τοῖς ὑπὲρ αὐτοῦ γράψασι μὴ ἀπιστῆσαι, καὶ μάλιστα ὅτι ὑμεῖς μὲν πόρρωθεν, ἐκεῖνοι δέ, ἐν τοῖς τόποις ὄντες καὶ εἰδότες τὸν ἄνδρα, καὶ τὰ ἐκεῖ γινόμενα πράγματα γράφουσι, μαρτυροῦντες αὐτοῦ τῷ βίῳ καὶ διαβεβαιούμε-

l. 207 γνώμην εἶναι ταύτην : *γ. τ. εἶ.* A^1*, Mon. Cou.* : *εἶ. γ. τ.* A^3*, Com.*
l. 213 ἔγραψαν *edd.* : -ατε *A* = *"You, the supporters of Eusebius, wrote earlier"*

and the surrounding regions.[24] I did not want to make all of them write letters, so they would not feel pressured by so many bishops. Now that the bishops have assembled at the appointed time and come to the verdict I here announce to you, I am again writing the letter myself. So, beloved, though I alone am sending out this letter, you should know that its opinions are those of all the bishops. This, then, is all I have to say about the excuses, both unfair and unworthy of trust, that some of you have quite unreasonably put forward.

(9) (27.) Though what we have already said should be sufficient to show you there was neither excessive indulgence nor lack of justice in our decision to receive our fellow bishops Athanasius and Marcellus into communion, it will be worthwhile to prove this through a brief review of the facts. Eusebius and his supporters wrote earlier against the Athanasian party, as you also have now written;[25] but a great number of bishops, both from Egypt and from other provinces, have written in support of Athanasius. First of all, there were contradictions in the letters you wrote against him, and your second letter does not in the least harmonize with the first; in many instances the first was negated by the second, and the second discredited by the first. Since the letters are in such disagreement, we can put no faith in their contents. But if you think we should trust the letter you have written, it follows that we should extend the same trust to those who have written on his behalf, especially since you live far away while these others live on the spot and write from their knowledge of the man and local events.[26] They have testified to Athanasius' way of life

letter (R^1): 1) he had addressed himself to a small group of bishops, rather than to the council as a whole, and 2) Julius had written in his own name, rather than in that of a council. Consequently, they claimed, his letter and invitation to come to Rome bore the appearance of a private, rather than an official, communication. He replies to both complaints in sec. 8.

24. We have no information about this previous Roman council, but Julius implies that it was similar to the council that had just met in 341, *i.e.*, it was attended by bishops from all of Italy, Sardinia, Corsica, and Sicily.

25. The second letter is certainly the latest one from the east (E^4). The prior letter is probably that carried by Macarius and the two deacons (E^2), but it might also be the one sent after Athanasius' condemnation at Tyre and Jerusalem in 335 (E^1).

26. These "others" are the Egyptian clergy who have come to testify on Athanasius' behalf.

νοι ἐν πᾶσιν αὐτὸν συσκευὴν πεπονθέναι. καὶ πάλιν Ἀρσένιός τις ἐπίσκοπος ἐλέχθη ποτὲ ὡς ἀναιρεθεὶς παρὰ Ἀθανασίου· ἀλλὰ τοῦτον ἐμάθομεν ζῆν, ἀλλὰ καὶ φιλίαν ἔχειν πρὸς αὐτόν.

(10) Τὰ ὑπομνήματα τὰ ἐν Μαρεώτῃ γενόμενα διεβεβαιώσατο κατὰ μονομέρειαν γεγενῆσθαι· μήτε γὰρ ἐκεῖ παρεῖναι Μακάριον τὸν πρεσβύτερον τὸν κατηγορούμενον, μήτε αὐτὸν τὸν ἐπίσκοπον αὐτοῦ Ἀθανάσιον. καὶ τοῦτο οὐ μόνον ἐκ τῶν αὐτοῦ λόγων, ἀλλὰ καὶ ἐκ τῶν ὑπομνημάτων ὧν ἐκόμισαν ἡμῖν οἱ περὶ Μαρτύριον καὶ Ἡσύχιον ἔγνωμεν. ἀναγνόντες γὰρ εὕρομεν ὅτι ὁ μὲν κατήγορος Ἰσχύρας ἐκεῖ παρῆν, οὔτε δὲ Μακάριος, οὔτε ὁ ἐπίσκοπος Ἀθανάσιος· ἀλλὰ καὶ τοὺς πρεσβυτέρους Ἀθανασίου ἀξιοῦντας παρεῖναι καὶ μὴ συγχωρηθέντας. ἔδει δέ, ἀγαπητοί, εἴπερ μετὰ ἀληθείας ἐγίνετο τὸ κριτήριον, μὴ μόνον τὸν κατήγορον, ἀλλὰ καὶ τὸν κατηγορούμενον παρεῖναι. ὥσπερ γὰρ ἐν τῇ Τύρῳ Μακάριος παρῆν ὁ κατηγορούμενος καὶ Ἰσχύρας ὁ κατήγορος, καὶ οὐδὲν ἐδείχθη, οὕτως ἔδει καὶ ἐν τῷ Μαρεώτῃ μὴ μόνον ἀπελθεῖν τὸν κατήγορον, ἀλλὰ καὶ τὸν κατηγορούμενον ἵνα παρὼν ἢ ἐλεγχθῇ ἤ, μὴ ἐλεγχθείς, δείξῃ τὴν συκοφαντίαν. νῦν δέ, τούτου μὴ γενομένου, ἀλλὰ μόνου ἀπελθόντος τοῦ κατηγόρου μεθ' ὧν παρῃτήσατο Ἀθανάσιος, ὕποπτα τὰ πράγματα φαίνεται. *(28.)* ᾐτιᾶτο δὲ καὶ τοὺς ἀπελθόντας εἰς τὸν Μαρεώτην παρὰ γνώμην αὐτοῦ ἀπεληλυθέναι· ἔλεγε γὰρ ὅτι Θεόγνιον, καὶ Μάριν,

and have declared that, throughout, he has been the victim of a conspiracy. Again, although it was previously claimed that Athanasius did away with a certain bishop Arsenius, we have discovered that he is, in fact, alive and remains in friendship with him![27]

(10) Arsenius also declared that the reports from the Mareotis were composed with only one of the two parties in attendance. For neither the accused priest Macarius[28] nor his bishop Athanasius was present at the investigation. We learned this not only from his own statement, but also from the official records brought to us by the delegation of Martyrius and Hesychius.[29] In reading these, we found that the accuser Ischyras was present, but neither Macarius nor Bishop Athanasius, and, what is more, that the priests of Athanasius had wanted to be present but were not admitted. Beloved, if the tribunal had been seeking the truth, not only the accuser but also the accused should have been present. For just as at Tyre the accused Macarius and the accuser Ischyras were present, but nothing was proven, it was not only the accuser but also the accused who was obliged to travel to the Mareotis, either to be convicted in person or, if not convicted, to prove the accusations false. As this did not take place, but only the accuser and others to whom Athanasius objected went there, the proceedings lack credibility. (28.) Athanasius also complained that those who went out to the Mareotis did so despite his protests. Ac-

27. By early 334 some Melitians had forwarded to the Eusebians a charge that Athanasius had arranged the murder of Arsenius, bishop of Hypsele. Arsenius, however, was found alive and well in Tyre (Ath., *Apol. sec.* 8, 65; Soz., *H. e.* 2.25.10). Julius uses the case of Arsenius as an example of a charge leveled against Athanasius that was later found to be baseless.

28. The rural district of the Mareotis, close to Alexandria, was under the direct supervision of the bishop of the metropolis (Ath., *Apol. sec.* 85). There, in the winter of 331/32, the priest Macarius, a supporter of Athanasius (*i.e.*, not to be confused with the Eusebian priest who bore E^2 to Rome), was accused of smashing a chalice and overturning an altar that were being used by the Melitian priest Ischyras, all on the orders of Athanasius himself (*ibid.*, 63f.). This charge, often repeated by his enemies, proved the most difficult for Athanasius to dispel. In *Apol. sec.* 63f., he reproduces a letter, in which Ischyras states that he had been forced by some Melitians to testify falsely against Athanasius.

29. The report of the commission sent to the Mareotis (*v.* n. 10 above) must have been appended to the Eusebians' letter of 338 (E^2).

καὶ Θεόδωρον, Οὐρσάκιον, καὶ Οὐάλεντα, καὶ Μακεδόνιον, ὑπόπτους ὄντας, ἀπέστειλαν.

(11) Καὶ τοῦτο οὐκ ἐκ τῶν λόγων αὐτοῦ μόνον, ἀλλὰ καὶ ἐκ τῆς ἐπιστολῆς Ἀλεξάνδρου, τοῦ γενομένου ἐπισκόπου τῆς Θεσσαλονίκης, ἐδείκνυε. προήνεγκε γὰρ ἐπιστολὴν αὐτοῦ γραφεῖσαν πρὸς Διονύσιον, τὸν ἐν τῇ συνόδῳ κόμητα, ἐν ᾗ δηλοῖ φανερὰν συσκευὴν γενέσθαι κατὰ Ἀθανασίου. καὶ αὐτοῦ δὲ τοῦ κατηγόρου Ἰσχύρα προεκόμισε χεῖρα ὁλόγραφον αὐθεντικήν, ἐν ᾗ, μάρτυρα τὸν θεὸν τὸν παντοκράτορα ἐπικαλούμενος, μήτε ποτηρίου κλάσιν μήτε τραπέζης ἀνατροπὴν γεγενῆσθαι ἔλεγεν, ἀλλ᾽ ὑποβεβλῆσθαι ἑαυτὸν ὑπό τινων πλάσασθαι ταύτην τὴν κατηγορίαν. ἀπαντήσαντες δὲ καὶ πρεσβύτεροι τοῦ Μαρεώτου διεβεβαιώσαντο μήτε τὸν Ἰσχύραν πρεσβύτερον εἶναι τῆς καθολικῆς ἐκκλησίας, μήτε τι τοιοῦτον πεπλημμεληκέναι Μακάριον ὁποῖον ἐκεῖνος κατηγόρησεν. οἱ πρεσβύτεροι δὲ καὶ οἱ διάκονοι ἀπαντήσαντες ἐνταῦθα οὐκ ὀλίγα, ἀλλὰ καὶ πολλὰ ἐμαρτύρησαν ὑπὲρ τοῦ ἐπισκόπου Ἀθανασίου, διαβεβαιούμενοι μηδὲν ἀληθὲς εἶναι τῶν κατ᾽ αὐτοῦ λεγομένων, συσκευὴν δὲ αὐτὸν πεπονθέναι. καὶ

cording to him, they sent Theognis, Maris, Theodore, Ursacius, Valens, and Macedonius, none of whom were trustworthy.[30]

(11) And he supported this not solely by his own testimony, but also with a letter from Alexander, bishop of Thessalonica.[31] He presented a letter written by Alexander to Dionysius,[32] the imperial representative at the council, containing information that an intrigue against Athanasius had come to light. He also presented the original hand-written letter of the accuser Ischyras himself, in which the latter, calling Almighty God as witness, stated that there was no broken chalice or overturned altar, and that others had induced him to fabricate this accusation.[33] And when the priests of the Mareotis presented themselves, they declared that Ischyras was not a priest of the Catholic Church,[34] and that, despite the accusation, Macarius had committed no such offense. When the priests and deacons presented themselves, they provided not just a few, but numerous, testimonials on behalf of Bishop Athanasius; they declared that there was no truth in the accusations made against him, but that he was

30. All six members of the commission were determined opponents of Athanasius: Maris of Chalcedon, Macedonius of Mopsuestia, and Theodore of Heraclea figure among the leaders of the Eusebian camp to whom Julius addresses this letter (*v.* n. 8 to the introduction to *ep.* 2); Theognis of Nicaea had refused to subscribe to the anathema pronounced against Arius at Nicaea. Ursacius and Valens, Pannonian bishops who sided with the Eusebian camp, would later be condemned by the western Council of Sardica (*v. ep.* 6 below).

31. Alexander was bishop of Thessalonica by 324, when Athanasius' predecessor (also named Alexander) wrote him an exposé of Arius' teachings (reproduced by Thdt., *H. e.* 1.4, where the addressee is wrongly identified as Alexander of Byzantium). The council was that held at Tyre in 335. The bishop of Thessalonica was one of the few non-Egyptian bishops who objected to the proceedings against Athanasius. His letter is reproduced in *Apol. sec.* 80.

32. The imperial *comes* (count) Flavius Dionysius, earlier governor of Syria, was sent as Constantine's representative to the council of Tyre (*V. C.* 4.42.3f.). Dionysius appended Alexander's letter to his own letter to the council, in which he warned the commissioners to present a fair report. Both documents are reproduced in Ath., *Apol. sec.* 81.

33. This letter is preserved in Ath., *Apol. sec.* 64.

34. *V.* the discussion regarding Ischyras in the letter of the Egyptian bishops preserved in Ath., *Apol. sec.* 74. The term "Catholic Church" here stands in contrast to the local Melitian sect.

οἱ ἀπὸ τῆς Αἰγύπτου δὲ καὶ Λιβύης πάντες ἐπίσκοποι γράφοντες διεβεβαιώσαντο καὶ τὴν κατάστασιν αὐτοῦ ἔννομον καὶ ἐκκλησιαστικὴν γεγονέναι, καὶ πάντα τὰ παρ᾽ ὑμῶν λεγόμενα κατ᾽ αὐτοῦ εἶναι ψευδῆ· οὔτε γὰρ φόνον γεγενῆσθαι, οὔτε τινὰς ἀναιρεθῆναι δι᾽ αὐτόν, οὔτε κλάσιν ποτηρίου γεγενῆσθαι, ἀλλὰ πάντα εἶναι ψευδῆ.

(12) Καὶ ἐκ τῶν ὑπομνημάτων δὲ τῶν ἐν Μαρεώτῃ κατὰ μονομέρειαν γενομένων ἐδείκνυεν ὁ ἐπίσκοπος Ἀθανάσιος ἕνα κατηχούμενον ἐξετασθέντα καὶ εἰπόντα ἔνδον εἶναι μετὰ Ἰσχύρα ὅτε Μακάριος, ὁ πρεσβύτερος Ἀθανασίου, ὡς λέγουσιν, *Ἐπέστη τῷ τόπῳ,* καὶ ἄλλους δὲ ἐξετασθέντας καὶ εἰπόντας τὸν μὲν ἐν κελλίῳ μικρῷ, τὸν δὲ ὄπισθεν τῆς θύρας κατακεῖσθαι τὸν Ἰσχύραν τότε νοσοῦντα ὅτε Μακάριον λέγουσιν ἀπηντηκέναι ἐκεῖ. ἀπὸ δὴ τούτων ὧν ἔλεγε, καὶ ἡμεῖς ἀκολούθως στοχαζόμεθα ὅτι πῶς οἷόν τε τὸν ὄπισθεν τῆς θύρας νόσῳ κατακείμενον τότε ἑστηκέναι, καὶ λειτουργεῖν, καὶ προσφέρειν; ἢ πῶς οἷόν τε ἦν προσφορὰν προκεῖσθαι, ἔνδον ὄντων τῶν κατηχουμένων; εἰ γὰρ ἔνδον ἦσαν οἱ κατηχούμενοι, οὔπω ἦν ὁ καιρὸς τῆς προσφορᾶς. ταῦτα, ὥσπερ εἴρηται, ἔλεγεν ὁ ἐπίσκοπος Ἀθανάσιος καὶ ἐκ τῶν ὑπομνημάτων ἐδείκνυε, διαβεβαιουμένων καὶ τῶν σὺν αὐτῷ μηδὲ ὅλως αὐτὸν πρεσβύτερον γεγενῆσθαί ποτε ἐν τῇ καθολικῇ ἐκκλησίᾳ, μηδὲ συνῆχθαι αὐτόν ποτε ἐν τῇ ἐκκλησίᾳ ὡς πρεσβύτερον· οὐδὲ γάρ, ὅτε Ἀλέξανδρος ἐδέχετο κατὰ φιλανθρωπίαν τῆς μεγάλης συνόδου τοὺς ἀπὸ τοῦ σχίσματος Μελιτίου, ὠνομάσθαι αὐτὸν ὑπὸ Μελιτίου μετὰ τῶν αὐτοῦ διεβεβαιοῦντο. ὃ καὶ μέγιστόν ἐστι τεκ-

l. 273 γενομένων : γεγενη- A^{3}, *Com. Mon. Cou.* **l. 287** συνῆχθαι A^{1pc} (*cf.* σεσυνῆχθαι $A^{2,3}$, A^{1ac}, *Op. Bre.*), *Com. Mon. Cou.* : συναχθῆναι $A^{4,5}$ οὐδὲ γὰρ *Op.* : οὐ. γ. οὐδὲ A, *Com. Mon. Cou. Bre.* = *"Nor did they declare that Melitius named him as one of his followers even when Alexander"*

the victim of a conspiracy. In addition, all the bishops writing from Egypt and Libya declared that his consecration was lawful and canonical, and that all your accusations were false:[35] there had been no murder, no one was done away with for his benefit, no chalice was broken. In fact, all these charges were untrue.

(12) Even from the one-sided official reports from the Mareotis Bishop Athanasius was able to show that, upon examination, one catechumen had reported that he was inside the church with Ischyras when Athanasius' priest Macarius, as they allege, "set upon the place."[36] Among the others who were examined, one said that Ischyras was in a small room, another that he was lying sick behind the door when, as they allege, Macarius presented himself. In light of this testimony, we are trying to make out how a man lying sick behind the door was able to stand up, conduct the liturgy, and offer the sacrament. Or how could it be that the offering was on the altar with catechumens still present? If the catechumens were still inside, it was not yet time for the offering.[37] This, as I have said, was the statement Bishop Athanasius made and which he supported from the official reports, while those with him also declared that Ischyras had never been ordained a priest in the Catholic Church, nor had ever been received into the communion of the Church as a priest. They declared that Melitius did not name him as one of his followers when Alexander, in accordance with the charity of the great council, was admitting the Melitian schismatics.[38] This is the most compelling proof that he

35. This letter, addressed to the investigative delegation sent to Mareotis by the Council of Tyre (*v.* n. 10 above), is reproduced by Athanasius in *Apol sec.* 73.

36. *Cf.* Ath., *Apol sec.* 83.

37. The offerings presented by the congregation at the beginning of the service were stored in an adjacent room until the celebration of the sacrament. After the dismissal of the catechumens, they were brought to the altar for consecration and distribution. Julius is questioning the chronology for the alleged desecration of the Eucharist; *cf. Const. apost.* 8 and Wybrew, pp. 38–45.

38. For Melitius of Lycopolis and his sectaries, *v.* n. 68 to the Introduction. The Council of Nicaea had tried, with little success, to heal the schism by readmitting the Melitians into communion. Although Athanasius had made it a priority to end the division, his Melitian opponents accused him of using compulsion. As Ischyras' name did not appear on a list of clergy (reproduced in Ath., *Apol. sec.* 71) that

μήριον μὴ εἶναι αὐτὸν μήτε Μελιτίου· εἰ γὰρ ἦν, πάντως καὶ αὐτὸς αὐτοῖς συνηριθμεῖτο. ἄλλως τε καὶ ἐν ἄλλοις ὁ Ἰσχύρας ψευσάμενος ἐδείκνυτο ὑπὸ Ἀθανασίου ἐκ τῶν ὑπομνημάτων· κατηγορήσας γὰρ ὡς βιβλίων κεκαυμένων ὅτε, ὡς λέγουσι, *Μακάριος ἐπέστη*, ἠλέγχθη ὑφ᾽ ὧν αὐτὸς ἤνεγκε μαρτύρων ψευσάμενος.

(13) *(29.)* Τούτων τοίνυν οὕτως λεγομένων, καὶ τοσούτων μὲν ὄντων τῶν μαρτύρων τῶν ὑπὲρ αὐτοῦ, τοσούτων δὲ δικαιωμάτων προφερομένων ὑπ᾽ αὐτοῦ, τί ἔδει ποιεῖν ἡμάς; ἢ τί ὁ ἐκκλησιαστικὸς κανὼν ἀπαιτεῖ ἢ μὴ καταγνῶναι τοῦ ἀνδρός, ἀλλὰ μᾶλλον ἀποδέξασθαι καὶ ἔχειν αὐτὸν ἐπίσκοπον ὥσπερ καὶ εἴχομεν; καὶ γάρ, πρὸς τούτοις πᾶσι, παρέμεινεν ἐνταῦθα ἐνιαυτὸν καὶ ἓξ μῆνας, ἐκδεχόμενος τὴν παρουσίαν ὑμῶν ἢ τῶν βουλομένων ἐλθεῖν· τῇ δὲ παρουσίᾳ ἐδυσώπει πάντας, ὅτι οὐκ ἂν παρῆν εἰ μὴ ἐθάρρει. καὶ γὰρ οὐκ ἀφ᾽ ἑαυτοῦ ἐλήλυθεν, ἀλλὰ κληθεὶς καὶ λαβὼν γράμματα παρ᾽ ἡμῶν καθάπερ καὶ ὑμῖν ἐγράψαμεν. καὶ ὅμως μετὰ τοσαῦτα ὑμεῖς ὡς παρὰ κανόνας ποιήσαντας ἡμᾶς ἐμέμψασθε.

(14) Σκοπεῖτε τοίνυν τίνες εἰσὶν οἱ παρὰ κανόνα πράξαντες· ἡμεῖς οἱ μετὰ τοσούτων ἀποδείξεων τὸν ἄνδρα δεξάμενοι, ἢ οἱ ἀπὸ τριάκοντα καὶ ἓξ μονῶν ἐν Ἀντιοχείᾳ ὀνομάσαντές τινα ὡς ἐπίσκοπον ξένον καὶ ἀποστείλαντες εἰς τὴν Ἀλεξάνδρειαν μετὰ στρατιωτικῆς ἐξουσίας; ὅπερ οὐ γέγονεν, οὐδὲ εἰς Γαλλίας αὐτοῦ ἀποσταλέντος· ἐγεγόνει γὰρ ἂν καὶ τότε εἰ ὄντως ἦν καταγνωσθείς. ἀμέλει ἐπανελθὼν σχολάζουσαν καὶ ἐκδεχομένην αὐτὸν τὴν ἐκκλησίαν εὗρεν.

l. 306 παρὰ κανόνας : π. -να *coni. Gilb.* = *"acting uncanonically"* **l. 307** παρὰ κανόνα *A^{-3}* : π. -νας *A^{3}, edd.*

was not a priest or a Melitian. For if he had been, he would surely have been listed with the others. Besides, Athanasius showed from the official records that Ischyras had lied in other matters as well. For Ischyras had also made accusations that, after Macarius had allegedly "set upon the place," he had burned some books, but Ischyras' charge was proven false by the very witnesses he had himself produced.

(13) (29.) Now then, given this testimony, with so many witnesses speaking on his behalf and himself bringing forward so many justifications, what were we to do? What does church law demand but that we not condemn the man, but rather accept and consider him a bishop, just as we have done? In addition to all this, he remained here a year and a half, awaiting your appearance or that of whoever might wish to come. By his mere presence he put all of you to shame, because he would not be here if he were not confident. He did not come on his own, but called by the letter he received from us, in the same way we wrote to you.[39] Nevertheless, after all this, you have blamed us for acting contrary to the laws of the Church.

(14) Consider now which side is acting contrary to church law—we who have received this man after hearing such conclusive proof, or those in Antioch (a thirty-six day journey from Egypt![40]), who named some stranger bishop and sent him to Alexandria with a military escort? That did not happen even when Athanasius was sent to Gaul.[41] And it would have happened then as well, if he had, in fact, been convicted. Of course, when he returned, he found the church vacant and awaiting him.

Melitius had drawn up, perhaps for the council of Nicomedia in late 327, Julius sides with Athanasius in declaring that Ischyras was not a clergyman at all, not even among the Melitians.

39. Julius must have dispatched his first letter calling for a council (R^1) in summer or fall of 338, his second (R^2) in late 339 or early 340. Athanasius arrived in Rome in the summer of 339 after the first letter had been sent (*ep. encycl.* 7 and *H. ar.* 9). Although Athanasius had been forced to flee Egypt, Julius claims that he had come to Rome in response to his invitation.

40. The third-century *Itin. Ant.* (vol. 1, p. 21, ##147.1–154.5), lists thirty-six stations from Antioch to Alexandria, the fourth-century (?) *Tab. peut.* (coll. 801–14 and 870f.) thirty-nine. On these ancient itineraries, *v.* Burian, pp. 1023f.

41. Barnes notes that Athanasius' time in Gaul (*v.* sec. 8 of the Introduction) "was

(30.) Ἀλλὰ νῦν οὐκ οἶδα ποίῳ τρόπῳ γέγονε τὰ γενόμενα. πρῶτον μὲν γάρ, εἰ δεῖ τἀληθὲς εἰπεῖν, οὐκ ἔδει, γραψάντων ἡμῶν σύνοδον γενέσθαι, προλαβεῖν τινας τὴν ἐκ τῆς συνόδου κρίσιν. ἔπειτα οὐκ ἔδει τοιαύτην καινοτομίαν κατὰ τῆς ἐκκλησίας γενέσθαι. ποῖος γὰρ κανὼν ἐκκλησιαστικὸς ἢ ποία παράδοσις ἀποστολικὴ τοιαύτη ὥστε, εἰρηνευούσης ἐκκλησίας, καὶ ἐπισκόπων τοσούτων ὁμόνοιαν ἐχόντων πρὸς τὸν ἐπίσκοπον τῆς Ἀλεξανδρείας Ἀθανάσιον, ἀποσταλῆναι Γρηγόριον, ξένον μὲν τῆς πόλεως, μήτε ἐκεῖ βαπτισθέντα μήτε γινωσκόμενον τοῖς πολλοῖς, μὴ αἰτηθέντα παρὰ πρεσβυτέρων, μὴ παρ' ἐπισκόπων, μὴ παρὰ λαῶν· ἀλλὰ κατασταθῆναι μὲν ἐν Ἀντιοχείᾳ, ἀποσταλῆναι δὲ εἰς τὴν Ἀλεξάνδρειαν, οὐ μετὰ πρεσβυτέρων, οὐ μετὰ διακόνων τῆς πόλεως, οὐ μετὰ ἐπισκόπων τῆς Αἰγύπτου, ἀλλὰ μετὰ στρατιωτῶν; τοῦτο γὰρ ἔλεγον καὶ ᾐτιῶντο οἱ ἐνταῦθα ἐλθόντες. εἰ γὰρ καὶ μετὰ τὴν σύνοδον ὑπεύθυνος ἦν εὑρεθεὶς ὁ Ἀθανάσιος, οὐκ ἔδει τὴν κατάστασιν οὕτως παρανόμως καὶ παρὰ τὸν ἐκκλησιαστικὸν κανόνα γενέσθαι, ἀλλ' ἐπ' αὐτῆς τῆς ἐκκλησίας ἀπ' αὐτοῦ τοῦ ἱερατείου, ἀπ' αὐτοῦ τοῦ κλήρου τοὺς ἐν τῇ ἐπαρχίᾳ ἐπισκόπους ἔδει καταστῆσαι, καὶ μὴ νῦν τοὺς ἀπὸ τῶν ἀποστόλων κανόνας παραλύεσθαι. ἆρα γάρ, εἰ καθ' ἑνὸς ὑμῶν ἐγεγόνει τὸ τοιοῦτον, οὐκ ἂν ἐβοήσατε, οὐκ ἂν ἠξιώσατε, ὡς παραλελυμένων τῶν κανόνων, ἐκδικηθῆναι; ἀγαπητοί, ὡς θεοῦ παρόντος, μετὰ ἀληθείας φθεγγόμεθα καὶ λέγομεν, *Οὐκ ἔστι τοῦτο εὐσεβές, οὐδὲ νόμιμον, οὐδὲ ἐκκλησιαστικόν.* καὶ γὰρ καὶ τὰ λεγόμενα γεγενῆσθαι παρὰ Γρηγορίου ἐν τῇ εἰσόδῳ αὐτοῦ δείκνυσι τὴν τῆς καταστάσεως τάξιν· ἐν γὰρ τοιούτοις *εἰρηνικοῖς καιροῖς,* ὡς αὐτοὶ οἱ ἐλθόντες ἀπὸ τῆς Ἀλεξανδρείας ἀπήγγειλαν, καθὼς καὶ οἱ

ll. 340f. οἱ ἐλθόντες ἀπὸ τῆς Ἀλεξανδρείας : οἱ ἀπὸ τῆς Ἀ. ἐλ. $A^{1,2}$

(*30.*) But I cannot comprehend how these events ever happened. First, to be frank, when we wrote that there was to be a council, it was not right for people to assume beforehand what the council's decision would be. Second, it was improper to impose such innovations on the Church. After all, what church law or what apostolic tradition could have this result: While the Church is enjoying peace, and the majority of bishops are living in harmony with Athanasius, the bishop of Alexandria, Gregory is sent, a stranger to the city, a man not baptized there, not known to the people, not requested by the priests, the bishops, or the laity, but appointed in Antioch and sent to Alexandria, not escorted by the priests and deacons of the city and the bishops of Egypt, but by troops![42] These are the statements, these the charges of those who have come here. And even if the council had found Athanasius guilty, a successor should not have been appointed in a way so irregular and contrary to church law. Rather, the proper thing would have been for the bishops within the province to appoint someone over the church, some one from among their own priests, their own clergy, not for canons in force since the apostolic age to be contravened now.[43] If anything of the sort had been done to one of you, I suppose you would have cried out in protest and demanded vindication from this breach of church law! Beloved, as God is present, we lift our voices and speak the truth: This action was neither pious, nor in accord with church custom or ecclesiastical practice. In addition, the nature of this appointment is shown by the actions Gregory is reported to have taken when he entered the city. During such a "peaceful time," according to the account of those who came

---

not the normal exile imposed ... on a bishop who had been condemned and deposed by a church council"; the emperor had "merely suspended him from his duties pending further investigation"; *v. Athanasius and Constantius,* p. 24. Thus, as Julius argues, he was not deposed, and no new bishop was appointed for Alexandria.

42. On Gregory, *v.* n. 13 above. Athanasius (*ep. encycl.* 2–5) gives a detailed account of Gregory's entry into Alexandria and of his first acts; he was supported by military forces under the command of the recently reappointed prefect Philagrius.

43. Even when a council had deposed a bishop for heresy or behavior unworthy of office, the local populace and clergy retained the right to elect his replacement; *v.* Norton, p. 19.

ἐπίσκοποι ἔγραψαν, ἡ ἐκκλησία ἐμπρησμὸν ὑπέμεινε· παρθένοι ἐγυμνώθησαν, μονάζοντες κατεπατήθησαν, πρεσβύτεροι καὶ πολλοὶ τοῦ λαοῦ ᾐκίσθησαν καὶ βίαν πεπόνθασιν, ἐπίσκοποι ἐφυλακίσθησαν, περιεσύρησαν πολλοί, τὰ ἅγια μυστήρια, ἐφ' οἷς ᾐτιῶντο Μακάριον τὸν πρεσβύτερον, ὑπὸ ἐθνικῶν διηρπάζετο καὶ εἰς γῆν ἐβάλλετο ἵνα τὴν Γρηγορίου τινὲς κατάστασιν δέξωνται. τὰ δὲ τοιαῦτα δείκνυσι τοὺς παραλύοντας τοὺς κανόνας· εἰ γὰρ νομίμη ἦν ἡ κατάστασις, οὐκ ἂν διὰ παρανομίας ἠνάγκαζε πείθεσθαι τοὺς νομίμως ἀπειθοῦντας αὐτῷ. καὶ ὅμως, τοιούτων γενομένων, γράφετε *Εἰρήνην μεγάλην γεγενῆσθαι ἐν τῇ Ἀλεξανδρείᾳ καὶ τῇ Αἰγύπτῳ.* ἐκτὸς εἰ μὴ ἀντιμεταβέβληται τὸ ἔργον τῆς εἰρήνης, καὶ τὰ τοιαῦτα *εἰρήνην* ὀνομάζετε;

(15) *(31.)* Κἀκεῖνο δὲ ὑμῖν ἀναγκαῖον ἐνόμισα δηλῶσαι, ὅτι Ἀθανάσιος διεβεβαιοῦτο Μακάριον ἐν Τύρῳ ὑπὸ στρατιώτας γεγενῆσθαι, καὶ μόνον τὸν κατήγορον ἀπεληλυθέναι μετὰ τῶν ἀπελθόντων εἰς τὸν Μαρεώτην, καὶ τοὺς μὲν πρεσβυτέρους ἀξιοῦντας παρεῖναι ἐν τῇ ἐξετάσει μὴ συγκεχωρῆσθαι, τὴν δὲ ἐξέτασιν γεγενῆσθαι περὶ ποτηρίου καὶ τραπέζης ἐπὶ παρουσίᾳ τοῦ ἐπάρχου καὶ τῆς τάξεως αὐτοῦ, παρόντων ἐθνικῶν καὶ Ἰουδαίων. τοῦτο δὲ κατὰ τὰς ἀρχὰς ἄπιστον ἦν εἰ μὴ καὶ ἐκ τῶν ὑπομνημάτων ἐδείκνυτο, ἐφ' ᾧ καὶ ἐθαυμάσαμεν, νομίζω δὲ καὶ ὑμᾶς ἔτι θαυμάζειν, ἀγαπητοί· πρεσβύτεροι μὲν οὐκ ἐπιτρέπονται παρεῖναι οἱ καὶ τῶν μυστηρίων λειτουργοὶ τυγχάνοντες, ἐπὶ δὲ ἐξωτικοῦ δικαστοῦ, παρόντων κατηχουμένων, καί, τό γε χείριστον, ἐπὶ ἐθνικῶν καὶ Ἰουδαίων, τῶν διαβεβλημένων περὶ τὸν Χριστιανισμόν, ἐξέτασις περὶ αἵματος Χριστοῦ καὶ σώματος Χριστοῦ γίνεται. εἰ γὰρ καὶ ὅλως ἐγεγόνει τι πλημμέλημα, ἔδει ἐν τῇ ἐκκλησίᾳ ὑπὸ κληρικῶν νομίμων ἐξετάζεσθαι τὰ τοιαῦτα, καὶ μὴ ὑπὸ ἐθνικῶν,

l. 347 ἐβάλλετο : κατε- A^{3ac}, *Com. Mon. Cou.* **ll. 362f.** ἔτι θαυμάζειν : ἐπιθαυμάζειν *Com. Mon. Cou.* **l. 369** νομίμων : -ως *Com. Mon. Cou.* = *"the investigation ought to have been lawfully conducted within the Church, by clergymen"* **ll. 369–72** καὶ μὴ … τοιαῦτα *om. per homotel.* A^{3-5}, *Com.* = *om. "not by heathen … concerning Athanasius"*

from Alexandria and that provided by the bishops in their letter, the church was engulfed in a conflagration: virgins were stripped naked, monks trampled, priests and many of the laity tortured and beaten, bishops imprisoned, many people dragged off, the holy sacrament—the very charge laid against the priest Macarius—seized by the heathen and thrown upon the ground. All this was done so a few could welcome the appointment of Gregory.[44] Events such as these show which side is disregarding church law. Had his appointment been lawful, he would not have broken the law to compel obedience from those who lawfully refused to submit to him. And yet, though this is what happened, you write, "A profound peace reigns in Alexandria and the rest of Egypt." Only if the meaning of "peace" be turned on its head can you call such violence "peace"!

(15) (*31.*) I decided I must inform you also regarding the following: Athanasius declared that Macarius was kept under military guard while in Tyre, that only his accuser went with those going to the Mareotis, and that, while the priests who wished to be present at the inquiry were not admitted, the inquiry into the matter of the communion chalice and altar took place in the presence of the imperial prefect and his staff with heathen and Jews in attendance. At first we could not believe this, but the proof was in the official reports. We were astonished at this, and I think, beloved, you must also be astonished! Although priests entrusted with the celebration of the sacrament are not permitted to be present, an inquiry about the body and blood of Christ takes place in front of a secular judge with catechumens in attendance, and, even worse, in the presence of heathen and Jews, the slanderers of Christianity! If some offense had been committed, the investigation ought to have been conducted within the Church and, as usual, by clergymen, not by heathen who

44. Though there was bloodshed when the two sides clashed over control of the churches, the rhetorical hyperbole of this account is evident. It is unclear whether Julius' description depends on an oral account received from Athanasius or on a reading of Ath., *ep. encycl.* 3.

τῶν τὸν λόγον βδελυσσομένων καὶ μὴ εἰδότων τὴν ἀλήθειαν.[f] τοῦτο δὲ τὸ ἁμάρτημα ἡλίκον καὶ ὁποῖόν ἐστι, συνορᾶν καὶ ὑμᾶς καὶ πάντας πεπίστευκα. περὶ μὲν Ἀθανασίου τοιαῦτα.

(16) *(32.)* Περὶ δὲ Μαρκέλλου, ἐπειδὴ καὶ περὶ αὐτοῦ ὡς ἀσεβοῦντος εἰς τὸν Χριστὸν ἐγράψατε, δηλῶσαι ὑμῖν ἐσπούδασα ὅτι, ἐνταῦθα γενόμενος, διεβεβαιώσατο μὲν μὴ εἶναι ἀληθῆ τὰ περὶ αὐτοῦ γραφέντα παρ᾽ ὑμῶν, ὅμως δέ, ἀπαιτούμενος παρ᾽ ἡμῶν εἰπεῖν περὶ τῆς πίστεως, οὕτως μετὰ παρρησίας ἀπεκρίνατο δι᾽ ἑαυτοῦ ὡς ἐπιγνῶναι μὲν ἡμᾶς ὅτι μηδὲν ἔξωθεν τῆς ἀληθείας ὁμολογεῖ. οὕτως γὰρ εὐσεβῶς περὶ τοῦ Κυρίου καὶ σωτῆρος ἡμῶν Ἰησοῦ Χριστοῦ ὡμολόγησε φρονεῖν ὥσπερ καὶ ἡ καθολικὴ ἐκκλησία φρονεῖ· καὶ οὐ νῦν ταῦτα πεφρονηκέναι διεβεβαιώσατο, ἀλλὰ καὶ ἔκπαλαι ὡσπεροῦν καὶ οἱ ἡμέτεροι πρεσβύτεροι τότε ἐν τῇ κατὰ Νίκαιαν συνόδῳ γενόμενοι ἐμαρτύρησαν αὐτοῦ τῇ ὀρθοδοξίᾳ. καὶ γὰρ καὶ τότε καὶ νῦν κατὰ τῆς αἱρέσεως τῶν Ἀρειανῶν πεφρονηκέναι διϊσχυρίσατο· ἐφ᾽ ᾧ καὶ ὑμᾶς ὑπομνῆσαι δίκαιόν ἐστιν ἵνα μηδεὶς τὴν τοιαύτην αἵρεσιν ἀποδέχηται, ἀλλὰ βδελύττηται ὡς ἀλλοτρίαν τῆς ὑγιαινούσης διδασκαλίας. ὀρθὰ τοίνυν αὐτὸν φρονοῦντα καὶ ἐπὶ ὀρθοδοξίᾳ μαρτυρούμενον τί πάλιν καὶ ἐπὶ τούτου ἔδει ποιεῖν ἡμᾶς ἢ ἔχειν αὐτόν, ὥσπερ καὶ εἴχομεν, ἐπίσκοπον καὶ μὴ ἀποβάλλειν τῆς κοινωνίας;

(17) Ταῦτα μὲν οὖν ἐγὼ οὐχ ὡς ὑπεραπολογούμενος αὐτῶν γέγραφα, ἀλλ᾽ ἕνεκα τοῦ πιστεῦσαι ὑμᾶς ὅτι δικαίως καὶ κανονικῶς ἐδεξάμεθα τοὺς ἄνδρας, καὶ μάτην φιλονεικεῖτε. ὑμᾶς δὲ δίκαιόν ἐστι σπουδάσαι καὶ πάντα τρόπον καμεῖν ἵνα τὰ μὲν παρὰ κανόνα γενόμενα διορθώσεως τύχῃ, αἱ δὲ ἐκκλησίαι εἰρήνην ἔχωσι πρὸς τὸ τὴν τοῦ Κυρίου εἰρήνην τὴν δοθεῖσαν ἡμῖν παραμεῖναι, καὶ μὴ

l. 378 ὡς ἐπιγνῶναι : ὥστ᾽ ἐπιγνῶναι *coni. Gilb.*

f. *Cf.* 1Cor 6.1–6.

detest the *Logos* and know nothing of the truth.[45f] I trust that you, like everyone else, are aware of the enormity of this sin. This, then, is all I have to say concerning Athanasius.

(16) (32.) Now about Marcellus. Since you have charged him also with impiety toward Christ,[46] I thought it imperative to inform you that, upon his arrival, he categorically denied the truth of the charges laid against him.[47] Nevertheless, when we demanded he state his faith to us, he spoke so frankly in his own words that we determined that he confesses nothing but the truth. Concerning our Lord and Savior Jesus Christ, he confessed that he holds the same pious beliefs as the Catholic Church. He declared that he had not adopted these convictions just now, but had long held them, an assertion confirmed by the fact that our own priests who had attended the Council of Nicaea testified to his orthodoxy.[48] He emphasized that he opposed the heresy of the Arians both then and now. And, in connection with this, I think it right to remind you that, rather than give credence to such heresy, everyone should detest it as foreign to sound teaching. Now then, since he was confirmed correct and orthodox in his belief, what action were we to take in his case, or how were we to treat him if not as we have? We recognized him as bishop and did not expel him from communion.

(17) My purpose in this letter is not to defend these men but rather to convince you that we have received them in accordance with justice and canonical practice, and that there was no good reason for your contentiousness. Instead, you should quickly do everything possible to correct these violations of church law so the churches may live in peace, and the peace of the Lord that has been granted

45. In 1Cor 6.1–6, Paul admonishes Christians to settle their differences among themselves without recourse to secular courts.

46. This may refer to E^2 or to Eusebius of Caesarea's attacks on Marcellus in *Marcell.* and *E. th.*

47. Opitz (*Athanasius Werke*, vol. 2, pt. 1, p. 110, n. on ll. 20ff.) suggests that Julius here echoes Marcellus' rejection of the charges brought against him (*ep.* 1.1), and that Julius' subsequent account of Marcellus' doctrine depends on the exposition of faith Marcellus had provided in *ep.* 1.

48. The two Roman priests present at Nicaea, Vito (Βίτων in the Greek sourc-

σχίζεσθαι τὰς ἐκκλησίας, μηδὲ ὑμᾶς, ὡς αἰτίους σχίσματος, μέμψιν ὑπομεῖναι. ὁμολογῶ γὰρ ὑμῖν, τὰ γενόμενα οὐκ εἰρήνης, ἀλλὰ σχίσματος προφάσεις εἰσίν.

(18) *(33.)* Οὐ γὰρ μόνον οἱ περὶ Ἀθανάσιον καὶ Μάρκελλον οἱ ἐπίσκοποι ἐληλύθασιν ἐνταῦθα, αἰτιώμενοι κατ᾽ αὐτῶν ἀδικίαν γεγονέναι, ἀλλὰ καὶ πλεῖστοι ἄλλοι ἐπίσκοποι ἀπὸ Θρᾴκης, ἀπὸ Κοίλης Συρίας, ἀπὸ Φοινίκης καὶ Παλαιστίνης. καὶ πρεσβύτεροι μὲν οὐκ ὀλίγοι, ἄλλοι δέ τινες ἀπὸ Ἀλεξανδρείας καὶ ἄλλοι ἐξ ἄλλων μερῶν, ἀπήντησαν εἰς τὴν ἐνταῦθα σύνοδον <καὶ> ἐπὶ πάντων τῶν συνελθόντων ἐπισκόπων, πρὸς τοῖς ἄλλοις οἷς ἔλεγον, ἔτι καὶ ἀπωδύροντο βίαν καὶ ἀδικίαν τὰς ἐκκλησίας πεπονθέναι, καὶ ὅμοια τῶν κατὰ Ἀλεξάνδρειαν καὶ <κατὰ> τὰς ἑαυτῶν καὶ ἐν ἄλλαις ἐκκλησίαις γεγενῆσθαι διεβεβαιοῦντο οὐ λόγῳ μόνον, ἀλλὰ καὶ πράγμασι. καὶ ἐξ Αἰγύπτου δὲ καὶ τῆς Ἀλεξανδρείας πάλιν ἐλθόντες νῦν, πρεσβύτεροι μετὰ γραμμάτων ἀπωδύροντο ὅτι πολλοὶ ἐπίσκοποι καὶ πρεσβύτεροι θέλοντες ἐλθεῖν εἰς τὴν σύνοδον ἐκωλύθησαν. μέχρι γὰρ νῦν καὶ μετὰ τὴν τοῦ ἐπισκόπου Ἀθανασίου ἀποδημίαν ἔλεγον ἐπισκόπους ὁμολογητὰς κατακόπτεσθαι πληγαῖς, καὶ ἄλλους φυλακίζεσθαι, ἤδη δὲ καὶ ἀρχαίους, πλεῖστον ὅσον χρόνον ἔχοντας ἐν τῇ ἐπισκοπῇ, εἰς λειτουργίας δημοσίας παραδίδοσθαι, καὶ σχεδὸν πάντας τοὺς τῆς καθολικῆς ἐκκλησίας κληρικοὺς καὶ λαοὺς ἐπιβουλεύεσθαι καὶ διώκεσθαι. καὶ γὰρ καί τινας ἐπισκόπους καί τινας ἀδελφοὺς ὑπερορίους ἔλεγον γεγενῆσθαι δι᾽ οὐδὲν ἕτερον ἢ ἵνα, καὶ ἄκοντες,

l. 402 γεγονέναι : γενομένην $A^{1,4,5}$ **ll. 403f.** πρεσβύτεροι μὲν : π. μ. αὐτόθεν *coni. Schd.* = *"More than a few priests from there as well as some from Alexandria and from other regions"* **ll. 405f.** <καὶ> ἐπὶ πάντων *suppl. Schd.* : ἐπὶ πάντων *A, edd.* **l. 407** ἔτι *coni. Mon., scr. Op.* : ὅτι *A, Com. Mon. Cou.* **l. 408** <κατὰ> τὰς ἑαυτῶν *suppl. Schd.* : τὰς ἑαυτῶν *A, edd.*

us may endure, and the churches not be split, nor you incur censure for causing schism. As far as I can see, your actions were meant to bring not peace but schism.

(18) (*33.*) Furthermore, it was not only Athanasius, and Marcellus, and the bishops associated with them who came here complaining of the injustices they had suffered, but also many more from Thrace, Coele-Syria, Phoenicia, and Palestine.[49] A great many priests as well, both from Alexandria and from other regions, presented themselves at the council, and, in the presence of all the assembled bishops, in addition to other statements, protested against the violence and injustice done to the churches and declared, with facts, not just words, that what had happened in Alexandria was also happening in their own and other churches. And, yet again, priests recently arrived with letters from Egypt and Alexandria protested that many bishops and priests who had wished to come to the council had been prevented from doing so. They stated that, from the time of Bishop Athanasius' exile to the present, bishop confessors are being savagely beaten, others held in prison,[50] even the elderly, with long service in the office of bishop, assigned to do public labor, and nearly all the clergy and laity of the Catholic Church subjected to plots and persecution. They stated as well that some bishops and brethren have been sent into exile for no other reason than to compel them against their will to enter

es) and Vincentius, had confirmed Marcellus' claim about his stance at Nicaea; *v. EOMIA*, vol. 1.1.1, pp. 36f. and 1.1.2, p. 97. These two priests were probably chosen to serve as envoys to the council, because they spoke Greek. A decade later, when Athanasius came to Rome, he may have been Vito's guest, either because they had become acquainted at Nicaea or because of Vito's facility with Greek. If so, this relationship might underlie Julius' choice of Vito's parish church as the site of the council; *v.* Ath., *Apol. sec.* 20.

49. The other deposed eastern bishops who fled to Rome included Lucius of Adrianople in Thrace, Asclepius of Gaza (Socr., *H. e.* 2.15.2), Euphration of Balanea in Syria, and Hellanicus of Tripolis in Phoenicia (Ath., *H. ar.* 5).

50. *Confessor* is a technical term for a Christian who has suffered, but not died, for his faith. Originally applied in the context of the persecution of Christians by pagans and Jews, it was extended also to the mistreatment of the orthodox at the hands of heretics. In *H. ar.* 12, Athanasius applies the title to the Egyptian bishops Sarapammon and Potammon, signatories of the creed of the Council of Nicaea, who suffered violence from the Arians.

ἀναγκάζωνται κοινωνεῖν Γρηγορίῳ καὶ τοῖς σὺν αὐτῷ Ἀρειανοῖς. καὶ ἐν Ἀγκύρᾳ δὲ τῆς Γαλατίας οὐκ ὀλίγα γεγενῆσθαι, ἀλλὰ τὰ αὐτὰ πάλιν τοῖς κατὰ Ἀλεξάνδρειαν γενομένοις ἠκούσαμεν καὶ παρ᾽ ἑτέρων, καὶ Μάρκελλος δὲ ὁ ἐπίσκοπος διεμαρτύρατο. πρὸς δὲ τούτοις, καὶ τοιαύτας κατηγορίας καὶ οὕτω δεινὰς κατά τινων ἐξ ὑμῶν, ἵνα μὴ λέγω τὰ ὀνόματα, οἱ ἀπαντήσαντες εἰρήκασιν, ἃς ἐγὼ μὲν γράψαι παρῃτησάμην· ἴσως δὲ καὶ ὑμεῖς παρ᾽ ἑτέρων ἀκηκόατε. διὰ τοῦτο γὰρ μάλιστα καὶ ἔγραψα, προτρεπόμενος ὑμᾶς ἐλθεῖν ἵνα, καὶ παρόντες, ἀκούσητε, καὶ πάντα διορθωθῆναι καὶ θεραπευθῆναι δυνηθῇ. ἐπὶ δὲ τούτῳ προθυμοτέρως ἔδει τοὺς κληθέντας ἀπαντῆσαι καὶ μὴ παραιτήσασθαι, ἵνα μήτε ὡς ὕποπτοι περὶ τὰ λεχθέντα, ἐὰν μὴ ἀπαντήσωσι, νομισθῶσι μήτε ὡς μὴ δυνάμενοι ἐλέγξαι ἃ ἔγραψαν.

(19) *(34.)* Τούτων τοίνυν οὕτως λεγομένων, καὶ οὕτως τῶν ἐκκλησιῶν πασχουσῶν καὶ ἐπιβουλευομένων, ὡς οἱ ἀπαγγέλλοντες διεβεβαιοῦντο, τίνες εἰσὶν *οἱ φλόγα διχονοίας ἀνάψαντες;* ἡμεῖς οἱ λυπούμενοι ἐπὶ τοῖς τοιούτοις καὶ συμπάσχοντες τοῖς πάσχουσιν ἀδελφοῖς, ἢ οἱ τὰ τοιαῦτα ἐργασάμενοι; θαυμάζω γὰρ πῶς, τοιαύτης καὶ τοσαύτης ἐκεῖ ἀκαταστασίας καθ᾽ ἑκάστην ἐκκλησίαν οὔσης, δι᾽ ἣν καὶ οἱ ἀπαντήσαντες ἦλθον ἐνταῦθα, γράφετε ὑμεῖς Ὁ*μόνοιαν γεγενῆσθαι ἐν ταῖς ἐκκλησίαις*. τὰ δὲ τοιαῦτα οὐκ ἐπὶ οἰκοδομῇ τῆς ἐκκλησίας, ἀλλ᾽ ἐπὶ καθαιρέσει ταύτης γίνεται.[g] καὶ οἱ ἐν τούτοις δὲ χαίροντες οὔκ εἰσιν εἰρήνης υἱοί,[h] ἀλλὰ ἀκαταστασίας· ὁ δὲ θεὸς ἡμῶν οὐκ *ἔστιν ἀκαταστασίας* … *ἀλλ᾽ εἰρήνης*.[i] διόπερ, ὡς οἶδεν ὁ θεὸς καὶ πατὴρ τοῦ Κυρίου ἡμῶν Ἰησοῦ Χριστοῦ, κηδόμενος μὲν καὶ τῆς ὑμῶν ὑπολήψεως, εὐχόμενος δὲ καὶ τὰς ἐκκλησίας μὴ ἐν ἀκαταστασίᾳ εἶναι, ἀλλὰ διαμένειν ὥσπερ ὑπὸ τῶν ἀποστόλων ἐκανονίσθη, γράψαι ὑμῖν

l. 430 προθυμοτέρως : προθυμοτέρους *A*[4,5?] **ll. 431–33** μήτε ὡς ὕποπτοι … μήτε ὡς μὴ δυνάμενοι *Op.* : μὴ τέως ὕ. … μ. ὡς μὴ δ. *A*: μὴ τέως ὕ. … ὡς μὴ δ. *Com. Mon. Cou.* = *"for, during the period of their absence, they would be presumed guilty of the charges laid against them in as much as they would appear unable to back up their own accusations"*

g. *Cf.* 1Cor 14.12; 2Cor 10.8; 13.10.
h. *Cf.* Lk 10.6.
i. 1Cor 14.33

into communion with Gregory and his fellow Arians. Bishop Marcellus also bore witness to what we heard from others—that many of the crimes committed in Alexandria have been committed also at Ancyra in Galatia. Furthermore, those who presented themselves uttered terrible accusations against some of you—I refrain from naming names—which I forbear to set down in writing. You have probably heard them from others. It was especially so you would hear them firsthand, and everything could be set right and healed that I wrote and urged you to come. And those who were summoned for this purpose, far from refusing, should have been all the readier to present themselves, for if they did not present themselves, they would be presumed guilty of the charges laid against them and appear unable to back up their own accusations.

(19) (*34.*) Therefore, given these statements and the sufferings and conspiracies endured, as our informants declared, by the churches, who is it who is "fanning the flames of discord"?[51] We, who are aggrieved by these events and suffering together with our suffering brethren, or those who have committed such crimes? Indeed, I am amazed how you could write that "there is a oneness of mind in the churches" while in church after church there is so much disorder that those who presented themselves decided to come here. Such behavior tends not to the edification of the Church, but to her destruction.[g] And those who rejoice in these events are not sons of peace but of disorder.[h] But our God "is not a God of disorder but of peace."[i] Therefore, as the God and Father of our Lord Jesus Christ knows, with concern for your reputation and prayer for the churches—that they no longer be troubled but remain, as they were, under the law

51. In this section, Julius is probably quoting from the Eusebians' most recent letter (E^4).

ταῦτα ἀναγκαῖον ἡγησάμην ἵνα ἤδη ποτὲ δυσωπήσητε τοὺς διὰ τὴν πρὸς ἀλλήλους ἀπέχθειαν οὕτω διαθεμένους τὰς ἐκκλησίας· ἤκουσα γὰρ ὅτι τινές εἰσιν ὀλίγοι οἱ τούτων πάντων αἴτιοι τυγχάνοντες· καὶ σπουδάσητε, ὡς *σπλάγχνα ἔχοντες οἰκτιρμοῦ,*[j] διορθώσασθαι, ὡς προεῖπον, τὰ παρὰ κανόνα γενόμενα ἵνα, εἰ καί τι προελήφθη, τοῦτο τῇ ὑμετέρᾳ σπουδῇ θεραπευθῇ.

(20) Καὶ μὴ γράφητε, ὅτι *Τὴν Μαρκέλλου καὶ Ἀθανασίου ἢ τὴν ἡμῶν ἑλοῦ κοινωνίαν.* οὐ γὰρ εἰρήνης, ἀλλὰ φιλονεικίας καὶ μισαδελφίας τὰ τοιαῦτα γνωρίσματα. διὰ τοῦτο οὖν κἀγὼ τὰ προειρημένα ἔγραψα, ἵνα, μαθόντες ὅτι οὐκ ἀδίκως ἐδεξάμεθα αὐτούς, παύσησθε τῆς τοιαύτης ἔριδος. εἰ μὲν γάρ, ἐλθόντων ὑμῶν, ἦσαν καταγνωσθέντες εἰ μὴ εὐλόγους ἀποδείξεις ἔχειν ἐφαίνοντο ὑπὲρ ἑαυτῶν, καλῶς ἂν τὰ τοιαῦτα γεγραφήκειτε. ἐπειδὴ δέ, ὡς προεῖπον, κανονικῶς καὶ οὐκ ἀδίκως τὴν πρὸς αὐτοὺς ἔσχομεν κοινωνίαν, παρακαλῶ ὑπὲρ Χριστοῦ, μὴ ἐπιτρέψητε διασχισθῆναι τὰ μέλη τοῦ Χριστοῦ[k] μηδὲ τοῖς προλήμμασι πιστεύσητε, ἀλλὰ τὴν τοῦ Κυρίου εἰρήνην προτιμήσατε. οὐ γὰρ ὅσιον οὐδὲ δίκαιον δι᾽ ὀλίγων μικροψυχίαν τοὺς μὴ καταγνωσθέντας ἀπορρίπτειν καὶ *λυπεῖν* ἐν τούτῳ *τὸ πνεῦμα.*[l]

(21) Εἰ δὲ νομίζετε δύνασθαί τινα κατ᾽ αὐτῶν ἀποδεῖξαι καὶ εἰς πρόσωπον αὐτοὺς ἐλέγξαι, ἐλθέτωσαν οἱ βουλόμενοι· ἑτοίμους γὰρ ἑαυτοὺς καὶ αὐτοὶ εἶναι ἐπηγγείλαντο ὥστε καὶ ἀποδεῖξαι καὶ διελέγξαι περὶ ὧν ἡμῖν ἀπήγγειλαν. *(35.)* σημάνατε οὖν ἡμῖν, ἀγαπητοί, περὶ τούτου ἵνα κἀκείνοις γράψωμεν καὶ τοῖς ὀφείλουσι πάλιν συνελθεῖν ἐπισκόποις πρὸς τό, πάντων παρόντων, τοὺς

l. 452 καὶ σπουδάσητε A^{-3} : καὶ σπουδάσατε A^{3}, *Com. Op. Bre. (*τὰς ἐκκλησίας. ἤκουσα γὰρ ὅτι τινές εἰσιν ὀλίγοι οἱ τούτων πάντων αἴτιοι τυγχάνοντες. καὶ σπουδάσατε = *"to this state. For, as I have heard, it is only a few who are responsible for all this trouble. And, as I have already said, … act quickly")* : σπουδάσατε *Cou. Mon. (*τ. ἐκκλησίας. ἤ. γ. ὅ. τ. εἰ. ὀ. οἱ τ. π. αἴ. τυγχάνοντες. σπουδάσατε*)* *οἰκτιρμοῦ* : οἰκτιρμῶν $A^{3,5}$, *Com.*

j. Col 3.12 k. *Cf.* 1Cor 6.15, 12.25. l. Eph 4.30

laid down by the apostles—I decided I must write, so that you might yet put to shame those who, in their mutual hatred, have brought the churches to this state (for, as I have heard, it is only a few who are responsible for all this trouble), and, as I have already said, having "a merciful heart,"[j] act quickly to set right any breach of church law and promptly bring healing to any that have already occurred.

(20) And you should not have written, "Choose communion with Marcellus and Athanasius or with us." Such words are indicative not of a desire for peace, but of partisanship and hatred toward brethren. I have written the above so you would desist from such dissension when you learned that we did no wrong in receiving these men. If you had come, and they had been condemned when it was shown they had no reasonable defense for themselves, you would have had good reason for your accusations. But since, as I have already said, when we received them into communion, we acted in accordance with church law and not in defiance of justice, I beg you for the sake of Christ, do not permit the members of Christ to be divided[k] or believe those prejudicial statements, but rather choose first the peace of the Lord. It is neither pious nor just, on account of a petty minded few, to repudiate men never previously condemned and, in this way, "grieve the Spirit."[l]

(21) But if you think you can prove any charge against these men and refute them face-to-face, let anyone come who wishes to. For they promised that, in the matters they have reported to us, they stand ready to prove their own position and confute their opponents. (35.) Therefore, beloved, just say the word, and we shall write to them and the bishops, who will be obliged to gather again, so that

ὑπευθύνους καταγνωσθῆναι καὶ μηκέτι ἀκαταστασίαν ἐν ταῖς ἐκκλησίαις γενέσθαι.

Ἀρκεῖ γὰρ τὰ γενόμενα· ἀρκεῖ ὅτι, παρόντων ἐπισκόπων, ἐπίσκοποι ἐξωρίζοντο, περὶ οὗ οὐδὲ μακρηγορεῖν δεῖ ἵνα μὴ βαρεῖσθαι οἱ παρόντες τότε δοκῶσιν. εἰ γὰρ δεῖ τἀληθὲς εἰπεῖν, οὐκ ἔδει μέχρι τούτων φθάσαι οὐδὲ εἰς τοσοῦτον ἐλθεῖν τῆς μικροψυχίας. ἔστω δέ· *Ἀθανάσιος καὶ Μάρκελλος*, ὡς γράφετε, *μετετέθησαν ἀπὸ τῶν ἰδίων τόπων*. τί καὶ περὶ τῶν ἄλλων ἄν τις εἴποι τῶν ἐκ διαφόρων τόπων, ὡς προεῖπον, ἐλθόντων ἐνταῦθα ἐπισκόπων καὶ πρεσβυτέρων; καὶ αὐτοὶ γὰρ πάλιν ἡρπάσθαι ἑαυτοὺς καὶ τοιαῦτα πεπονθέναι ἔλεγον.

(22) Ὦ ἀγαπητοί, οὐκέτι κατὰ τὸ εὐαγγέλιον, ἀλλὰ λοιπὸν ἐπὶ ἐξορισμῷ καὶ θανάτῳ αἱ κρίσεις τῆς ἐκκλησίας εἰσίν. εἰ γὰρ καὶ ὅλως, ὥς φατε, γέγονέ τι εἰς αὐτοὺς ἁμάρτημα, ἔδει κατὰ τὸν ἐκκλησιαστικὸν κανόνα, καὶ μὴ οὕτως, γεγενῆσθαι τὴν κρίσιν. ἔδει γραφῆναι πᾶσιν ἡμῖν ἵνα οὕτως παρὰ πάντων ὁρισθῇ τὸ δίκαιον. ἐπίσκοποι γὰρ ἦσαν οἱ πάσχοντες, καὶ οὐχ αἱ τυχοῦσαι ἐκκλησίαι αἱ πάσχουσαι, ἀλλ᾽ ὧν αὐτοὶ οἱ ἀπόστολοι δι᾽ ἑαυτῶν καθηγήσαντο. διὰ τί δὲ περὶ τῆς Ἀλεξανδρέων ἐκκλησίας μάλιστα οὐκ ἐγράφετο ἡμῖν; ἢ ἀγνοεῖτε ὅτι τοῦτο ἔθος ἦν, πρότερον γράφεσθαι ἡμῖν καὶ οὕτως ἔνθεν ὁρίζεσθαι τὰ δίκαια; εἰ μὲν οὖν τι τοιοῦτον ἦν ὑποπτευθὲν εἰς τὸν ἐπίσκοπον τὸν ἐκεῖ, ἔδει πρὸς

l. **479** εἰς τοσοῦτον … τῆς μικροψυχίας *coni. J.P., scr. Thomp.* : εἰς τοσοῦτον … τὰς μικροψυχίας *codd., edd.* l. **491** οἱ ἀπόστολοι δι᾽ ἑαυτῶν : δι᾽ ἑαυτῶν οἱ ἀπόστολοι $A^{1,2}$ l. **492** ἐκκλησίας : πόλεως A^{3-5}, *Com.* = *"especially in the case of the city of Alexandria?"*

the guilty might be condemned with everyone present, and the disorder within the churches come to an end.

Enough has happened already. We have had enough of bishops being sentenced to banishment in the presence of other bishops. To avoid seeming too hard on those present on those occasions, I shall not continue at length. But to speak truthfully, you should not have gone so far or descended to such mean-spiritedness. Let us grant for a moment that, as you write,[52] "Athanasius and Marcellus were properly removed from their sees." Even then, as I have already said, what of the other bishops and priests who have come here from other places? They stated that they too were seized and submitted to similar outrages.

(22) My beloved, church decisions are no longer made according to the gospel, but with a view to banishment and death. If, as you say, they actually committed some sin, a verdict should have been reached in accord with church law, not like this. You should have written us all, so that a just decision could have been rendered by all. Those under attack were bishops, and the congregations under attack were no ordinary ones, but those the apostles themselves had governed.[53] Why were we not informed especially in the case of the church of Alexandria?[54] Certainly, you cannot be unaware that, according to custom, we must be informed in writing before a just verdict can be determined.[55] If there was some such suspicion in regard to the bishop there, this church should have been

52. This probably refers to the Eusebians' letter of 341 (E[4]).

53. The Eusebians had failed to consult the wider Church before deposing the bishops of sees as ancient and important as Alexandria and Ancyra. It was widely believed that the Christian community of Alexandria had been founded by the evangelist Mark (Eus., *H. e.* 2.16) while Ancyra was associated with St. Paul through his ministry and the epistle to the Galatians (Hier., *in Gal.* 2, *praef.*).

54. The ties between the churches of Roman and Alexandria were both close and long-standing; *v.* n. 2, p. xxviii for the exchange of letters in the mid-third century between Dionysius of Rome and Dionysius of Alexandria (Eus., *H. e.* 7.7.6–7.8; Ath., *Decr.* 26 and *Dion.* 13–15).

55. Brightman (p. 159) regards καὶ οὕτως ἔνθεν as a literal translation of the Latin *et sic deinde.*

τὴν ἐνταῦθα ἐκκλησίαν γραφῆναι· νῦν δὲ οἱ ἡμᾶς μὴ πληροφορήσαντες, πράξαντες δὲ αὐτοὶ ὡς ἠθέλησαν, λοιπὸν καὶ ἡμᾶς, οὐ καταγνόντας, βούλονται συμψήφους εἶναι. οὐχ οὕτως αἱ Παύλου διατάξεις, οὐχ οὕτως οἱ πατέρες παραδεδώκασιν· ἄλλος τύπος ἐστὶν οὗτος,[m] καὶ καινὸν τὸ ἐπιτήδευμα. παρακαλῶ, μετὰ μακροθυμίας ἐνέγκατε· ὑπὲρ τοῦ κοινῇ συμφέροντός ἐστιν ἃ γράφω. ἃ γὰρ παρειλήφαμεν παρὰ τοῦ μακαρίου Πέτρου τοῦ ἀποστόλου, ταῦτα καὶ ὑμῖν δηλῶ.[n] καὶ οὐκ ἂν ἔγραψα, φανερὰ ἡγούμενος εἶναι ταῦτα παρὰ πᾶσιν, εἰ μὴ τὰ γενόμενα ἡμᾶς ἐτάραξεν. ἐπίσκοποι ἁρπάζονται καὶ ἐκτοπίζονται, ἄλλοι δὲ ἀλλαχόθεν ἀντιτίθενται, καὶ ἄλλοι ἐπιβουλεύονται ὥστε ἐπὶ μὲν τοῖς ἁρπασθεῖσιν αὐτοὺς πενθεῖν, ἐπὶ δὲ τοῖς πεμπομένοις ἀναγκάζεσθαι ἵνα οὓς μὲν θέλουσι μὴ ἐπιζητῶσιν, οὓς δὲ μὴ βούλονται δέχωνται. ἀξιῶ ὑμᾶς μηκέτι τοιαῦτα γίνεσθαι· γράψατε δὲ μᾶλλον κατὰ τῶν τὰ τοιαῦτα ἐπιχειρούντων ἵνα μηκέτι τοιαῦτα πάσχωσιν αἱ ἐκκλησίαι, μηδέ τις ἐπίσκοπος ἢ πρεσβύτερος ὕβριν πάσχῃ, ἢ παρὰ γνώμην, ὥσπερ ἐδήλωσαν ἡμῖν, ἀναγκάζηταί τις ποιεῖν ἵνα μὴ καὶ παρὰ τοῖς ἔθνεσι γέλωτα ὀφλήσωμεν καί, πρό γε πάντων, ἵνα μὴ τὸν θεὸν παροξύνωμεν·[o] ἕκαστος γὰρ ἡμῶν *ἀποδώσει … λόγον ἐν ἡμέρᾳ κρίσεως*[p] περὶ ὧν ἐνταῦθα ἔπραξε. γένοιτο δὲ πάντας κατὰ θεὸν φρονῆσαι ἵνα καὶ αἱ ἐκκλησίαι, τοὺς ἐπισκόπους αὐτῶν ἀπολαβοῦσαι, χαίρωσι διὰ παντὸς ἐν Χριστῷ Ἰησοῦ τῷ Κυρίῳ ἡμῶν, δι' οὗ τῷ πατρὶ *ἡ δόξα εἰς τοὺς αἰῶνας τῶν αἰώνων. ἀμήν.*[q] ἐρρῶσθαι ὑμᾶς ἐν Κυρίῳ εὔχομαι, ἀγαπητοὶ καὶ ποθεινότατοι ἀδελφοί.

ll. 496f. μὴ πληροφορήσαντες $A^{1,3,4}$, A^{2pc}, *edd.* : π. A^{5}, A^{2ac} = *"But those who have informed us"* **ll. 500f.** μακροθυμίας : προ- A^{3}, *Com. Mon. Cou.* = *"accept this gladly"* **l. 507** αὐτοὺς : τοὺς λαοὺς *coni. Stäh.* **ll. 513f.** ἵνα μὴ τὸν θεὸν παροξύνωμεν $A^{1,2}$, *Mon. Cou. Op.* : τ. θ. π. A^{3-5}, *Com.*

m. *Cf.* Rom 6.17. n. *Cf.* 1Cor 11.23.
o. *Cf.* Nm 15.30; Dt 9.18, 22; Mal 2.17.
p. Mt 12.36
q. *Cf.* 4Mc 18.24; Gal 1.5; Phil 4.20; 2Tm 4.18; Heb 13.21.

contacted by letter. But those who have neglected to inform us and acted according to their own wishes now desire us to cast our vote with them against men whom we have not condemned! This is not the rule received from Paul or the practice handed down from the fathers; this follows a different pattern[m] and a novel procedure. I beg of you, accept this patiently; what I write is for the common good. I am setting forth for you the tradition we have received[n] from the blessed apostle Peter. As I imagined this was evident to everybody, I would not have written if we had not been so troubled by the events: bishops seized and exiled, men from elsewhere appointed in their stead, others made the victims of conspiracy, so that while the people mourn for their exiled leaders, they are compelled to accept those sent to replace them, so they will be prevented from seeking out those they wish and be forced to welcome those they do not desire. I implore you not to let anything of this sort continue, but rather bring accusation against those who set their hands to this mischief, so the churches might no longer suffer, no bishop or priest endure outrage, nor, as they assured us has happened, anyone be forced to act contrary to his own will. We must not become a laughingstock among the heathen, and, above all, we must not provoke God to anger.[56] [o] "On the day of judgment, each of us will render an account"[p] of what he has done on earth. Let us all conform to the will of God, so the churches may regain their own bishops and rejoice always in Jesus Christ our Lord, through whom "be glory" to the Father "forever and ever. Amen."[q] It is my prayer that you fare well in the Lord, my beloved and greatly missed brethren.

56. The English "provoke" does not catch the gravity of the Greek παροξύνω as used in connection with God (*v.* Nm 14.11; Dt 9.18). One who provokes God cuts himself off from God's people (Nm 15.30).

LETTER III

To Julius, Bishop of Rome,
from Hosius of Cordova and Protogenes of Sardica
(Meminimus, et tenemus)

Introduction

Julius' letter to the eastern bishops was not warmly received. If anything, it caused a further hardening of the eastern position. Since the bishop of Rome and his Italian synod had reaffirmed communion with both Athanasius and Marcellus and declared invalid the deposition of both, the easterners decided to petition the western emperor to support their decisions by preventing the deposed bishops from being reinstalled. They sent four of their number carrying a statement of faith, known as the fourth creed of Antioch, to Constans at Trier. Though they were not granted an audience, Constans issued no decree in support of the decisions of their western opponents.[1]

Meanwhile, events in his capital city drove home to the eastern emperor Constantius II the threat to public order posed by these ecclesiastical controversies. As the reader will recall,[2] the rightful possession of the see of Constantinople had been in dispute since the death of Bishop Alexander in 337, when Constantius put aside the election of Paul, the choice of the Nicene party, and arranged the transferral to the capital of Eusebius of Nicomedia. Upon Eusebius' death in late 341, the exiled Paul, perhaps with the encouragement

1. The situation is described, and the creed reproduced in Ath., *Syn.* 25; *v.* also Socr., *H. e.* 2.18 and Soz., *H. e.* 3.10. The delegation was made up of Narcissus of Neronias, Maris of Chalcedon, Theodore of Heraclea, and Marcus of Arethusa; on the first three, *v.* n. 8 to the introduction to *ep.* 2. Marcus was bishop of the Syrian see of Arethusa. He supported the *homoean* theological position at the Council of Seleucia in 359. Having suffered for his faith under Julian, he died a confessor; *v.* Wermelinger, p. 323. Emperor Constans and Maximinus, bishop of Trier, refused to receive the bishops or accept the creed they carried (Hil., *fragg. histt.* A.4.1.27; *v.* also Parvis, pp. 206–10). Yet, the mere appearance of the delegation may have confirmed the seriousness of the situation; at least, in the following year, Constans insisted on organizing a council. On the four creeds of Antioch, *v.* Hanson, *The Search*, pp. 284–92. Noting the importance of this creed in these negotiations, Tetz attempts to reconstruct from it the charges missing in *ep.* 3; *v.* c. n. to ll. 4–6.

2. *V.* sec. 8 of the Introduction and n. 77.

of Constans, tried to reclaim the episcopal seat, but his opponents elevated Macedonius, Paul's Arian rival in the election following the death of Alexander. Riots ensued.[3] Early in 342 the general Hermogenes, one of the highest ranking commanders in the east, was killed while trying to restore order (Amm., 14.10.2; Socr., *H. e.* 2.13). Constantius himself hurried to the city and reasserted his authority. Paul was again removed and sought refuge with Constans at Trier. Macedonius was allowed to remain, but without the official recognition of the emperor (Lib., *Or.* 59.94 and Ath., *H. ar.* 7.3.).

Constans used this opportunity to convince his brother that they must seek a more permanent settlement. The emperors called a joint council of eastern and western bishops to meet in 343.[4] The site, chosen to be as neutral as possible, was Sardica, now Sofia, the capital of Bulgaria. This city, on the eastern edge of the western empire, lay just 300 miles west of the eastern capital. Nearly one hundred western, and more than seventy-five eastern, bishops traveled to the synod. Had it met, it would have been the most representative ecumenical council to date.[5]

The synod, however, never truly got started. The anti-Nicene par-

3. On the complicated chronology of Paul's career, *v.* Barnes, *Athanasius and Constantius,* pp. 212–17 and Parvis, pp. 200–07.

4. The year of the council of Sardica (also spelled "Serdica") is still in dispute. Both Socrates (*H. e.* 2.20) and Sozomen (*H. e.* 3.12) record that it took place during the consulship of Rufinus and Eusebius, eleven years after the death of Constantine, *i.e.*, in 347. In 1848, however, with the aid of newly discovered material, Cureton was able to establish a more accurate chronology of Athanasius' career. These documents comprised many of Athanasius' festal letters, previously known only in a few Greek fragments, and an index to the letters (also dating to the fourth century), both letters and index preserved in a Syriac translation. Cureton's discovery has been supplemented by Lefort's publication of additional letters in Coptic translation. Profiting from this new information and drawing on the so-called *Hist. aceph.* (1.1), Girardet has argued (p. 108) for 342, Parvis (pp. 210–17) for 343. Following Barnes' (*Athanasius and Constantius,* pp. 68–71) reconstruction of Athanasius' movements, I prefer 343; on the *epp. festt.*, *v.* Barnes, *ibid.*, App. 1, pp. 183–91. For the *Hist. aceph.*, *v.* below, App. A, item Td.

5. Parvis (pp. 218–24) calculates that the eastern delegation consisted of two or three bishops each from twenty-eight different provinces; on the western delegation, *v. ibid.*, pp. 224–29.

ty was now led by Narcissus of Neronias, Theodore of Heraclea, Stephen of Antioch, Acacius of Caesarea, Ursacius of Singidunum, and Valens of Mursa. In firm control of the eastern delegation, they were in no mood to compromise on what they saw as the two key issues: the depositions of Marcellus and Athanasius, the first for his seemingly Sabellianizing christology, the second for malfeasance in office.[6] Given Julius' recent letter to those same eastern leaders (*ep.* 2) and his acceptance of Marcellus' confession (*ep.* 1), these were issues on which the western bishops could not compromise. When Constans gave permission for Athanasius and the other exiled bishops to take part in the council, the eastern bishops immediately protested that the deposed bishops had been ousted in accord with church law; hence they were no longer bishops and could not participate in the council.[7] The western bishops argued that, until the council decided their fate, they had a right to be seated.

The two sides never officially met. The eastern bishops first composed and signed a synodal letter, which included both the fourth creed of Antioch and a new excommunication of Athanasius and Marcellus. Along with these, they excommunicated also their supporters, Hosius of Cordova, Protogenes of Sardica, Gaudentius of Naissus, and Julius of Rome, whom they denounced as the "chief and leader of the wicked" (*ut principem et ducem malorum,* Hil., *fragg. histt.* A.4.1.27). A few days later, they reconvened in eastern territory at Philippopolis (modern Plovdiv in south-central Bulgaria), where their decisions were officially ratified.[8]

The western bishops, divided into several groups, perhaps by lan-

6. As Löhr (pp. 17–25) has emphasized, the eastern bishops focused more on Marcellus' alleged modalism than on the debate over the creedal formula of Nicaea.

7. Socrates (*H. e.* 2.20) records objections to the participation of Athanasius and Paul of Constantinople, but makes no mention of Marcellus. Yet, the bishop of Ancyra did attend the western council; *v.* Parvis, *Marcellus of Ancyra,* p. 228.

8. The letter of condemnation is preserved by Hilary, *fragg. histt.* A.4.1. From the introduction, it is clear that the easterners drew up the document, not at Philippopolis, but while still at Sardica (*v.* Brennecke, *Hilarius,* pp. 35f.). The translation is that of Stevenson (p. 16).

guage since many delegates were Greek-speaking, continued to meet at Sardica.[9] Under the shared chairmanship of Hosius of Cordova and the host bishop, Protogenes of Sardica, they focused on the fight against the perceived Arianism of the east.[10] In the course of debate, it was proposed that a theological tract targeting Arian heresies be produced and circulated to serve as a supplement to, and explanation of, the Nicene formula.

To explain the rationale for this new theological document and seek his support, the two chairmen then wrote our *ep.* 3 to Julius.[11] They report that the bishops assembled at Sardica have all unequivocally confessed the Nicene faith. But since the disciples of Arius have continued to spread their teachings, it is necessary to elaborate the true teaching with a longer explanation. In this way, the truth will be confirmed, teachers within the Church will be freed from confusion, and the heretical opposition will be overcome.

There is some question as to whether Hosius and Protogenes ever dispatched this letter. Maassen argued that *ep.* 3 was only a draft, which was never sent.[12] De Clercq more elaborately hypothesized that the doctrinal statement was voted on, defeated, and hence never promulgated, but that the draft letter and creed were still entered into the proceedings of the council.[13] Bardy suggested that letter and creed were tabled and never sent.[14] Yet, as Pietri, Hess, Tetz, and Hanson have all argued, it is unlikely that the letter would have been preserved if it had not been sent.[15] In addition, this must be

9. *V.* Parvis, pp. 234f.

10. Prior to this council Protogenes, who had written against Marcellus of Ancyra, appears to have sympathized with the easterners (Hil., *fragg. histt.* A.4.1.3).

11. Parvis (p. 237) suggests that Julius, informed of the proceedings by his representatives, had objected to a new theological formulation. *Ep.* 3 would thus be an attempt to gain his approval for their actions and for the proposed supplementary and explanatory document.

12. *Geschichte der Quellen,* vol. 1, p. 64.

13. De Clercq, p. 369.

14. "The Eusebian reaction," p. 151.

15. *V.* Pietri, "La question," p. 115; Hess, p. 66; Tetz, "Ante omnia," p. 249. Hanson (*The Search,* p. 305) thinks *ep.* 3 was the cover letter to *ep.* 4, the encyclical of the council. Going a step further, Parvis (p. 237) argues that *ep.* 3 was the beginning

the letter which Sozomen describes as follows: "Hosius and Protogenes, at that time the leaders of the western bishops gathered at Sardica, perhaps because they feared incurring suspicion of changing the enactments of the council of Nicaea, wrote a letter to Julius, in which they declared that, though they regarded those doctrines as normative, given the need for clarity, they had provided a fuller treatment of their meaning; in this way they intended to prevent the Arians from taking advantage of the brevity of the formula and leading those inexperienced in debate to improper conclusions" (*H. e.* 3.12.6).[16]

It is difficult to derive from the ancient sources a coherent account of the doctrinal tract proposed at the council. According to Athanasius, the council "was indignant and determined not to write any other statement of faith, but to regard as sufficient the faith confessed by the fathers at Nicaea" (ἡ δὲ ἁγία σύνοδος … ἠγανάκτησε, καὶ ὥρισε μηδὲν ἔτι περὶ πίστεως γράφεσθαι, ἀλλ' ἀρκεῖσθαι τῇ ἐν Νικαίᾳ παρὰ τῶν Πατέρων ὁμολογηθείσῃ πίστει, *Tom.* 5). Yet, Sozomen writes that "they set forth at that time another statement of faith more extensive than that of Nicaea, which preserved the same sense and made only slight changes of wording" (ἐξέθεντο δὲ καὶ αὐτοὶ τηνικαῦτα πίστεως γραφὴν ἑτέραν, πλατυτέραν μὲν τῆς ἐν Νικαίᾳ, φυλάττουσαν δὲ τὴν αὐτὴν διάνοιαν καὶ οὐ παρὰ πολὺ διαλλάττουσαν τῶν ἐκείνης ῥημάτων, *H. e.* 3.12.5). Socrates states that "by confirming the definition of the Nicene faith and rejecting the term *anomoion* (unlike), they clarified the *homoousion* (of the same substance). They set this out in a letter, which they sent everywhere" (τὸν ὅρον τε τῆς πίστεως τὸν ἐν Νικαίᾳ κρατύναντες καὶ

of *ep.* 4, "which lacks an opening paragraph." But the two letters do not fit neatly together, and Parvis' theory lacks any support in the manuscript tradition.

16. ἀμέλει Ὅσιος καὶ Πρωτογένης, οἳ τότε ὑπῆρχον ἄρχοντες τῶν ἀπὸ τῆς δύσεως ἐν Σαρδικῇ συνεληλυθότων, δείσαντες ἴσως, μὴ νομισθεῖέν τισι καινοτομεῖν τὰ δόξαντα τοῖς ἐν Νικαίᾳ, ἔγραψαν Ἰουλίῳ καὶ ἐμαρτύραντο κύρια τάδε ἡγεῖσθαι, κατὰ χρείαν δὲ σαφηνείας τὴν αὐτὴν διάνοιαν πλατῦναι, ὥστε μὴ ἐγγενέσθαι τοῖς τὰ Ἀρείου φρονοῦσιν ἀποκεχρημένοις τῇ συντομίᾳ τῆς γραφῆς εἰς ἄτοπον ἕλκειν τοὺς ἀπείρους διαλέξεως.

τὸ ἀνόμοιον ἐκβαλόντες τὸ ὁμοούσιον φανερώτερον ἐκδιδόασιν, ἐγγράψαντές τε καὶ αὐτοὶ πανταχοῦ διαπέμπονται, *H. e.* 2.20.10). Perhaps we may infer that 1) the idea of a new creed was rejected; 2) the proposal of a longer explanation of the Nicene teaching was accepted, at least by some; and 3) this longer explanation was incorporated into the letter sent out by the council. Thus, the doctrinal tract that stands at the conclusion of the encyclical letter in Verona, Bibl. cap., *60* (foll. 86r–88r) and in Theodoret's *Ecclesiastical History* (2.8.37–52) must be that new explanation.[17]

If we take Athanasius' account to refer to a general opposition to any new formulation, those of Sozomen and Socrates clearly indicate that many favored an expanded explanation of the Nicene position. In these circumstances, it would have been logical for the two chairmen to write *ep.* 3 to explain their rationale to Julius and to seek his support. This would have occurred while the council was still in session, perhaps even before the final wording was determined.[18] Thus, the council did approve the tract and, as Socrates asserts, it was circulated with the encyclical letter, thus finding its way into Theodoret's history and the Verona codex. The extant text of *ep.* 3 does not indicate whether a draft of the tract was sent along with this letter.

The question arises why Athanasius (*Apol. sec.* 42–47) and Hilary (*fragg. histt.* B.2.1) preserve the synodical letter but without the

17. Though this document contains some credal formulations, it is a brief treatise, rather than a creed. For a critical edition, *v.* Tetz, "Ante omnia," pp. 252–58, and for an English translation and discussion, Hanson, *The Search,* pp. 301–05; *v.* also Barnes' comments (*Athanasius and Constantius,* pp. 76f.).

18. Chapman (p. 65) thought it "highly probable that the canons proposed to the Council by Hosius had been previously drawn up in Rome, under the direction of Pope Julius." He speaks of "verbal reminiscences" and agreement in content with Iul., *ep.* 2, but provides no detailed or convincing argument. Clearly, Julius had thought through the issues and sent concrete proposals with his delegation; he would have expected and received reports on the proceedings. He and Hosius viewed each other as key allies. This letter, however, would have been unnecessary if Chapman's hypothesis were correct. Yet, the letter makes perfect sense if the papal representatives were unwilling to support a new creed-like statement without Julius' prior agreement.

theological tract. Indeed, we find no mention of the tract in their extant works. In the *Tomus ad Antiochenos*, written twenty years later (in 362), Athanasius denied that the Council of Sardica had approved another credal statement. This denial is understandable in the light of his efforts to heal the schism in Antioch by calling all sides to unite behind the Nicene Creed.[19] But why did he omit the brief treatise when reporting the encyclical letter in his *Apologia secunda* of 349? Why did Hilary transcribe the encyclical in a work directed against Ursacius and Valens without citing at least the beginning of that tract, which addresses the heretical teachings of those very bishops, "two vipers recently brought forth by the Arian asp" (ὑπόγυιον δὲ δύο ἔχεις ἀπὸ τῆς ἀσπίδος τῆς Ἀρειανῆς ἐγεννήθησαν, Thdt., *H. e.* 2.8.38).[20] Very likely, by the time they composed their works, both had perceived its theological inadequacies.

Barnes rightly describes the tract as "rambling, outspoken and incautious," but then wrongly concludes that "the western bishops decided to omit this section of the draft from the final form of" their encyclical and that, "though discarded," it "soon began to embarrass its proposers," Hosius and Protogenes.[21] The witness of Theodoret and the Verona manuscript suggest rather that it was adopted and entered into the official *acta*. Later, when its failings became apparent, Athanasius and Hilary would deliberately avoid mentioning it.

The original Latin letter, of no lasting importance in the West, was not preserved. Our corrupt and fragmentary Latin text is a

19. On the dating and situation, *v.* Barnes, *Athanasius and Constantius*, pp. 156–59.

20. As only fragments of this work survive, it is possible, though not probable, that Hilary had included the tract.

21. *V. Athanasius and Constantius*, pp. 76f. His assumption, probably based on *ep.* 3, that the two chairmen proposed this doctrinal statement is unsubstantiated. In fact, it would be highly unlikely for those chairing the meeting to make any such proposal. Nonetheless, as there may well have been some disagreement on the advisability of any new statement, it seems likely that the two chairmen would have sought the advice of the Roman bishop before putting the proposed tract to a vote. Parvis (pp. 235–38) believes that disagreements arose because the western council met in several subgroups. She postulates, but with little evidence, that the final decision was left to Rome.

re-translation into Latin from a no longer extant Greek translation.[22] Perhaps, *ep.* 3 fell into the hands of the eastern bishops, who planned to exploit it in further polemics. At least, as we have seen, Sozomen had accurate knowledge of its contents.[23] *Ep.* 3 has been preserved in just one manuscript.[24]

The most important editions are those by P. and G. Ballerini (*Bal.*), Opitz (*Op.*) in the *EOMIA*, and, more recently, Tetz (*Tetz*), and Brennecke (*Bre.*).[25] Of the three most recent reconstructions of this lacunose and puzzling document (Tetz', Brennecke's, and my own), Brennecke's follows the manuscript most closely. All editors posit a lacuna following the statement that three issues were discussed at Sardica (ll. 5f.), since what follows lists only one of these. While Brennecke, like Opitz, simply indicates the lacuna, Tetz suggests a supplement that I also adopt, though I suggest an alternative of my own. In the middle section (*ratio quaedam … consententientem,* ll. 8–10), Brennecke, following the Ballerini brothers, accepts the change of *renouent* to the singular and the change of the nonsensical *nefia* to *ne fiat.* This reconstruction requires only two very obvious conjectures and produces an entirely natural word order (verb followed by direct object, verb followed by subject, verb followed by predicate adjectives) in the three clauses *renouet fidem … longior.* Yet, as his translation indicates, this requires interpreting

22. The fragmentary nature of the letter is clear. Noting that three problems were raised, it mentions only one and then jumps to the rationale for the new tract. It also lacks the prayers for good health that normally appear in the conclusion of a letter between bishops; *v.* Telfer, n. 30, p. 182. The conclusion that it is a retroversion into Latin from a Greek translation is the scholarly consensus. Indeed, the other documents of the series within which *ep.* 3 is preserved are all retroversions; *v.* Schwartz, "Über die Sammlung," n. 5, p. 6 and p. 10; Telfer, pp. 182f., 199f.; Tetz, p. 247; Field, p. 61 and n. 85, p. 76.

23. *V.* Telfer, p. 182, and n. 30. In this period a letter from western bishops to the bishop of Rome would certainly have been written in Latin. On Sozomen's knowledge of it, *v.* n. 16 above.

24. On the transmission of this letter, *v.* sec. 5 of the Introduction and App. A, item Td.

25. For information on the editors and their editions, *v.* sec. 6 of the Introduction.

quis as referring to an ecclesiastical council, separating *quis* from the following singular verbs *excludatur* and *fiat,* understanding these as governed by an understood nominative *fides,* taking *spolium* as equivalent to *spolium fidei* ("a theft of the faith"), and referring the comparative adjectives *latior* and *longior* to the faith rather than to its exposition (*v.* n. 3 to the translation). The interpretations of *quis* and *spolium* to me seem very strained. Tetz would change *renouent* to *remoueat, nefia* to *nefas,* and the comparative adjectives *latior* and *longior* to adverbs. In his reconstruction, as in Brennecke's, the verb *excludatur* is dissociated from *quis* and is governed by the noun phrase that follows, though now the noun phrase is not just *eorum spolium* but *eorum spolium et nefas.* Like Brennecke, he accepts the manuscript reading *consentientes,* but unlike Brennecke, places a sentence end at *exponere.* I do not see that Tetz' *excludatur eorum spolium et nefas* (*v.* n. 3 to the translation) is susceptible of any convincing translation. I have preferred Opitz' emendations *rennuerit* and *ne fiat* and regard the three verbs *rennuerit, excludatur,* and *fiat* as all bound to the subject *quis.* I have accepted Tetz' change of the comparative adjectives into adverbs, and, like Tetz, I take these as modifying the infinitive *exponere.* In addition, I have followed Opitz' emendation *consentientem* (modifying *fidem*) and the consequent binding of the participial clause to the sentence beginning with *ratio quaedam.* In marking a sentence end at the participle *consentient-*, I agree with Brennecke against Tetz. In l. 12, Brennecke accepts Opitz' emendation *priora;* Tetz and I adhere to the reading of the manuscript (*plura*).

III

Epistula Osii cordubensis et Protogenis serdicensis ad Iulium, episcopum urbis Romae

Dilectissimo fratri Iulio Osius et Protogenes.

Meminimus, et tenemus, et habemus illam scripturam quae continet catholicam fidem factam apud Niceam, et consenserunt omnes qui aderant episcopi. tres enim quaestiones motae sunt: <quod de non exstantibus est filius Dei uel ex alia substantia, et non ex Deo, et> quod erat <aliquando> quando non erat. sed quoniam post hoc discipuli Arrii blasphemias conmouerunt, ratio quaedam coegit—ne quis, ex illis tribus argumentis

l. 1 et Protogenes *Bal. Op. Tetz* : et pro et P. *Td* **ll. 4–8** episcopi. tres enim quaestiones motae sunt: quod erat quando non erat. sed quoniam post hoc discipuli Arrii blasphemias conmouerunt *hunc codicis Td ordinem sequuntur Bal. Tetz Bre.* : episcopi. sed … conmouerunt; tres enim … erat *transp. Op.* **ll. 4–6** motae sunt <quod de … et> *suppl. Tetz ex Hil.,* Syn. *34* : motae sunt <quod non uerum Verbum Dei est Filius Iesus Christus, sed ex alia substantia aliena a Patre, et erat Pater ante Filium, et> *coni. Thomp. ex ep. 1.2* = *"that the Son, Jesus Christ, is not the true Logos of God but of substance different from the Father, and that the Father existed before the Son"* : motae sunt *Td, Bre.* **l. 6** quod *Bal. Op. Tetz Bre.* : quad *Td* erat <aliquando> quando *coni. Bal., suppl. Tetz.* : erat quando *Td, Op. Bre.* : e. <aliquando tempus> q. *coni. Tetz ex Ath.,* Syn. *25* = *"there was once a time when he did not exist"* : e. <aliquando tempus aut saeculum> q. *coni. Tetz ex Hil.,* Syn. *34* = *"there was once a time or an age when he did not exist"* non erat. : non erat, <et quia ex nullis existentibus factus est, aut ex alia substantia uel essentia dicunt esse conuertibilem, aut mutabilem Filium Dei> *suppl. Bal.* (*ex anathemate nicaeno*) = *"he did not exist, and, since he was made from nothing or from another substance or essence, they say that the Son of God is changeable or mutable"* : *lacunam signif. Op. Bre.* **l. 7** blasphemias *coni. Bal., scr. Op. Tetz.* : -ae *Td* **ll. 8–11** ratio quaedam coegit, ne quis … rennuerit fidem et excludatur eorum spolium et ne fiat, latiorem et longiorem exponere priori consentientem ut igitur nulla reprehensio fiat, haec significamus tuae bonitati *Op.* : r. q. c. ne quis … renouet f., et ex. eor. spolium et ne fiat latior et longior, exponere priori consentientes. ut i. n. r. f., h. s. t. b. *Bre.* = *"a reasonable foresight compels us to*

III

To Julius, Bishop of Rome, from Hosius of Cordova and Protogenes of Sardica

Hosius and Protogenes to our dearest brother Julius.

We keep in mind, hold to, and retain the document produced at Nicaea[1] that contains the catholic faith, and all the bishops present agreed with it. Three disputed points were raised: <that the Son of God came into being from nothing or from another substance, and that he was not from God, and>[2] that there was a time when he did not exist. But because, since then, the disciples of Arius have raised these blasphemous teachings, reason itself compels us (so no one, deceived by these three arguments, reject the faith, be divided from the Church, and fall prey to them[3]) to set forth a formula

1. This is the earliest known reference to the Nicene Creed as authoritative in the west; *v.* Brennecke, p. 159.

2. Tetz ("*Ante omnia,*" p. 248) supplied the two missing issues (*quaestiones*) from Hil. *Syn.* 34, a transcription of a Latin translation of the so-called "fourth formula of Antioch," the creed produced at the Dedication council of 341, whose rejection of Julius' offer of mediation (R^2) occasioned the dispatch of *ep.* 2 (R^3). For the original Greek text, *v.* Ath., *Syn.* 25. Tetz' supplement presupposes an ommision due to *homoioarcton;* the eye of the scribe, confronted with two successive lines beginning with the same word, would have jumped from the first, to the second, *quod.* The Ballerini suggested inserting words from the anathema appended to the Nicene Creed (*v.* the critical note to l. 6). Since Marcellus played an important role at the Council of Sardica, I have suggested supplying the missing lines from Marcellus' analysis of Arian doctrine in *ep.* 1.2.

3. The meaning of the phrase *eorum spolium* is perhaps the most problematic aspect of this corrupt passage. In this translation, *eorum* = "their" is taken to refer either to the Arians or to the three mistaken propositions they espouse; the unfortunate believer, deceived by these, is like a fallen warrior stripped of his armor by his enemy or the prey devoured by a lion or a wolf; *v. OLD, sub uoce,* esp. secc. 2f. My reconstruction of ll. 6–8 is based on the framework provided by Opitz, though, in his own edition, Opitz provides little punctuation and, therefore, little clue to his understanding of the passage. I understand the following clause division: *ratio . . . coegit ne quis . . . rennuerit fidem, et excludatur, eorum spolium et ne fiat.* In the last

circumuentus, rennuerit fidem, et excludatur, eorum spolium et ne fiat—latius et longius exponere priori consentientem. ut igitur nulla reprehensio fiat, haec significamus Tuae Bonitati, frater dilectissime: plura placuerunt firma esse et fixa, et haec plenius cum quadam sufficientia ueritatis dictari ut omnes docentes et catechizantes clarificentur, et repugnantes obruantur et teneant catholicam et apostolicam fidem.

---

expound the faith (*or "creed"* ?) *in agreement with the earlier one, to prevent any future council, because of these three contested issues, from introducing novelties into the faith, to prevent the faith from falling prey to those people, and to see that it be neither extended nor expanded. So then, to avoid ground for censure, we make the following known to your Excellency"* : r. q. c. (ne quis … renouet f.) ut ex. eor. scholium <aduersus Nicaenam fidem>, et fiat latior et longior expositio p. consentiens. ut i. n. r. f., h. s. t. b. *coni. Bal.* = *"reason itself compels us (so no one … may introduce novelties into the faith) to see that their teaching contrary to the Nicene formula of faith be rejected, and that there be produced an exposition that would be more comprehensive yet in agreement with the previous formulation. So then, to avoid ground for censure, we make the following known to your Excellency"* : r. q. c. (ne quis … remoueat f. et ex. eor. s. et nefas) latius et longius e. p. consentientes, ut i. n. r. f., h. s. t. b. *Tetz* = *"reason itself compels us (so no one … put aside the faith, and to see that their violent criminality [?] be debarred) to set out a more comprehensive formula of faith. In agreement with the previous formulation, to avoid ground for censure, we make the following known to your Excellency"* : r. q. c. ne quis … renouent f., et ex. eor. spolium, et nefia latior et longior exponere priori consentientes. ut i. n. r. f., h. s. t. b. *Td*
l. 9 circummentus *Td*[ac] rennuerit *Op.* : renouet *Bal. Bre.* : remoueat *Tetz* : renouent *Td* **l. 12** plura *Td, Bal. Tetz* : priora *scr. Op. Bre.* = *"We agreed that the previous questions have been defined"* **l. 14** catechizantes *Thomp.* : caticiz. *Td, Op. Tetz Bre.* repugnantes *coni. Bal., scr. Op. Tetz* : propug- *scr. Bal.* : prepug- *Td*

of faith that would be more comprehensive yet in agreement with the previous formulation. So then, to avoid ground for censure, we make the following known to your Excellency, dearest brother: We agreed that additional questions have been defined for certain, and that these should be formulated more fully to express the truth in a more sufficient manner, so that teachers and catechists may be freed from confusion, and those who oppose the truth confounded and adhere to the catholic and apostolic faith.

---

clause, I admit, the predicate *eorum spolium* would stand, in a notable hyperbaton, before, rather than after, the conjunction + negative *et ne.* Tetz' ("*Ante omnia,*" p. 248) reconstruction demands taking *eorum spolium et nefas* as a compound subject bearing the sense "their violent criminality." *Spolium,* however, refers to something taken by violence, and is, consequently, a term suggestive of passive suffering, rather than active injustice. Tetz argues that the Latin *spolium et nefas* is meant to be the translation of a Greek hendiadys τὸ ἁρπαγμὸν καὶ τὸ ἀδίκημα. While the stem ἁρπαγ- could bear the active sense of "despoiling" that Tetz desires, the Greek noun is either ἅρπαγμα or ἁρπαγμός not ἁρπαγμόν. Though the two terms ἅρπαγμα and ἀδίκημα occur in parallelism in the Septuagint at Lv 6.4 (LXX) = 5.23 (MT), the *TLG* offers no parallel for either τὸ ἅρπαγμα καὶ τὸ ἀδίκημα or ὁ ἁρπαγμὸς καὶ τὸ ἀδίκημα, and Tetz produces no parallels for the alleged equivalence of the Latin and the Greek phrases. Brennecke's understanding of *et excludatur eorum spolium* is open to the same objection regarding the sense of *spolium;* furthermore, it is very hard to see how the reader could be expected to make the connection between *spolium* and *fides.* The Ballerini had suggested that *spolium* was a corruption of the transliterated Greek term *scholium* (σχόλιον) = "a little tract." In support of this emendation, one might cite the authority of Atticus and Cicero (*Att.* 16.7.3), who had imported the Greek word into a Latin context; *v. LSJ, sub uoce.*

LETTER IV

To Julius, Bishop of Rome, from the Synod of Sardica (Quod semper credidimus)

Introduction

After several months, the western bishops ended their deliberations at Sardica with the promulgation of some new canons[1] and the condemnation of eleven bishops.[2] The council then detailed its work in letters sent to the church of Alexandria and to the bishops of Egypt and Libya and in an encyclical to the Church at large.[3] In addition, they addressed a special letter (*ep.* 4), to Julius.[4]

Greeting Julius as their "dearest brother," the bishops acknowledge the necessity of his absence lest the "schismatic wolves" and "heretical dogs" wreak havoc at Rome. They wish to report on their actions "to the head, that is to the see of the apostle Peter" (sec. 1). It is quite evident that Athanasius and Marcellus have received an unjust treatment from the Eusebians, who have been condemned by a council of eighty Egyptian bishops and have refused to come to Rome to accuse Athanasius before Julius (sec. 2). The agenda of the council has consisted of the following three items: purity of doctrine, the charges against the exiled bishops, and crimes committed against the orthodox (sec. 3). In particular, the scandalous activities of Ursacius and Valens have been investigated and condemned (sec. 4). The bishops request that Julius communicate the council's decisions to the bishops of Sicily, Sardinia, and Italy (sec. 5).

1. *V.* Turner's edition of these canons, *EOMIA*, vol. 1.2.3, pp. 452–531 and Hess, *The Canons of the Council of Sardica*.

2. Athanasius lists those condemned in *Apol. sec.* 36, 49. Besides the three judged to have been illegitimately installed in Alexandria, Ancyra, and Gaza, eight of the Eusebian party were declared deposed and excommunicated: Theodore of Heraclea and the seven listed at the close of *ep.* 4. On the decisions of the western council in general, *v.* Parvis, pp. 234–45; for the signatories, *v. ibid.*, table 8, pp. 263f.

3. Athanasius (*Apol. sec.* 36–50) preserves all three letters. He omits, however, *ep.* 4, probably because he judged it redundant.

4. I reject (*v.* n. 15 to the introduction to *ep.* 3) Parvis' theory that *ep.* 4 was actually the body of *ep.* 3.

Letter IV

A decade later, when Hilary of Poitiers became involved in the Arian struggle, he began composing a richly documented work on the origin and development of the controversy in the western empire. Though bits of this survive only in a jumbled and truncated state among the *fragmenta historica*, it is clear that Hilary took a special interest in the Council of Sardica, the topic of almost one third of the extant material.[5] He probably acquired his copy of *ep.* 4 through Hosius of Cordova or some other elder statesmen of the Nicene party. Though not impossible, it is unlikely that he requested a copy from his contemporary, Liberius of Rome. Hilary had lost respect for the exiled Roman bishop, who, in 357, acquiesced to the Eusebians' demands to accept the deposition of Athanasius and to sign a creed omitting the Nicene term *homoousion*.[6]

Hilary's historical work seems to be the basis for all the many extant manuscript copies of *ep.* 4. These include 1) copies preserved within the context of the *fragg. histt. (H)* and 2) copies preserved within collections of canonical material. Of the first, the most ancient and most important is the ninth-century codex Paris, Bibliothèque d'Arsenal, *483* (H^1). Yet, the earliest editions of the *fragg. histt.*, those of Faber and Coustant, were based on much later sources. In the last decade of the sixteenth century, the classicist and theologian Pierre Pithou (1539–96) discovered a 15th- or 16th-century copy (H^3) and set about editing Hilary's historical work from this sole source. Two years after Pithou's premature death, Nicolaus Faber brought his work to completion and saw it through the press. Almost a century later (1693), Coustant was able to make use of the *Pithoeanus,* which has since disappeared. Yet, the text of H^3 was copied, perhaps by Pithou himself, into another manuscript that in 1680 entered the collection of J.B. Colbert, the finance minister of Louis XIV. This (H^4) has survived and today resides in the Bibliothèque Nationale.

5. It is unclear how many anti-Arian historical works Hilary composed and how many are represented by the extant fragments; *v.* Quasten, vol. 4, p. 47. Wickham provides a translation and introduction to the *fragg. histt.,* to which he gives the title *Against Valens and Ursacius.*

6. *V.* "Liberius," *ODCC,* p. 979.

In the early seventeenth century, the Jesuit philologist and patristic scholar Jacques Sirmond (1559–1651) had discovered another manuscript of Hilary in the monastery of St. Remigius in Rheims (H^2). From this, he compiled a collection of variants, which he used in editing the canons of early councils. Coustant did not see H^2, but, thanks to the assistance of the ecclesiastical historian Étienne Baluze (1630–1718), he was able to have access to Sirmond's collations. Unfortunately, H^2, which seems to have transmitted many early readings, had also vanished by the end of the eighteenth century.[7]

Hilary's text of *ep.* 4 was copied also into four early western collections of canons and decretals: 1) the early sixth-century Italian *Collection of St. Blaise* (*B*), which survives in seven manuscripts, of which five contain our letter; 2) the mid-seventh-century *Collection of Diessen* (*Di*), surviving in only one codex, whose text is very like that of *B;* 3) the late sixth-century French *Collection of St. Maur* (*M*), extant in three manuscripts; 4) the later eighth- or early ninth-century Italian *Expanded Dionysiana Collection* (*E*), represented by six codices, of which two contain our letter.[8]

While there are many sources for *ep.* 4, for most passages of the text, there are only two, for some three, independent witnesses. According to Feder's stemma,[9] the ninth-century H^1 constitutes the first. Though we can recover from Faber's edition readings of the much later, and now lost, *Pithoeanus* (H^3), this manuscript, apparently a mere copy of H^1, is irrelevant to the recension. Of course, H^4, the apograph of the apograph, is even less significant. I cite H^3 and H^4 only where they disagree with H^1, and in those places, their readings should be regarded as conjectures, not bits of the medieval tradition.

The manuscript discovered by Sirmond at St. Remigius in Rheims

7. For H^3 and H^4, *v.* Feder, pp. xx, xxxviif., for H^2, pp. xxxvf.; for the shelfmarks of these manuscripts and further details, App. A, item H. On Pithou, Sirmond, and Baluze, *v.* the articles in the *ODCC*, pp. 1291, 1506f., 148.

8. For the manuscripts of these canonical collections, *v.* App. A, items B, Di, M, and E.

9. Feder, p. xlv

(H^2) was not a descendent of H^1, and so constitutes a second witness. It is available only in the relatively few places where Sirmond noted its reading. Furthermore, according to Feder, Sirmond's reports are not entirely reliable, since he included his own conjectures among the variants culled from that lost codex.[10]

As the shared lacunas at lines 11, 43, 73f. indicate, the conciliar collections all descend from a single archetype; thus, together they constitute just one independent witness, our third.[11] As the text carried by the *Collection of Diessen* (*Di*) is derived from the same archetype as that from which the manuscripts of the *Collection of St. Blaise* (*B*) descend, it is of use only insofar as it helps to reconstruct the exemplar of *B*. Therefore, it will be cited only at places where there is dissension within *B*. A reading attested by just one of the concilar collections or by manuscripts within just one collection will not normally be cited unless it may be correct. In that case, the reading must be understood to represent a conjecture.

The principal editors of *ep.* 4 have been Baronius (*Bar.*), Faber (*Fab.*), Coustant, Feder (*Fed.*), and Brennecke (*Bre.*). Coustant produced two rather different editions, first for the complete works of Hilary (*Cou.*^{1}), then for the collection of early papal correspondence (*Cou.*).[12] In an attempt to regularize the syntax of the Latin or to extract a meaning from difficult passages, the earlier editors made some ingenious, if overly bold, conjectures. Feder's text, far more heedful of the medieval tradition, is the basis of my own.

I have departed from the usage of both Feder and Brennecke in the orthography of proper nouns and in several readings. Regardless of the medieval tradition, I have followed classical Greek usage,

10. Feder, p. xxxv

11. Baronius edited *ep.* 4 from a Cassinese manuscript that neither Feder nor I have been able to identify. As, in that codex, the letter was preserved within the *Collectio crescentiana*, perhaps a now-lost canonical collection, the form of text may have been related to that borne by *B Di M E; v.* n. 59 to the Introduction above.

12. For information on the editors and their editions, *v.* sec. 6 of the Introduction.

i.e., the orthography most likely employed by the bilingual fathers of Sardica, in the transliteration of Greek place and personal names. In this, I follow the example of Coustant and the usage (*v.*, *e.g.*, Rv 1.10) of Weber and Gryson in *Biblia sacra iuxta vulgatam versionem*. The most significant difference, however, is my restoration of the text of the second half of the introductory period to the form carried by the manuscripts. After *locutus est*, Feder and Brennecke, following earlier editors, insert a scriptural quotation: Feder, the Vulgate text of 2Cor 13.3 suggested by Baronius, and Brennecke Col 2.5 suggested by Wickham (*v.* n. 1 to the translation). In addition, as the greeting of this letter has been lost, I have supplied one by conjecture. I have printed one other conjecture of my own (l. 25) and recorded another, palaeographically quite plausible, suggested by Gilbert (l. 51).

IV

Epistula synodi serdicensis ad Iulium, episcopum urbis Romae

<Dilectissimo fratri Iulio, episcopo urbis Romae, episcopi congregati in urbem serdicensem.>

(1) Quod semper credidimus, etiam nunc sentimus; experientia enim probat et confirmat quae quisque auditione audiuit; uerum est enim quod beatissimus magister gentium Paulus apostolus de se locutus est—quamquam utique, quia in ipso dominus Christus habitauit, dubitari non possit spiritum per animam eius locutum et organum corporis personasse[a]—et tu itaque, dilectissime frater, corpore separatus, mente concordi ac uoluntate adfuisti.[b] et honesta fuit et necessaria excusatio absentiae ne aut lupi scismatici furtum facerent et raperent per insidias, aut canes heretici, rabido furore exciti, insani oblatrarent, aut certe serpens diabolus blasphemiorum uenenum effunderet. hoc enim optimum et ualde congruentissimum esse uidebitur: si ad caput, id est ad Petri

ll. 1f. <Dilectissimo … serdicensem> Quod semper *suppl. Thomp.* : Quod semper *codd., edd.* **l. 4** quisque H^4, *Bar. Fab. Cou.* : quique H^1, *Fed. Bre.* **l. 6** locutus est : l. e. <an *(quia Fed.)* experimentum quaeritis eius, qui in me loquitur Christus> *suppl. Bar. Cou.*[1] *Fed. (ex Vulgata, 2Cor 13.3)* : l. e. <nam etsi corpore absens sum, sed spiritu uobiscum sum> *suppl. Wick. Bre. (ex Vulgata, Col. 2.5); v. notam 1 ad interpretationem* **l. 7** animam : -um B^{-3} *Di M E, Bar. Cou.* **l. 11** furtum … insidias *om. B M E, Bar.* = *"so the schismatic wolves or the heretical dogs … go on barking"*

a. 2Cor 13.3
b. *Cf.* 1Cor 5.3f.; 2Cor 4.13; Col 2.5.

IV

To Julius, Bishop of Rome, from the Synod of Sardica

<The bishops gathered in the city of Sardica, to our dearest brother Julius, bishop of Rome.>

(1) We are now perceiving what we have always believed, for our experience shows and confirms what each of us has heard with his own ears. What the most blessed teacher of the gentiles, the apostle Paul, said about himself is truly the case[1]—to be sure, since Christ the Lord dwelt in him, there can be no doubt that the Spirit spoke through his breath and resounded through the trumpet of his mouth[a]—you also, dearest brother, though separated in body, have been present with us, united in mind and will.[b] The reason for your absence was both honorable and compelling: so the schismatic wolves might not steal or treacherously waylay any of the flock, or the heretical dogs, rabid with anger, go on barking madly, or, indeed, that serpent, the devil, pour forth the venom of his blasphemies.[2] This will certainly seem the best and most fitting course: that

1. Taking the reference to Paul to refer to the words, "dwelt in him" and "spoke through his breath," Baronius, without manuscript authority, inserted into the long opening period the first half of 2Cor 13.3 in a variant of the Vulgate version. Yet, as the conclusion of the sentence indicates, the bishops are primarily concerned to draw the parallel that Julius, like the apostle, though absent in body, is present in spirit to his correspondents. While there is certainly reference to 2Cor 13.3 (*cf.* also 2Cor 4.13), the more important connection of thought is to passages such as Col 2.5 and 1Cor 5.3f. Indeed, Brennecke, following the suggestion of Wickham, inserts the first half of the former. That addition, though more to the point, lacks manuscript authority, and the text, as it stands, would be easily comprehensible to any churchman thoroughly familiar with Scripture.

2. There is no evidence for religious strife in Rome at this time; hence the reason given for Julius' absence rings hollow. The bishop of Rome is not known to have attended councils outside the vicinity of Rome; instead he would send representatives. By the end of the fourth century, this had become the established usage. A list of sixty bishops who attended the western council has been preserved. Though it mentions no priests or deacons of Rome, it does contain the names of

apostoli sedem, de singulis quibusque prouinciis domini referant sacerdotes.

(2) Quoniam ergo uniuersa quae gesta sunt—quae acta, quae constituta—et chartae continent, et uiuae uoces carissimorum fratrum et conpresbyterorum nostrorum, Arcydami et Filoxeni, et carissimi filii nostri, Leonis diaconi, uerissime et fideliter exponere poterunt, paene superuacuum uidetur eadem his inferre litteris. patuit apud omnes, qui conuenerunt ex partibus orientis, qui se appellant episcopos—quamquam sint ex his certi auctores quorum sacrilegas mentes arriana heresis pestifero tinxit ueneno—<eos> diu tergiuersatos propter diffidentiam, ad iudicium uenire noluisse tuamque et nostram reprehendere communionem, quae nullam habebat culpam, quia non solum octoginta episcopis testantibus de innocentia Athanasi pariter credimus, sed, et conuenti per presbyteros tuos et per epistulam ad synodum quae futura erat in urbe Roma, uenire noluerunt, et satis erat iniquum, illis contemnentibus, tot sacerdotibus testimonium perhibentibus, Marcello et Athanasio denegare societatem.

(3) Tria fuerunt quae tractanda erant. nam et ipsi religiosissimi imperatores permiserunt ut de integro uniuersa discussa

l. 21 uidetur : -eatur *B M E, Bar. Fab. Cou.*^{2} = *"it would seem almost unnecessary"* **l. 22** conuenerunt : -rint *coni. J.P.* **l. 25** <eos> diu tergiuersatos *suppl. Thomp.* : d. t. *codd., edd.* diffidentiam : differentiam *B M E* = *"these had hesitated for a long time because of a difference"* **l. 26** reprehendere : -disse *Bar. Cou.*^{2} **l. 28** credimus : -didimus *Bar. Fab. Cou.*^{2} = *"It is not just that we trusted the eighty bishops"* **l. 29** ad synodum : et -do *H*^{1} : a -do *B*$^{-3}$ *Di M, Fab.* **l. 30** et satis : s. *B M E, Bar.* = *"It was quite wrong"*

the priests of the Lord from each and every province report to the head, that is, to the see of the apostle Peter.[3]

(2) It seems almost unnecessary to report the same things again in this letter since everything that transpired—all that has been acted upon and decided—is contained in the official documents, and our dearest brethren and fellow priests, Arcydamus and Philoxenus, and our dearest son, the deacon Leo, will be able to set them forth in person with complete accuracy. It was apparent to all that those who had assembled from the eastern provinces, who call themselves bishops (although some were instigators whose sacrilegious minds had been contaminated with the fatal poison of the Arian heresy) hesitated for a long time because of their mistrust; they then refused to come for a hearing and even censured our communion with you, although there was no reason for this. It is not just that we share your trust in the eighty bishops who testified to the innocence of Athanasius, but they refused to come even after they had been summoned by your priests and by letter to a synod to be held in Rome.[4] When so many bishops were testifying on behalf of Marcellus and Athanasius, it would have been quite wrong to deny them fellowship, solely because of the opposition of the easterners.

(3) Three matters had to be dealt with. Our most devout emperors had themselves entrusted us with discussing afresh the entire

ten Italian bishops, including the three Campanians, Vincent of Capua, Januarius of Beneventum, and Calepodius of Naples, who were probably Julius' official representatives. For the complete list, *v.* Brennecke, *Dokumente*, pp. 227–30. I have not included this in my edition. Most likely, it was attached to the encyclical letters of the council rather than to that addressed to Julius.

3. This sentence has been the object of much discussion. Despite its presence in all the manuscripts, some critics, including Percival (p. 434) and Caspar (p. 587) have argued that it must be a later interpolation, since it contrasts with the logical development of the letter. Jalland (p. 223) and Chapman (n. 1, p. 63) have defended its authenticity; *v.* also the discussion by Pietri (n. 4, p. 229). In order to assure Julius' approval of the decisions of the council, the authors remind him of their willingness to look for leadership to Rome. This reflects no more than the consensus among the western bishops as to the traditional leadership of the Roman bishop and his primacy of honor in the west.

4. Julius' correspondents refer to A^1, the letter sent in 338, by an Egyptian

disputarentur et, ante omnia, de sancta fide et de integritate ueritatis, quam uiolauerunt; secunda de personis quos dicebant esse deiectos de iniquo iudicio ut, si potuissent probare, iusta fieret confirmatio; tertia uero quaestio, quae uere *quaestio* appellanda est, quod graues et acerbas iniurias intolerabiles etiam et nefarias contumelias ecclesiis fecissent cum raperent episcopos, presbyteros, diacones, et omnes clericos in exilium mitterent, ad deserta loca transducerent, fame, siti, nuditate, et omni egestate necarent; alios clausos carcere et squalore et putore conficerent, nonnullos ferreis uinculis ita ut ceruices eis artissimis circulis strangularentur. denique ex ipsis quidam uincti in eadem iniusta defecerunt poena, quorum ambigi non potest martyrio gloriosam mortem extitisse. adhuc quoque audent quosdam retinere, nec ulla causa fuit criminis nisi quod repugnarent et clamarent quod execrarentur arrianam et eusebianam heresim et nollent habere cum talibus communionem; qui autem saeculo seruire maluerunt, prodesse. et qui ante fuerant deiecti non solum recepti sunt, sed etiam ad clericalem dignitatem promoti et acceperunt praemium falsitatis.

l. 35 et de integritate : i. *B M E, Bar.* **l. 37** ut *H^{4pc}, Fab. Fed.* : uel *H^{1}, H^{4ac}, B M E, Bar. Cou.^{2}* **l. 39** iniurias : -iis *H^{1}, B^{-3} Di M E* **l. 43** necarent : neg- *H^{1}, B^{1ac} Di M* alios … conficerent *om. B M E, Bar.* = *"killing them … and every sort of deprivation, some they strangled"* **l. 44** nonnullos : -llo *$B^{1,4,7}$ Di M* uinculis : u. stringerent *coni. Cou.^{1}* artissimis *scr. Bar.* (arct-) *Fab. Cou.* (arct- *Cou.^{1}*) *Fed.* : partiss- *H^{1}, $B^{1,4,7}$ Di M E* : paruiss- *$B^{2,3}$* **l. 45** strangularentur *E, Cou.^{2} Fab.* (stragull-) : strangularetur *H^{4pc}* : stranguilarentur *H^{1}, B M, Fed. Bre.* : stranguilaretur *H^{4ac}* **ll. 50–52** qui autem (aut *H^{1}, H^{2}*) saeculo (in s. *H^{1}, H^{2}, $B^{1,7}$ Di M E*) seruire maluerunt, prodesse (-deesse *$B^{1,2,7}$ Di M^{-2}*). et qui ante fuerant deiecti … recepti sunt *H^{1}, B M E^{2}* : q. a. sae. ser. noluerunt prodesse. et q. a. f. d. … r. s. *Fab.* = *"Those who refused to serve it were the ones who conferred benefit on the world. Furthermore, those who had previously been deposed were not only received once more into fellowship"* : iis autem qui secum sentire m., prodesse. et q. a. f. d. … r. s. *Bar. Cou.^{1}* = *"that those who preferred to share their opinions might find profit in their communion. Furthermore, those who had previously been deposed were not only received once more into fellowship"* : q. a. in sae. ser. m., quam in Ecclesia p., et q. a. f. d. … r. s. *coni. Cou.* = *"Those who preferred to serve in this age rather than to be of service in the Church and those who had previously been deposed were not only received once more into fellowship"* **l. 51** maluerunt : -rint *coni. Eng.* prodesse : -esset *coni. Gilb.*

spectrum of disputed topics: first and foremost, the holy faith and the purity of the truth, which those men have profaned; second, those who are said to have been unjustly deposed. If they were able to prove their case, they were to be duly reinstated. The third inquiry might in strict usage be termed an inquiry into criminal charges, for they had committed serious and cruel offenses, indeed intolerable and wicked acts of violence against the Church: kidnapping bishops, priests, and deacons, sending clergy of all levels into exile, transporting them to remote locations, killing them with starvation, thirst, exposure, and every sort of deprivation. They finished off some in the filth and stench of prison; they strangled others with iron chains, pulled tight around their necks. And then, there were those who succumbed in prison in the midst of this unjust punishment, and there can be no doubt that their death was really a glorious martyrdom.[5] Even now they still dare detain men against whom there was no cause for accusation except that they persisted in their refusal and loudly proclaimed that they detested the Arian and Eusebian[6] heresy and would not commune with such as these, but those who preferred to serve the world could find profit in their communion. Furthermore, those who had previously been deposed were not only received once more into fellowship but even promoted among the ranks of the clergy and rewarded for their lies.[7]

---

synod of "nearly one hundred bishops" (ἐπισκόπων ἐγγὺς ἑκατόν; Ath., *Apol. sec.* 1; *v.* p. 28 above). For the text of this, *v. Apol. sec.* 3–19. The synod to which the easterners refused to come was the Roman council of 341 (*v. ep.* 2 above).

5. *Cf.* the description of the persecution of the orthodox in Egypt in *ep.* 2.14. Acts of violence and bloodshed must often have occurred during the seizure of a see by the opposing party.

6. Even after the death in late 342 of Eusebius of Nicomedia/Constantinople, his name continued to be used to denote the moderate Arian position popular in the east.

7. Arius had been readmitted to communion at Nicomedia in 327, and again at Jerusalem in 335; he died in mid-336 at Constantinople, where his supporters were trying to force Bishop Alexander to admit him to communion; *v.* Barnes, *Constantine and Eusebius*, p. 242. Theonas of Marmarica and Secundus of Ptolemais were also condemned at Nicaea (Thdt., *H. e.* 1.8) and later readmitted. According to canon 5 of Nicaea, clergy excommunicated by a bishop or a council were required to seek readmission from the diocese or the provincial council that had pronounced the excommunication.

(4) Quid autem de impiis et de imperitis adulescentibus Vrsacio et Valente statutum sit, accipe, beatissime frater, quia manifestum erat eos non cessare adulterinae doctrinae letalia semina spargere et quod Valens, relicta ecclesia, ecclesiam aliam inuadere uoluisset. eo tempore, quo seditionem commouit, unus ex fratribus nostris qui fugere non potuit, Viator, obrutus et conculcatus, in eadem aquiliensium ciuitate tertia die defecit. causa utique mortis fuit Valens, qui perturbauit, qui sollicitauit. sed ea quae beatissimis Augustis significauimus cum legeritis, facile peruidebitis nihil nos praetermisisse, quantum ratio patiebatur. et, ne molesta esset longa narratio, quae fecissent et quae commisissent insinuauimus.

(5) Tua autem Excellens Prudentia disponere debet ut per tua scripta in Sicilia, in Sardinia, in Italia fratres nostri, quae acta sunt et quae definita, cognoscant et ne ignorantes eorum accipiant litteras communicatorias, id est epistolia, quos iusta sententia degradauit. perseuerent autem Marcellus, et Athanasius,

l. 56 eos : eum *B M E* = *"he was clearly continuing"* non cessare : concessare *B M E* = *"as he was clearly ceasing to sow the lethal seeds"* **l. 57** relicta ecclesia ecclesiam aliam : r. ecclesia a. *B M E, Bar. Fab.* **l. 59** Viator *Bar. Fab. Cou.*^{2} *Fed* : uiator *Bre.* = *"one of our brethren who was traveling (i.e., through Aquileia)"* : Victor *coni. Bar.* **l. 60** aquiliensium $B^{1,2,7}$ *Di* M^{-2}, *Bar. Cou.*^{2} ciuitatem H^{1}, *B M* E^{4} **l. 61** fuit Valens : Valens *B M E, Bar.* **l. 64** et quae commisissent *om.* B^{7} *M E, Bar.* **l. 67** in Sicilia in Sardinia : qui in Sic. qui in Sar. *B M E, Bar. Fab. Cou.* (q. in Sic. in Sar. *Cou.*^{1}) in Italia *coni. Eng., scr. Fed. Bren.* : (<et> *coni. Bar., scr. Cou.*) in I. sunt H^{1}, *B M E, Bar. Fab. Cou.*^{2} **l. 69** epistolia : -tola $H^{1,4ac}$ (-ulas) : episcopalia H^{2}, H^{4pc}, B^{3} (-alis) B^{4} *Di M E* = *"to prevent them from unwittingly accepting letters of communion, that is the office of bishop"* **ll. 70f.** Marcellus, et Athanasius, et Asclepius : M., Ath., et Ascl. *B M E, Bar. Fab. Cou.*

(4) We have also, most blessed brother, taken a decision concerning the irreligious and ignorant youths Ursacius and Valens, as they were clearly continuing to sow the lethal seeds of their spurious teaching, and Valens, having abandoned his own church, had tried to take possession of another. At the time when he was inciting a riot in Aquileia, one of our brethren, Viator, was unable to escape; knocked down and trampled, he died there three days later. Valens was the cause of his death, Valens the rabble-rouser, Valens the instigator.[8] When you read our report to the most blessed emperors, you will promptly perceive that we have omitted nothing that could be reasonably expected. To avoid annoying you with a lengthy narrative, we have only stated the nature of the crimes committed by these men.

(5) Your Surpassing Farsightedness must, therefore, make provision for letters to be sent to our brethren in Sicily, Sardinia, and Italy to inform them of our decisions and definitions,[9] to prevent them from unwittingly accepting letters of communion, so-called *epistolia*, from those whom our just sentence has removed from office.[10]

8. Brennecke takes *uiator* as a common noun ("a traveller") in apposition to *unus ex fratribus nostris* ("one of our brethren"), but the Christian name *Viator* is securely attested in this period; *v.* Pietri and Pietri, vol. 2, pp. 2268f. There is no other mention of this event in the extant sources.

9. Julius' correspondents refer to the role of the bishop of Rome as metropolitan of Italy; *v.* sec. 7 of the Introduction.

10. Commendatory letters (*litterae communicatoriae*) used in the early Church were of two main sorts. The first was a letter attesting that the bearer was a member in good standing of his home congregation. This allowed him to participate in worship with other orthodox Christians while traveling. The second, that referred to in the synod's letter to Julius, was a letter announcing the selection and installation of a new bishop that was dispatched to other churches. By accepting such a letter, the other churches confirmed their communion or fellowship with the new bishop and his church. For this latter sort, *v. ep.* 2.4 and n. 14. Letters announcing the installation of a new bishop are first attested *ca.* 250 by Cyprian of Carthage (*ep.* 36.4). Subsequently, they are mentioned in canons 7 and 10 of the Council of Arles (314; *v.* Munier, pp. 10f.) and in canons 25 and 58 of the Council of Elvira (mid-fourth century; *v.* Martínez Díez, pp. 250, 260). For references by Augustine, *v. epp.* 43.1, 7f., 16, 19; 44.3. In this last passage, he speaks of "letters of communion which we call regular," *i.e.*, canonical (*epistulas communicatorias, quas formatas dicimus*). *Epistolia* = "short notes" is another technical expression equivalent to *litterae communicatoriae*.

et Asclepius in nostra communione, quia obesse eis non poterat iniquum iudicium, fuga, et tergiuersatio eorum qui ad iudicium omnium episcoporum, qui conuenimus, uenire noluerunt. cetera, sicuti superius commemorauimus, plena relatio fratrum, quos Sincera Caritas Tua misit, Vnanimitatem Tuam perdocebunt. eorum autem nomina qui pro facinoribus suis deiecti sunt subicere curauimus ut sciret Eximia Grauitas Tua qui essent communione priuati. ut ante praelocuti sumus, omnes fratres et coepiscopos nostros litteris tuis admonere digneris ne epistolia, id est litteras communicatorias eorum, accipiant.

Item nomina hereticorum: Vrsacius a Singiduno, Valens a Mirsa, Narcissus ab Irenopoli, Stephanus ab Antiochia, Acacius a Caesarea, Menophantus ab Epheso, Georgius a Laodocia.

l. 72 iudicium, fuga, et tergiuersatio : i., et f., et t. H^{4pc}, *B Di M E, Fab. Cou.*^{2} **ll. 73f.** cetera ... commemorauimus *om. B M E, Bar.* = *om. "As for ... previously,"* **l. 75** perdocebunt: -bit B^{3}, *Fab. Cou.*^{2} **l. 78** ut ante: uti a. H^{4}, *B* (uti i ante B^{3}) M^{-2} *E, Cou.*^{2} *Fed.* **l. 81** Item ... hereticorum *om. M* = *om. "Herewith ... the heretics:"* **ll. 81–83** Vrsacius ... Valens ... Narcissus ... Stefanus ... Acacius ... Menofantus ... Georgius : Acacius ... Vrsacius ... Menofantus ... Valens ... Georgius ... Narcissus ... Stefanus *B M E, Bar. Cou.* (Menoph-, Steph-)

Therefore, let Marcellus, Athanasius, and Asclepius[11] remain within our communion. We cannot penalize them for the unjust judgment or the flight and subterfuge of those who were unwilling to appear before the tribunal of all the bishops who convened. As for the other matters, as we mentioned previously, your Concord will receive a full report from the brethren whom your True Charity has sent. Nonetheless, we have had appended to this the names of those who have been deposed for their crimes, so your Excellency might know who has been excluded from communion. As we stated earlier, it is our hope that you will deign to send a letter admonishing all our brethren and fellow bishops not to accept from them *epistolia,* that is, letters of communion.

Herewith the names of the heretics: Ursacius of Singidunum, Valens of Mursa, Narcissus of Irenopolis, Stephen of Antioch, Acacius of Caesarea, Menophantus of Ephesus, and George of Laodicea.[12]

11. The early career of Asclepius of Gaza is the subject of contradictory reports in the ancient sources (*v.* Hanson, *The Search*, pp. 277–79). About 330, he was deposed, apparently for reasons other than his theology, and, in 337, he returned to his see. By 340, he had been ousted again, and, like other ecclesiastical refugees from the east, sought and received hospitality from Julius in Rome. He attended the western Council of Sardica and, by 347, had returned to Gaza (Socr., *H. e.* 2.23). He appears to have died by 358 (Ath., *Fug.* 3).

12. In all the manuscript sources, the text of the letter concludes, not with the expected valediction, but with the list of the leading heretics condemned by the council. For Ursacius and Valens, *v.* the introduction to *ep.* 6 below. For Narcissus, *v.* n. 8 to the introduction to *ep.* 2. Stephen of Antioch, an Arian sympathizer driven from the city by Eustathius (bishop of Antioch from *ca.* 325 to *ca.* 330), was elected bishop shortly before the Council of Sardica. Soon after his return from the council, he was deposed after being implicated with a prostitute in a plot to incriminate the visiting bishop Euphrates (Ath., *H. ar.* 2.20; Thdt., *H. e.* 2.7). Acacius succeeded Eusebius as bishop of Caesarea in 339. He was a leader at the Dedication Synod (341) and was probably also present among the eastern bishops at Sardica. Later he feuded with Cyril of Jerusalem and helped to depose him (357). He became one of Constantius' chief ecclesiastical advisors and presided at the Council of Constantinople (360). He died *ca.* 365. Jerome (*Vir. ill.* 98) wrongly connects him with the elevation of Felix as the successor of Liberius; *v.* "Acacius of Caesarea," *ODCC,* p. 8. Menophantus was a supporter of the Arian faction from the Council of Nicaea at least until the Council of Antioch in 351. In the western bishops' letters to Constantius and to the churches at large, he is listed among the

continued on page 116

leaders of the Eusebians at Sardica (*Or. syn. serd.* 1.5; Hil., *fragg. histt.* B.2.1.7f.). George of Laodicea is not to be confused with the Eusebian of the same name, who was appointed bishop of Alexandria in 338 and continued in office until 345. A priest of Alexandria, George became an adherent of the Arian party and was dismissed *ca.* 320, by Bishop Alexander. Athanasius preserves extracts from two of his early letters (*Syn.* 17). About ten years later, after a stay in Antioch, he succeeded Theodotus as bishop of Laodicea. He did not come to the Council of Sardica, at which he was condemned by the western bishops (Hil., *fragg. histt.* B.2.1.7f.). In 349, George, Theodore of Heraclea, and Narcissus of Neronias made an unsuccessful attempt to convert Paul of Constantinople to their theological position (*Hist. aceph.* 1.1f.). In 358, he attended the Council of Sirmium (Epiph., *Haer.* 73.12.3) and, perhaps with the assistence of Basil of Ancyra, composed a *homoeousian* statement of faith preserved by Epiphanius (*Haer.* 73.12; *v.* Hanson, *Search*, pp. 365–71). His death is placed in 360.

LETTER V

To the Priests, Deacons, and Laity of Alexandria
from Julius, Bishop of Rome
(Συγχαίρω κἀγὼ ὑμῖν)

Introduction

Neither Constans nor Constantius was happy with the debacle of Sardica. A century later the historian Socrates still regarded the failed council as a turning point in the relations of east and west: "From then on the east was cut off from the west, and Mount Soucis, which divides the Illyrians from the Thracians, also became the dividing line of communion. On each side of the mountain, communion remained unbroken, with no disagreement about the faith. But when someone crossed the mountain, he was no longer in his own communion" (*H. e.* 2.22).[1] Yet, the increasing pressures on the borders of the empire necessitated a united defense. If Christianity was to be the religion of the empire, peace had to be reestablished within the Church.

Upon the death of Gregory, the Eusebians' replacement for Athanasius, in June, 345, Constans seized the opportunity to pressure Constantius to recall Athanasius to his see.[2] Constantius finally relented. He directed Athanasius to meet with him on the way,[3] and the reconciliation took place at Antioch in April, 346. Constantius himself then provided letters announcing Athanasius' rehabilitation to the Alexandrians, the prefect of Egypt, Nestorius, and the Church at large (Ath., *Apol. sec.* 54–56; *H. ar.* 23). Furthermore, in what may

1. διεσπᾶτο οὖν ἡ ἀνατολὴ ἐκ τῆς δύσεως, καὶ ἦν ὅρος τῆς κοινωνίας αὐτοῖς τὸ ὄρος τὸ λεγόμενον Συύκεις, ὅπερ ἐστὶν Ἰλλυριῶν τε καὶ Θρᾳκῶν, καὶ ἕως μὲν τοῦ ὄρους τούτου ἀδιάφορος ἦν ἡ κοινωνία ἀδιαφόρου τυγχανούσης καὶ τῆς πίστεως, περαιτέρω δὲ ἀλλήλοις οὐκ ἐκοινώνουν. The translation is my own.

2. On Gregory, *v.* n. 13 to the translation of *ep.* 2. According to Socrates (*H. e.* 2.22), Constans, after making this request several times, finally threatened to invade the east and himself restore Athanasius and Paul of Constantinople; *v.* also Soz., *H. e.* 3.20 and the discussion of Barnes, *Athanasius and Constantius*, pp. 63, 89f.

3. This time it was Athanasius' turn to demur and delay. Theodoret says (*H. e.* 2.10.3) that Constantius wrote three times before Athanasius agreed to return; *cf.* also Ath., *H. ar.* 21.

have been a gesture meant to pacify the easterners, Constantius passed new laws exempting the clergy from supplementary taxes, postal requisitions, and the poll tax (*Cod. theod.* 16.2.10). To avoid accusations for past misconduct, he dispatched an official with orders to remove from the records of the prefect and the military commander of Egypt all previous edicts issued against Athanasius (Ath., *Apol. sec.* 56; *H. ar.* 23). On October 23, 346, the exiled bishop re-entered his see in triumph.

Athanasius, who had spent Easter of 345 at Aquileia, passed through Rome on his voyage back to the east.[4] There he celebrated the propitious turn of events with his faithful ally, Julius, who provided him with our *ep.* 5. This takes the form of a letter of congratulations to the clergy and laity of Athanasius' see.

Addressing himself to "the priests, deacons, and laity of Alexandria," Julius lauds the return of their bishop as "the fruit of your faith." As his flock devoutly continued to believe that he was always with them in spirit, Athanasius was never, even for a moment, forgetful of their love (sec. 1). During his exile he has "trampled underfoot all the deceit of the Arian heresy" (sec. 2) and now returns home "proclaimed innocent not only by us, but by the entire council" (παρὰ πάσης τῆς συνόδου, sec. 3).[5] Therefore, the church of Alexandria should welcome the returning prelate with joyous thanksgiving (sec. 3). Julius closes with a prayer that God reward the faithful Alexandrians for their unwavering support of their persecuted leader (sec. 4).

Julius' letter, composed in Greek for its Alexandrian audience,[6] was transmitted through two independent traditions. Athanasius (*A*), the subject and bearer of the letter, doubtless had either the

4. *V.* Bardy's account (*DHGE*, vol. 4, col. 1327) of his movements after the Council of Sardica.

5. *V.* n. 3 to the translation.

6. So Amman, col. 1917. The letter is full of biblical pictures and terminology but has only one clear quotation. If Julius was thinking in the language of his Latin bible, it may be that some quotations and allusions were obscured when his ideas were translated into Greek; *cf.* the differences between the *apparatus fontium* of the Greek original and that of Epiphanius' Latin translation (App. C).

original or an accurate copy. Nonetheless, he inserted only a shortened version into his *Apol. sec.* (52f.). Socrates (*Sc*) clearly had access to an independent source, for he included the complete letter in his history (2.23.15–32). The section omitted by Athanasius, mainly devoted to a panegyric on his faith and courageous endurance of the sufferings of exile, seemed to Opitz a later addition.[7] Yet, it is far more likely that here, as elsewhere, Athanasius simply abridged a letter for inclusion in his apologetical work.[8] His motivation was probably the desire for brevity, not, as de Montfaucon suggested, his personal modesty.[9]

This edition takes Athanasius' *Apol. sec.* as its base for secc. 1 and 3f., Socrates for the second section that Athanasius did not transcribe. To reconstruct the text of the letter as reported by Athanasius, I identify two witnesses, for, of the five manuscripts, one (A^{2}) stands apart from the other four ($A^{1,3-5}$).[10] Socrates' text is cited from three independent witnesses ($Sc^{1,2,4}$). Where the reading of Sc^{1} cannot be determined, the editor can draw on its apograph, Sc^{3}.[11]

For Socrates' text of *ep.* 5 we have also the direct witness of Nicephorus (*N*) and the Latin translation of Epiphanius Scholasticus commissioned by Cassiodorus (*C*).[12] *N* survives in a single, but very reliable, copy.[13] Epiphanius' translation of *ep.* 5 was copied, amidst other supplementary material, into two manuscripts bearing the Pseudo-Isidorian decretals (*P*).[14] In Appendix C, I provide

7. *Athanasius Werke*, vol. 2.4, p. 133

8. *V.* Barnes, *Athanasius and Constantius*, p. 31 for another example.

9. De Montfaucon's comment is reproduced in PG, vol. 25, col. 345, n. 23; *cf.* Coustant, col. 399, n. a.

10. For the shelf-marks of these manuscripts, Opitz' discussion of their relationships, and further details, *v.* App. A, item A.

11. For the shelf-marks of these manuscripts and further details, *v.* App. A, item Sc.

12. *V.* sec. 6 of the Introduction.

13. *V.* App. A, item N.

14. For the shelf-marks of these manuscripts and further details, *v.* App. A, item P. On Ps.-Isidore, *v.* Introduction, p. xxxvi.

an edition of this translation based on both the *C* and *P* traditions. These witnesses are called upon when there is dissension within *Sc*. They are also cited on a few occasions where they disagree with *Sc*, and their readings are perhaps correct.

Among the modern editors, the most important are Coustant, the editor of the early papal correspondence, and the editors of the works of Athanasius (Commelinus, de Montfaucon, and Opitz) and of Socrates (Valesius, Hussey, and Hansen). For Nicephorus, I cite the edition of Ducaeus.[15]

Throughout the volume, I have departed from the usage of my predecessors in capitalizing honorific titles in the ancient text. In sec. 3 of this letter, that orthographic change brings out more clearly the meaning of an entire sentence (*v.* n. 6 to the translation). Earlier in that section, I have recorded a supplement conjectured by Gilbert and Petruccione (*v.* n. 4 to the translation). Their conjecture points to the possible preservation in the Latin translation of a meaningful pun that has vanished from the direct tradition of the Greek text.

15. For information on the editors and their editions, *v.* sec. 6 of the Introduction.

V

Epistula Iulii, episcopi urbis Romae, ad presbyteros, diaconos, et populum alexandrinum

Ἰούλιος πρεσβυτέροις, καὶ διακόνοις, καὶ λαῷ παροικοῦντι Ἀλεξάνδρειαν, ἀγαπητοῖς ἀδελφοῖς, ἐν Κυρίῳ χαίρειν.

(1) Συγχαίρω κἀγὼ ὑμῖν, ἀγαπητοὶ ἀδελφοί, ὅτι τὸν καρπὸν τῆς ἑαυτῶν πίστεως ἐπ᾽ ὀφθαλμῶν λοιπὸν ὁρᾶτε· τοῦτο γὰρ καὶ ἀληθῶς ἄν τις ἴδοι γενόμενον ἐπὶ τοῦ ἀδελφοῦ καὶ συνεπισκόπου μου Ἀθανασίου, ὃν διὰ τὴν καθαρότητα τοῦ βίου καὶ διὰ τὰς ὑμετέρας εὐχὰς θεὸς ὑμῖν ἀποδίδωσιν. ἐκ δὴ τούτου συνορᾶν ἔστι καθαρὰς ὑμᾶς καὶ μεστὰς ἀγάπης ἀεὶ τὰς εὐχὰς ἀνενηνοχέναι πρὸς τὸν θεόν· μνήμονες γὰρ ὄντες τῶν οὐρανίων ἐπαγγελιῶν καὶ τῆς πρὸς αὐτὰς ἀγωγῆς, ἣν ἐκ τῆς διδασκαλίας τοῦ προειρημένου ἀδελφοῦ μου ἐπαιδεύθητε, ἔγνωτε ἀληθῶς καὶ κατὰ τὴν προσοῦσαν ὑμῖν ὀρθὴν πίστιν κατειλήφατε ὡς οὐκ ἂν εἰς τέλος ἀφ᾽ ὑμῶν ἀποσχοινισθήσεται οὗτος, ὃν ταῖς θεοσεβεστάταις ὑμῶν ψυχαῖς ἀεὶ ὡς παρόντα ἐσχήκατε. οὐκοῦν οὐ πολλῶν μοι χρεία λόγων πρὸς ὑμᾶς ἐπιστέλλοντι· ὅσα γὰρ ὑμῖν ἂν λεχθῇ παρ᾽ ἐμοῦ, ταῦθ᾽

ll 1f. Ἰούλιος πρεσβυτέροις … Ἀλεξάνδρειαν *om.* A^5, Sc^2, *N* = *om.* "Julius, to the priests, deacons, and laity of Alexandria" **l. 1** πρεσβυτέροις : ἐπισκόποις καὶ π. Sc^{-2} = *"to the bishops, priests, deacons," etc.* **l. 2** ἀγαπητοῖς … χαίρειν *om. A*, Sc^2, *N* = *om. "greetings … in the Lord!"* **l. 3** ἀγαπητοὶ αδελφοί : ἀδ. ἀγ. Sc^{-4}, *Val.*^{1} **ll. 4f.** καὶ ἀληθῶς : ἀληθῶς *Sc* **l. 6** διὰ τὰς : διά τε τὰς *Sc* **l. 7** θεὸς : ὁ θεὸς *Sc* **l. 8** ὑμᾶς : ὑμῶν *Sc* **l. 10** ἀγωγῆς : ἀγαπῆς *Sc* = *"Mindful of the heavenly promises and the love that is in accord with them"* **ll. 10f.** τοῦ … ἀδελφοῦ μου : fratris mei Athanasii *CP* = *"by my aforementioned brother Athanasius"* **l. 12** κατειλήφατε : κ. τοῦτο *Sc* = *"really did understand this: that he who was always present"* **ll. 12f.** ἀφ᾽ ὑμῶν ἀποσχοινισθήσεται οὗτος : οὗ. ἀφ᾽ ὑ. ἀπ. *Sc* **l. 13** ταῖς … ψυχαῖς : ἐν τ. … ψ. *Sc* θεοσεβεστάταις : θεοσεβέσιν *Sc* **l. 14** ἀεὶ ὡς παρόντα ἐσχήκατε : ἐ. ὡς π. ἀ. *Sc* **l. 15** ὅσα … ἂν λεχθῇ *A, C* (quaecumque … potuerint loqui) *P* (q. … poterunt l.) : ὅσα … λέλεκται Sc^{-4} = *"whatever I have said to you"*

V

To the Priests, Deacons, and Laity of Alexandria from Julius, Bishop of Rome

Julius, to the priests, deacons, and laity of Alexandria, greetings to our beloved brethren in the Lord!

(1) Beloved, I join you in rejoicing that now, at last, you are able to behold the fruit of your faith with your own eyes. For one might see this coming true in the case of my brother and fellow bishop Athanasius, whom God is returning to you because of his holy life and your prayers. This is the proof that your unceasing prayers to God were pure and full of love. You kept before you the heavenly promises and the life they require, just as you were taught by my aforementioned brother. You really did know and, thanks to your adherence to the true faith, really did understand that he who was always present in your pious hearts could not be permanently separated from you. Consequently, I need not write at length, for your faith has anticipated whatever I might say to you, and, by the grace

ἡ ὑμετέρα πίστις προὔλαβε, καὶ πεπλήρωται κατὰ θεοῦ χάριν τὰ τῆς κοινῆς πάντων ἡμῶν εὐχῆς. συγχαίρω τοίνυν ὑμῖν, *πάλιν* γὰρ *ἐρῶ*,[a] ὅτι τὰς ψυχὰς ἀκαταμαχήτους ἐν τῇ πίστει τετηρήκατε, καὶ αὐτῷ δὲ τῷ ἀδελφῷ μου Ἀθανασίῳ οὐκ ἔλαττον συγχαίρω, ὅτι, καίπερ πολλὰ πάσχων λυπηρά, οὐδεμίαν ὥραν ἐπιλήσμων γέγονε τῆς ὑμετέρας ἀγάπης καὶ τοῦ ὑμετέρου πόθου. εἰ γὰρ καὶ τῷ σώματι πρὸς καιρὸν ἔδοξεν ἀφ' ὑμῶν ἀφελκυσθῆναι, ἀλλὰ τῷ πνεύματι διαπαντὸς ὡς συνὼν ὑμῖν διῆγεν.[b]

(2) Καὶ ἔγωγε, ἀγαπητοί, τὸν γενόμενον κατ' αὐτοῦ *πάντα πειρασμὸν*[c] οὐκ ἄδοξον ἡγοῦμαι γεγενῆσθαι· καὶ γὰρ καὶ ἡ ὑμετέρα καὶ ἡ τούτου πίστις ἐγνώσθη παρὰ πᾶσιν[d] καὶ δεδοκίμασται. εἰ γὰρ μὴ τοσαῦτα συμβεβήκει, τίς ἂν ἐπίστευσεν ἢ ὑμᾶς τοσαύτην κρίσιν καὶ τοσαύτην ἀγάπην περὶ τὸν τηλικοῦτον ἐπίσκοπον ἔχειν, ἢ ἐκεῖνον τοσαύταις ἀρεταῖς περιβεβλῆσθαι, δι' ἃς καὶ τῆς ἐν οὐρανοῖς ἐλπίδος οὐκ ἀλλότριος γένοιτο; ἐπέτυχε τοίνυν οἵῳ δήποτε τρόπῳ, καὶ ἐν τῷ νῦν καὶ ἐν τῷ μέλλοντι, καὶ ὁμολογίας ἔνδοξον μαρτυρίαν·[e] διαφόρως γὰρ κατά τε γῆν καὶ κατὰ θάλατταν πολλὰ χειμασθείς, τὴν σκευωρίαν πᾶσαν τῆς ἀρειανῆς αἱρέσεως κατεπάτησεν καὶ πολλάκις, διὰ φθόνον καὶ εἰς κίνδυνον ἐπιβουλευθείς, κατεφρόνησεν θανάτου,[f] φρουρούμενος ὑπὸ τοῦ παντοκράτορος θεοῦ καὶ τοῦ Κυρίου ἡμῶν Ἰησοῦ Χριστοῦ,[g] ἐλπίζων ἅμα καὶ τὰς ἐπιβουλὰς ἐκκλινεῖν καὶ ἀποκα-

l. 16 προὔλαβε : iam ... praecessit *C* = *"your faith has already anticipated"* πεπλήρωται *Sc* : πεπλήρωκε *A, CP* (compleuit) = *"and, by the grace of God, your faith has fulfilled everything for which we prayed together"* θεοῦ *A, CP* (diuina) : Χριστοῦ *Sc* = *"by the grace of Christ"* **l. 17** πάντων ἡμῶν : ὑμῶν πάντων *Sc* = *"everything for which you prayed together"* **l. 21** ὑμετέρας ... ὑμετέρου : ἡμετέρας ... ἡμετέρου A^{3-5}, A^{1ac} = *"forgetful of our love and our yearning for his return"* **ll. 24–42** Καὶ ἔγωγε ... παρ' ὑμῶν ἀγαπώμενος *om. A* = *om. "Indeed, beloved ... loved by you"* **l. 24** ἀγαπητοί: carissimi fratres *CP* = *"Indeed, beloved brethren,"* **l. 33** χειμασθείς : πειρασθεὶς *Val.*^{1} *Cou.* = *"though tried by many and varied temptations on land and sea"* **ll. 36f.** τοῦ Κυρίου ἡμῶν Ἰησοῦ Χριστοῦ : Iesu Christo saluatore nostro *CP* = *"protected ... by ... our savior Jesus Christ"*

a. Phil 4.4 b. *Cf.* 1Cor 5.3; Col 2.5. c. Lk 4.13
d. *Cf.* 1Thes 1.8; Rom 1.8. e. *Cf.* 1Tm 6.12f. f. *Cf.* Heb 12.2.
g. *Cf.*, *e.g.*, 1Pt 1.5.

of God, everything for which we prayed together has been fulfilled. Therefore, "again I say," I "rejoice" with you[a] that you have preserved your souls unwavering in the faith, and I rejoice no less with my brother Athanasius; though suffering so much, he was never, for even a single moment, forgetful of your love and your yearning for his return. Even if, for a time, it seemed that in body he had been dragged from your sight, in spirit he continued to be ever among you.[b]

(2) Indeed, beloved, it is my opinion that "every trial"[1c] set in his path has added to his honor. Both your faith and his have been made known and commended to all the world.[d] After all, had he not been beset by so many troubles, who would have believed that you were possessed of such judgment or of such love for this great bishop, or that he was clothed with such heroic virtues. And, because of these, may he never be deprived of his heavenly reward![2] Moreover, one might say that, both now and for the future, he has achieved the rank of a glorious confessor of the faith.[e] Though tossed by many and varied tempests on land and sea, he trampled underfoot all the deceit of the Arian heresy; though often the victim of malicious conspiracy, he scorned death,[f] protected, as he was, by almighty God and our Lord, Jesus Christ.[g] His hope was to escape those plots

1. The phrase πάντα πειρασμὸν occurs in Lk 4.13, but there the noun bears the common biblical sense of "temptation." Here, as is clear from the context and the subsequent use of δεδοκίμασται, it signifies "trial"; *cf.* 1Pt 4.12.

2. Julius uses a turn of phrase suggestive of citizenship: "may he not be a foreigner to the hope residing in heaven"; for a similar use of the adjective ἀλλότριος, *v. epp.* 1.2, 5; 2.1, 16.

τασταθήσεσθαι πρὸς ὑμετέραν παράκλησιν, φέρων ὑμῖν ἅμα ἐκ τῆς ὑμετέρας συνειδήσεως μείζονα τὰ τρόπαια. ἐν οἷς καὶ ἄχρι τερμάτων πάσης τῆς γῆς ἔνδοξος ἐγνώσθη, δοκιμασθεὶς ἐκ τοῦ βίου, παρρησιασάμενος μὲν τῇ προθέσει καὶ τῇ οὐρανίῳ διδασκαλίᾳ, ἀποδειχθεὶς δὲ ἀθανάτῳ κρίσει, παρ᾽ ὑμῶν ἀγαπώμενος.

(3) Ἐπανέρχεται τοίνυν πρὸς ὑμᾶς λαμπρότερος νῦν ἢ ὅτε παρ᾽ ὑμῶν ἀπεδήμησεν· εἰ γὰρ καὶ τὰς τιμίας ὕλας, χρυσὸν δὴ καὶ ἄργυρον, εἰς καθαρότητα τὸ πῦρ δοκιμάζει,[h] τί ἄν τις εἴποι κατ᾽ ἀξίαν τοῦ τοσούτου ἀνδρός, ὅς, κινδύνους τοσούτων θλίψεων νικήσας, ἀποδίδοται ὑμῖν, ἀθῷος οὐ παρ᾽ ἡμῶν μόνον, ἀλλὰ καὶ παρὰ πάσης τῆς συνόδου ἀποδειχθείς; ὑποδέξασθε τοίνυν, ἀγαπητοὶ ἀδελφοί, μετὰ πάσης τῆς κατὰ θεὸν δόξης καὶ χαρᾶς τὸν ἐπίσκοπον ὑμῶν Ἀθανάσιον μετὰ τούτων οἵτινες αὐτῷ καὶ τῶν τοσούτων καμάτων κοινωνοὶ γεγόνασι[i] καὶ χαίρετε τῶν εὐχῶν ἑαυτῶν ἀπολαύοντες οἳ τὸν ποιμένα τὸν ὑμέτερον, ἵν᾽ οὕτως εἴπω, ποθοῦντα καὶ διψῶντα Τὴν Ὑμετέραν Θεοσέβειαν,[j] σωτηρίοις γραφαῖς ἐθρέψατε καὶ ἐποτίσατε· καὶ γὰρ τῆς ἐπὶ ξένης αὐτοῦ διατριβῆς ὑμεῖς παραμυθία γεγόνατε καὶ διωκόμενον ἐθάλψατε ταῖς πιστοτάταις ἑαυτῶν ψυχαῖς καὶ διανοίαις. ἐμὲ δὲ ἤδη εὐφραίνει, ἐννο-

l. 41 οὐρανίῳ : -ίᾳ Sc^{1}, *Val.*^{1} *Cou. Hus.*^{1} *Duc.* **l. 43** τοίνυν : τοιγαροῦν *Sc* **l. 44** χρυσὸν δὴ *A* : χρυσὸν δὴ λέγω *Sc, CP* (id est aurum) **l. 46** κινδύνους τοσούτων θλίψεων : τοσούτων θλίψεων πυρὰν *(i.e.,* πεῖραν*?)* καὶ κινδύνους $Sc^{1,4}$ Sc^{2pc}, *C* (tantas tribulationes et pericula) = *"victorious in the trial (*πεῖραν *= "trial";* πυρὰν *= "funeral pyre") and the dangers arising from such terrible tribulations"* : -ον θλίψεων πυρ/δυνους Sc^{2ac} **l. 47** ἀποδίδοται : ἀ. νῦν *Sc* = *"is being restored to you"* **l. 49** δόξης καὶ χαρᾶς : δ. τε καὶ χ. *Sc* **ll. 49f.** τὸν ἐπίσκοπον ὑμῶν Ἀθανάσιον : pastorem uestrum ac praesulem tamquam uere Athanasium *CP* = *"welcome home your pastor and bishop as though truly 'Athanasius'" (i.e., Athanasius = "undying," "immortal")* : τ. ἐ. καὶ προϊστάμενον ὑμῶν ὡς ἀληθῶς Ἀ. *coni. Gilb. J.P.* **ll. 50f.** αὐτῷ … καμάτων : αὐτῶν Sc^{-4} = *"as well as those who were their companions."* : αὐτῷ *N* = *"as well as those who were his companions."* **l. 51** τῶν εὐχῶν ἑαυτῶν : τῶν εὐχῶν *Sc* **l. 52** οἳ τὸν : ὅτι *N* **l. 54** ἐθρέψατε καὶ ἐποτίσατε: ἐθ. τε καὶ ἐπ. Sc^{-4} ἐποτίσατε : potastis assidue *P* = *"you have attentively provided food and drink to your shepherd"* καὶ γὰρ : κ. γ. καὶ *Sc* **l. 55** διωκόμενον : δ. καὶ ἐπιβουλευόμενον *Sc* = *"comforted him while he was the victim of persecution and conspiracy"*

h. *Cf.* 1Pt 1.7. i. *Cf.* 2Cor 1.7; Phil 3.10. j. *Cf.* Mt 5.6.

and be sent back to bring you comfort and award you even greater trophies for your faithfulness. Because of these events he has come to be known and praised to the ends of the earth: winning commendation for the life he has lived, boldly asserting his teaching and his godly instruction, approved by the judgment of God, loved by you.

(3) Therefore, he returns to you more illustrious now than when he left. If fire reveals the purity of valuable metals such as gold and silver,[h] what words of praise could be worthy of this man, who, victorious over dangers arising from such terrible tribulations, has been restored to you and proclaimed innocent not only by us, but by the entire council?[3] Therefore, my beloved brethren, with all godly honor and joy, welcome home your bishop, Athanasius,[4] as well as those who have been with him and shared in his labors.[i] Rejoice in the fruition of your prayers. Through your letters of support you have provided food and drink to your shepherd who, if you will permit my bold metaphor,[5] was yearning and thirsting for your Reverence.[6][j] You were his consolation even while he dwelt in a foreign land; remaining faithful in heart and mind, you comforted

3. Julius is referring to the Council of Sardica of 343. Though he declares that Athanasius was exonerated "by the entire council" (παρὰ πάσης τῆς συνόδου), the entire council never met; *v.* the introduction to *ep.* 3. It was the western part that confirmed the judgment rendered on Athanasius' case two years earlier at the synod chaired by Julius in Rome.

4. The phrase *pastorem uestrum ac praesulem tamquam uere Athanasium* presented by the witnesses to the Latin translation suggests that, in the sixth century, Epiphanius Scholasticus read something more than τὸν ἐπίσκοπον ὑμῶν Ἀθανάσιον ("welcome home your bishop, Athanasius"), perhaps τὸν ἐπίσκοπον καὶ προϊστάμενον ὑμῶν ὡς ἀληθῶς Ἀθανάσιον ("welcome home your pastor and bishop as though truly 'Athanasius'"). If so, Julius, applying to Athanasius a trope common in martyr literature, was pointing out that, by his resilience in the face of suffering and persecution, Athanasius had lived up to the implications of his name ("Athanasius" = "undying," "immortal"). For an elaborate example of this sort of etymological pun on the name conferred at the baptism of water and certified by the baptism of blood, *v., e.g., M. Agap.* 2.2f. Though Athanasius was not, of course, a martyr, Julius presents him as a confessor, one who suffers for his witness to Christ, but without sheddding blood; *v.* sec. 2.

5. Brightman (p. 159) identifies ἵν᾽ οὕτως εἴπω as a "flagrant Latinism" = *ut ita dicam,* the idiom that is, in fact, used here by Epiphanius. Latin prosaists make frequent use of *ut ita dicam* to beg the readers' indulgence for a novel turn of phrase or a bold metaphor; *v. OLD, sub uoce,* sec. 8d.

ούμενον καὶ προορῶντα τῷ λογισμῷ τὴν ἐπὶ τῇ ἐπανόδῳ ἑκάστου ὑμῶν χαράν, καὶ τοῦ πλήθους τὰς θεοσεβεστάτας ἀπαντήσεις, καὶ τὸ ἔνδοξον τῆς τῶν συντρεχόντων ἑορτῆς. καὶ τίς ἐκείνη ἡ ἡμέρα ὑμῖν καὶ ποία ἔσται, ἐπανερχομένου μὲν τοῦ ἀδελφοῦ μου, παυομένων δὲ τῶν προγενομένων, καὶ τῆς πολυτιμήτου καὶ κατ' εὐχὴν ἐπανόδου εἰς εὐφροσύνην τινα πληρεστάτης χαρᾶς συναπτούσης τοὺς πάντας; ἡ τοιαύτη δὲ χαρὰ κατὰ τὸ μέγιστον μέχρις ἡμῶν φθάνει εἰ θεόθεν καὶ τοῦτο συγχωρεῖσθαι συνέστηκεν ὅπως εἰς γνῶσιν τοῦ τηλικούτου ἀνδρὸς ἐλθεῖν δυνηθῶμεν. εἰς εὐχὴν δὴ οὖν τὴν ἐπιστολὴν τελειῶσαι καλόν.

(4) Ὁ θεός, ὁ παντοκράτωρ, καὶ ὁ τούτου υἱός, ὁ Κύριος καὶ σωτὴρ ἡμῶν Ἰησοῦς Χριστός, διηνεκῆ τὴν χάριν ὑμῖν παράσχοι, διδοῦς ἔπαθλον τῇ θαυμαστῇ ὑμῶν πίστει, ἣν περὶ τὸν ἐπίσκοπον ὑμῶν ἐνδόξῳ μαρτυρίᾳ ἐνεδείξασθε ἵνα ὑμῖν τε καὶ τοῖς μεθ' ὑμᾶς

l. 59 τὸ ἔνδοξον τῆς τῶν συντρεχόντων ἑορτῆς : τὴν ἔ. τ. σ. ἑορτήν *Sc* **ll. 60f.** παυομένων : παυσα- *Sc* **ll. 61f.** τῆς πολυτιμήτου καὶ κατ' εὐχὴν ἐπανόδου : τ. π. κατ' εὐ. ἐπ. *Sc* **l. 63** ἡ τοιαύτη δὲ χαρὰ : ἡ τ. χ. *Sc* **l. 64** εἰ *A* : οἷς *Sc* συγχωρεῖσθαι : -κεχωρῆσθαι *Sc* **ll. 65f.** εἰς εὐχὴν δὴ οὖν : εἰς εὐ. οὖν A^{3}, *Sc*, *Com.* **l. 67** Ὁ θεός : θεός A^{3-5}, *Val.*[1] ὁ τούτου υἱὸς : huius unigenitus filius *CP* = *"May almighty God and his only begotten Son,"* etc. **l. 68** Ἰησοῦς : ὁ Ἰ. A^{2}, A^{1pc}, *Sc* τὴν χάριν : τ. χ. ταύτην *Sc* **l. 69** ἔπαθλον : dignum … praemium *CP* = *"award you a prize commensurate with your admirable faith"* **ll. 70f.** ἵνα ὑμῖν τε καὶ τοῖς μεθ' ὑμᾶς … τὰ βελτίονα νέμοι : ut et uos et qui uobiscum sunt … meliora possideatis *CP* = *"may you and those with you possess those better things"*

him during his persecution. I am already delighted[7] to picture in my imagination and look forward to the joy each of you will feel at his return, the holy welcomings of the throngs, and the glorious celebration of those who will run to greet him. Indeed, what a day you will have when my brother returns, as the previous troubles are laid to rest, and his home-coming, so wonderful an event, the answer to your prayer, unites everyone in complete happiness and joy! That same joy has already come, and in large measure, upon us. Perhaps God has permitted this[8] just so we might come to know that great man. Therefore, it is well to end this letter with a prayer.

(4) May almighty God and his Son, our Lord and Savior, Jesus Christ, confirm forever his favor for you and award you the prize for the admirable faith you have exhibited by your glorious witness

6. When Julius refers to Athanasius' "yearning and thirsting" (ποθοῦντα καὶ διψῶντα), he may be playing a variation on Christ's blessing of those who hunger and thirst for justice (πεινῶντες καὶ διψῶντες τὴν δικαιοσύνην, Mt 5.6); indeed, the direct object of these participles, as in the beatitude, is an abstract noun τὴν ὑμετέραν θεοσέβειαν. Yet, the substitution of a form of ποθέω ("yearn") for πεινάω ("hunger") shows that Julius is thinking not of Athanasius' desire for the spiritual welfare of his flock (as Robertson and Zenos, the translators of Athanasius and Socrates for the NPNF understood ποθοῦντα καὶ διψῶντα τὴν ὑμετέραν θεοσέβειαν), but of his yearning for his absent friends. In fact, the article + possessive + abstract should be capitalized, as it is a form of address common in epistolography. For Ἡ Ὑμετέρα Θεοσέβεια as an honorific title, *v.*, *e.g.*, Thdt., *epp.* 75 (vol. 2, p. 162, ll. 14f.), 77 (*ibid.*, p. 172, l. 1), and 138 (vol. 3, p. 140, ll. 24f.); *cf.* Τῇ Θεοσεβείᾳ Σου in *ep.* 1.1 above. For the use of the root ποθ- to signify "missing" a friend, *v.* Thdt., *epp.* 24 (vol. 2, p. 80, l. 21), 58 (*ibid.*, p. 134, l. 19), and 81 (*ibid.*, p. 192, l. 2).

7. Brightman (p. 159) regards εὐφραίνει as another Latinism = *iuuat,* used impersonally.

8. Brightman (p. 159) identifies συνέστηκεν as yet another Latinism here = *constat; cf.* Epiphanius' rendering: *hoc constat esse concessum.* The variant οἷς (dative relative pronoun) for εἰ (the conditional conjunction) may suggest that this passage has puzzled readers since antiquity. It is particularly difficult to determine the reference of the demonstrative pronoun τοῦτο. In his translation for the NPNF ("since it has been granted to us by God, to be able to make the acquaintance of so eminent a man") Robertson takes τοῦτο to anticipate and sum up the content of the following clause introduced by ὅπως, but that empties that clause of any nuance of purpose. My translation interprets the demonstrative as looking back to the exile of Athanasius and his flight to Rome in 339: God has permitted an apparent evil so that good might ensue.

ἐνταῦθα καὶ ἐν τῷ μέλλοντι τὰ βελτίονα νέμοι *ἃ ὀφθαλμὸς οὐκ εἶδε, καὶ οὖς οὐκ ἤκουσε, καὶ ἐπὶ καρδίαν ἀνθρώπου οὐκ ἀνέβη, ἃ ἡτοίμασεν ὁ θεὸς τοῖς ἀγαπῶσιν αὐτὸν*[k] *διὰ τοῦ Κυρίου ἡμῶν Ἰησοῦ Χριστοῦ,*[l] δι' οὗ τῷ παντοκράτορι θεῷ *ἡ δόξα εἰς τοὺς αἰῶνας τῶν αἰώνων. ἀμήν.*[m] ἐρρῶσθαι ὑμᾶς ἐν Κυρίῳ εὔχομαι, ἀγαπητοὶ ἀδελφοί.

l. 71 νέμοι : μένοι *Sc* **l. 74** δι' οὗ : per quem et cum quo *CP* = *"through whom and with whom be glory"* **l. 75** ἐρρῶσθαι … ἐν Κυρίῳ : ἐρρῶσθαι *Sc* = *"I pray that you fare well, my beloved brethren"*

k. 1Cor 2.9 l. *Cf.* Rom 5.1, 11; 15.30; 1Cor 15.57; 1Thes 5.9.
m. *Cf.* 4Mc 18.24; Gal 1.5; Phil 4.20; 2Tm 4.18; Heb 13.21.

on behalf of your bishop. Both now and in the future, may he grant you and your descendants those better things, which "no eye has seen, nor ear heard, nor have entered into the heart of man: those things that God has prepared for those who love him,"[k] "through our Lord Jesus Christ,"[l] through whom be "glory" to almighty God "forever and ever. Amen."[9][m] I pray that you fare well in the Lord, my beloved brethren.[10]

9. Julius appropriates a formula found at the conclusion of several Pauline letters.

10. *Cf.* the valediction of *ep.* 2: ἐρρῶσθαι ὑμᾶς ἐν Κυρίῳ εὔχομαι, ἀγαπητοὶ καὶ ποθεινότατοι ἀδελφοί.

LETTER VI

To Julius, Bishop of Rome,
from Valens of Mursa and Ursacius of Singidunum
(Quoniam constat nos)

Introduction

The careers of Valens of Mursa and Ursacius of Singidunum spanned almost the entire Arian conflict. Throughout they espoused the *homoean* position.[1] While still quite young—the church historian Eusebius referred to them as "the fairest of God's youthful flock" among the Pannonians and Moesians (*V. C.* 4.43.3)[2]—they attended the Synod of Tyre (335), where Athanasius was eventually condemned and deposed. Both were members of the committee sent to the Mareotis to investigate the charges against him (Socr., *H. e.* 1.31; Ath., *Apol. sec.* 13; Iul., *ep.* 2.10).[3] When Athanasius fled to Constantinople and attempted to gain the support of Constantine, Ursacius and Valens were among those who approached the emperor on behalf of the council and succeeded in having Athanasius sent to Trier (Soz., *H. e.* 2.28; Socr., *H. e.* 1.35; Ath., *Apol. sec.* 87). In the following year, the two took part in the Council of Constantinople, chaired by Eusebius of Nicomedia, at which Marcellus of Ancyra was excommunicated and deposed.[4] Some years later, Valens tried

1. If Philostorgius is correct in naming Illyricum as the site of the exile of Arius, Secundus, and Theognis (*H. e.* 1.9c; *v.* n. 15 to the translation to *ep.* 2 above), it is easy to understand how these young bishops came into contact with anti-Nicene views. Athanasius reports that they were instructed by Arius (*ep. Aeg. Lib.* 7.4). Maris and Theognis served with Ursacius and Valens on the commission sent by the Council of Tyre to the Mareotis; *v.* n. 8 to the introduction to *ep.* 2 and nn. 4, 8, and 30 to the translation of *ep.* 2 above.

2. τὰ ... ἀνθοῦντα κάλλη τῆς τοῦ θεοῦ νεολαίας.

3. Eight years later (343) the Council of Sardica still refers to them as "irreligious and ignorant youths" (*ep.* 4.4). The presence of these western bishops at Tyre was, in itself, extraordinary; it was equally surprising that, at their age, they played such a prominent role.

4. For Marcellus' condemnation at this council, *v.* the introduction to *ep.* 1. Socrates' narrative (*H. e.* 1.35f.) presents the Council of Constantinople of 336, not as a distinct gathering, but as a continuation of the Council of Tyre-Jerusalem, which resulted in the exile of Athanasius in November of 335. Sozomen (*H. e.* 2.33.1) explicitly speaks of two different councils (2.33.1f.), though he provides no clear date (ἐν δὲ τῷ τότε = "at that time") for the second.

unsuccessfully to take the more prominent see of Aquileia by the violent intrigue described and condemned in *ep.* 4 (sec. 4), the letter sent to Julius from the Council of Sardica.

In its encyclical to the bishops of Egypt and Libya, the western Council of Sardica names Ursacius and Valens among the Eusebian leaders who ensured that the ecumenical convocation intended by the emperors never took place (Ath., *Apol. sec.* 48). At Sardica, the two Pannonians met only with the eastern delegation. They were among those who joined in the excommunication not only of Athanasius and Marcellus but also of Julius, Hosius of Cordova, and Paul of Constantinople.[5] The westerners replied by including Ursacius and Valens among the bishops they excommunicated and deposed (Hil., *fragg. histt.* B.2.1.8; Ath., *Apol. sec.* 36, 49; Iul. *ep.* 4.4). Constans and Constantius each accepted and backed the decisions taken by the bishops from his part of the empire (Ath., *Apol. sec.* 51–56).

As westerners condemned by the western council supported by Constans, Valens and Ursacius now realized that their hold on their sees had become tenuous. Further, in 345, after the death of the Eusebian Gregory, their enemy Athanasius was allowed to return to Alexandria. Hence, they began to come to terms with the western pro-Nicene and pro-Athanasian positions. That their change was strictly one of policy, not belief, is apparent from their renewed dedication to the eastern position immediately after the death of Constans in early 350.

The chronology of their rapprochement is not entirely clear. Nonetheless, it is agreed that the process began at a council held in Milan in 345. The main concern of this synod was the modalist teaching of Photinus, a former deacon of Marcellus who had recently been appointed bishop of Sirmium. Ursacius and Valens, presumably in attendance, must have been glad to concur with the condemnation of a pupil of the bishop of Ancyra whom the easterners, in general, re-

5. *V.* sec. 24 of the encyclical of the eastern Council of Sardica (Hil., *fragg. histt.* A.4.1); in the list of seventy-three signatories (A.4.3), the name of Valens is the last, that of Ursacius does not appear.

garded as the principal threat to orthodoxy. As the council was deliberating, a delegation of bishops brought from Antioch a lengthy document known as the *Ekthesis makrostichos* ("the Creed of Long Lines"), in which the easterners endeavored to explain to the westerners their mildly subordinationist Trinitarian theology. This document, which nowhere includes the Nicene term *homoousios,* had been rejected by the western council.[6] Ursacius and Valens do not seem to have taken a stand in support of the delegation that was presenting a theology very like, or perhaps identical to, their own.[7]

The Pannonians took a further step toward solidarity with the west two years later. Photinus, though condemned, had not been dislodged from Sirmium, and a second council was called to depose him. Though Hilary, our principal source for these events, does not explicitly state the site of this synod of 347, it is natural to assume that it too met in Milan, the only city mentioned in the sentence in which he refers to both gatherings.[8] Here, Ursacius and Valens are reported to have begged for a reconciliation with Julius. As appears from our *ep.* 6, they complemented their direct appeal with a written declaration that included anathemas of radical Arian positions.[9] It was probably later in that same year that the two Pannonians went

6. For the Creed of Long Lines, *v.* Ath., *Syn.* 26 and Socr., *H. e.* 2.19.7–28, and for an annotated translation, Stevenson, pp. 22–25. This document unites the fourth creed of Antioch and its anathemas with five anathemas produced by the eastern Council of Sardica and eight new paragraphs of explanation. The fourth creed of Antioch was that which, in the aftermath of Julius' synod in Rome, a delegation of easterners had tried to present to Constans at Trier; *v.* the introduction to *ep.* 3.

7. For this council of 345, *v.* Hil., *fragg. histt.* B.2.5.4 (*Fotinum, qui ante biennium iam in Mediolanensi synodo erat hereticus damnatus*); also Meslin, pp. 264–66; Hanson, *The Search,* pp. 309–14; and Barnes, *Athanasius and Constantius,* p. 231.

8. *V.* Hil., *fragg. histt.* B.2.5.4: *igitur ad tollendum ex episcopatu Fotinum, qui ante biennium iam in Mediolanensi synodo erat hereticus damnatus, ex plurimis prouinciis congregantur sacerdotes.* Löhr, (pp. 34–36), Meslin (pp. 266–68), and Hanson (*The Search,* p. 313) assume that this council met in Milan. Barnes (*Athanasius and Constantius,* p. 231) places it in Rome.

9. *V. ep.* 6: "just as in the written statement we presented at Milan, … we declare that we have now, as always, anathematized the heretic Arius as well as his supporters."

to Rome and presented to Julius *ep.* 6 itself.[10] According to Hilary, the petition of the two bishops was to be received back into the Church, but, as they had never, despite the western declaration at Sardica, been deposed from their sees, the issue was probably that of re-establishing communion between the church of Rome and those of Mursa and Singidunum.[11] They read their letter before Julius and his assembled clergy. This was a local synod, not a council attended by a large number of bishops, like those in Milan.[12]

Addressing themselves to "our most blessed Lord, Pope Julius," the bishops admit that they have previously made many grave accusations against Athanasius and that, when summoned by Julius to justify them, they had failed to reply. They excuse their previous conduct with the claim that they had been misinformed. Now that they know the charges are false, they are "very glad to embrace communion with Athanasius, especially since, in keeping with your usual kindliness, your Holiness has deigned to pardon our error." If either Athanasius or the easterners should in the future bring a malicious charge against them, they will seek the pope's advice before taking any action. Finally, now again, they publicly condemn the heretic Arius and his supporters, just as they had at the Council of Milan. In particular, they reject several propositions regarding the

10. Hilary (*fragg. histt.* B.2.6: *Exemplum epistulae quam … in urbe Roma olografa manu Valens perscripsit, etc.*), Athanasius (*H. ar.* 26), and Hosius (*v.* the letter preserved in *H. ar.* 44) place the reconciliation in Rome. Brennecke (pp. 62f.), referring to Hil., *fragg. histt.* B.2.9.1, has suggested that the Pannonians were readmitted to communion with the westerners at a synod held in Sirmium. As Barnes has shown (*Athanasius and Constantius,* p. 231), this is an unlikely interpretation; furthermore, the passage on which Brennecke depends may be lacunose.

11. Speaking of the council of 347, Hilary reports (B.2.5.4) *quam opportunitatem nancti Vrsacius et Valens Romanae plebis episcopum adeunt, recipi se in ecclesiam deprecantur et in communionem per ueniam admitti rogant.* Ursacius and Valens must have addressed themselves to Julius through his legates, as the bishop of Rome would not himself have attended this synod; *v.* n. 2 to the translation of *ep.* 4. Hilary's *recipi se in ecclesiam* is probably hyperbolic; *v.* Meslin, p. 268.

12. *V. ep.* 6: "we publicly declare before your Holiness, in the presence of all our fellow priests."

temporal creation of the Son.[13] The letter, composed by Valens, is signed also by Ursacius.[14]

As Hilary states, Julius received the Pannonians back into communion two years after the Romans, *i.e.,* the westerners, had condemned the teaching of Photinus (*fragg. histt.* B.2.7 and B.2.9.1; *v.* also Socr., *H. e.* 2.12).[15] Shortly afterward, Valens and Ursacius wrote Athanasius a brief letter, in which they offered to re-establish peace and communion (Hil., *fragg. histt.* B.2.8; Soz., *H. e.* 3.24; Ath., *Apol. sec.* 58).[16] For a brief time, the acrimonious controversy seemed to be settling in a manner favorable to the Nicene party.

13. They had subscribed to the same articles already in 343; *cf.* the anathemas of *ep.* 6 with those appended to the fourth creed of Antioch, which were incorporated into the creed produced by the eastern Council of Sardica; *v.* Stevenson, pp. 14f.; Meslin, p. 267; Hanson, *The Search*, pp. 298f.

14. *V.* the c. n. *ad loc.* and n. 7 to the translation.

15. On the chronology, *v.* Schwartz, "Zur Kirchengeschichte," pp. 144f. and Löhr, pp. 34–36. Barnes, who places the council of 347 in Rome, rather than Milan, assumes that Ursacius and Valens first repudiated their accusations against Athanasius at the Council of Milan in 345 and then, two years later, presented our *ep.* 6 to a second council in Rome; *v. Athanasius and Constantius,* p. 97. Yet this entails the difficulty of a hiatus of two years between the Pannonians' offer, and Julius' acceptance, of a rapprochement. Furthermore, the placement of the second council in Rome cannot claim any support from Hilary. Finally, the obvious sense of Hilary's narrative is that the Pannonians first approached the bishop of Rome at the council (*i.e.,* with their *libellus*) and shortly thereafter with their letter (*ep.* 6). Both events must have taken place in 347, *i.e.,* two years after the condemnation of Photinus by the westerners.

16. Barnes (*Athanasius and Constantius,* p. 97) postulates that, on their way home from Rome, Ursacius and Valens passed through Aquileia, where they met the priest Moses, who was carrying to Athanasius a letter of communion (*i.e., litterae communicatoriae, v. ep.* 4, sec. 5 and n. 10 *ad loc.*) from Paulinus, the newly elected bishop of Trier. The Pannonian bishops there gave Moses a copy of their letter to Julius and an additional short letter for Athanasius. This would explain several difficulties in the sources: Athanasius' statement (*H. ar.* 26) that he received a copy of the letter of Ursacius and Valens from Paulinus, Hilary's comment that the letter to Athanasius was sent "from Aquileia somewhat later" than the letter to Julius (*post aliquantum temporis ab Aquileia, postea quam hanc superiorem Roma emiserant; fragg. histt.* B.2.8), and the reference in the letter itself to a priest named Moses coming from Aquileia. Hosius must have been mistaken in his report that the letter to Athanasius was written before that to Julius; *v.* Ath., *H. ar.* 44. If, as Barnes believes, there was such a meeting in Aquileia, it is possible that Ursacius made the Greek translation of *ep.* 6 on the spot and then had Valens sign it. This

Letter VI

As one would expect, Ursacius and Valens composed their letter in Latin (Ath., *H. ar.* 26). It was probably cited frequently during the following decades when the two Pannonian bishops rejoined the anti-Nicene party.[17] Indeed, Sozomen (*H. e.* 4.11.7) tells us that, in 356 during his interview with Constantius in Milan, Pope Liberius referred to this letter and its acknowledgement of the untruthfulness of the charges against Athanasius.[18] Yet our sole witness to the Latin text is in the fragments of the anti-Arian historical work of Hilary of Poitiers (*fragg. histt.* B.2.6).[19]

In addition to the witness of Hilary, we have the Greek translation made by or for Athanasius (*Apol. sec.* 58.1–4).[20] Of the five *A* manuscripts, however, A^2 is defective and lacks *ep.* 6. Sozomen and Nicephorus copied this translation into their own church histories. For the relevant sections of Sozomen's history (3.23.2–5), we have two independent witnesses ($Sz^{1,3}$), and for those of Nicephorus one.[21] For the reconstruction of the translation, Sozomen and Nicephorus will be cited only where they differ from *A* and might more accurately reflect the original wording of Athanasius' translation. The stemma, thus, divides into two trunks: one direct source (Hilary) and one indirect (the translation of Athanasius). The major editors have been Faber (*Fab.*), Coustant (*Cou.*), and Feder (*Fed.*).[22] I have not differed from Feder in my choice of readings.

---

would explain the discrepancy between the subscription of the Latin original and that of the Greek translation; *v.* c. n. *ad* l. 21.

17. Athanasius cited it in *Apol. sec.* 1.

18. Theodoret (*H. e.* 2.16.11) mistakenly presents this letter as a petition for pardon submitted to the Council of Sardica.

19. On this work and the manuscript tradition of Hilary (*H*), *v.* the introduction to *ep.* 4 and App. A, item H.

20. If, as Barnes surmises (*v.* n. 16 above), the Panonnian bishops sent the letter to Athanasius themselves, they may have provided him with a Greek version. For an edition of the translation made by or for Athanasius, *v.* App. D. Athanasius cited the letter also in *H. ar.* 26.3, but the scribes of the extant manuscripts, rather than recopying the text, merely refer the reader to its earlier occurrence in the corpus.

21. *V.* App. A, items A, N, Sz.

22. For information on the editors and their editions, *v.* sec. 6 of the Introduction. I do not cite Baronius, because, as far as I can determine, he had no access to manuscript sources for the Latin text.

VI

Epistula Valentis mursensis et Vrsacii singidonensis ad Iulium, episcopum urbis Romae

Domino beatissimo papae Iulio Valens et Vrsacius.

Quoniam constat nos antehac multa grauia de nomine Athanasii episcopi litteris nostris insinuasse atque, litteris Sanctitatis Tuae conuenti, eius rei, de qua significauimus, non praestitisse rationem, profitemur apud Sanctitatem Tuam, praesentibus cunctis presbyteris fratribus nostris, omnia quae antehac ad aures nostras peruenerunt de nomine praedicti falsa nobis esse insinuata atque omnibus uiribus carere, atque ideo nos libentissime amplecti communionem praedicti Athanasii, maxime cum Sanctitas Tua, pro insita sibi beniuolentia, errori nostro ueniam fuerit dare dignata. profitemur etiam quod, si aliquando nos orientales uoluerint, uel idem Athanasius, malo animo ad causam uocare, citra Conscientiam Tuam non adfuturos.

l. 1 Valens et Vrsacius : Οὐρσάκιος καὶ Οὐάλης *A* = "*Ursacius and Valens*" **l. 3** litteris nostris : γραμμάτων ὑμῶν *SzN* : γ. *A* = "*in previous letters*" **l. 4** praestitisse *scr. Fab. Cou. Fed.* : praestitit se H^1 **ll. 6f.** nostras H^1, $Sz^{1,4}$ (*ἡμῶν*) : ues- *A* (*ὑμῶν*), *Cou.* = "*everything that had previously come to your ears*" **l. 7** de nomine praedicti : περὶ τοῦ ὀνόματος τοῦ προειρημένου Ἀθανασίου *A* = "*regarding the reputation of the aforementioned Athanasius*" **ll. 7f.** falsa nobis esse insinuata atque omnibus uiribus carere : ψευδῆ καὶ πλαστά ἐστι πάσῃ τε δυνάμει ἀλλότρια αὐτοῦ τυγχάνει· *A* = "*was only misinformation and fabrication entirely foreign to his character.*" **l. 12** ad causam uocare : περὶ τούτου εἰς κρίσιν καλέσαι *A* = "*summon us to a hearing for this*"

VI

To Julius, Bishop of Rome, from Valens of Mursa and Ursacius of Singidunum[1]

Valens and Ursacius, to our most blessed Lord, Pope Julius.

It is well known that, in our previous letter, we brought many serious accusations against the reputation of Bishop Athanasius, and that, though summoned by a letter of your Holiness,[2] we did not explain the basis of our charges. Therefore, we now publicly declare before your Holiness, in the presence of all our fellow priests,[3] that everything that had previously come to our ears regarding the reputation of the aforementioned was only second-hand misinformation completely devoid of validity. For this reason we are very glad to embrace communion with Athanasius, especially since, in keeping with your usual kindliness, your Holiness has deigned to pardon our error.[4] We further declare that, if at any time in the future the eastern bishops or Athanasius himself should maliciously decide to summon us to a hearing, we shall not present ourselves without informing Your Knowledge.

1. Hilary (B.2.6) introduces the letter with the heading: *Exemplum epistulae, quam post renuntiationem orientalium Athanasium reum non esse, in urbe Roma olografa manu, Valens perscripsit et Vrsacius subscripsit* = "a copy of the letter, which, after the easterners issued a statement that Athanasius was innocent of the charges brought against him, Valens composed in Rome, with his own hand, and to which Ursacius added his signature."

2. We have no other record of a letter sent by Julius to the Pannonians, unless they are referring to the summons to the Roman synod of 341.

3. The letter was written for public presentation at a local synod.

4. Julius must have given some indication that he was ready to accept their repudiation of the charges against Athanasius.

Hereticum uero Arrium sed et satellites eius qui dicunt *erat tempus, quando non erat filius,*[a] et qui dicunt ex nihilo filium,[b] et qui negant Dei filium ante saecula fuisse, sicut per priorem libellum nostrum, quem apud Mediolanum porreximus, et nunc et semper anathematizasse hac manu nostra, qua scripsimus, profitemur. et iterum dicimus heresim arrianam, ut superius diximus, et eius auctores in perpetuum damnasse.

Ego Vrsacius episcopus huic professioni nostrae subscripsi.

ll. 14–19 Hereticum uero Arrium sed et satellites eius … anathematizasse hac (hac *scr. Fab. Cou.* : ac H^1) manu nostra … profitemur. et iterum dicimus : Τὸν δὲ αἱρετικὸν Ἄρειον καὶ τοὺς ὑπερασπίζοντας αὐτοῦ … ἀναθεματίζομεν. ταῦτα δὲ τῇ χειρὶ ἑαυτῶν γράψαντες, ὁμολογοῦμεν πάλιν *A* = "*we … anathematize the heretic Arius and his supporters. Setting this down with our own hand, we again publicly state*" **l. 15** filium : Χριστὸς *SzN* (ὁ Χ.) = "*that Christ was created out of nothing*" **l. 16** Dei filium ante saecula fuisse : τὸν Χριστὸν θεὸν εἶναι θεοῦ υἱὸν πρὸ αἰώνων *A* = "*that Christ is God the Son of God before all ages*"
l. 21 Ego Vrsacius (Vrsac- *scr. Fab. Cou.* : Vrsat- *H*) episcopus huic professioni nostrae subscripsi : Ἐγὼ Οὐρσάκιος, τῇ ὁμολογίᾳ μου ταύτῃ παρών, ὑπέγραψα· ὁμοίως καὶ Οὐάλης *A* = "*I Ursacius have signed this confession of mine in person, as has also Valens*"

a. *Symb. nic.* (325)
b. *Symb. nic.* (325)

Furthermore, just as in the written statement we presented at Milan,[5] by this our hand, with which we have set down this letter, we declare that we have now, as always, anathematized the heretic Arius as well as his supporters, who say that "there was a time when the Son did not exist,"[a] and who say that the Son was created out of nothing,[b] and who deny that the Son of God existed before all ages.[6] Again we state, as we stated above, that we condemn for all time the Arian heresy and its originators.

I, Bishop Ursacius, have signed this, our confession.[7]

5. This statement has not survived.

6. Note that this last anathema takes a rather different form in the Greek; *v.* the c. n.

7. At the conclusion, Hilary adds *et manu Vrsaci:* ("and written in Ursacius' own hand:") to introduce the subscription *Ego Vrsacius episcopus huic professioni nostrae subscripsi.* Though it is apparent from the Latin original that Valens wrote the document, and Ursacius added his signature, in the Greek translation, their roles are reversed; *v.* the c. n.

Appendices and Indices

APPENDIX A

Manuscript Descriptions

Appendix A lists the literary and documentary sources and the manuscripts in which the correspondence of Julius was transmitted from antiquity. Each entry begins with a brief introduction to the source in which a letter (or the letters) has (or have) been preserved. The introduction often ends with a summary statement of the number of independent witnesses to that source. Following is a description of the relevant manuscripts. In each description, the first line contains the *siglum* used in this volume, the current location (city, library), and shelf-mark of the codex; in some cases, earlier shelf-marks are listed in parentheses. In the following lines, I provide, when possible, the approximate date of the manuscript, its provenance (a question mark indicates more uncertainty than usual), the number of folios (or pages, if the manuscript is so numbered), the number of columns per page and lines per column, the approximate size of the codex in millimeters, and the type of script. Unless stated otherwise, it is to be assumed that the manuscripts are made of parchment. These details are followed by other information relevant to this edition, especially the contents of the manuscript, its use by previous editors, and its relationship to other manuscripts. The description concludes, where applicable, with the volume and inventory number of images reproduced in the *CLA*.[1] The alphabetical portion of each *siglum* enables the reader to identify the source (the corpus of an author or collection of documents) within which each letter is transmitted; the superscript numbers place the manuscripts in rough chronological order. Manuscripts of a given source that do not contain pieces of the correspondence of Julius are not listed in this catalogue.

1. Lowe, *Codices latini antiquiores*. 11 voll. and *Supplement* (Oxford 1934–71).

Appendix A

A Athanasius, *Apologia secunda* or *Apologia contra Arianos*

Athanasius included copies of *epp.* 2 (*v.* secc. 20–35), 5 (*v.* secc. 52f.), and 6 (*v.* sec. 58) in his *Apol. sec.* Barnes has argued that Athanasius produced two editions of this work, the first to present his case to the Council of Antioch in 349 and a later revised edition to which he added two new chapters (89f.).[2] Our reconstruction of these letters as transmitted through the *Apol. sec.* depends on the five manuscripts listed below, which, according to Opitz, all descend from a collection of Athanasius' works made in fifth-century Constantinople.[3] Opitz has identified two subgroups: the first containing A^1 and A^2 (his *R* and *E*), the second A^{3-5} (his *B, O,* and *K*). I note, however, that in the case of our letters, these alignments show some variation.[4]

A¹ Paris, Bibliothèque Nationale, *gr. 474* (*Reg. 2284*)[5]

Copied in the 11th c. in Constantinople. 457 foll., with 1 column of 31 lines per page. 300 × 200 mm. Written in formal *Perlschrift* minuscule.[6] Contains various works of Athanasius, including the *Apol. sec.* (foll. 211–77). This manuscript was used by de Montfaucon and Coustant.

A² El Escorial, Real Biblioteca de San Lorenzo, *gr. Ω.III.15* (*548*)[7]

Copied in the 12th c. in Constantinople. x + 348 foll., with 1 column of 29 lines per page. 260 × 218 mm. Written in a formal ornamented minuscule.[8] Contains the *Apol. sec.* incomplete and disordered (foll. 165r–167r and 251v–313r). *Ep.* 6 is not found in this manuscript.

A³ Basel, Universitätsbibliothek, *A.III.4* (*gr. 32*)[9]

Copied in the late 12th / early 13th c. on Mt. Athos. i + 595 foll., paper, with 1 column of 30 lines per page. 335 × 250 mm. Written in a personal mi-

2. *Athanasius and Constantius,* pp. 99f.
3. *V. Untersuchungen,* p. 157.
4. See the introduction of each letter for details.
5. *V.* Opitz, *Untersuchungen,* pp. 54–57.
6. For this script, *v.* Barbour, p. xx.
7. *V.* Opitz, *Untersuchungen,* pp. 61–65; also de Andrés, vol. 3, pp. 195–97.
8. For this script, *v.* Barbour, p. xx.
9. *V.* Opitz, *Untersuchungen,* pp. 28–36. He lists (pp. 36f.) three fifteenth-century

nuscule.[10] Contains various works of Athanasius, including the *Apol. sec.* (foll. 346–83). This manuscript was the basis for the edition published by Commelinus.[11]

A^4 El Escorial, Real Biblioteca de San Lorenzo, *gr. X.II.11 (371)*[12]

Copied in the 13–14th c. 435 foll., with 1 column of *ca.* 33 lines per page. 285 × 210 mm. Written in a formal ornamented minuscule.[13] Contains various works of Athanasius, including the *Apol. sec.* (foll. 236–81).

A^5 Athos, Μονὴ Βατοπαιδίου, *6*[14]

Copied in the 14th c. in Constantinople. 361 foll., with 1 column of 30 lines per page. 300 × 220 mm. Written in an archaizing minuscule. Contains various works of Athanasius, including the *Apol. sec.* (foll. 119–64).

B *Collectio sanblasiana* (*Collection of St. Blaise*)[15]

This collection takes it name from codex B^1, which once belonged to the library of the Abbey of St. Blaise in the Black Forest. Compiled in Italy in the early sixth century, it contains our *ep.* 4 (the Synod of Sardica to Julius). As its latest items are five apocryphal pieces from the time of Pope Symmachus (498–514),[16] Wurm dated the collection to about 525.[17] Maassen thought that *B* was used by Dionysius Exiguus (*ca.* 470–*ca.* 556) for the collection known as the *Collectio dionysiana*, in which he combined canons of Latin and Greek councils and fourth- and fifth-century papal decretals.[18] Wurm and Turner, however, regarded the *Collection of St. Blaise* as dependent on the *Dionysiana.*[19] *B* was itself incorporated into the *Collection of Diessen*

---

apographs of A^3: Vienna, Öster. Nationalbib., *theol. gr. 2;* Vatican, BAV., *Ottob. gr. 456;* and Oxford, Bodl. Libr., *Roe gr. 29.*

10. For this script, *v.* Barbour, p. xxii.

11. De Montfaucon cites readings from this manuscript, but only as reported in the edition published by Commelinus; *v.* Opitz, *Untersuchungen,* p. 30.

12. *V. ibid.,* pp. 68–72; also de Andrés, vol. 2, pp. 278–81.

13. For this script, *v.* Barbour, p. xx.

14. *V.* Opitz, *Untersuchungen,* pp. 37–42.

15. *V.* Maassen, *Geschichte,* pp. 504–12 and Kéry, pp. 29–31.

16. *V.* Stürner, p. 81; and Fournier and Le Bras, vol. 1, p. 26.

17. *V. Studien und Texte,* pp. 88f.

18. *V. Geschichte,* pp. 436, 512. On Dionysius, *v.* Rist, "Dionysius [55] Exiguus," p. 494.

19. According to Turner ("Chapters . . ., VI," p. 19), its indebtedness to the *Dionysiana* is "occasional only"; *v.* also Wurm, p. 89.

(*Di*) and the so-called *Colbert Collection.*[20] It may have been a source also for the *Collection of St. Maur* (*M*).[21]

This collection is now preserved in seven manuscripts, of which only five contain *ep.* 4.[22] As their shared errors indicate, the Lavanttal and Lucca manuscripts were copied from one exemplar, the *Coloniensis* and *Parisinus 3836* from another.[23] The collection contains both canons and decretals. Though the latter follow no discernible order, Turner believed that the compiler thought he was arranging them chronologically.[24] No complete edition of this collection has ever been published. Turner edited the Greek councils and Damasus' letter *Post concilium nicaenum,*[25] and Wurm the *incipits* and *explicits* of each document.[26]

B[1] St. Paul in Lavanttal (Austria), Stiftsbibliothek, *7/1* (*XXIX Kassette I; XXV.a.7*)[27]

Copied in the 8th c. in Italy; belonged to the Abbey of Reichenau, transferrred in 1768 to St. Blaise in the Black Forest (Baden-Württemberg, Germany), in 1807 to St. Paul. 195 foll., with 1 column of 27–28 lines per page.

20. *V.* Stürner, pp. 81f. Maassen (*Geschichte,* pp. 536–42) coined the name "*Colbert Collection*" ("Sammlung der Colbert'schen Handschrift") for the compilation found in Paris, BN, *lat. 1455,* in which excerpts from the *Quesnel Collection* are appended to the *Collection of St. Blaise.* Since that manuscript is a unique hybrid, I do not follow this designation, but list the portion that contains *B* as my witness *B*[7]. On the *Quesnel Collection,* compiled *ca.* 500 in Gaul or at Rome and a source for Dionysius Exiguus, *v.* Van der Speeten, p. 384 and Kéry, pp. 27–29.

21. *V.* Wurm, p. 98; and Stickler, vol. 1, p. 98.

22. There may be another fragmentary witness to *B; v.* the description of *M*[1] below.

23. *V. EOMIA,* vol. 1.1.2, p. vi.; vol. 1.2.1, p. viii.; vol. 2.1, p. 34; Wurm, pp. 89, 265f.; Stürner, p. 80 and n. 59, p. 81.

24. Turner, "Chapters …, VI," p. 16. On the peculiarities of the collection, *v.* Stürner, pp. 79–82; Feder, *Studien,* vol. 1, pp. 24f.; Silva-Tarouca, pp. 664f.; Rius, p. 556; Fournier and Le Bras, vol. 1., pp. 51f., 98; Van Hove, pp. 161f.; Stickler, vol. 1, pp. 51f.; Turner, *EOMIA,* vol. 1.2.1, p. viii; vol. 1.2.3, p. 444; *id.,* "Chapters …, VI," pp. 9f. *Cf.* also Schwartz' review of *EOMIA,* p. 602, and *ACO,* vol. 2.2.2, pp. v–viiii.

25. *V. EOMIA,* vol. 1.2.1, pp. 281–95. Turner used *B*[1–3] and the former Phillipps *17849,* now in private hands. On that codex, *v.* Stürner, p. 81; Bischoff, "Frühkarolingische Handschriften," pp. 306–14; Munby, pp. 108f.; Schenkl, #2040, pp. 139–41; H.P. Kraus (firm), pp. 16–18; Plotzek and von Euw, pp. 35–40.

26. *V.* pp. 261–64.

27. *V.* Stürner, n. 53, p. 79; *EOMIA,* vol. 1.1.1, p. xii, where Turner refers to this manuscript as "*Codex Augiensis.*"

260 × 180 mm. Written in uncial (foll. 1–154) and early Italian caroline minuscule (foll. 154–95); corrections in several hands of the 9th c. *V. CLA*, vol. 10, #1457. Contains *B* (foll. 1r–154r).

B² Paris, Bibliothèque Nationale, *lat. 3836* (*Colb. 784, Reg. 3887.3.3*)[28]

Copied in the second half of 8th c. in northern France, perhaps at Corbie. 104 foll., with 1 column of 26 lines per page. 325 × 275 mm. Written in Corbie minuscule. Contains *B* (foll. 1–102). The first hand refers to a shorter text in Capua (fol. 34v), and another scribe mentions an exemplar at Trier (fol. 89r).[29] *V. CLA*, vol. 5, #554 and *CLA, Sup.*

B³ Cologne, Erzbischöfliche Diözesan- und Dombibliothek, *213* (*Darmstadt 2336*)[30]

Copied in the early 8th c. in England, Ireland, or Echternach; in Cologne already in the 8th c. ii + 143 + i foll., with 1 column of 25 lines per page. 328 × 230 mm. Written by several hands mostly in Anglo-Saxon majuscule and some minuscule; some corrections and notes in insular minuscule. Contains *B* (foll. 1r–143r). *V. CLA*, vol. 8, #1163 and *CLA, Sup.*

B⁴ Lucca, Biblioteca Capitolare, *490* (89)[31]

Copied *ca.* 800 in Lucca. 355 foll., with 1 column of 50 lines per page. 265 × 195 mm. Written, by at least thirty hands, in uncial and pre-caroline script. Contains the *Collection of St. Blaise* (foll. 236r–71v) and the *Epitome hispana* (foll. 288–309). *V. CLA*, vol. 3, #303b and *CLA, Sup.*

28. *V.* Burn, pp. xxxv–xxxviii; Turner, "Latin Lists," p. 77; von Dobschütz, pp. 157f.

29. *V.* Turner, "Chapters . . ., VI," p. 9; Maassen, p. 508.

30. *V.* Hofmann, pp. 36, 42–44; Turner, "Latin Lists," p. 77 and "Chapters . . ., VI," pp. 9f.; Bischoff, *Mittelalterliche Studien*, vol. 2, p. 327. Rufinus' letter to Pope Anastasius *Audivi quosdam*, carried by *B³* alone of the seven codices, must be considered a later addition to the *Collection of St. Blaise*. The entire manuscript with a description by von Euw is available online (http://www.ceec.uni-koeln.de/).

31. *V.* Schiaparelli, *Il codice 490;* Maassen, *Bibliotheca latina*, vol. 1, pp. 380f.; Stürner, n. 58, p. 81; Bischoff, "Panorama," pp. 249, 252.

B[7] Paris, Bibliothèque Nationale, *lat. 1455*
(*Colb. 3368, Reg. 3887.1.1.A*)[32]

Copied in the second half of 9th c. in the region of Rheims. 199 foll., with 2 columns, each of 42–44 lines, per page. 330 × 250 mm. Written in caroline minuscule. Contains the *Collection of St. Blaise* (foll. 1–77r) to which is appended excerpts from the *Collection of Quesnel* and the *Collection of St. Amand* (foll. 80–199).

C Cassiodorus, *Historia ecclesiastica tripartita*

In a distinguished public career of twenty years, Flavius Magnus Aurelius Cassiodorus filled numerous high offices in the government of the Ostrogothic kings of Italy. In about 550, he retired to his monastic foundation at Vivarium in the boot of Italy, where he dedicated himself to scholarly interests. There he sponsored the translation into Latin of important Greek works, including a continuation of the ecclesiastical history of Eusebius composed of excerpts from the works of Socrates Scholasticus, Sozomen, and Theodoret. This, the *Historia ecclesiastica tripartita,* was translated into Latin by the Greek monk Epiphanius Scholasticus. Among the materials excerpted from Socrates was his recension of Julius' letter to the Alexandrians (*ep.* 5). For our purposes, Cassiodorus provides an early indirect witness to the manuscript tradition of Socrates.

Walter Jacob (*Die handschriftliche Überlieferung*) lists the extant manuscripts and studies their relationships. These, numbering 138, are found to fall into six major families and their subgroups. Jacob concludes that an edition of the *Hist. trip.* should be founded only on the first family, which consists of twenty-seven members, divided into six subgroups.[33] In their

32. *V.* Maassen, *Bibliotheca latina,* vol. 1, pp. 195–98; von Dobschütz, p. 157; and Mordek, pp. 127f.

33. *V.* "Zusammenfassung," p. 160. Hanslik (*Cassiodori-Epiphanii H. e. trip.*, pp. xvi–xviii) reduces Jacob's six subgroups to just three: Ia, Ib, and Ic–f. The names of both Jacob and Hanslik appear on the edition of the *H. e. trip.* and the separately published study of the manuscripts, *Die handschriftliche Überlieferung.* By his death, Jacob had completed the main body of the latter; Hanslik added a summary and saw the volume through the press. While Jacob laid out the recension that underlies the edition, it was Hanslik who made the final choice of readings.

edition for the CSEL, Jacob and Hanslik make consistent use of only three of the twenty-seven (my *C*^{2}, *C*^{5}, and *C*^{13}) and cite two others (*C*^{3} and *C*^{10}) in places where these are defective.[34] To provide a broader spectrum of evidence from the direct tradition,[35] I have collated fifteen of the manuscripts, including most of the oldest representatives of Jacob's favored family I and at least one representative of each of the six subgroups of that class. In addition I have studied one each from classes III and IV.

C^1 Paris, Bibliothèque Nationale, *nouv. acq. lat. 1746*[36]

Copied in the 10th c. 183 foll., with 1 column of 32 lines per page. 320 × 240 mm. Written in caroline minuscule. Contains the complete *Hist. trip.* (foll. 1–180). A member of Jacob's family Ia.

C^2 Naples, Biblioteca Nazionale Vittorio Emanuele III, *VI.D.18*[37]

Copied in the 10th c. in southern France or Spain. 200 foll., with 1 column per page. 240 × 160 mm. Written in caroline minuscule. Contains the *Hist. trip.* through 11.1 (foll. 3–200); the last gatherings have been lost. A member of Jacob's family Ia, this manuscript is cited as *N* in the CSEL edition.

C^3 Leiden, Universiteitsbibliotheek, *Voss. lat. fol. 62*[38]

Copied in the mid-10th c. in southern France. 170 foll., with 1 column of 40–42 lines per page. 305 × 200 mm. Written in caroline minuscule; two hands (foll. 2–92 and 93–170). Contains the complete *Hist. trip.* (foll. 2–170). A member of Jacob's family Ia, it is cited as *L* in the CSEL edition.

C^4 London, British Library, *Harley 3630*[39]

Copied in the 13th c. in southern France; belonged to the church of St. Nazarc in Carcassonne. 191 foll., with two columns, each of 32 lines, per page. 350 × 250 mm. Written in gothic textual. Contains the complete *Hist. trip.* (foll. 1–179). A member of Jacob's family Ia.

34. *V.* their introduction to the text, pp. xvi–xviii.

35. *Cf.* the introduction to the Latin version of *ep.* 5 in App. C.

36. *V.* Jacob and Hanslik, *Die handschriftliche Überlieferung,* p. 8. For a fuller description, *v.* Zechiel-Eckes, *Rebellische Kleriker,* pp. 3–6.

37. Jacob and Hanslik, *Die handschriftliche Überlieferung,* pp. 8f.

38. *ibid.*, p. 9

39. *ibid.*, p. 10

C[5] St. Petersburg, National Library (Saltykov-Shchedrin), *F.v.I.11*[40]

Copied between 814 and 821 probably at Noirmoutier in the estuary of the Loire; belonged to the monastery of St. Peter of Corbie 11–17th c. 250 foll., with 2 columns, each of 31 lines, per page. 330 × 230 mm. Written, by numerous hands, in Corbie minuscule. Contains the complete *Hist. trip.* (foll. 1–248). A member of Jacob's family Ib, this manuscript is cited as *C* in the CSEL edition. *V. CLA*, vol. 11, #1606.

C[6] Paris, Bibliothèque Nationale, *lat. 17581*[41]

Copied in the 11th c. in France; belonged to the Collège de Navarre until 1796. 135 foll., with 2 columns, each of 37 lines, per page. 330 × 235 mm. Written in caroline minuscule. Contains the complete *Hist. trip.* (foll. 1–135). A member of Jacob's family Ib.

C[7] Angers, Bibliothèque Municipale, *676*[42]

Copied in the 11th c.; belonged to the monastery of Saint-Aubin at Angers; ii + 184 foll., with 2 columns, each of 34–38 lines, per page. 330 × 220 mm. Written in caroline minuscule. Contains the complete *Hist. trip.* (foll. 1–184). A member of Jacob's family Ib.

C[8] Vienna, Österreichische Nationalbibliothek, *3141*[43]

Copied in 1432 in Basel; 284 foll., with 1 column of 38 lines per page. 285 × 210 mm. Written in gothic cursive. Contains the complete *Hist. trip.* (foll. 1–163). A member of Jacob's family Ib.

C[9] Charleville-Mézières, Bibliothèque Municipale, *lat. 4*[44]

Copied in the 12th c.; belonged to the Abbey of Belval (Ardennes). 161 foll., with 1 column of 35 lines per page. 250 × 140 mm. Written in gothic textual. Contains the complete *Hist. trip.* (foll. 1–161). A member of Jacob's family Ic.

40. On this ms. *v.* Dobiaš-Roždestvenskaja, pp. 98–101; and Jacob, pp. 10f. In the *CSEL* edition, Jacob (p. xvii) erroneously reports the shelf-number as *1.10*.

41. *V.* Jacob and Hanslik, *Die handschriftliche Überlieferung*, p. 11.

42. *V. ibid.*, p. 13, where this manuscript is mistakenly identified as ms. *673*.

43. *ibid.*, p. 13

44. *ibid.*, p. 14

C[10] Monte Cassino, Archivio dell'Abbazia, *302*[45]

Copied in the 10th (foll. 2–133), 11th (foll. 134–57), and 12th cc. (foll. 158–89). 189 foll., with 1 column of 34 lines per page. 330 × 240 mm. The first two sections are written in 10th- and 11th-c. caroline minuscule, the third in beneventan script. Contains the complete *Hist. trip.* (foll. 2–189), but the original copy of the conclusion (from 7.24.22 on) was replaced in the 11–12th c. A member of Jacob's family Id, it is cited as *M* in the CSEL edition.

C[11] London, British Library, *add. 19961*[46]

Copied in the 10th c. in France (?). 215 foll., with 1 column of 27 lines per page. 270 × 210 mm. Written in caroline minuscule. Contains a lacunose text of the *Hist. trip.* (foll. 1–215). The sole member of Jacob's family Ie.

C[12] Florence, Biblioteca Medicea Laurenziana, *San Marco 383*[47]

Copied in the 10th c. 178 foll., with 1 column of 36 lines per page. 330 × 240 mm. Written in caroline minuscule. Contains the complete *Hist. trip.* (foll. 1–177). A member of Jacob's family If.

C[13] Chartres, Bibliothèque Municipale, *lat. 10*[48]

Copied in the 10th c.; belonged to the monastery of St. Peter of Chartres of the Benedictine Congregation of St. Maur. 164 foll., with 1 column of 42 lines per page. 340 × 250 mm. Written in caroline minuscule. Contained the complete *Hist. trip.* (foll. 8–164); now missing two gatherings (between foll. 103 and 104 and between foll. 143 and 144). A survivor from the bombardment of the library in World War II, this codex is extremely fragile; the binding was destroyed, and all the folia singed. A member of Jacob's family If, it is cited as *A* in the CSEL edition.

C[14] Vatican, Biblioteca Apostolica Vaticana, *Vat. lat. 1970*[49]

Copied in the 10th c. in Italy (?). 196 foll., with 1 column of 29 lines per page. 320 × 230 mm. Written in caroline minuscule. Contained the complete *Hist. trip.*, though the last lines of book 7 are now missing (foll. 1–193). A member of Jacob's family IIIf.

45. *V. ibid.*, p. 14; and Inguanez, pp. 123–25.
46. *V.* Jacob and Hanslik, *Die handschriftl. Überlieferung*, p. 15.
47. *ibid.*, pp. 15f.
48. *ibid.*, p. 17
49. *ibid.*, p. 31

C[15] Vatican, Biblioteca Apostolica Vaticana, *Pal. lat.* 823[50]

Copied in the 10th c. 158 foll., with 1 column of 30 lines per page. 295 × 225 mm. Written in caroline minuscule. Contains the *Hist. trip.* 1.9–8.13 (foll. 1–158) with some lacunae. A member of Jacob's family IVc.

Di *Collectio diessensis (Collection of Diessen)*[51]

This collection contains *ep.* 4 (the Synod of Sardica to Julius). As the latest item in this collection is a record of the acts of the Council of Clichy (626), all agree that it was produced in the middle, or toward the end, of the seventh century. Its place of origin is, however, controversial. Without discussion, Maassen and Kéry identify this as a Gallic collection.[52] Stickler specifies the region of the Rhone.[53] Stürner argues that the interest in Gallic councils indicates France as the likely place of origin.[54] Turner, however, suggested Reichenau.[55]

At the end of *Di,* a copyist has left a note in which he states that the documents have been drawn from three sources.[56] These have been identified as the collections of Chieti, St. Blaise, and Rheims.[57] The decretals were edited in 1757 by Amort.[58]

50. *ibid.,* p. 34

51. *V.* Maassen, *Geschichte,* pp. 624–36.

52. *V.* Kéry, pp. 3f.

53. p. 99

54. p. 85

55. Turner, *EOMIA,* vol. 1.2.1, p. vii. In his edition of Hilary, Feder, following Turner, classed it as a descendant of the *Collection of St. Blaise; v.* his stemma (CSEL 65, p. xlv) of *ep.* 4.

56. *V.* fol. 130v: *Expliciunt canones ex tribus libris editae quod inchoaui kl. apr. et consummui idus setb. id est diebus CLXVI ebdomatibus XXIII.* Unfortunately, he does not indicate the year.

57. The *Chieti Collection* (*Collectio teatina*) is found in Vatican, BAV, *Reg. lat. 1997,* the *Rheims Collection* in Berlin, Staatsbibl., *lat. 84*. Maassen (*Geschichte,* pp. 625, 631), followed by Scharnagl (p. 136), believed the third source to be the *Dionysiana. V.* also Mordek, p. 241. According to Stürner (n. 81 to p. 85), Turner was the first to identify the *Rheims Collection,* rather than the *Dionysiana,* as the third source. Turner's identifications of *B* and the *Rheims Collection* as sources of *Di* have won general support; *v.* Schwartz, *ACO,* vol. 1.2, pp. viiiif; Turner, *EOMIA,* vol. 1.2.1, pp. vif.; Wurm, pp. 99–101; Van Hove, p. 276.

58. vol. 2, pp. 273–594

Di Munich, Bayerische Staatsbibliothek, *Clm 5508* (Diessen 8)

Copied at the end of 8th c. at Salzburg; transferred to Diessen by the 15th c. 218 foll., with 2 columns, each of 30–33 lines, per page. 345 × 240 mm. Written, by several hands, in early caroline minuscule.[59] Contains the ninety-two items of the *Diessen Collection* (foll. 1–130); then three unnumbered items; then twenty-eight items (numbered 95 and following), a later addition, drawn mostly from the collection known as *Frisingensis prima. V. CLA,* vol. 9, #1247 and *CLA, Sup.*, p. 63.[60]

E *Collectio dionysiana aucta (Expanded Dionysiana Collection)*[61]

This collection takes its name from the fifth-sixth-century scholar Dionysius Exiguus, who compiled one of the first collections of conciliar canons and papal decretals, which became known as the *Collectio dionysiana.*[62] A later expanded version of the *Dionysiana,* presented by Hadrian I (pope from 772–95) in 774 to the court of Charlemagne, is known as the *Dionysio-Hadriana.* The *Expanded Dionysiana* is the name given to a collection that consists of the *Dionysio-Hadriana* plus an appendix of seventy-three more items. This recension was produced in the third quarter of the ninth c. in Rome or Ravenna.[63] It is a valuable source for much fourth-century papal correspondence, including that of Liberius, Damasus, and Siricius. Two manuscripts, E^2 and E^4, also transmit *ep.* 4, the letter of the Synod of Sardica to Julius.[64]

E^2 and E^4 derive from similar exemplars and present a closely similar

59. The script of the first pieces shows a strong French influence; *v.* Bischoff, *Die Südostd. Schreibschulen,* vol. 2, pp. 56f., 87–89.

60. *V.* also Stürner, pp. 84f.; von Dobschütz, pp. 146f.; Silva-Tarouca, pp. 662f. On the *Collectio frisingensis prima, v.* Kéry, pp. 2f.

61. *V.* Maassen, *Geschichte,* pp. 454–65; Kéry, pp. 20f.

62. *V.* the introduction to item B and n. 18 above.

63. For the date and provenance, *v.* Fowler-Magerl, pp. 44f.

64. There has also been debate over the relationship of the *Expanded Dionysiana* to the *Vatican Collection.* Wurm thinks that the compiler drew from the *Vatican Collection,* while others have postulated that the *Expanded Dionysiana* and the *Vatican Collection* descend from a common source; *v.* Wurm, pp. 35, 90 and Stürner, pp. 152f.

text of that letter. In the case of other papal letters, the first hand of E^2 tends to agree with the first hand of E^1 (Rome, Bibl. Vallicelliana, *A.5*).[65] The *Expanded Dionysiana* has never been printed.

E² Munich, Bayerische Staatsbibliothek, *Clm 14008* (*St. Emmeram A.8*)[66]

Copied sometime from the middle to the last third of the 9th c., perhaps in northern Italy;[67] in 885, it was brought to St. Emmeram in Regensburg. 259 foll., with 2 columns, each of 36 lines, per page. 440 × 325 mm. Written, by at least six hands, in caroline minuscule; many corrections, some Old Slavonic glosses. Contains the *Collectio Dionysio-Hadriana* (foll. 21r–149r) and expansions (foll. 149r–259v).

E⁴ Vatican, Biblioteca Apostolica Vaticana, *Vat. lat. 5845*[68]

Copied between 915 and 934 at Capua by monks who had fled Monte Cassino.[69] 327 foll., with 2 columns, each of 27 lines, per page. 300 × 225 mm. Written in beneventan script. Contains the *Collectio dionysiana* (foll. 1–135), then additions to form the *Dionysio-Hadriana* (foll. 135–58), then further additions to form the *Expanded Dionysiana. Ep.* 4 appears within the last section (foll. 189v–90v), after the letters of Liberius and before the letter of Damasus *Post concilium nicaenum.*

65. On this codex, *v.* Wurm, p. 35; Maassen, *Bibliotheca latina,* vol. 1, p. 407; Reifferscheid, vol. 53, pp. 339–46; von Dobschütz, p. 165; Turner, *EOMIA,* vol. 1.2.1, pp. ixf.

66. *V.* Wurm, n. 25, p. 36; Massigli, pp. 363–83; Bischoff, *Die Südostd. Schreibschulen,* vol. 1, pp. 225f.; Lettenbauer, pp. 246–69. Landau (pp. 62f.) discusses the role of this manuscript in the study of canon law at the monastery of Regensburg.

67. Bischoff (*Mittelalterliche Studien,* vol. 1, pp. 88–92) dates the manuscript to the last third of the ninth century and locates its origin in Rome rather than in northern Italy. This may have been the manuscript that Pope John VIII sent to the missionary Methodius.

68. This manuscript was described by the Ballerini (*v.* sec. 6 of the Introduction), who first named it *Collectio Additionum Dionysii;* their discussion and description is reprinted in PL, vol. 56, coll. 211–18. *V.* also Massigli, pp. 363–83.

69. *V.* Lowe, *Scriptura Beneventana,* vol. 1, plate 40.

Ep Epiphanius, *Panarion* or *Adversus LXXX haereses* (*Haer.*)

Epiphanius of Salamis composed his compendium of heresies (*Panarion* = "medicine chest," *praef.*) in the 370s. He quoted a copy of Marcellus of Ancyra's letter to Julius, our *ep.* 1, in ch. 72.2f. Of the extant manuscripts containing the section on Marcellus, the Jena manuscript is our only independent witness to the text of Epiphanius.

Ep¹ Jena, Universitätsbibliothek, *Bose 1*[70]

Copied in 1304. 174 foll., with 1 column of 46 lines per page. 320 × 225 mm. Written in a formal *Perlschrift.*[71] This is the second of two volumes of which the first is lost. Contains the last book of *Haer.* (foll. 1–112), *Exp. fid.* (foll. 113–20), *Anc.* (foll. 121–52), *Anac.* (foll. 152–61), *Mens.* (foll. 161–68), and passages from works of Chrysostom and the *Chronographia* of Nicephorus I.

Ep² Wroclaw, Biblioteka Uniwersytecka, *Rehdiger 240* (lost)[72]

Copied in the 15th c. Belonged to Bessarion and through him came to the Marciana in Venice. 327 foll., with 1 column of 46 lines per page. 375 × 260 mm. Contains *Haer.*, *Anc.*, the *Anac.*, and several smaller works. This is an apograph of *Ep¹* and its now-lost first volume.[73]

H Hilary of Poitiers, *Fragmenta historica*

The *fragg. histt.* are a collection of fragments drawn from one or more anti-Arian polemics composed by Hilary of Poitiers. They may be, or may include, portions of the work *Against Valens and Ursacius* (*liber aduersus Valentem et Ursacium*) mentioned by Jerome (*Vir. ill.* 100). Two pieces of the

70. *V.* Holl, *Die handschriftl. Überlieferung*, pp. 75–80.

71. For this script, *v.* Barbour, p. xx.

72. *V.* Holl, *Die handschriftl. Überlieferung*, pp. 63–68; also *Catalogus codicum graecorum*, pp. 63–65. Jan Gromadzki of the Department of Manuscripts has informed me that the manuscript was lost in 1945. I have not been able to learn whether this manuscript has been microfilmed. I have cited its readings from the reports of earlier editors.

73. Paris, BN, *gr. 835* (16th c.) also contains the end of the *Panarion* but is of no value as a witness to our text, for it is an apograph of Rome, Bibl. Angelica, *94*, itself a copy of *Ep²*. The *angelicanus* no longer contains the relevant sections; *v.* Holl, *Die handschriftl. Überlieferung*, pp. 69–72; also Omont, vol. 1, p. 157.

correspondence of Julius, *ep.* 4, from the Council of Sardica, and *ep.* 6, from Valens and Ursacius, are preserved amidst this material. Three copies of this collection survived until the sixteenth century and were used by early modern editors. Of the two still extant, only H^1 is an independent witness.[74] This codex was not, however, known to any editor prior to Feder. For a discussion of the relationships among the codices, *v.* the introduction (above) to *ep.* 4.

H¹ Paris, Bibliothèque de l'Arsenal, *483*[75]

Copied in the early 9th c. By 1778 it was in the possession of Baron von Heiss; from 1781 it was owned by the Marquis de Paulmy, whose library became the core of the collection of the Bibliothèque de l'Arsenal. 116 foll., with 1 column of 30 lines per page. 310 × 235 mm. Written in caroline minuscule. Contains Cassian, *Incarn.*, Ath., *ep. ad Epictetum;* Hil., *fragg. histt.* (foll. 76r–113v).

H² Rheims, Biblioteca Sancti Remigii, ms. (12th c.; lost)[76]

This manuscript was discovered by Jacques Sirmond in the monastic library of St. Remigius in Rheims and is now lost.

H³ *Cod. Pithoeanus* (15th c.; lost)[77]

Copied *ca.* 1400 (Coustant, *Hilarii … opera,* p. 1290) or *ca.* 1500 (Faber, *B. Hilarii … fragmenta,* p. 15) in France. This manuscript was discovered by Pithou and provided the basis for his editon of the *fragg. histt.*, which was completed and published by Faber. Coustant also drew from it for his edition of the complete works of Hilary. It was an apograph of H^1, which was not known to either Faber or Coustant.[78]

H⁴ Paris, Bibliothèque Nationale, *lat. 1700*[79]

Copied in the last decade of 16th c.; i + 270 pp., paper, with 1 column of 25 lines per page. Contains Hil., *fragg. histt.* (pp. 1–131) copied from H^3 for the use of Faber, whose annotations are written in the text and margins.

74. On the *fragg. histt.*, *v.* Feder, *Studien,* voll. 1–3; also Smulders, *Hilary of Poitiers' Preface;* and Wickham (*v.* Bibliography, Hilarius pictauiensis), pp. ix–xxvi.

75. *V.* the description by Schiktanz, pp. 22–29.

76. *V. ibid.*, pp. 21f. I have cited H^2 from Coustant's reports of its readings.

77. *V.* Schiktanz, p. 14–19.

78. *ibid.*, p. 29; Feder, *Studien,* vol. 1, p. 11

79. *V.* Schiktanz, pp. 19f.

M *Collectio Sancti Mauri* (*Collection of St. Maur*)[80]

The *Collection of St. Maur* contains our *ep.* 4 (the Council of Sardica to Julius). In its present form, its latest item is the decree of the Roman Synod of 595. Maassen, however, has suggested that in its original form the latest item was the Acts of the Synod of Orléans of 549. In either case the collection certainly dates to the latter half of the sixth century.

It was probably compiled in Gaul; the regions of Narbonne, Arles, Bourges, and Tours have all been suggested as its place of origin.[81] Its sources probably include the *Collection of Quesnel*[82] and, perhaps, the *Collection of St. Blaise.*[83] It was named from M^2, which once belonged to the monastery at Saint-Maur-des-Fossés near Paris. There are three extant manuscripts, but no published edition.[84]

M^1 The Hague, Museum Meermanno-Westreenianum, *10.B.4* (*9; Clarom. 562; Meerm. 583*)

Copied in the late 8th (foll. 1–30, 54–197) and 8–9th cc. (foll. 31–53 = restoration) in northern or central France.[85] 197 foll., with 1 column of 27 lines per page. 285 × 185 mm. Contains the *Collection of St. Maur* (foll. 1–30). Written in late 8th-c. minuscule and early caroline minuscule (foll. 31–53). *V. CLA*, vol. 10, #1572a.[86]

80. *V.* Maassen, pp. 613–24; Kéry, pp. 45f.

81. Duchesne (*Fastes épiscopaux,* n. 6, p. 144) suggested Narbonne, Turner ("Chapters . . ., VII," p. 9) Arles, Stürner (p. 84 and n. 76) the region of Bourges or Tours.

82. *V.* Stürner, p. 84.

83. *V.* Turner, "Chapters . . .,VII," pp. 6f.; Wurm, p. 98; and Stickler, vol. 1, p. 98. Turner (*ibid.,* p. 7) regards the *Collectio hispana* as an additional source.

84. There is a description of a fourth manuscript (Laon, last decade of the 8th c.), now lost, by the church historian É. Baluze in Paris, BN, *Baluze 2*; *v.* Mordek, n. 81, p. 55.

85. Lowe (*CLA*, vol. 10, #1572a) suggests Rheims, Bischoff ("Panorama," p. 241 and n. 57) the vicinity of Bourges.

86. Turner concludes that only one leaf of the collection, the last of signature D (which now ends at canon 19 of Nicaea, "On deacons") is missing. He points out ("Chapters . . ., VII," p. 5) that foll. 31–53 "form an intrusive element which interrupts the original arrangement of the gatherings, is written in a quite different hand, and takes up more space on the page." These are connected with the

M^2 Paris, Bibliothèque Nationale, *lat. 1451* (*Colb. 1868; Reg. 3887.9.9*)

Copied between 800 and 816, in the region of Tours; belonged to the monastery of Saint-Maur-des-Fossés near Paris. 108 foll., with 2 columns, each of 35 lines, per page. 320 × 230 mm. Written in caroline minuscule (foll. 25v–108v). *V. CLA,* vol. 5, #528.[87]

M^3 Vatican, Biblioteca Apostolica Vaticana, *Reg. lat. 1127*

Copied in the second quarter of 9th c. in Gaul; at the Abbey of St. Cybar in Angoulême by the 11th c.;[88] 165 foll., with 2 columns, each of 27–28 lines, per page. 373 × 310 mm. Written in caroline minuscule.[89]

N Nicephorus Callistus, *Historia ecclesiastica*

In the early fourteenth century, the monk Nicephorus Callistus Xanthopulus wrote a work of ecclesiastical history that incorporated documents from the works of the earlier Greek church historians. He transcribed our *ep.* 5 (Julius to the priests, deacons, and laity of Alexandria) from Socrates (Socr. 2.23.15–32 = Niceph. 9.22) and Athanasius' Greek translation of *ep.* 6 (Valens and Ursacius to Julius) from Sozomen (Soz. 3.23.2–5 = Niceph. 9.27).[90] His history survives in a single independent manuscript.[91]

Collection of St. Blaise; v. also Levison, pp. 513–18; Turner, *EOMIA,* vol. 1.2.3, p. ix; Stürner, p. 83 and n. 72.

87. Turner ("Chapters . . ., VII," p. 3), believed that M^1 was the "common ancestor" of both M^2 and M^3. Lowe first agreed that M^2 was a direct copy of M^1 (*CLA,* vol. 5, #528) and then later opined that it was "closely related" to M^1 (*CLA,* vol. 10, #1572a). Yet, from my own examination of the text of the *tomus Damasi* presented by these manuscripts, I conclude that M^{1-3} were all copied from a common exemplar. For a complete description of contents of M^2, *v.* Maassen, *Geschichte,* pp. 614–22, and *Bibliotheca,* vol. 2, pp. 173–84.

88. *V.* Turner, "Chapters . . ., VII," pp. 1f.

89. Dr. Paolo Vian, Director of the Manuscript Division of the BAV, has kindly provided the dimensions of this manuscript for which no full codicological description has yet been published. A few pages of *Reg. lat. 1127* have been copied into another manuscript written at Angoulême, now Paris, BN, *lat. 2400* (early 11th c.). The bulk of this book is occupied by the *Herovalliana* and the *Canones ad Hugonem et Robertum eius filium Francorum reges; v.* Mordek, n. 12, p. 5; n. 81. p. 55; and n. 65, p. 112.

90. *V.* PG, vol. 146, coll. 315–18 and 327–30.

91. On the editons of Nicephorus, *v.* Gentz, esp. pp. 1–3 and 201–08.

N Vienna, Österreichische Nationalbibliothek, *hist. gr.* 8[92]

Copied *ca.* 1320. iii + 501 foll., with 1 column of 40–43 lines per page. 340 × 250 mm. Written in renaissance minuscule. Contains Nicephorus' history (foll. 1–498). Gentz suggests that the copying and illustration of this book were commissioned by the author himself; it would have been a presentation copy for Emperor Andronicus II (1282–1328).[93] Paris, BN, *suppl. gr.* 515 (17th c.) is an apograph of this codex.

P The Pseudo-Isidorian Decretals

The collection known as the Pseudo-Isidorian decretals was compiled in France *ca.* 850. In its standard recension, this contains only one genuine fourth-century letter, Damasus' *Per filium meum.* Neveretheless, two manuscripts that carry the decretals contain additional materials, including the Latin translation of Iul., *ep.* 5 (Julius to the priests, deacons, and laity of Alexandria = Socr. 2.23.15–32).[94] Both descend from a source independent of the extant manuscripts of Cassiodorus.

P¹ Florence, Biblioteca Nazionale Centrale, *Conv. soppr. J.3.18*[95]

Copied in the 10th–11th c. 174 foll., with 1 column of 39–40 lines per page. 335 × 270 mm. Written in gothic textual. Contains, in addition to the first and third parts of the Pseudo-Isidorian decretals, Iul. *ep.* 5 (foll. 111r–v), a letter of Liberius, and three letters of Damasus.

P² Bernkastel Kues, St. Nikolaus-Hospital/Cusanusstift, Bibliothek, 52[96]

Copied in the 12th c. at St. Jakobskloster in Lüttich. 331 foll., with 2 columns, most of 70 lines, per page. 280 × 195 mm. Written in gothic textual. Contains (foll. 1–82) part of the Pseudo-Isidorian decretals with additional material including Iul., *ep.* 5 (foll. 37v–38r).

92. For a description, *v.* Hunger, vol. 1, p. 14.

93. *V.* pp. 1f.

94. On this collection and its manuscripts *v.* S. Williams, *Codices Pseudo-Isidoriani;* and Kéry, pp. 100–114. *Cf.* sec. 4 of the Introduction above.

95. *V.* S. Williams, pp. 21–23.

96. *ibid.*, pp. 9f.

Appendix A

Sc Socrates Scholasticus, *Historica ecclesiastica*

Socrates intended his church history, completed in Constantinople about 440, to serve as a continuation of Eusebius', and like Eusebius, he incorporated numerous primary sources into the narrative. One of these was our *ep.* 5 (Julius to the priests, deacons, and laity of Alexandria; 2.23.15–32). We have three manuscripts (*Sc¹*, *Sc²*, and *Sc⁴*) that are independent of each other. In addition, *Sc³*, an apograph of *Sc¹*, can be consulted for places where the reading of its parent is in doubt.[97]

Sc¹ Florence, Biblioteca Medicea Laurenziana, *plut.* 69.5[98]

Copied in the 11th c.; belonged to the monastery of St. Michael at Sosthenion. 290 foll., with 1 column of 35 lines per page. 280 × 210 mm. Written in formal plain minuscule. Contains books 1–6 (foll. 1–190) followed by Euag. Schol., *H. e.* This codex was originally part of a book that contained also Eus., *H. e.*, but the section containing Eusebius' work has been detached and is now Florence, Bibl. Med. Laur., *plut. 70.20*. For their editions of Socrates, Valesius and Hussey had to rely on collations of this manuscript made by others; those used by Hussey were inaccurate. There are four apographs of this manuscript: Patmos, Library of the Monastery of St. John, *gr. 688* (13th c.), Alexandria, Patriarchal Library, *60* (*v. Sc³* below), Venice, Bibl. Naz. di S. Marco *gr. 337* (mid-14th c.),[99] and Florence, Bibl. Med. Laur., *plut. 69.7* (15th c.).

Sc² Florence, Biblioteca Medicea Laurenziana, *plut. 70.7*[100]

Copied in the 10th c. 391 foll., with 2 columns, each of 34 lines, per page. 350 × 275 mm. Written in early angular minuscule. Contains Eus., *H. e.* (foll. 1–172) and *M. P.* (foll. 173–87), Socr. *H. e.* (foll. 188–391). Hussey had to rely on inaccurate collations of this manuscript.

97. On the manuscript tradition of Socrates, *v.* Hansen, *Sokrates Kirchengeschichte*, pp. ix–xxxiii.

98. *ibid.*, pp. ix–xi

99. Paris, BN, *gr. 1443* and El Escorial, Real Bibl. de San Lorenzo, *gr. Y.I.2* (*295*), both of the 16th c., are copies of Marciana *gr. 337; v. ibid.*, p. xii.

100. *V.* Hansen, *Sokrates Kirchengeschichte*, pp. xii–xviii.

Sc^{3} Alexandria, Patriarchal Library, *Alex. 60* (*Cairo 86*)[101]

Copied in the 13th c. 447 foll., paper, with 1 column of 38 lines per page. 275 × 210 mm. Written in a personal minuscule. Contains Soz., *H. e.* (foll. 12–144), Thdt., *H. e.* (foll. 145–243), Socr., *H. e.* (foll. 247–394), and Euag. Schol., *H. e.* (foll. 403–47). The text of Socrates, copied directly from *Sc*^{1}, was in turn copied into Venice, Bibl. Naz. Marc. *gr. 339* (mid-14th c.).

Sc^{4} Athos, Μονὴ Ξηροποτάμου, *226* (*Athos 2559*)[102]

Copied in the 14th c. 293 foll., paper, with 1 column of 26 lines per page. Written in a formal ornamented minuscule. Contains the chronicle of Michael Glykas, Socrates' *H. e.* (foll. 57–293), incomplete and lacunose.

Sz Sozomen, *Historia ecclesiastica*[103]

In his continuation of Eusebius' church history, completed about 450, Sozomen included a transcription (*H. e.* 3.23.2–5) of Athanasius' translation of *ep.* 6 (Valens and Ursacius to Julius). Though Sozomen's history has survived in numerous manuscripts, there are only three independent witnesses to the text (*Sz*$^{1-3}$). As *Sz*^{2} (Venice, Bibl. Naz. di San Marco *gr. 917*)[104] does not contain book 3, we must depend on *Sz*^{1} and *Sz*^{3} for the reconstruction of the Greek translation of *ep.* 6 as transmitted by Sozomen. *Sz*^{4}, an apograph of *Sz*^{1}, can be consulted for places, where the reading of its parent is in doubt.

Sz^{1} Alexandria, Patriarchal Library, *Alex. 60* (*Cairo 86*)[105]

V. Sc^{3} above. The text of Sozomen was copied into *Vat. gr. 976* (*v. Sz*^{4} below).

101. *V. ibid.*, pp. xif.; also Moschonas, pp. 50f.

102. Hansen, *Sokrates Kirchengeschichte,* pp. xviiif.

103. On the extant manuscripts, *v.* Hansen, *Sozomenus Kirchengeschichte*, pp. ix–xxxiii.

104. On this codex, *v. ibid.*, pp. xxi–xxiii.

105. *V. ibid.*, pp. xiv–xvi and Moschonas, pp. 50f.

Sz^3 Oxford, Bodleian Library, *Baroc. 142*[106]

Copied in the 14th c. 292 foll., with 1 column of 27–28 lines per page. 250 × 165 mm. Witten in a personal minuscule. Contains Soz., *H. e.* (foll. 9–153) and Euag. Schol., *H. e.* (foll. 155–204) with other miscellaneous items. In the 16th c., the text of Sozomen was copied into Brit. Libr., *Egerton 2626* and Paris, BN, *gr. 1444*.[107]

Sz^4 Vatican, Biblioteca Apostolica Vaticana, *Vat. gr. 976*[108]

Copied in the 14th c. 248 foll., paper, with 1 column of 26–31 lines per page. 300 × 205 mm. Witten in a personal minuscule. Contains Soz., *H. e.* (foll. 1–244) copied directly from *Sz^1*. In the 15th c., the text of Sozomen was copied into Venice, Bibl. naz. Marc., *gr. 691*.[109]

Td *Collectio Theodosii diaconis* (*Collection of Theodosius the Deacon*)[110]

This collection is our only source for many items, including our *ep.* 3 (Hosius and Protogenes to Julius), belonging to the earliest papal correspondence. It is named after the scribe who wrote his name at the conclusion of the archetype of our sole copy.[111] The main components of the collection are a rather extensive series of Greek canons and a dossier of documents centering around the Council of Sardica. As the collection begins with the acts of the Council of Carthage of 419 and contains other material

106. *V.* Hansen, *Sozomenus Kirchengeschichte,* pp. ix–xii.

107. On these two manuscripts, *v. ibid.,* pp. xii–xiv.

108. *ibid.,* pp. xviif.

109. *V. ibid.,* pp. xix–xxi. There are three 16th–17th-c. apographs of Venice, Marciana *691*: Leiden, Universiteitsbibliotheek, *gr. bibl. publ. 33A*; Paris, BN, *gr. 1445*; and El Escorial, Real Bibl. de San Lorenzo, *gr. Y.I.2* (*295*).

110. On this collection, *v.* esp. Maassen, *Geschichte,* pp. 546–51; Kéry, p. 38; Schwartz, "Über die Sammlung des Codex Veronensis LX" and "Die Sammlung des Theodosius"; Telfer, "The Codex Verona LX (58)"; Muzzioli, "Il codice Veronese LX (58)"; Munier, "Cinq canons inédits," p. 22; and the monograph of Field.

111. In this colophon, Theodosius tells us that he copied this material "from faulty copies" (*de mendosis exemplaribus transtuli*). Yet as this colophon is itself carelessly written, it is obviously not in Theodosius' own hand. It is unclear what, if any, role he played in the collection of the documents.

regarding North Africa, it is usually regarded as North African in origin. Yet, as Field suggests, it may have been assembled in its present form in Verona sometime between the eighth and tenth centuries.[112] There is no complete published edition of this manuscript.[113] The *Historia acephala,* a Latin translation of a truncated Greek biography of Athanasius, is preserved in the same manuscript as the canonical collection.

Td Verona, Biblioteca Capitolare, *LX* + Rome, Biblioteca casanatense, *378 (A.III.24)*

Copied in the second half of 8th c., probably at Bobbio; in Verona by the 10th c. 126 foll. (+ 7 in Rome),[114] with 1 column of 28–30 (foll. 1–35) and 26–28 lines per page (foll. 37–126). 265 × 205 mm. Written in half-uncial. *V. CLA,* vol. 4, ##416 and 510 and *CLA, Sup.*

112. *V.* pp. 115, 58–62.

113. Turner has used parts of the collection in his edition of the early councils in *EOMIA*. Field (*On the Communion of Damasus and Meletius*) provides a description of the codex and a critical edition of foll. 43v–47r.

114. The seven folios now in Rome originally formed part of the eight-folio signature D, of which one folio has been lost. This signature, which should stand between foll. 71 and 72, carries the *Canones apostolorum; v.* Ceresi, vol. 4, pp. 105f.

APPENDIX B

Items Falsely Attributed to Julius

In sec. 4 of the Introduction, I reviewed the items that have been falsely attributed to Julius.[1] Here I provide supplementary information bearing mostly on the transmission of each text and the edition(s), if any, in which it has been printed. For each item (labeled A–Z as above), I provide a heading with the Greek or Latin *incipit,* or another commonly used title, followed by the numerical designation of Jaffé-Kaltenbrunner.[2] Where relevant, I provide that of the *CPG*. Though I have listed all known letters or excerpts from letters falsely attributed to Julius, I have not been able to provide an exhaustive account in every case.[3]

The Apollinarian Forgeries (A–J)

A. Ἅγιον ἐξ ἀρχῆς / *De unione* (JK †191; *CPG* #3646)[4]

Lietzmann has edited the Greek text on the basis of BAV, *Vat. gr. 1431* and

1. The only text attributed to Julius not included in this appendix is the Jacobite liturgy that has been edited by Raes (vol. 3.1, #22, pp. 73–101). This was excluded on the ground that it is not a letter. Although other texts here listed no longer appear in the context of letters, they were preserved because they were believed to have been taken from papal letters and decrees, and, thus, to have the same validity as conciliar canons. Translations of all the pseudonymous writings attributed to Julius here listed are available at www.fourthcentury.com.

2. A dagger (†) indicates that Jaffé-Kaltenbrunner identified the item as a forgery.

3. There are so many unpublished florilegia and patristic manuscripts that it is not yet possible to enumerate all the contexts in which a piece has been, at least partially, preserved. For example, Graf ("Zwei dogmatische Florilegien," pp. 354f.) states, with no further detail, that a collection of material on monophysite christology in BAV, *Vat. arab. 178* (13th c.) contains some citations attributed to Julius.

4. *V.* the discussion in Lietzmann, pp. 133–35. Mai (Script. vet., vol. 7, pp. 165–68), prints the Greek text under the page heading *Scripta Supposita.* Migne, however, reprints the text at the beginning of the *Monumenta genuina* of Julius (PL, vol. 8, coll. 873–75).

Vat. gr. 1455 and Munich, Bayer. Staatsbibl., *gr. 207*.[5] The letter is preserved also in two different Syriac translations, both of which have been edited by Flemming and Lietzmann from London, Brit. Libr., *add. 14597* (dated to 569; beginning on fol. 101v) and *add. 14604* (7th c.; beginning on fol. 106v).[6] The last sentence of sec. 6 through sec. 8 was spread widely as an independent citation.[7] Other brief citations are found in a variety of patristic works.[8]

5. Lietzmann (pp. 185–93), prints the text under the title Περὶ τῆς ἐν Χριστῷ ἑνότητος τοῦ σώματος πρὸς τὴν θεότητα. He reports that the passage extending from the last sentence of sec. 6 through sec. 8 appears twice in two of these manuscripts.

6. *V., ibid.*, pp. 16–24.

7. This excerpt also appears in:

1) Tim. II al., *Constan.*, which is preserved in three translations, two Syriac (1.a–b) and one Ethiopic (1.c): a) within Zach. Mit., *H. e.* 4.12; *v.* CSCO, vol. 83, p. 191 (Syriac text) and vol. 87, p. 132 (Latin translation); Hamilton and Brooks, p. 86 (English translation); b) within a compilation of Timothy Aelurus' treatises in London, Brit. Libr., *add. 12156* (dated to 562); *v.* Ebied and Wickham, p. 335 (Syriac text) and p. 354 (English translation); c) in Paris, BN, *eth. 113; v.* Zotenberg, pp. 129f.;
2) Seu. ant., *Cens.; v.* CSCO, vol. 244, p. 75 (Syriac text) and vol. 245, p. 57 (French translation);
3) an anonymous Greek florilegium of the ninth or tenth century (Lietzmann, p. 96) on fol. 302v in BAV, *Vat. gr. 1431,* under the title Ἐκ τοῦ περὶ σαρκώσεως λόγου;
4) *Die Bekenntnis der Väter* (*v.* item C below); for a description of the excerpt, *v.* Graf, "Zwei dogmatische Florilegien," p. 273, #52, and his German translation in "Unechte Zeugnisse," pp. 222f.;
5) Mich. Syr. (*v.* item E below), *Chron.* 9.1; *v.* Chabot, *Chronique,* vol. 4, p. 245 (Syriac text) and vol. 2, p. 134 (French translation).

8. These include:

1) citations in the works of Seu. ant.: a) the second half of sec. 4 through the first third of sec. 5 in *Gram.* (*or.* 3.23); *v.* CSCO, vol. 101, p. 16 (Syriac text) and vol. 102, p. 11 (Latin translation); b) the first third of sec. 5 in *Gram.* (*or.* 3.6, 14, 17, 22, and 41); *v.* CSCO, vol. 93, pp. 72f., 237, 278, 286, and vol. 101, pp. 3, 298 (Syriac text) and vol. 94, pp. 51, 166, 196, 201, and vol. 102, pp. 2, 220 (Latin translation); c) the first third of sec. 5 also in *Serg. gram.* (*Seu., ep.* 1); *v.* CSCO, vol. 119, p. 88 (Syriac text) and vol. 120, pp. 64f. (Latin translation); d) the first two thirds of sec. 5 in *Gram.* (*or.* 3.17); *v.* CSCO, vol. 93, pp. 280, 301f. (Syriac text) and vol. 94, pp. 197, 212 (Latin translation); e) all of sec. 5 in *Gram.* (*or.* 3.40); *v.* CSCO, vol. 101, p. 267 (Syriac text) and vol. 102, p. 196 (Latin translation); f) sec. 7 in *Gram.* (*or.* 3.6); *v.* CSCO, vol. 93, pp. 71f. (Syriac text) and vol. 94, pp. 50f. (Latin translation); g) sec. 8 in *Serg. gram.* (*Seu., ep.* 2); *v.* CSCO, vol. 119, pp. 131f. (Syriac text) and vol. 120, p. 99 (Latin translation); h) the last line of sec. 15 through the first third of sec. 17 in *Gram.* (*or.* 3.40); *v.* CSCO, vol. 101, p. 272 (Syriac text) and vol. 102, p. 200 (Latin trans-

lation); i) sec. 17 in *Neph.* (*or.* 2); *v.* CSCO, vol. 119, p. 29 (Syriac text) and vol. 120, p. 22 (Latin translation); j) sec. 17 in *Serg. gram.* (*Seu., ep.* 1); for text and translation, *v.* c above; k) the last two thirds of sec. 17 in *Gram.* (*or.* 3.40); *v.* CSCO, vol. 101, p. 266 (Syriac text) and vol. 102, p. 196 (Latin trranslation);

2) excerpts from secc. 2 and 8 in Leont. Byz., *Apoll.*, where Leontius cites Tim. ber., *ep. ad Hom.; v.* Mai, Spic., vol. 10.2, pp. 138–40 (rpt. PG, vol. 86.2, col. 1961);

3) the first two thirds of sec. 5 (Gray, pp. 122f. and 132f.), a short sentence from the middle of sec. 12 (pp. 132f.), and the last words of sec. 17 (pp. 74f. and 94f.) in Leont. H., *Monoph.;* on the composite nature of this work, *v.* Gray, p. 15;

4) two excerpts from Tim. II al., *Contra eos,* preserved only in Armenian: a) the last line of sec. 6 through sec. 8 (Ter-Merkerttschian and Ter-Minassiantz, pp. 9f.; Schwartz, *Codex Vat. gr. 1431,* p. 99); b) sec. 8 (Ter-Merkerttschin and Ter-Minassiantz, p. 187; Schwartz, *Codex Vat. gr. 1431,* p. 113);

5) sec. 17, quoted in a work of Ephraem of Antioch (bishop 526–44) excerpted by Phot. constan., *Bibl., cod.* 229 (sec. 265b); Coustant prints the Greek text (Ὅθεν ἐξ ἀνάγκης; App., vol. 1, col. 81) and his Latin translation (*ibid.*, col. 82);

6) excerpts from sec. 5 in two Syriac works preserved in London, Brit. Libr., *add. 12155* (8th c.): a) on foll. 142r–v in a tract (foll. 136r–142v) against the monophysite views of Probus written by the monks of Antioch in 596 (a second copy of this tract is preserved on foll. 107r–115r of *add. 14533; v.* Wright, #859); b) on foll. 167r–v in a letter (foll. 164r–169v) written in support of Peter of Callinicum, patriarch of Antioch (581–91), in response to five propositions from the monks of the monastery of Maro at Armanaz; *v.* Wright, #857;

7) excerpts from secc. 4f. (*v.* Lietzmann, p. 187, ll. 3–8), in Syriac translation in a synodal letter of John VI Sarigta, Jacobite patriarch of Antioch (965–85), to Minas II, Coptic patriarch of Alexandria (956–74); *v.* the Latin translation by Renaudot (p. 360), rpt. Achelis (frag. ii, p. 281), who apparently confuses these fragments, which he mistakenly states are drawn from "*Reg.* 432," with those in J (*v.* below);

8) the first sentence of sec. 7 on fol. 9v in BAV, *Vat. arab. 121* (16th c.); *v.* Pitra, vol. 2, p. xxxiii, #xi (rpt. Achelis, p. 285, frag. xiv);

9) an excerpt from sec. 4 and the last half of sec. 5 in sec. 3 of the *Pearl of Great Price*, an unedited, anonymous, Arabic florilegium produced within the Coptic church sometime between the eighth and thirteenth centuries; *v.* Graf, "Zwei dogmatische Florilegien," p. 74, #130;

10) the same excerpts from sec. 4 and the last half of sec. 5 (*v.* #9 above) in Arabic translation in Sev. Ibn al-Muqaffaʿ, *Lib. Con.* (10th c.); *v.* PO, vol. 3, p. 188, ll. 4–10;

11) Citations in the works of Mich. Syr. (*v.* item E below): a) the same excerpts from sec. 4 and the last half of sec. 5 (*v.* #9 above) in Syriac translation in an unedited work preserved in BAV, *Vat. arab. 136* (f. 29r); *v.* Graf, "Zwei dogmatische Florilegien," p. 74; b) sec. 17 and the first two thirds of sec. 5 in *Chron.* 8.13; *v.* vol. 4, p. 234 (Syriac text) and vol. 2, p. 115 (French translation).

Appendix B

B. *De fide et incarnatione* (JK †193; *CPG* #3647)

Of the nine extant sections, only secc. 3–7 survive in the original Greek, first edited by Mai and then re-edited by Lietzmann;[9] thus the *incipit* Μηδεὶς is actually the first word of sec. 3. The Syriac translation, which preserves the sections missing from both the beginning and the end of the Greek fragment, was edited by Flemming and Lietzmann. It is found complete in London, Brit. Libr, *add. 14604* (7th c.; beginning on fol. 103v) and *add. 18813* (7th c.; beginning on fol. 79r);[10] incomplete in Brit. Libr., *add. 14608* (7th c.; secc. 3–7 on foll. 121v–122v, and secc. 8f. on foll. 122v–123v), Brit. Libr., *add. 17183* (10th c.; secc. 3–7 on foll. 176v–177v, and secc. 8f. on foll. 177v–178r), and in the so-called *Florilegium edessenum anonymum* in Brit. Libr., *add. 12156* (6th c.; secc. 3–7 on foll. 69r–80r).[11] A Latin version of secc. 3–7 is preserved in Novara, Bibl. Cap. di Santa Maria, *30*, from which it was first edited by Amelli and then re-edited by Schwartz.[12] Other passages have been excerpted in a variety of contexts.[13]

9. For the *editio princeps, v.* Script. vet., vol. 7, pp. 168f. (PL, vol. 8, coll. 876f., where B, like A, is placed among Julius' genuine works). For Lietzmann's edition, *v.* pp. 194–99.

10. *V.* Flemming and Lietzmann, pp. 24–32.

11. The name *Florilegium edessenum* is that given by its editor Rucker to this collection of testimonies produced in the sixth century (before 562); secc. 3–7 are found on foll. 74r–75r (#61 in Rucker's edition). Brit. Libr., *add. 12156* also preserves citations of B in the works of Tim. II al.: a) secc. 6f. in the Syriac translation of Tim. II al., *Ref. syn.* on foll. 48v–49r; for the text, *v.* Ebied and Wickham, "Timothy Aelurus," pp. 132f.; b) secc. 8f. in an abbreviated version of Tim. II al., *Contra eos* on foll. 5r–v; for the text, *v.* Flemming and Lietzmann, p. 30.

12. *V.* Amelli, vol. 1, pp. 94f.; *ACO*, vol. 2.2.1, pp. 36f.

13. These include:

1) an excerpt from the end of sec. 6 through the beginning of sec. 7 in Philox., *Monach.; v.* CSCO, vol. 231, p. 37 (Syriac text) and vol. 232, p. 30 (French translation);
2) citations in the works of Seu. ant. a) the second half of sec. 6 through the beginning of sec. 7 in *Apol. phil.* 101; *v.* CSCO, vol. 318, pp. 63f. (Syriac text) and vol. 319, pp. 53f. (French translation); b) the last lines of sec. 6 in *Nephal.* (*or.* 2); *v.* CSCO, vol. 119, p. 50 (Syriac text) and vol. 120, p. 37 (Latin translation); c) the last lines of sec. 6 and the opening of sec. 7 in Seu. ant., *Gram.* (*or.* 3.41); *v.* CSCO, vol. 101, p. 298 (Syriac text) and vol. 102, p. 220 (Latin translation); d) the end of sec. 6 in *Serg. gram.* (*Seu., ep.* 1); *v.* CSCO, vol. 119, p. 87 (Syriac text) and vol. 120, p. 64 (Latin translation); e) the second half of sec. 7 in *ibid.; v.* CSCO, vol. 119, pp. 60f. (Syriac text) and vol. 120, p. 45 (Latin translation) and in *Serg. gram.* (*Seu., ep.* 1), vol. 119, p. 88 (Syriac text) and vol. 120, p. 64 (Latin translation);

C. Θαυμάζω πυνθανόμενος (JK †190; *CPG* #3669)

This letter, containing thirteen sections, was attributed to Julius in the superscriptions of numerous manuscript copies and by Gennadius in his catalogue of early Christian authors.[14] Muratori edited the Greek text and translated it into Latin, and his text and translation were reprinted by Coustant.[15] Lietzmann has re-edited C from BAV, *Vat. gr. 1431*, and Milan, Bibl. Ambros., *M 88 sup.*[16] A full Armenian version is preserved in the Armenian translation of Tim. II al., *Contra eos.* In addition, most of the letter is excerpted in previous sections of this work.[17] There is also a Syriac translation from the Syriac version of *Contra eos* that has been edited by

---

3) an excerpt from sec. 6 in Anast. S., *Doct. patr.* 41.46; *v.* Diekamp and Chrysos, p. 315;

4) the last two thirds of sec. 8 through sec. 9 in *Sigillum fidei* (early 7th c.), a florilegium of patristic citations attributed to the Armenian catholicos Komitas (612–28); for the text, *v.* Ter-Merkerttschian, pp. 341f., and for a description of the patristic citations, *v.* Chabot, "Les citations patristiques";

5) quotations in an unedited anoymous florilegium of patristic and scriptural citations preserved on foll. 28r–57v of BAV, *Vat. syr. 135* (7th or 8th c.): a) the central part of sec. 6 on fol. 39r; *v.* the last six lines of Mösinger, frag. A.1 (Syriac text, pp. 1f.; Latin translation, p. 4); b) secc. 8f. on foll. 48v–49r; *v.* Mösinger, frag. A.1.3 (Syriac text, pp. 2f.; Latin translation, pp. 4f.);

6) an excerpt from sec. 6 (fol. 35r) in a florilegium of testimonies "on the Incarnation of God the Word" preserved on foll. 33r–46r in Brit. Libr., *add. 12155* (*v.* n. 8.6 above); *v.* Wright, #857, vol. 2, p. 923;

7) an excerpt from sec. 6 in a synodal letter of John of Antioch to Minas of Alexandria (*v.* n. 8.7 above); *v.* the Latin translation by Renaudot (p. 360; rpt. Achelis, frag. i, p. 281);

8) The second half of sec. 6 (Lietzmann, pp. 198f.) and secc. 8f. (Lietzmann, pp. 200–03) in the unedited Arabic florilegium called by Graf *Die Bekenntnis der Väter; v. id.*, "Zwei dogmatische Florilegien," p. 373, ##53f. (description of the text) and "Unechte Zeugnisse," pp. 223–25 (German translation).

14. *V.* n. 24 of the Introduction.

15. For Muratori's *editio princeps, v. Anecdota graeca,* pp. 341–46; for Coustant's reprint, *v.* App., vol. 1, coll. 62–70.

16. For the text, *v.* pp. 256–62, and, for discussion, pp. 121–23, 147–49. Though there is no obvious lacuna in this Greek text, it may not be complete, *v.* n. 21.5 below.

17. Timothy's work is a florilegium of patristic citations. He quotes the entire letter once (pp. 259–62) and sections of the letter at numerous points, in each case with an attribution to Julius of Rome: a) secc. 1f. (pp. 186f.); b) secc. 2–6 (pp. 8f. and pp. 132f.); c) sec. 3–beginning of 5 (p. 177); d) secc. 6f. (pp. 156f.); e) the first two thirds of sec. 8 (p. 133); f) sec. 8–the first half of 9 (p. 178); g) the first half of sec. 9 (p. 187); h) sec. 12 (p. 178).

Flemming and Lietzmann from a copy preserved in Brit. Libr., *add. 12156* (foll. 3r–4v).[18] The entire text is preserved also in an Arabic translation in the unedited florilegium called by Graf *Die Bekenntnis der Väter* (*The Confession of the Fathers,* 11th c.).[19] The first seven of the thirteen sections are preserved in two Latin translations, the first transmitted within the Latin translation of the *Florilegium of Eutyches,* and the second in a document appended to a manuscript collection of the letters of Leo I.[20] Short excerpts appear in many eastern writings.[21]

18. *V.* Flemming and Lietzmann, pp. 35–39. For the ms., *v.* n. 11 above.

19. *V.* Graf, "Zwei dogmatische Florilegien," p. 372, item #48, and his German translation in "Unechte Zeugnisse," pp. 214–19. A note in the manuscripts states that the Arabic is a translation from the Coptic, but it is uncertain whether the translator worked with a pre-existing Coptic florilegium or assembled the *Bekenntnis* from various Coptic sources ("Unechte Zeugnisse," p. 204). According to Graf (*ibid.,* p. 199), there is also an Ethiopic version of this collection.

20. The complete Latin version of the florilegium is preserved only in Novara, Bibl. Cap. di Santa Maria, *30* (10–11th c.); for C 1–7, *v. ACO,* vol. 2.2.1, pp. 35f. The second version of the letter, made from the same Greek original, was transmitted in Monte Cassino, Archivio dell'Abbazia, *2* (13th c.); for C 1–7, *v. ACO,* vol. 2.4.1, pp. 149f. For the complete florilegium, *v.* Amelli, pp. 91–100, and for both versions (that transmitted in the florilegium and that transmitted in the appendix to the letters of Leo I) printed side-by-side, *v.* Amelli, pp. 91–93. The last two lines of sec. 7 are lacking in both the *nouarensis* and the *casinensis.* The latter and BAV, *Vat. lat. 1319* (12th c.) contain the same collection of Leo's letters, but the *vaticanus* is now incomplete and lacks the final item containing letter C. In both manuscripts, however, there are short fragments of secc. 5f. within an anonymous letter on the beliefs of Eutyches; *v. ACO,* vol. 2.4, p. 147. Coustant (App., vol. 1, coll. 57–70) discussed the relationship between the Greek and Latin texts. For Eutyches' florilegium, *v.* the discussion of item D in sec. 4 of the Introduction.

21. These include:

1) an excerpt from sec. 2 in Tim. II al., *Constan.,* fourth among the patristic testimonies following Timothy's introduction. This work survives in the two Syriac versions (*v.* n. 7.1 above): a) within Zach. Mit., *H. e.* 4.12; *v.* CSCO, vol. 83, pp. 191f. (Syriac text) and vol. 87, pp. 132f. (Latin translation); and Hamilton and Brooks, pp. 86f. (English translation); b) within a compilation of Timothy Aelurus' treatises in Brit. Libr., *add. 12156; v.* Ebied and Wickham, p. 335 (Syriac text) and p. 354 (English translation);
2) citations in Philox., *Monach.:* a) from secc. 2, 4, and 6; *v.* CSCO, vol. 231, p. 37 (Syriac text) and CSCO vol. 232, p. 30 (French translation); b) sec. 2, the last sentence of sec. 3 and the second half of sec. 7 through the first third of sec. 9; *v.* CSCO, vol. 231, pp. 37f. (Syriac text) and vol. 232, pp. 31f. (French translation);
3) the salutation and an excerpt from sec. 6 in Iustn., *Monoph.,* sec. 71;
4) the first few lines of sec. 2, the second half of sec. 5, and all of sec. 6 in Seu.

D. Τὸ φρόνημα (JK 189; *CPG* #3726)[22]

This document purports to be a letter from Julius to a certain Prosdocius. The original Greek was published by Coustant[23] and re-edited by Lietz-

ant., *Nephal.* (*or.* 2); *v.* CSCO, vol. 119, pp. 28f. (Syriac text) and vol. 120, pp. 21f. (Latin translation);

5) citations in Leont. Byz., *Apoll.:* a) an excerpt from a letter to Dionysius (*i.e.*, presumably from item C, though the citation does not match any part of the letter as preserved) = the third citation following the introduction; for the context in *Apoll.*, *v.* Mai, Spic., vol.10.2, p. 129 (rpt. PG, vol. 86.2, col. 1949); for this excerpt incorporated into C, *v.* Lietzmann, p. 262; b) an excerpt from sec. 1 = the fourth citation following the introduction; *v.* Mai, *ibid.*, p. 130 (rpt. PG, vol. 86.2, col. 1949); Lietzmann, p. 256; c) an excerpt from sec. 10 = the fifth citation following the introduction; *v.* Mai, *ibid.* (rpt. PG, vol. 86.2, *ibid.*); Lietzmann, p. 260;

6) part of sec. 6, in *De sectis* (*actio* 8.3), an anonymous work (*v.* Krausmuller, "Leontius of Jerusalem") of the late sixth-century; *v.* Lietzmann, p. 258; *v.* Gallandi, vol. 12, p. 651 (PG, vol. 86.1, col. 1253);

7) citations in Leont. H., *Monoph.:* a) the end of sec. 2 and all of sec. 3 (Gray, pp. 122–25); b) sec 6 (pp. 124f.); c) sec. 8 and the first two thirds of sec. 9 (*ibid.*);

8) the salutation and an excerpt from sec. 6, probably quoted indirectly from Iustn. (*v.* n. 21.3 above), in Anast. S., *Doct. patr.* 9.10; *v.* Diekamp and Chrysos, p. 63;

9) excerpts from secc. 2 and 6 in the eighth-century christological florilegium preserved in Brit. Libr., *add. 12155* (*v.* n. 8.6 above), beginning (according to Lietzmann, p. 102) on fol. 35r;

10) an excerpt from sec. 6 in a synodal letter of John of Antioch to Minas *II* of Alexandria (*v.* n. 8.7 above); *v.* the Latin translation by Renaudot (p. 360; rpt. Achelis, frag. iii, p. 282);

11) secc. 5b–6 in BAV, *Vat. syr. 135* (11th c.), fol. 34 in a florilegium of patristic and scriptural passages (foll. 28r–57v); edited by Mösinger, frag. A.1.2 (*v.* p. 2 for the Syriac text, and p. 4 for Mösinger's Latin translation) and re-edited by Flemming and Lietzmann (p. 36);

12) sec. 2 in Mich. Syr. (*v.* item E below), *Chron.* 9.1; *v.* Chabot, *Chronique,* vol. 4, pp. 245f. (Syriac text) and vol. 2, p. 135 (French translation);

13) excerpts from secc. 7, 9f. and 13 on foll. 7f. in a florilegium of patristic passages preserved in BAV, *Vat. arab. 121* (16th c.); *v.* Pitra, vol. 2, p. xxxii, ##i–iii (rpt. Achelis, pp. 282f., fragg. iv–vi);

14) secc. 5f. in sec. 6 of the *Pearl of Great Price* (*v.* n. 8.9 above); Graf ("Zwei dogmatische Florilegien," p. 74, #129) provides only the *incipit* and *explicit* encompassing these sections. This Arabic translation is different from that preserved in the *Bekenntnis der Väter.*

22. Some manuscripts omit the first paragraph and begin Κηρύσσεται δὲ. As Jaffé and Kaltenbrunner considered this letter a forgery, their omission of the † must have been an oversight.

23. *V.* App., vol. 1, coll. 73–80. Coustant (coll. 71f.) attributed to Lequien (died

mann, who based his text on Oxford, Bodl. Libr., *Laud. 92b.*[24] The Armenian translation preserved in the Armenian version of Tim. II al., *Contra eos* has been published by Ter-Merkerttschian and Ter-Minassiantz,[25] and the Syriac translation from the Syriac version by Flemming and Lietzmann on the basis of Brit. Libr., *add. 12156.*[26] Sections 1–3 appear in the Latin translation of the florilegium of Eutyches, preserved in Novara, Bibl. Cap. di Santa Maria, *30.*[27] It has been preserved also in the Arabic *Bekenntnis der Väter.*[28] Shorter citations have been preserved in a variety of other works.[29]

1733) the Greek text, edited from an ancient manuscript in an English collection (*ex antiquo exemplari Anglicano*); this was probably Oxford, Bodl. Libr., *Laud. 92b.* Coustant provided the Latin translation.

24. For the text, *v.* pp. 283–86, and, for discussion, p. 156.

25. For the complete text of the letter, *v.* pp. 262–64. Citations from the letter also occur earlier in the collection: a) middle of sec. 2 (pp. 60, 155f.); b) another part of sec. 2 (pp. 67f.); c) the first half of sec. 3 (p. 156); d) secc. 5f. (except the last line of sec. 6; pp. 10, 156).

26. *V.* Flemming and Lietzmann, pp. 39–41. The Syriac heading that introduces this letter is repeated on fol. 71v, but the brief text that follows is not part of item D; *v. ibid.*, p. 41, and, for a German translation, *v.* Lietzmann, p. 286.

27. *V.* the editions of Amelli, p. 97, and *ACO,* vol. 2.2.1, pp. 39f.

28. *V.* Graf's description of this letter in "Zwei dogmatische Florilegien," p. 373, #49, and his German translation in "Unechte Zeugnisse," pp. 219–21.

29. These include :

1) an excerpt from the middle of sec. 2 cited a) in several places among the acts of the Council of Ephesus: a1) in a florilegium of patristic sources read into the acts of the Council by Peter the notary; *v. ACO,* vol. 1.1.2, p. 41; 1.1.7, p. 91 (Greek text) and vol. 1.2, pp. 45f.; 1.3, p. 123 (Latin translation); a2) in a quotation of Cyr., *Apol. xii cap.* contained within the *Collectio atheniensis,* a thirteenth-century collection of Greek documents from the Council of Ephesus; v. *ACO,* vol. 1.1.7, pp. ii and vii for the contents and date of the collection; pp. 17–167 for a text of the collection; pp. 33–65 for Cyril's treatise; and p. 45 for the excerpt from D; a3) in a Latin translation of Cyr., *Apol. xii cap.* contained within the *Collectio palatina,* a sixth-century collection of Latin translations of documents from the Council of Ephesus; v. *ACO,* vol. 1.5, pp. viif. for the contents and date of the collection; pp. 3–181 for the text of the collection; pp. 116–42 for Cyril's treatise; and p. 126 for the excerpt from D; b) in the acts of the Council of Chalcedon, which contain the acts of the Council of Ephesus, including the florilegium of Peter the notary; *v. ACO,* vol. 2.3.1, p. 205; c) in the Latin translation of Cyr., *Apol. xii cap.* contained within the *Collectio vaticana* of the early sixth century (*v.* Maassen, pp. 512–26, for a description of the collection and p. 516, where he lists Cyril's treatise as part of item #xxii); d) in the Latin translation of a patristic florilegium on the incarnation contained in the *Collection of St. Maur* of the later sixth century (*v.* Maassen, pp. 613–24 for a description of the collection and p. 617 for the relevant portion of the florilegium);

E. Περὶ πίστεως / *De fide* (*CPG* #3705)

The original Greek has been edited by both Schwartz and Lietzmann: by Schwartz as it appears in Cyr., *Arcad.*, and by Lietzmann as a work of the Apollinarist Vitalis.[30] There are three Syriac translations: 1) in the truncated version of the *Contra eos* transmitted in Brit. Libr., *add. 12156* (*v.* fol. 7v);[31] 2) in the Syriac epitome of Zach. Mit., *H. e.*;[32] 3) in Mich. Syr., *Chron.* 9.1.[33] E is preserved also in the Armenian translation of *Contra eos;* here it appears twice.[34] The entire letter, except for the final anathema, is quoted also in the

2) the middle part of sec. 2 (same as in n. 29.1 above) and the second half of sec. 4 through the middle of sec. 5 in the Syriac translation of Seu. ant., *Gram.* (*or.* 3.41); *v.* CSCO, vol. 101, pp. 297f. (Syriac text) and vol. 102, pp. 219f. (Latin translation);

3) a brief excerpt from a letter of Julius to Prosdocius, the supposed recipient of D, in the *Florilegium edessenum anonymum* (*v.* n. 11 above; this excerpt does not, however, match any extant section of D); *v.* Rucker, ##27 and 61 (pp. 25 and 47f.);

4) the first sentence of sec. 3 in the unedited anonymous florilegium of patristic and scriptural citations preserved on foll. 28r–57v of BAV, *Vat. syr. 135* (*v.* n. 13.5 above); *v.* Mösinger, frag. A.1.4 (Syriac text, p. 3; Latin translation, p. 5) and Lietzmann, p. 156 (I have not been able to reconcile conflicting reports of the location of this excerpt);

5) parts of secc. 1 and 5 in Anast. S., *Doct. patr.* 42.5; *v.* Diekamp and Chrysos, pp. 316f.;

6) excerpts from secc. 2f. (foll. 48v–49r) and sec. 6 (foll. 165v–167r) in an eighth century christological florilegium preserved in British Library, *add. 12155* (*v.* n. 8.6 above);

7) excerpts of secc. 1–5 on foll. 8v–9r and 63 in BAV, *Vat. arab. 121* (*v.* n. 21.13 above); *v.* Pitra, vol. 2, p. xxxii, ##iv–viii and xiv (rpt. Achelis, pp. 283f., fragg. vii–xi and xvii).

30. *V. ACO,* vol. 1.1.5, pp. 67f.; Lietzmann, p. 273, frag. 172.

31. *V.* Wright, #729; this version has not been published.

32. Brooks, CSCO, vol. 83, pp. 195f. (Syriac text) and vol. 87, pp. 135f. (Latin translation); for an English translation, *v.* Hamilton and Brooks, p. 90. E is here cited from Tim. II al., *Constan.*, but this letter is not contained in Brit. Libr., *add. 12156,* from which Ebied and Wickham produced their edition of *Constan.* Zach. Mit., *H. e.* is transmitted in Brit. Libr., *add. 17202,* letter E on foll. 88v–89r. This manuscript was the basis for Flemming and Lietzmann's edition of E; *v.* pp. 54f., #2 (172).

33. *V.* Chabot, *Chronique,* vol. 4, p. 248 (Syriac text) and vol. 2, pp. 138f. (French translation). Michael the Syrian was the monophysite patriarch of Antioch (1166–99). His chronicle, covering world history from the creation to 1195, is a valuable source of information for Arab-Byzantine relations and rivalries; *v.* the notice by Griffith.

34. *V.* Ter-Merkerttschian and Ter-Minassiantz, pp. 7f. and 191. At the second

Arabic *Bekenntnis der Väter.*[35] In all of these except the epitome of Zach. Mit., *H. e.* and Mich. Syr., *Chron.,* E is attributed to Vitalis.[36]

F. Πέπεισμαι μὲν (JK †192; *CPG* #3735)

In the manuscripts, this letter bears the title "Encyclion." Lietzmann placed it among the Apollinarian forgeries of unknown authorship. Mai provided the *editio princeps* of the Greek text, which was reprinted by Migne.[37] Lietzmann re-edited the Greek from three patristic miscellanies: Munich, Bayer. Staatsbibl., *gr. 207* (15th c.; fol. 155v); BAV, *Vat. gr. 1431* (9–10th c.; fol. 258v); and BAV, *Vat. gr. 1455* (14th c.; fol. 198v).[38]

Timothy Aelurus included F in his *Contra eos,* so the entire letter survives also in Syriac and Armenian translations.[39] It is also found in a florilegium in Univ. of Birmingham, *Mingana syr. 481* (17th c.).[40] A Latin translation has been transmitted within the florilegium of Eutyches found in Novara, Bibl. Cap. di Santa Maria, *30,* from which it was first edited by Amelli and then re-edited by Schwartz.[41] The entire text is preserved also in the Arabic *Bekenntnis der Väter.*[42] Short citations appear in Arabic sources.[43]

---

occurence, there is a note in the manuscript stating that the letter was taken from Cyril's *Arcad.*

35. On the *Bekenntnis, v.* item C above. For the place of E in the *Bekenntnis, v.* Graf, "Zwei dogmatische Florilegien," p. 374, #79, and, for his German translation, "Unechte Zeugnisse," p. 230, and, on the missing anathema, p. 233.

36. *V.* the discussion of E in sec. 4 of the Introduction. Schwartz (*Vat. gr. 1431,* p. 99) postulated that the misattribution arose from the error of a Syriac copyist, who wrote *jvljus* for *vjtljvs; v.* also Graf, "Unechte Zeugnisse," pp. 205f.

37. It seems likely that Mai used BAV, *Vat. gr. 1431; v.* Script. vet. 7, p. 163 (rpt. PL, vol. 8, col. 876). Migne numbered F (as also A and B) among the genuine letters of Julius.

38. For the text, *v.* Lietzmann, pp. 292f.; for discussion, p. 158.

39. For the Syriac, *v.* Flemming and Lietzmann, pp. 41f. They based their text on Brit. Libr., *add. 12156* (fol. 5r). For the Armenian, *v.* Ter-Merkerttschian and Ter-Minassiantz, pp. 264f.

40. *V.* Graf, "Zwei dogmatische Florilegien," p. 355.

41. *V.* Amelli, pp. 96f. (*Cf.* n. 20 above); and *ACO,* vol. 2.2.1, p. 39.

42. *V.* Graf's description of this letter in "Zwei dogmatische Florilegien," p. 373, #51, and his German translation in "Unechte Zeugnisse," pp. 221f. In manuscripts of the *Bekenntnis,* F is attributed to a bishop of Rome variously identified as Julius, Bulis, or Hippolytus.

43. An excerpt starting at the beginning of sec. 2 is preserved on fol. 9r in BAV, *Vat. arab. 121* (16th c.); *v.* Pitra, vol. 2, p. xxxiii, #x (rpt. Achelis, pp. 284f., frag. xiii).

G. "The Third Letter" (*CPG* #3739)

No one has ventured a guess as to the author of this letter. It survives only in Syriac, Arabic, and Armenian versions. Flemming and Lietzmann have edited one Syriac version from Brit. Libr., *add. 17183* (10th c.; foll. 177v–78r) and Brit. Libr., *add. 14608* (7th c.; foll. 123v–24r), of which only the first contains the complete text.[44] In addition, Mösinger has edited a Syriac epitome from BAV, *Vat. syr. 135* (11th c.), p. 39.[45] It is preserved also in the Arabic *Bekenntnis der Väter*[46] and in two Armenian versions.[47] Two fragments are cited in other Syriac works.[48]

H. Περὶ πίστεως / *De fide* (*CPG* #3740)

In the ninth century, this fragment was copied in isolation on the last two folios (43v–44v) of the Syriac manuscript, London, Brit. Libr., *add. 14555* (7th–8th c.).[49] It has been edited by Flemming and Lietzmann.[50]

44. *V.* pp. 49–51. For Lietzmann's discussion of the "Third Letter," *v.* p. 161, and, for his German translation, pp. 307–10. The name of this document is derived from these manuscripts in which G is placed directly after B. In these, the last two chapters of B (8f.) are separated from the first seven and designated "The Second Letter of Julius." Letter G is thus introduced with the title "The Third Letter of Julius."

45. *V.* frag. A.1.1 (Syriac text, p. 1, and Latin translation, pp. 3f.). This fragment consists of Lietzmann, *Apollinaris,* p. 307, ll. 1–3; p. 308, ll. 5–21; p. 309, ll. 5–17, 18–20. In his edition, Mösinger attaches to G an excerpt that Lietzmann regards as belonging to sec. 6 of B.

46. *V.* Graf's description in "Zwei dogmatische Florilegien," p. 373, #55, and his German translation in "Unechte Zeugnisse," pp. 225–28.

47. These two translations appear:
1) in the Armenian translation of Tim. II al., *Contra eos*; *v.* Ter-Merkerttschian and Ter-Minassiantz, pp. 266f.;
2) in the *Sigillum fidei* (*v.* n. 13.4 above); for the text, *v.* Ter-Merkerttschian, pp. 342–45, and, for a description of the document, *v.* Chabot, "Les citations patristiques," p. 29.

48. These comprise:
1) an excerpt from sec. 2 in Seu. ant., *Adu. apol. Iul.* 2.32; *v.* CSCO, vol. 301, p. 328 (Syriac text) and vol. 302, p. 287 (French translation);
2) perhaps an excerpt from the beginning of sec. 4 in Tim. II al., *Contra eos* preserved on fol. 5r in Brit. Libr., *add. 12156; v.* Flemming and Lietzmann, p. 54 for the Syriac text (= *CPG* #3741.1) and Lietzmann, p. 318 (frag. 185) for a German translation. This may, however, be an excerpt of a different work; *v.* Lietzmann, p. 162.

49. *V.* Wright, #609.

50. For the Syriac text, *v.* pp. 51–54, and, for Lietzmann's German translation,

Appendix B

I. Four Arabic fragments (*CPG* #3741.4)

These four fragments survive only in Arabic. Their subject matter is christology, and all derive from sources—BAV, *Vat. arab. 121* and the *Bekenntnis der Väter*—that carry materials attributed to Julius.[51] It is, therefore, an easy inference that they probably belong to the same corpus of Apollinarian forgeries as items A–H. Indeed, they may represent fragments of one or more of the incomplete pieces already catalogued. Three of the four, it is true, are attributed to Hippolytus (in a form equivalent to "Bulides" or "Bulidus"), rather than to Julius, but this must be due to scribal error. Drawing from foll. 9r, 10v, and 65r of the *Vaticanus,* Pitra produced Latin translations of all four fragments, which he numbered ix (*Confitemur creatum*), xii (*Et ipse est*), xiii (*Sit anathema*), and xv (*Nos credimus*). His fragg. ix and xii appear also in the *Bekenntnis der Väter* (Graf's ##50 and 57), the former in what appears to be a slightly longer redaction.[52] There may be a fifth fragment that belongs to the same group. This appears in the *Bekenntnis* after G ("The Third Letter"), which explicitly claims to be the work of Julius. While the heading of the fragment attributes the piece to a Pope Methologon, that name looks like a scribal error, perhaps a corruption of the Greek phrase μετ' ὀλίγον ("and a bit later"), which is frequently used to introduce the quotation of a passage that occurs "a bit later" in a document from which one has already been quoting. If so, the citation would

---

Apollinaris, pp. 310–18. Lietzmann (p. 161) dates H to the first half of the fifth century.

51. *V.* the references to BAV, *Vat. arab. 121* in nn. 8.8 (item A); 21.13 (item C); 29.7 (item D); and 43 (item F) above; and the references to the *Bekenntnis der Väter* in nn. 7.4 (item A); 13.8 (item B); 19 and 21.14 (item C); 28 (item D); 35 (item E); 42 (item F); and 46 (item G).

52. Pitra's Latin versions were reprinted by Achelis (fragg. xii, xv, xvi, and xviii, pp. 284–86) and by Lietzmann (fragg. 188–91; *v.* pp. 321f.). For Graf's German translation of the two fragments in the *Bekenntnis der Väter, v.* "Unechte Zeugnisse," pp. 221, 228f. The following *comparatio locorum* gives the *incipits,* attributions, and numbers assigned by the various editors.

Incipit	Attribution	Pitra	Achelis	Lietzmann	*Bekenntnis*
Confitemur creatum	*Et dixit* (*i.e., Bulidus patriarcha Romae*) *in sua epistula ad Dionysium*	IX	XII	188	50

likely be derived from a document containing writings of Julius. The fifth fragment does not, however, appear to come from the text of G as it has been preserved elsewhere; at present it remains unidentified.[53]

J. Two additional Arabic fragments (JK †194)

Renaudot provided Coustant with a Latin translation of these fragments that, according to Coustant, his informant had discovered in two sources: a monophysite treatise written in Arabic by Īsā, son of Zaraa (certainly ʿĪsā Ibn Zurʿa, d. 1007) and in an Arabic florilegium preserved in a codex belonging to the royal library that then bore the shelf-mark *432*.[54] The first

footnote 52 continued

Incipit	Attribution	Pitra	Achelis	Lietzmann	*Bekenntnis*
Et ipse est	*Et dixit sanctus Bulides patriarcha Romae in epistola ad Seuirianum sanctum episcopum Galliae*	XII	XV	189	57
Sit anathema	*Anathemata quae protulit Bulidus archiepiscopus Romae ex iis, de quibus testatur Timotheus in suo libro*	XIII	XVI	190	—
Nos credimus	*De anathematibus, quae protulit archiepiscopus Romae causa fidei, ex iis quae scripsit Cyrillus ad reges ad probandum quod Christus sit deus.*	XV	XVIII	191	—

53. *V.* Graf, "Zwei dogmatische Florilegien," p. 373, #56; "Unechte Zeugnisse," pp. 208f. (further discussion) and p. 228 (his German translation).

54. Coustant reports that the fragments were drawn "cum *ex tractatu Arabico Isa filii Zaraa apologetico sententiae Jacobitarum seu Monophysitarum circa incarnati Verbi mysterium,* tum ex codice Regio 432. item Arabico, in quo varia patrum testimonia in ejusdem opinionis gratiam proferuntur" (App., n. a, col. 81). I have not been able to confirm this description of the work by ʿĪsā Ibn Zurʿa or to discover the whereabouts and shelf-mark of the manuscript, which, like the rest of the royal collection, must have entered the Bibliothèque Nationale. The Arabic manuscript bearing the number *432* (among the *codices manuscripti orientales*) in vol. 1 of the *Catalogus codicum manuscriptorum Bibliothecae Regiae* (Paris, 1739–44) could not be Renaudot's source. Mansi, who reprints (vol. 2, coll. 1253f.) these two

fragment, beginning *Cum ipse Deus* is introduced by a rubric identifying it as an excerpt from "The Fifth Letter" of Julius (*Julius Romae patriarcha in epistola V. ita scribit*). The second, beginning *Non inuenitur*, is ascribed, without further information, to St. Julius (*Sanctus Julius*).[55]

The Pseudo-Isidorian Forgeries (K–N)

K. *Sanctae sedi*[56]

This purports to be a synodal letter issued by a Roman council of about 120 bishops, which reaffirms the Nicene Creed and its condemnation of Arius.

L. *Decuerat uos fratres* (JK †195)

This purports to be a letter to the eastern bishops, in which Julius claims the support of Scripture and canon law for the principle that the bishop of Rome must be consulted on the deposition of other bishops and in affairs involving the relationships between dioceses.

M. *Licet circa omnes*

This purports to be the response of the eastern bishops to Julius, *ep.* 2 and perhaps also to L. Julius is chastised for readmitting into communion Athanasius and other deposed bishops.

N. *Decuerat uos aduersus* (JK †196)

This purports to be Julius' response to M. He reasserts the authority of the see of Peter and the innocence of Athanasius and renews his condemnation of the acts of the eastern bishops.

These letters (K–N) belong to a collection known as the *Decretals of Pseudo-Isidore* or *The False Decretals*. Composed between 835 and 850 and

---

texts (along with that listed in n. 8.5 above), repeats (col. 1253), without comment, the citation "*Regius 432*."

55. *V.* Coustant, App., vol. 1, coll. 81f.

56. The standard edition of the Pseudo-Isidorian decretals is that of Hinschius; for the four letters attributed to Julius, *v.* pp. 454–74. In Hinschius' edition, the *incipit* of the first is *Sanctae sedi* (*sedis, u. l.*). In the online edition of Schon and Zechiel-Eckes (http://www.pseudoisidor.mgh.de/html/129.htm [accessed 4 February 2014]), the *incipit* is *Sanctae dei*. I cite the letter according to the traditional *incipit*.

circulated within the Carolingian empire, the *Decretals of Pseudo-Isidore* were part of an effort to devolve more authority from metropolitans onto their subordinate bishops.[57] As they are subdivided into nineteen continuous sections (K = 1, L = 2–9, M = 10, and N = 11–19), it is clear that the four were regarded as a group. Though the letters were composed in the ninth century, the forgers incorporated many citations from earlier works.[58] The new collection spread widely and was very influential; more than a hundred manuscripts are extant.[59]

The Pseudo-Isidorian corpus was soon exploited as a source. The compilers of the Pseudo-Isidorian collection were among the last to incorporate entire conciliar canons and papal decretals. Subsequent compilers produced collections in which documents were excerpted, and the excerpts systematically arranged by topic. Dozens of these collections were made, circulated, copied, and combined; Gratian's *Decretum* represents the culmination of this process. While the collection continued to circulate as a whole, excerpts, large and small, of the letters attributed to Julius were incorporated into many of these systematic compilations.

Due to the volume and complexity of the material, almost entirely still unpublished, it has been impossible to make even generalizations concerning the frequency of such citation and the relationships between the col-

57. The corpus was first printed by Merlin (Paris 1523) on the basis of a rather late manuscript, which deviated considerably from the original form of the collection. A later edition (Cologne 1530) was reprinted by Migne and much influenced Hinschius' mid-nineteenth-century edition, which has yet to be replaced. Currently Schon and Zechiel-Eckes are re-editing the collection for the *MGH*. On the dating and origins of the collection, *v.* Zechiel-Eckes, "Ein Blick."

58. *V.*, *e.g.*, Zechiel-Eckes' analysis of the sources of N (pp. 89f.); the sources of that one false decretal include genuine decretals of Siricius (d. 399), Innocent I (d. 417), Zosimus (d. 418), Boniface I (d. 422), Celestine I (d. 432), Leo I (d. 461), Gelasius I (d. 496), Anastasius II (d. 498), and Gregory I (d. 604); canons of Arles (314), Neocaesarea (315), Nicea (325), Antioch (341), Sardica (343), Carthage (397, 429, and 475), Mileve (402), Chalcedon (451), Rome (502), Orléans (549), and Toledo (633, 675, and 681); letters of Bishop Ennodius of Pavia (d. 521), several works of Isidore of Seville (d. 636), the *Capitulary of Ansegisus* (827), the *Liber Pontificalis*, the *Theodosian Code*, the *Lex romana Visigothorum*, and the *Hist. trip.* of Cassiodorus (d. 580).

59. The standard work on the manuscripts of the collection has been that of S. Williams. Schon provides an updated list of 105 manuscripts at the MGH website for the *Projekt Pseudoisidor:* http://www.pseudoisidor.de/html/Handschriftenverzeichnis.html (accessed 4 February 2014).

lections sharing the same excerpts. Thanks to the work of Linda Fowler-Magerl, we can now begin to discern some patterns in the use and dispersion of this material. My references to the unedited, *i.e.*, to the large majority, of the medieval collections cited in K–Y come from her *Clavis canonum*, an electronic database containing the *incipits* and *explicits* of approximately 100,000 canons from over 125 different collections made prior to 1140. In the database, some of these collections are represented in various recensions. This material permits us to make preliminary assessments of the date and the way in which the name of Julius became attached to later canons. Still, given the frequency with which the inscriptions of individual canons were added, dropped, or changed in the manuscript tradition, our conclusions remain tentative.

Sanctae sedi (K) provides the historical context for the other letters. As it was not useful for medieval controversies or penitential practice, it was never cited in the later collections. *Licet circa omnes* (M), was equally irrelevant to contemporary concerns and was copied into only one systematic collection.[60] In contrast, L and N were widely cited.[61] Around 869, Hincmar, the bishop of Laon in northeastern France, incorporated two excerpts from *Decuerat uos fratres* (L) and eleven from *Decuerat uos aduersus* (N) into the small collection known as the *Pittaciolus*.[62] Much of sec. 5 of L and a citation from secc. 13–15 of N were quoted in the *Collectio XLIV capitulorum* (also referred to as the *De episcoporum transmigratione*) compiled in northeastern France in the mid-870s.[63] Before the end of the ninth century, eight selections of L and six from N were excerpted into the northern Italian *Collectio Anselmo dedicata*.[64]

60. The entire letter is reproduced in the early eleventh-century *Collectio XII partium*, produced probably at the Bavarian monastic center of Freising; *v. Clavis* database TX04.237; and, for the collection, Fowler-Magerl, *Clavis*, pp. 91–93.

61. Much preliminary material has been posted on the internet, including preliminary editions of all four letters attributed to Julius; *v.* Schon and Zechiel-Eckes, *Projekt Pseudoisidor.* For the edition of N (*cf.* n. 58 above), *v.* Zechiel-Eckes, "Ein Blick," pp. 62–90.

62. The title *pittaciolus* is a diminutive = "a bit of parchment." For the two excerpts from L, ch. 9, *v.* Zechiel-Eckes, "Ein Blick," p. 70; for the eleven from N, chh. 10–12 (pp. 70–72) and 20–22 (pp. 76–81). Berlin, Staatsbibl., *Phillipps 1764* contains five small collections from the same period, which are also associated with Hincmar; the first, dealing with the relationship between bishops, metropolitans, and the pope, also contains a long citation from secc. 12f. of N.

63. On this collection, *v.* Fowler-Magerl, pp. 49f.

64. On this collection, *v. ibid.*, pp. 70–74.

Our letters do not appear to have been cited in the handful of tenth-century collections. Nevertheless, they appear frequently in the many collections made in the eleventh century. These include that of Burchard of Worms, both recensions of the *Collectio XII partium*, the *Collection of Anselm of Lucca*, the *Collectio XIII librorum* in Berlin, *Savigny* 3, the *Collectio capituli ueronensis*, the *Liber canonum diuersorum sanctorum patrum* (also known as the *Collectio Sancte Marie Nouelle*), as well as the offshoots of these collections. In the twelfth century, the letters were excerpted in the *Collectio tripartita*, the *Decretum* of Ivo, and many other collections.[65]

Other Miscellaneous Forgeries (O–Z)[66]

O. *Quicumque enim tempore* (JK †197)

This is a passage consisting of two sentences dealing with usury (BU02.127). It first appears as Canon 17 in the *Capitulare missorum* of Nijmegen of 806 and is repeated in the *Capitulary of Ansegisus* of 827 (1.125) and in the collections of Benedictus Leuita (mid-ninth century; 1.265*)[67] and Regino of Prüm (late ninth or early tenth century; *Disc. eccl.* 1.287* = RP01.292).

It was Burchard of Worms who, in his canonical collection, the *Decretum* (2.127), composed between 1008 and 1012, first attributed O to Julius, rather than a capitulary. This is our first example of the process of deliberate falsification (*v.* sec. 4 of the introduction), of which we shall notice sever-

65. While not every part of these letters is cited, some sections are used in over thirty different collections; *v.* Fowler-Magerl's database, also n. 99 below and item Y[5].

66. Most of the sources for O–Z have not been edited, and, in the manuscripts of a given collection, the canons may be numbered differently or left unnumbered. Therefore, in the following discussions of the citations, I frequently mention specific manuscripts. Unless otherwise specified, my system of reference follows the key numbers from Fowler-Magerl's *Clavis* database. These consist of three parts: 1) two letters indicating the recension of a collection, 2) a number indicating the book or part, 3) the number of the canon; items two and three are separated by a period. Thus, #TX02.239 refers to a specific recension of the *Collectio XII partium*, book 2, canon #239. Where references to canons are followed by an asterisk, the reader is referred to editions reprinted in the PL.

67. This passage can be found in Hartmann and Schmitz' online edition of Benedictus (www.benedictus.mgh.de/edition/archiv/bl_20080226/libl.pdf [accessed 4 February 2014]). Baluze's edition (Paris 1677) remains the best printed edition, better than that of Pertz (Berlin 1837), reprinted by Migne.

al more examples, by which Burchard attributed to popes materials he had found in collections of canon and civil law. Burchard's excerpt with its new attribution found its way into numerous subsequent collections: the first recension of the *Collectio XII partium* (TX02.239), the *Liber canonum diuersorum sanctorum patrum* (NO060.09), the epitome of the *Liber canonum diuersorum sanctorum patrum* (the *Collectio V librorum* = NP01.36.03), the augmented recension of the *Collectio sinemuriensis* found in Orléans, Bibl. Mun., *306* (SO614), the *Collectio canonum* of Celle, Bibl. des Oberlandesgericht, *C.8* (CE02.047.01), the *Collectio canonum* of the canonry of St. Hilary the Great (HI02.068), the *Collectio II librorum / VIII partium* (VA02.232.01),[68] the *Decretum* (ID06.201) and *Panormia* (IP03.162) of Ivo of Chartres,[69] the *Polycarpus* (PX04.32.20), the *Collectio III librorum* (DR02.20.006), and, finally, Gratian (Part 2, C.14 q.4 c.9).

P. *Si presbyter poenitentiam* (JK †198)

This three-sentence text forbids priests to deny absolution to repentant sinners who are dying. It appears, without attribution, in the *Liber sacramentorum augustodunensis* compiled at the beginning of the ninth century (Heiming, #2354) and in the *Iudicium poenitentis* of the late tenth.[70] The first two sentences were incorporated into the anonymous penitential (*Liber poenitentialis ex scrinio romanae ecclesiae assumtus*) that Halitgar, bishop of Cambrai believed to derive from the archives of the church of Rome and which he used in his revision of the penitential of the Frankish

68. This collection is preserved in both Assisi, Bibl. Com., *227* and BAV, *Vat. lat. 3822* (foll. 1–99v and 199r). In the first, which, in the twelfth century, was divided into eight books, the relevant canon is 5.31. As the second presents the text without subdivision, Bernhard added his own in his edition of the *Collectio II librorum / VIII partium* from the *vaticanus*, and his numeration is followed by Fowler-Magerl; for this canon, *v.* Bernhard, pp. 443f.

69. For the sake of convenience, I adopt the convention of associating the *Panormia* and the *Tripartita* with Ivo. Brett has shown that Ivo made use of the *Tripartita* in his *Decretum* and that the *Decretum* was, in turn, used in the compilation of the *Panormia;* he denies Ivo's authorship of both *Tripartita* and *Panormia*; Rolker (esp., pp. 100–126) further develops his arguments.

70. For the *Iudicium poenitentis, v.* PL, vol. 138, col. 977a. Migne reprints the edition of Gerbertus, who derived his text from what he identified as a sacramentary of German provenance dating from about 1000 and belonging to the monastery of Rheinau (p. 12). Gerbertus remarks (first note, p. 23) that this passage reproduces ideas that appear in *ep. 2 Celestini I ad episcopos Galliae.* Indeed, *v.* sec. 2 of Celestine, *Cuperemus quidem* (JK 369; Hinschius, p. 560).

church (*ca.* 829). In that anonymous penitential, they are introduced with the heading *ex decretis Lucii papae, cap. 5.*[71] In the early eleventh century, Burchard incorporated all three sentences, with an attribution to Julius, into his *Decretum* (BU18.021). In this case also, Burchard's new attribution was maintained in numerous subsequent collections, including both recensions of the *Collectio XII partium* (TX12.022 and TW11.167), the *Collectio ambrosiana II* (MJ041), Ivo's *Decretum* (ID15.043) and *Tripartita* (IT03.28.101), the *Polycarpus* (PX08.01.10),[72] as well as Gratian (Part 2, C.26 q.6 c.12).

Q. *Si quis desponsauerit* (JK †199)

This single sentence forbids a man to marry a woman previously married to one of his blood relatives, even if that marriage remained unconsummated. It first appears about 1085 in the *Liber canonum diuersorum sanctorum patrum* (NO147.35), where it is falsely labeled as canon fifty-four of the Council of Laodicea. Soon afterward, Bonizo of Sutri (d. 1090) quotes it, without attribution, in the *Liber de uita christiana* (BO10.050).[73] Shortly after 1100, it is first associated with Julius in the *Polycarpus* collection, where it is said that he received this canon from a Council of Tibur (*ex concilio Triburiensi a Iulio papa confirmato;* PX06.04.34). From that collection, it is taken into the *Collectio III librorum* (*Triburiensi statuente Iulio papae;* DR03.43.002).[74] Gratian also attributes it to Julius (Part 2, C.27 q.2 c.15).

R. *Si quis ancillam suam* (JK †200)

This passage confirms the legitimacy of marriages between masters and slaves. In its longest form, it consists of five sentences. The first three appear in the *Code of Justinian* (5.4.26) at the beginning of an edict addressed *Iuliano p.p.*, "to Julian, the praetorian prefect."[75] This passage of the *Code* was incorporated into the third section of book 7 of the ninth-century *Collectio*

71. *V.* PL, vol. 105, col. 708. Note that the preceding item is a canon attributed to Julius; *v.* Y^7 below.

72. Here it is attributed to "Pope Julianus."

73. *V.* Schaefer's brief account of Bonizo.

74. The relationship between the *Collectio III librorum* and the *Polycarpus* has been the subject of debate; Fowler-Magerl (*Clavis*, p. 231) asserts that the former was dependent on the latter.

75. The *incipits* and *explicits* for the first three sentences are:

1) *Si quis alumnam suam … esse uideantur, an non.*

2) *Nos itaque uetustam … censemus.*

3) *Si enim ex adfectu … inhibendas existimauerimus.*

Anselmo Dedicata.[76] In the early eleventh century, in Burchard's *Decretum* (BU09.018), the three sentences are supplemented with two more, and the entire passage is introduced with the heading *Ex decretis Iulii papae, cap. 4.*[77] This five-sentence formulation and the attribution to Julius are repeated in Bonizo's *Liber de uita christiana* (BO08.28), the *Polycarpus* (PX06.04.08), the *Decretum* of Ivo (ID08.156), the *Panormia* (IP06.037), and many other collections.[78] The first recension of Gratian's *Decretum* (Part 2, C.29 q.2 c.1) contains a formulation, attributed to Julius, which consists of the last two and a new supplementary sentence (*Si autem omnes unam legem … dimitti poterit*). In the second recension, sentences 1–3 are added nearby (Part 2, C.29 q.2 c.3), and the ascription to Julius is repeated. Thus Gratian divides this citation into two separate items.[79]

S. *Nullum in utroque* (JK †201)

This passage, originally just one sentence proscribing the marriage of close relatives, is attributed to Julius only in the final two-sentence formulation found in Gratian's *Decretum*. The general content of the original sen-

76. Though the *Collectio Anselmo Dedicata* has never been edited, we can infer from the *explicit* ("*Lampadio et Oreste*") given in Fowler-Magerl's database (DE07.R.007), that the law was taken over intact, including the subscription, which had the consular date and the *A. Juliano p.p.* = "The emperor to Julianus praetorian prefect."

77. The source of the two additional sentences is still unknown (*v.* Hoffmann and Pokorny, p. 213). Their *incipits* and *explicits* are (PL, vol. 140, col. 818b):

4) *Omnibus uobis unus … daturi sunt.*

5) *Quapropter omnibus … non dubitamus.*

78. In de Vosmediano's edition of the *Panormia,* there is additional material (6.37f.; *v.* col. 1251). Nonetheless, in both the *Clavis* and the provisional online edition of Brasington and Brett (*v.* pp. 19f. of their PDF of *Panormia* 6), these sections of book six contain only the unit of five sentences. Other collections in which this five-sentence canon is attributed to Julius include the first version of the *Collectio caesaraugustana* (CA10.036), the *Collectio Sancte Genoveve* (preserved only in Paris, Bibl. Sainte-Geneviève, *166;* GE02.04.048), the *Liber canonum diuersorum sanctorum patrum* (NO147.51), the *Collectio pragensis* (PR087), the *Collectio XIII librorum* (preserved only in Berlin, Staatsbibl., *Savigny 3;* SA12.096), the *Collectio VII librorum* (preserved in several recensions; cited by Fowler Magerl according to Vienna, Öster. Nationalbibl., *2186;* SV06.042.14), the augmented version of the *Collectio XII partium* (TW08.019), the latter part of the *Collectio II librorum / VIII partium* (VB07.010), and the *Collectio decem partium* (ZE07.07.02). Several other collections have only one or two of the sentences.

79. *V.* De León, pp. 18–21.

tence can be traced at least to the Visigothic Law Code (12.3.8), where it has reference only to Jews.[80] In the mid-ninth century, the falsifier who used the pseudonym Benedictus Leuita incorporates it into *Additio* IV, where it is made to apply also to Christians.[81] The sentence is later found with slightly altered wording in two collections of the early eleventh century: Burchard's *Decretum* (BU07.014) and the *Collectio XII partium* (TX08.017); in these it follows an attribution to a Council of Orléans (*Ex concilio Aurelianensi, cap. 20*). In both Ivo's *Decretum* and the *Panormia,* the sentence and its inscription are repeated, though in these works, it is assigned to the tenth, rather than the twentieth, canon. In the first recension of Gratian's *Decretum* (Part 2, C.35 q.2–3 c.7), a second sentence is added, and the attribution is changed to Julius.[82] Neither the origin of the second sentence nor the reason for the attribution to Julius has been explained.[83]

T. *De fabrica* (JK †202)

This three-sentence passage discusses the proper procedures for reconsecrating church buildings that have been damaged or rebuilt. It originally formed part of a Pseudo-Isidorian forgery (JK †907), a letter purportedly addressed to a Bishop Eutherius (or Eleutherius) by Pope Vigilius (d. 555). These sentences, constituting the fourth chapter of the letter, were excerpted into at least thirty-one canonical collections.[84] Throughout this

80. For the citation in the Visigothic Code, *v.* Zeumer, p. 435.

81. For the citation in the work of Benedictus, *v.* the online edition of Hartmann and Schmitz. On Benedict, *v.* the brief account of Kirsch.

82. The second sentence runs: *Preterea illud quoque adiecimus, quia, sicut non licet cuiquam Christiano de sua consanguinitate, sic etiam nec licet de consanguinitate uxoris suae coniugem ducere propter carnis unitatem.* Winroth, who has distinguished between two recensions of the *Decretum,* lists this canon (App., p. 226) among the contents of the first recension. In the *editio princeps* of the *Panormia,* Brant added the additional sentence, seemingly without textual evidence; he must have borrowed it from Gratian.

83. The redaction consisting of a single sentence is found also in *Collectio Sancte Genoveve* (GE02.04.013), *Liber canonum diuersorum sanctorum patrum* (NO147.15), the second part of the *Collectio II librorum / VIII partium* (VB06.298), and the *Collectio decem partium* (ZE08.14.03.04). The compilers of the first two probably borrowed from Burchard, those of the last two from the *Panormia.* Three of the four have the attribution *Ex con. Aurel.;* in the *Liber canonum diuersorum sanctorum patrum,* this is changed, probably by scribal error, to *Ex con. Arelatensi* ("from the Council of Arles").

84. For ch. 4, *v.* Hinschius, *Decretales,* p. 711.

literature, the attribution to Vigilius is constant, with just four exceptions. In three, there is no attribution,[85] and in the fourth, the second part of the *Collectio II librorum / VIII partium* (Assisi, Biblioteca Comunale, *227*),[86] the excerpt is cited *ex epistola Iulii pp.* ("from a letter of Pope Julius"; VB06.112). This, most likely an error of transmission, appears also in some manuscripts of Gratian's *Decretum*, where this canon is appended to the *De consecratione* (D.1 c.24); the agreement in error probably indicates direct dependence on the *Assisiensis.*

U. *Cum omne crimen* (JK †203)

This twenty-sentence canon covers improprieties in the celebration of the Eucharist. It is actually the first canon from the third Council of Braga (675), which, like items O, P, and R, was first ascribed to Julius by Burchard of Worms. It is preserved in the *Collectio hispana* 65.1 (HO01.053.03) and is found also in the collection of Pseudo-Isidore[87] and the *Collectio Lanfranci* (LA02.053.003). When he incorporated this text into his *Decretum* (BU05.001), Burchard identified it as a letter sent by Julius to the bishops of Egypt. With this attribution it entered most subsequent collections: the *Collectio burdegalensis* (BG05.001), Ivo's *Decretum* (ID02.011), and the first recension of the *Collectio XII partium* (TX06.158). The last work is likely the source of this quotation, again assigned to Julius, in the *De consecratione* of Gratian (D.2 c.7).

There is, however, another line of transmission in which U is identified as a decree of Pope Lucius to the Egyptian bishops. This attribution appears in the longer recension of the *Collectio XII partium* (TW05.170) and in a number of other collections that transmit just the first nine of the twenty sentences: Ivo's *Panormia* (IP01.146a), the *Collectio XIII librorum* of BAV, *Vat. lat. 1361* (AH09.091a), the *Collectio decem partium* (ZE01.45.02), and the *Collectio ambrosiana II* (MJ162).[88]

85. These are the *Collectio hispana* (HO02.009.04), the early twelfth-century *Collectio Sancte Genoveve* (GE01.04.093.02), and the *Collectio canonum* that begins on fol. 10v of BAV, *Vat. lat. 3829* (PG38.005).

86. On this manuscript and its presentation of this work, *v.* n. 68 above.

87. For this canon *v. CCEH*, vol. 2, coll. 630–32 (rpt. PL, vol. 84, coll. 587f.); for the same canon in the collection of Pseudo-Isidore, *v.* PL, vol. 130, coll. 589f.; *v.* also the online edition of Schon and Zechiel-Eckes.

88. In the *Collectio II librorum / VIII partium* (VB06.236) and the collection of

V. *Ecclesia Graecum* (JK †204)

These two sentences discuss the meaning of the Greek word *ecclesia* and the designation "catholic" as applied to the Church. The first is excerpted from Isid., *Etym.* (8.1.1), the second from his *Eccl. off.* (1.1.2f.). This, like O, P, R, and U, appears to have been first attributed to Julius by Burchard (*Decretum* 3.1), who assigns it to chapter five of a papal decree. There are nine clearly interrelated collections, all of which reproduce Burchard's reference to "chapter 5" of Julius' decree: the collection in Paris, Bibl. de l'Arsenal, *721* (AS03.001), the *Collectio Sancte Genoveve* (GE01.04.001), Ivo's *Decretum* (ID03.003) and *Panormia* (IP02.001), the *Collectio decem partium* (ZE02.01.01), part II of the collection in BAV, *Vat. lat. 3829* (PG38.002), the first recension of the *Polycarpus* (PX03.01.01), the first recension of the *Collectio XII partium* (TX05.006), and the augmented recension of the latter (TW04.006).[89]

W. *Si quis ecclesiam* [*igne*] *comburit* (JK †205)

This brief canon regarding the proper penance for arson in the case of a church building is found without attribution in penitential collections of the early ninth century, including two redactions of an anonymous *liber poenitentialis*.[90] It does not appear again until the early eleventh century, when it is found in Burchard's *Decretum* (BU03.204), the earlier recension of the *Collectio XII partium* (TW04.050/TX05.036), and the *Collectio sinemuriensis* in Semur-en-Auxios, Bibl. Mun. *13* (SM02.153). In all, it is introduced with the phrase *Ex decretis Iulii pp.* In the following centuries,

BAV, *Vat. lat. 3829*, part 2 (PG38.004), the entire twenty-sentence canon is quoted without attribution. In several others, abbreviated redactions are assigned to Julius:

1) sentences 2–12b in the *Collectio canonum* of Celle, Bibl. des Oberlandesgerichts, *C.8* (CE02.023);
2) sentences 1–11 in the first version of the *Collectio tarraconensis* (TO313);
3) sentences 10f. in the *Polycarpus* (PX03.09.01).

89. Several collections cite this, in slightly variant forms, as derived from the *Etymologies: e.g.*, the *Collectio IX librorum* in BAV, *Vat. lat. 1349* (FY06.001.01), the *Collectio hibernensis* in Rome, Bibl. Vallicell., *Tom.* 18 (HS43.01), and the *Collectio VII librorum* in Turin, Bibl. Naz. Univ., *D.IV.33* (TU04.001).

90. For W in the first recension of the *Liber poenitentialis ex scrinio romanae ecclesiae assumtus, v.* ch. *De diuersis capitulis* (rpt. PL, vol. 105, col. 700); for W in the second, *v.* ch. *De diuersis capitulis* (rpt. PL, vol. 105, col. 722). Though this canon appears in some manuscripts of Halitgar's penitentiary, Schmitz, regarding it as a later addition, excluded it from his text; *v.* also Hoffmann and Pokorny, p. 197.

it is taken into nearly thirty other collections, always under the name of Julius.[91] Among the *paleae* of Gratian's *Decretum,* however, it is assigned to Hyginus (Part 2, C.17 q.4 c.14).[92]

X. *Et hoc quoque / Aequaliter uir* (JK †206)

This item, dealing with the eligibility of possible marriage partners, consists of four sentences that, despite Jaffé and Kaltenbrunner's listing, are never found in a single consecutive text. While all four appear under the name of Julius in the first recension of Gratian's *Decretum,* they are there divided into two canons. The first consists of sentences one through three: 1) *Et hoc quoque statutum est ut … in matrimonium sumat* forbidding marriage to the widow of one's father, brother, or son; 2) *Relictam consanguineorum … in uxorem sumat* forbidding marriage up to the third degree; and 3) *In quarta autem … non separentur* allowing marriage in the fourth and fifth degrees (Part 2, C.35 q.2–3 c.12). The fourth *Equaliter uir … consanguineis uxoris suae,* recorded in an adjacent but separate canon, directs that some undefined statute should be applied to cases of marriage to relatives of one's own and to those of a deceased wife (c. 13).

Before Gratian, the sentences circulated in various combinations. In the late seventh-century *Penitential of Theodore* (2.12.26b–28), the rough equivalent of sentences three, two, and four are cited without attribution. It was apparently from that source that this redaction was taken into the eighth-century *Pseudo-Cummeanus Penitential,* also know as the *Excarpsus Cummeani* (3.3.B.24f.). In these, however, sentences three and two, while bearing a meaning similar to that of the equivalent sentences of the *Decretum,* are worded quite differently.[93]

In the early eleventh century, sentence four, previously unattributed in the penitentials, was taken into Burchard's collection and assigned to Ju-

91. In these collections, both the *incipit* (sometimes *comburit,* sometimes *igne comburit*) and *explicit* (sometimes *distribuat,* sometimes *tribuat*) appear in various forms. In Bonizo's collection, this passage is cited twice; at the first occurence (4.128) it is assigned to Julius, at the second (10.29) it normally bears no attribution; for the exception, *v.* Perels, *Bonizo,* pp. 173, 318.

92. The term *paleae* is used to refer to twelfth-century additions to the *Decretum.* It may derive from the Latin noun *palea, -ae,* meaning "chaff."

93. For the *Penitential* of Pseudo-Theodore of Canterbury, *v.* Wasserschleben, p. 216 and the translation by McNeill and Gamer, pp. 210f. For the excerpt in the *Pseudo-Cummeanus Penitential, v.* Wasserschleben, p. 474; on its origins and authorship, *v.* the discussion in McNeill and Gamer, p. 266f.

lius (BU07.007). It was then copied, with this attribution, into the first (TX08.004) and second (TW08.089) editions of the *Collectio XII partium,* into Mantua, Bibl. Com. *318* containing the recension of the *Collectio canonum* of Anselm of Lucca known as *A Aucta* (ADMantua 10.046a), into Bonizo's *Liber de uita christiana* (BO09.012), Ivo's *Decretum* (ID09.043), the first recension of the *Polycarpus* (PX06.04.09), the *Collectio VII librorum* of Vienna, Öster. Nationalbibl., *2186* (SV06.021.01), and the *Collectio Sancte Genoveve* (GE02.04.007.01).

Concurrently, the first three sentences began circulating as a unit in a form in which, though the second and third had the wording that would later be adopted by Gratian, the first began *relictam, i.e.,* without the first six words *Et hoc quoque statutum est ut* ("And it has also been established that"). In this redaction, X1–3 was usually attributed to Innocent I. It appears in the late eleventh-century recensions of the *Collectio canonum* of Anselm known as *A Aucta* (AD10.063) and *B* (AE10.061), the early twelfth-century collections *IX librorum* in Vatican, Archivio di San Pietro, *C.118* (DS08.01.099a), Anselm's recension *A′* (AB10.050), the *III librorum* (DR03.42.001), the *XIII librorum* of BAV, *Vat. lat. 1361* (AH10.050), and the second part of the collection in BAV, *Vat. lat. 3829* (PG43.025).[94] In all but the last, the unit is attributed to Innocent.[95]

Finally, in the late eleventh century, the first three sentences, introduced by the words *et hoc quoque statutum est ut,* appear in the *Collectio VII librorum* of Turin, Bibl. Naz. Univ., *D.IV.33* (TU05.194).[96] Here, still attributed

94. There are three recensions of recension *A* of Anselm of Lucca's *Collectio canonum: A,* the original text composed by Anselm; *A Aucta,* an expansion of *A* probably due to Anselm himself (died 1086); *A′,* a different expansion probably dating to shortly after 1123; *v.* Fowler-Magerl, pp. 139f., 218f.

95. The first sentence also circulated as an individual canon under the name of Innocent I in the late eleventh-century *Liber canonum diuersorum sanctorum patrum* (NO147.24) and Bonizo, *Liber de uita christiana* (BO09.024), and the twelfth-century collections, the *VII librorum* of Vienna, Öster. Nationalbibl., *2186* (SV06.021.02), the first versions of *Polycarpus* (PX06.04.05), the *Collectio caesaraugustana* (CA10.082a), and the *Collectio pragensis* (PR084). In the early twelfth century, sentences two and three also appeared as an independent unit attributed to Innocent in the first version of the *Collectio caesaraugustana* (CA10.082c). None of these sentences corresponds to anything in the genuine decretals of Innocent or in the Pseudo-Isidorian forgeries attributed to him.

96. This introductory clause is a formula frequently used to string together canons of similar content. It may well have been inserted by the copyist of the *Taurinensis.*

to Innocent, they follow directly after sentence four (TU05.193), which is attributed to Julius. Quite likely, this was the source used by the compiler of the twelfth-century *Collectio casinensis* (RO218), in which the fuller form of sentences one through three, found in the Turin collection, is, for the first time, attributed to Julius.[97] Gratian then appears to be the first to place the sentences in the order in which the unit of three sentences, in which sentence one has the longer form, precedes the unit of one sentence and to attribute all four to Julius.

Y. Attributions not noticed by Jaffé and Kaltenbrunner.

The following attributions to Julius found in the medieval western collections are the result of scribal error or other similar factors that did not eventuate in further misattribution.

1. *Rerum ecclesiasticarum et facultatum raptores a ... iude proditori comparatur*

This canon anathematizes those who have stolen church property. In the original recension of the *Collectio XII partium* (TX10.050), compiled in the early eleventh century, this canon is attributed to Julius, but in fourteen other collections, it is assigned to Pope Lucius. It appears to come from a letter of Charles the Bald.[98]

2. *Devotas in pascha in epiphania aut ... apostolorum diebus consecrandas*

In the original recension of the *Collectio XII partium* (TX03.256), this canon is attributed to Pope Vigilius, in the second (TW03.201), to Julius.

3. *Episcopi vero per singulas provincias observent ... nec ecclesiastice reputabuntur*

This canon commands bishops to ensure that their subordinate clergy not interfere in matters above their station or outside their parish. It cir-

97. The *Collectio casinensis* does not contain the fourth sentence. Fowler-Magerl does not note the *Collectio VII librorum* as a source for the *Collectio casinensis*, but it would be easiest to account for the attribution to Julius of X1–3 by assuming that the copyist of the *casinensis* misread the attribution in the *Collectio VII librorum*.

98. *V. Epistola II synodalis ad episcopos et comites Galliae, sub nomine Caroli regis* in Labbe, *Sacrorum conciliorum, etc.*, vol. 8, p. 246 (rpt. PL, vol. 124, col. 866c–d).

culated under the name of Pope Lucius in at least fifteen collections, the earliest of which is Burchard's *Decretum* (BU01.054). Yet, in the second recension of the *Collectio XII partium*, it is attributed to Julius (TW09.029).

4. *Licet itaque summo pontifici Romano tollere ... hec enim reperitur* (TO553.01) *Nec enim reperitur dominus fecisse specialem ... nisi soli isti* (TO553.02) *Hac itaque ostensione quam dominus noster ... per malorum intemperantiam* (TO554)

In the first recension of the late eleventh-century *Collectio tarraconensis*, these three canons follow two excerpts from L, both of which are attributed to Julius: 1) sec. 6, ll. 9–20 (*Qui sanctam Romanam ecclesiam primatum ... deo placite perficiant;* TO551); and 2) a sentence from sec. 8 (TO552). Of the three canons in Y^4, the first (TO553.01) is lacking in attribution, and the second (TO553.02) and third (TO554) are introduced by *et iterum* ("and furthermore"). As a result of this confusing arrangement, Fowler-Magerl lists Julius as the author of all three items in Y^4.[99]

5. *Si quis desiderat in ecclesia militare ... vice legatione funguntur* (SM01.074)

This excerpt derives from secc. 7f. of the Ps.-Isidorian *Constitutum Siluestri* and deals with the requirements for episcopal office and the respect due to bishops. It was taken into the *Collectio sinemuriensis*, where it is the third in a series of eight citations attributed to Julius (SM01.072–079). The other items, 1f. and 4–7 (SM01.072–73; 075–078), are all excerpts from N.[100]

99. In the second recension of the *Collectio tarraconensis*, the two excerpts from L and abbreviated redactions of the first two canons of Y^4 (TA06.095.001 = TO551; TA06.095.002 = TO552; TA06.096 = TO553.01; TA06.097 = TO553.02) are repeated with the same inscriptions as in the first recension. The third item of Y^4 is omitted (TO554).

100. I have correlated Fowler-Magerl's catalogue numbers with the relevant passages of Hinschius' edition:

1) SM01.072 = ch. 11, ll. 34–38;
2) SM01.073 = ch. 11, ll. 101–03;
3) SM01.074 = *Constitutum Siluestri* ch. 7, l. 1 – ch. 8, l. 8;
4) SM01.075 = ch. 12, ll. 17f.;
5) SM01.076 = ch. 12, ll. 80f.;
6) SM01.077 = ch. 16, ll. 10–15;
7) SM01.078 = ch. 18, ll. 5–9;
8) SM01.079 = ch. 19, ll. 10–12.

6. *Que sunt que intellectu divinarum scripturarum ... locis ordini intentioni* (HS39.19c)

The passage contains a dialogue between students and teacher about the proper understanding of Scripture. It comes from the second book of *De partibus diuinae legis libri II*, by the sixth-century North African, Junilius. In Rome, Bibl. Vallicell., *Tom. 18* (mid-ninth century), there is an expanded recension of the *Collectio hibernensis* containing this canon attributed to Julius. This, however, is a copyist's error, as Oxford, Bodl. Libr., *Hatton 32*, a manuscript containing the same recension, offers the proper inscription: *Iunilius ait.*

7. *Ut nemo presbyterorum xenium ... et hominibus contrarium est*

This canon warns clergy against allowing gifts or partisanship to pervert the proper administration of penance. It appears in a dozen medieval collections, always under the name of Pope Alexander. Yet in one redaction of the anonymous *Liber poenitentialis ex scrinio romanae ecclesiae assumtus,* this is identified as a decree of Pope Julius (*ex decretis Julii papae*). In another recension of the same work, however, the canon is attributed to Lucius I.[101]

Z. Μέγας κόπος and Οὐ δύναμαι (*CPG* #3593)

These excerpts, two redactions of the same material, are derived from a letter purportedly written to Julius by a patriarch of Jerusalem who requests that the pope command that the records of the Jews, transported to Rome by Titus, be examined for information regarding the days on which Christ was born and baptized. In the first, cited in a letter of John of Nicaea (*Natiu.;* late tenth-century) to Zacharias, Catholicus of Greater Armenia,[102]

101. For the first recension, *v.* Gallandi, vol. 12, p. 551 (rpt. PL, vol. 105, col. 708), for the second PL, vol. 105, col. 729. This canon is quoted also in Reg. Prum., *Disc. eccl.* 1.212, where it is attributed to a Council of Nantes; on the question of the historicity of a seventh-century council at Nantes and the quotation of its alleged acts by Regino, *v.* Scudamore, p. 60, and Halfond, p. 240.

102. The letter, transmitted in the fifteenth-century manuscript Paris, BN, *gr. 900,* was first edited by Combefis (1672). Coustant, who reprints (coll. 83–86) Combefis' text, notes (col. 83f.). that it was transcribed "*ex codice Regio olim 696. nunc 2428. pag. 149.*" The same text was reproduced by Mansi (vol. 2, coll. 1255f.), and Mansi's edition was taken over by Migne, who printed the entire letter among the works of John of Nicaea (PG, vol. 96, coll. 1441f.) and our excerpt (without the rest of the letter) in the appendices to the works of Cyril of Jerusalem (PG,

the patriarch of Jerusalem is identified as Cyril, whose first five years as bishop (349–54) coincided with the last five of Julius. According to Coustant, the second redaction was found on fol. 120 of the same manuscript, in a work entitled Ἀναγκαία διήγησις (*Necessaria narratio*).[103] It is introduced by a heading that describes the passage as an excerpt of a letter to Julius from Juvenal, Patriarch of Jerusalem. Juvenal, however, was bishop *ca.* 422–458, a century after Julius. Of all those catalogued in this Appendix, the first redaction of Z is the piece that might most plausibly be regarded as a genuine fragment of the correspondence of Julius I. Nonetheless, scholars from Coustant to the present, considering the lateness of the transmission and the unstable form of the text, have judged authenticity unlikely.

---

vol. 33, coll. 1207–10). There may be a different recension of this letter in London, Brit. Libr., *add. 34060* (15th c.), which incorporates (foll. 511–579) a portion of a twelfth-century manuscript that contains a "homily of Joannes, Archbishop of Nicaea, on the Birth of our Lord, *etc.*, but differing from that printed, after Combefisius, in Migne"; *v.* the online catalogue.

103. The piece was first edited by Cotelerius in the notes to *Const. apost.* 5.13 (vol. 1, p. 313; rpt. PL, vol. 1, col. 861); on Jean-Baptiste Cotelier (1627–86), *v.* the notice by Weber.

APPENDIX C

The Latin Version of Letter V

This edition of the Latin translation by Epiphanius Scholasticus (Cass., *Hist. trip.* 4.28) is based on the collation of seventeen manuscripts. Fifteen belong to the tradition of the *Hist. trip.* (C^{1-15}). According to Jacob's analysis, thirteen of the fifteen belong to family I, which falls into six subgroups: Ia (C^{1-4}), Ib (C^{5-8}), Ic (C^{9}), Id (C^{10}), Ie (C^{11}), and If ($C^{12,13}$). The fourteenth represents Jacob's family III, and the fifteenth, his family IV. The other two carry the letter amidst materials appended to copies of the *Decretals of Pseudo-Isidore* (P^{1-2}). For the shelf-marks of these manuscripts and further details, *v.* Appendix A, items C and P.

As groups *C* and *P* represent two different branches, I report all cases where these disagree, and both offer even a possibly meaningful reading. When there is dissension among the members of the *C* groups, I report the variants if 1) they are widely attested (*i.e.*, represented by more than two of these groups) and could retain the truth; and 2) if they could be bearers of the truth even if represented less extensively.

In addition to the readings of the manuscripts, I cite readings and emendations from the editions of Beatus Rhenanus (*Rhe.*), Garet (*Gar.*), and Jacob and Hanslik (*Hansl.*). I note all places where I depart from the reading adopted by *Hansl.* I do not cite Baronius or Coustant. The first provided only his own Latin translation of Socrates' Greek, the latter an eclectic Latin translation, in which he drew from the translations of Epiphanius, Baronius, and Valesius. For information on these editors and their editions, see sec. 6 of the Introduction.

As the obvious meaning of this Latin translation often differs somewhat from that of the Greek, I have adopted a policy regarding variant readings different from that found in the *apparatus* to the original Greek. There I provide a translation of the variants that offer a meaning substantially different from that of the received text, which is represented by the English translation. Here I translate first the received Latin version, then the variant.

My collations have resulted in some surprises. First, they show that branch *P* preserves correct readings not attested in the direct tradition. The most important, the accusative pronoun *ipsum* at l. 47 restores good sense to a passage garbled in the direct tradition. As *P* reports, Athanasius' flock have fed him "with life-giving letters"; according to the absurd reading of *C* they have nourished themselves. In addition, at l. 16 P^1 carries *praecepit* ("anticipated"). This, a literal rendition of the Greek προὔλαβε, is far closer in meaning to the Greek than the *praecessit* (= surpassed) of the *C* manuscripts and had already been conjectured by Hanslik. At l. 11, *P* carries the phrase *in integrum* ("completely") similar to the *ad integrum* conjectured by Hanslik. A phrase like *ad* or *in integrum,* because clearly adverbial, is preferable to the unaccompanied accusative *integrum* of most of the direct tradition. At l. 26, *P* carries *quod* ("because"), which may be the original; at any rate, *quod,* when causal, is sometimes glossed by *quia* in medieval manuscripts.

Second, I have found in stray representatives of the *C* groups two correct readings conjectured by earlier scholars: *ratione,* l. 51, conjecturally restored by Garet and printed by Hanslik, and *sartis,* l. 54, the expected form of the perfect passive participle of the verb *sarcio,* conjectured by Beatus Rhenanus. While the good readings carried by P^1 or *P* may well represent genuine tradition, those appearing in only one member of *C* are most likely scribal emendations.

The Latin Version of Letter V

Epistula Iulii, episcopi urbis Romae, ad presbyteros, diaconos, et populum alexandrinum

Iulius archiepiscopus presbyteris, et diaconibus, et plebi habitantibus Alexandriam, dilectissimis fratribus, in Domino salutem.

(1) Congaudeo uobis et ego, dilectissimi fratres, quoniam fructum uestrae fidei ante oculos iam uidetis; hoc etenim uere gestum quilibet inspiciet in fratre et coepiscopo nostro Athanasio, quem propter puritatem suae uitae et uestras orationes restituit uobis Deus. ex hoc itaque creditur puras et caritate plenas orationes uestras ascendisse semper ad Deum; memores enim estis promissionum caelestium atque dilectionis, quam ex doctrina praedicti fratris mei Athanasii didicistis, et in integrum cognouistis secundum insitam uobis fidem, quam percepistis, quoniam non usque ad finem is a uobis possit abduci, cuius orationes in sanctissimis animabus uestris tamquam praesentes semper habuistis. ergo non plurimis mihi uerbis opus est uobis scribere; quaecumque enim uobis a me potuerint dici, haec iam fides uestra praecepit et diuina gratia communis orationis nostrae uota compleuit. congaudeo siquidem uobis; *iterum* enim *dico*, congaudeo,[a] quoniam inexpugnatas animas in fide seruastis, sed etiam ipsi fratri meo Athanasio non minus congaudeo, quia, licet multam sit passus tristitiam, neque una hora uestri desiderii et caritatis oblitus est.

l. 3 archiepiscopus = *"Julius, archbishop"* : a. sanctae catholicae et apostolicae Romanae ecclesiae *P* = *"Julius, archbishop of the holy catholic and apostolic Roman church"* presbyteris, et diaconibus, et plebi habitantibus = *"to the priests, deacons, and laity of Alexandria* : pr., et d., et pl., omnibus h. *P* = *"to the priests, deacons, and laity, to all who live in Alexandria"* **l. 4** Alexandriam C^{5pc} : -dria C^{-6}, *P, Rhe. Hansl.* : in -dria C^{6}, *Gar.* **l. 5** Congaudeo uobis et ego : C. u. C^{Ib}, *P* **l. 12** in integrum *P* : integrum C^{-14}, *Rhe. Gar.* : ad int. *scr. Hansl.* **l. 14** possit : potuit P^{1} orationes : -m *P* **ll. 16f.** quaecumque . . . potuerint dici = *"whatever I could have said"* : q. poterunt d. *P* = *"whatever I shall be able to say"* **l. 17** praecepit P^{1} (precae-), *scr. Hansl.* = *"your faith has already anticipated whatever I could have said to you"* : per- P^{2} : pr(a)ecessit *C, Rhe. Gar.* = *"your faith has already excelled . . . to you"*

a. Phil 4.4

nam licet corpore ad tempus sit a uobis abstractus, tamen spiritu uobiscum[b] semper degere uidebatur.

(2) Et ego quidem, carissimi fratres, *omnem temptationem*[c] contra eum surgentem reor sine gloria non fuisse; nam et uestra et eius fides cognita est uniuersis[d] et comprobata. si enim non tanta et talia prouenissent, quis crederet quia aut uos tale iudicium tantamque caritatem circa talem exhibuistis episcopum, aut ille potuisset tantis circumdari uirtutibus, per quas spe caelesti fraudatus non est? promeruit igitur quolibet modo et nunc et in futuro etiam confessionis gloriosum martyrium.[e] frequenter enim terra marique plurimum aestuatus, omnem prauitatem arrianae conculcauit haereseos et, crebro per inuidiam usque ad periculum impulsus, contempsit mortem,[f] munitus omnipotenti Deo et Domino Iesu Christo saluatore nostro, sperans et inimicitias declinare et consolationi uestrae restitui, deferens uobis maiora tropea ex fortissima conscientia. pro quibus et *usque ad terminos terrae*[g] totius apparuit gloriosus; fiduciam itaque habens sui propositus caelestisque doctrinae, clarificatus est inmortali iudicio et a uobis reuertitur ‡ diligendus.

(3) Igitur apud uos clarior nunc est quam tunc quando profectus a uobis est; nam si materias pretiosas, id est aurum atque argentum, ad purgandum ignis probat,[h] quid dignum dici poterit de tali tantoque uiro, qui, cum tantas tribulationes et pericula

ll. 27f. non tanta et talia prouenissent : tan. et tal. n. p. *P* **l. 28** quia : quod *P* **l. 29** exhibuistis : exhibuissetis C^{5pc}, C^{14}, *Rhe. Gar.* **l. 34** conculcauit : calcauit *P* **l. 40** propositus : -iti C^{6-7}, C^{11pc}, *Hansl.* **l. 41** a uobis reuertitur ‡ diligendus *locus deprauatus? uidetur uerbum* reuertitur (=Ἐπανέρχεται) *e posteriore in priorem periodum esse transpositum* : ad uos C^{4}, C^{6-7}, C^{9}, *Rhe. Gar.* = "*he returns, worthy of love, to you*" reuertitur ‡ diligendus = "*he returns worthy of love*" : reuertitur diligentibus *P* = "*he returns to you who love him*" **ll. 44f.** quid dignum dici poterit = "*what will be appropriate to say*" : q. dignius dici p. *P* = "*what will be truly appropriate to say*"

b. *Cf.* 1Cor 5.3; Col 2.5. c. Lk 4.13 d. *Cf.* 1Thes 1.8; Rom 1.8.
e. *Cf.* 1Tm 6.12f. f. *Cf.* Heb. 12.2. g. Mi 5.4; Sir 44.23
h. *Cf.* 1Pt 1.7.

deuicisset, redditur nunc uobis immaculatus, non a nobis solummodo, sed comprobatus ab omni concilio? suscipite siquidem nunc, fratres carissimi, cum omni diuina <gloria> gratiaque pastorem uestrum ac praesulem tamquam uere Athanasium cum his qui tantis laboribus eius participes sunt effecti[i] et gaudete, fruentes orationibus, qui pastorem uestrum, ut ita dicam, esuritis atque sititis[j] quando etiam ipsum propter Sanctitatem Vestram salutaribus scripturis cibastis atque potastis; nam cum degeret in peregrinis, uos ei consolatio fuistis et in persecutione atque periculis refouistis eum fidelissimis uestris animabus et mentibus. ego siquidem iam exulto, considerans et ratione prospiciens in eius reuersione uniuscuiusque uestrum gaudium, et plebis uotiuas occursiones, et concurrentium gloriosam festiuitatem. et qualis ille uobis erit dies et quantus, remeante scilicet fratre meo, et quiescentibus priscis malis quorundam machinatione sartis, nec non et pretiosa ac uotiua reuersione cunctos in quadam plenissimi gaudii laetitia copulante. huiusmodi uero gaudium usque ad nos magnitudine sua pertingit, quibus diuinitus etiam hoc con-

l. 46 redditur nunc = *"he is now being restored to you"* : redditur *P* = *"he is being restored to you"* **l. 48** cum omni diuina <gloria> gratiaque : *suppl. Jacob ex A et Sc* (μετὰ πάσης τῆς κατὰ θεὸν δόξης καὶ [τε καὶ *Sc*] χαρᾶς) = *"welcome home your pastor and bishop … with all godly glory and grace"* : cum o. d. gratiaque C^{2-3}, $C^{5,8}$, C^{10}, C^{11ac}, C^{13ac}, *Rhe.* : cum omni diuina gratia $C^{1,4}$, C^{6-7}, C^{9}, C^{11pc}, $C^{12,13pc}$, C^{14}, C^{15}, *P, Gar.* = *"welcome … with all godly grace"* **l. 52** ipsum propter Sanctitatem Vestram *P* = *"since, on your own behalf, your Reverence even satisfied his hunger and thirst with life-giving letters"* : ipsi V. S. *C* = *"since your Reverence even satisfied your hunger and thirst … letters by yourselves"* : ipsum Sanctitas Vestra *coni. J.P.* = *"since your Reverence even satisfied his hunger and thirst … letters"* **l. 53** potastis = *"since your Reverence even satisfied your hunger and thirst"* : p. assidue *P* = *"since, on your own behalf, your Reverence even constantly satisfied his hunger and thirst* **l. 56** ratione C^{8}, *scr. Gar. Hansl.* : -abiliter C^{7} : -em C^{Ia}, C^{5}, C^{9-10}, C^{13pc}, C^{14-15}, *P, Rhe.* : oratione C^{6} : orationem $C^{12,13ac}$ **l. 60** machinatione = *"the previous troubles, contrived by the scheming of a few"* : -nibus *P* = *"… contrived by the schemings of a few"* sartis C^{14} (-es artis), *scr. Rhe.* : sarcitis C^{Ia}, C^{6-7} (-ce-), C^{9-11}, C^{If}, C^{15}, *Gar. Hansl.* : sarces(s)itis $C^{5,8}$ **l. 61** quadam : quo- C^{Ia-1}, $C^{5-7,8ac}$, C^{9-11}, C^{13}, C^{14}, C^{15}, *Rhe.*

i. *Cf.* 2Cor 1.7; Phil 3.10. j. *Cf.* Mt 5.6.

stat esse concessum, quatenus et nos debeamus ad laudem tanti uiri consurgere. sed melius est ut epistulam oratione claudamus.

(4) Deus omnipotens et huius unigenitus filius, Dominus et saluator noster Iesus Christus, hoc gaudium uobis praebeat in aeternum, dignum tribuens praemium ammirabili uestrae fidei, quam circa pontificem uestrum glorioso testimonio demonstrastis ut et uos et qui uobiscum sunt hic et in futuro meliora possideatis quae *oculus non uidit, nec auris audiuit, nec in cor hominis ascendit, quae praeparauit Deus* diligentibus se[k] *per Dominum nostrum Iesum Christum,*[l] per quem et cum quo omnipotenti Deo *gloria in saecula saeculorum. Amen.*[m] ualere uos opto, carissimi fratres.

l. 73 Deo = *"through whom be glory to almighty God"* : Deo una cum Spiritu Sancto *P* = *"… to almighty God together with the Holy Spirit"*

k. 1Cor 2.9
l. *Cf.* Rom 5.1, 11; 15.30; 1Cor 15.57; 1Thes 5.9.
m. *Cf.* 4Mc 18.24; Gal 1.5; Phil 4.20; 2Tm 4.18; Heb 13.21.

APPENDIX D

The Greek Version of Letter VI

The following edition of the Greek version of *ep.* 6 is based on two recensions, those of Athanasius and Sozomen (*v.* sec. 6 of the Introduction). Since A^2 and Sz^2 do not contain this letter, the *sigla A* and *Sz* will refer to the agreement of manuscripts $A^{1,3-5}$ and $Sz^{1,3,4}$. *N* (Nicephorus) is a fourth independent witness to the tradition of Sozomen. For Athanasius, I have consulted the editions of Commelinus, (*Com.*), de Montfaucon (*Mon.*), and Opitz (*Op.*); for Sozomen, those of Valesius, Hussey (*Hus.*^{2}) and Bidez/Hansen. For Nicephorus' transcript of Sozomen, I cite Ducaeus (*Duc.*). I cite also Coustant's (*Cou.*) edition of the Greek text in the *Epistolae romanorum pontificum.*

As I am attempting to reconstruct the text as it was translated by Athanasius, my edition follows very closely that of Opitz. From Sozomen's recension I have adopted only the possessive pronoun ἡμῶν omitted by the direct tradition (l. 3). The ancient witnesses actually carry the second person pronoun ὑμῶν, identical in sound to the form of the first person, to which the editors have routinely emended it.

Κυρίῳ, μακαριωτάτῳ Πάπᾳ, Ἰουλίῳ Οὐρσάκιος καὶ Οὐάλης.

Ἐπειδὴ συνέστηκεν ἡμᾶς πρὸ τούτου πολλά τε καὶ δεινὰ περὶ Ἀθανασίου τοῦ ἐπισκόπου διὰ γραμμάτων ἡμῶν ὑποβεβληκέναι, γράμμασί τε Τῆς Σῆς Χρηστότητος μεθοδευθέντες τοῦ πράγμα-

l. 2 συνέστηκεν : συνέστησεν *SzN* πρὸ τούτου πολλά τε : πο. τε πρὸ τ. Sz^3N
l. 3 γραμμάτων ἡμῶν *scr. Duc. Hus.*^{2} *Hans.*^{2} : γ. ὑμ- *SzN, Val.*^{2} : γ. *A* =“*in previous letters*” **l. 4** γράμμασί τε : γράμμασι *SzN*

τος χάριν, περὶ οὗ ἐδηλώσαμεν, οὐκ ἠδυνήθημεν λόγον ἀποδοῦναι, ὁμολογοῦμεν παρὰ Τῇ Σῇ Χρηστότητι, παρόντων τῶν ἀδελφῶν ἡμῶν πάντων τῶν πρεσβυτέρων, ὅτι πάντα τὰ πρὸ τούτου ἐλθόντα εἰς ἀκοὰς ἡμῶν περὶ τοῦ ὀνόματος τοῦ προειρημένου Ἀθανασίου ψευδῆ καὶ πλαστά ἐστι πάσῃ τε δυνάμει ἀλλότρια αὐτοῦ τυγχάνει· διά τε τοῦτο ἡδέως ἀντιποιούμεθα τῆς κοινωνίας τοῦ προειρημένου Ἀθανασίου, μάλιστα ὅτι Ἡ Θεοσέβειά Σου κατὰ τὴν ἔμφυτον ἑαυτῆς καλοκἀγαθίαν τῇ πλάνῃ ἡμῶν κατηξίωσε συγγνώμην δοῦναι. ὁμολογοῦμεν δὲ καὶ τοῦτο, ὅτι, ἂν ποτε ἡμᾶς οἱ ἀνατολικοὶ θελήσωσιν ἢ καὶ αὐτὸς Ἀθανάσιος κακοτρόπως περὶ τούτου εἰς κρίσιν καλέσαι, μὴ ἀπέρχεσθαι παρὰ γνώμην Τῆς Σῆς Διαθέσεως.

Τὸν δὲ αἱρετικὸν Ἄρειον καὶ τοὺς ὑπερασπίζοντας αὐτοῦ τοὺς λέγοντας, *Ἦν ποτε ὅτε οὐκ ἦν ὁ υἱός,*[a] καὶ ὅτι, *Ἐκ τοῦ μὴ ὄντος ὁ υἱός ἐστι,*[b] καὶ τοὺς ἀρνουμένους τὸν Χριστὸν θεὸν εἶναι θεοῦ υἱὸν πρὸ αἰώνων, καθὼς καὶ ἐν τῷ προτέρῳ λιβέλλῳ ἑαυτῶν ἐν τῇ Μεδιολάνῳ ἐπιδεδώκαμεν, καὶ νῦν καὶ ἀεὶ ἀναθεματίζομεν. ταῦτα δὲ τῇ χειρὶ ἑαυτῶν γράψαντες, ὁμολογοῦμεν πάλιν ὅτι τὴν ἀρειανὴν αἵρεσιν, καθὰ προείπομεν, καὶ τοὺς ταύτης αὐθέντας κατεκρίναμεν εἰς τὸν αἰῶνα.

Ἐγὼ Οὐρσάκιος, τῇ ὁμολογίᾳ μου ταύτῃ παρών, ὑπέγραψα· ὁμοίως καὶ Οὐάλης.

l. 8 εἰς ἀκοὰς : εἰς τὰς ἀ. *SzN* ἡμῶν : ὑμ- *A, Sz^{3}N, Cou. Com. Mon. Duc. Hus.^{2}* = *"everything that had previously come to your ears"* **l. 10** διά τε τοῦτο *A*: δ. τοι τ. *SzN* **l. 12** ἑαυτῆς : αὐ- *SzN* **l. 13** κατηξίωσε συγγνώμην : σ. κ. *SzN* ὁμολογοῦμεν δὲ : ὁμ. *A^{5}, SzN* ἂν : ἐάν *SzN* **l. 14** Ἀθανάσιος : Εὐσέβιος *Com.* (*Cf. Hus.^{2}*, "Εὐσέβιος *Athanasii codices" et Annotationes, p. 104.*) = *"the eastern bishops or Eusebius himself should … decide"* **l. 19** *ὁ υἱός* : Χριστός *SzN* (ὁ Χ.) = *"that Christ was created out of nothing"* **ll. 19f.** θεοῦ υἱὸν : καὶ υἱ. θ. *SzN* **l. 21** Μεδιολάνῳ : -ων *SzN* **l. 22** ἑαυτῶν : αὐτῶν *Sz^{3}N* **l. 23** ἀρειανὴν : ἀρειανικὴν *SzN* **l. 26** ὁμοίως : ὡσαύτως δὲ *SzN*

a. *Symb. Nic.* (325) b. *Symb. Nic.* (325)

INDEX SCRIPTURISTICUS

1) We regard as "scriptural" works that were read and regarded as authoritative in early Christian churches.

2) Bold-faced numbers indicate direct quotation (*i.e.*, verbal equivalences; *v.* sec. 10 of the Introduction); those in normal typeface all other citations, whether paraphrases, allusions, or *comparanda.*

3) Citations appearing within the letters and the critical notes to the ancient text are listed by *ep.* or *ep.* and subsection. An asterisk (*) following reference to a passage in a letter extant in both the original and an ancient translation indicates that the quotation or citation of the biblical passage is found in the translation as well as in the original; the parenthetical notation "(Lat.)" that the quotation or citation is likely or possible only in the translation.

4) Citations appearing in the Introduction, the introductions to the individual letters, and the explanatory notes to the translation are listed by the number of the page or page and footnote.

5) Verses cited in the critical and explanatory notes are listed separately even if they are also cited in the text of the work. Thus, the entry "*ep.* 1.3, **1 n. 8**" indicates that the same biblical passage (Nm 24.14) is, or may be, referred to in the third subsection of *ep.* 1 and is quoted in the eighth explanatory note to this letter. The abbreviation c. n. indicates a critical, rather than an explanatory, note.

Old Testament

Index scripturisticus

New Testament

INDEX OF MANUSCRIPTS

This index lists all the manuscripts mentioned in this work, both those used and those not used in editing the correspondence of Julius I. For the latter, I list all references. The former are followed by a parenthesis containing the *siglum* (*sigla*) by which they are designated in the critical notes. The reader will find a description of each of these in Appendix A, where they are listed in the alphabetical order of their *sigla*. This index does not contain references to the main entries in Appendix A and to the *Conspectus siglorum*. For other details of organization and abbreviation, *v.* the introduction to the General Index.

Index of Manuscripts

Index of Manuscripts

Index of Manuscripts

GENERAL INDEX

In the General Index, the order of reference is 1) to the general introduction, cited by page, then footnote number; 2) to the individual letters and their introductions. The former are cited by section numbers, the latter by page and footnote numbers. References to both the body of the page and to a footnote on the same page are joined by "and." Thus, under the heading "Alexander, Bishop of Alexandria," the sequence "p. lxix; p. 10, n. 17; *ep.* 2.3f.; p. 49, nn. 12, 14; p. 61, n. 31" refers to page lxix of the general introduction, note 17 on page 10 of the body of the volume, the text and translation of subsections 3 and 4 of *ep.* 2, notes 12 and 14 on p. 49, and note 31 on p. 61. While a reference to "p. xxix, n. 4" would indicate that pertinent information is to be found only in note 4, not in the body, of page xxix, the reference "p. xxix and n. 4" would point to information on the page and in the note. The more complex articles are subdivided, sometimes with a collection of general references followed by more specific subheadings. The subheadings are arranged by a variety of criteria: alphabetical, chronological, thematic; to facilitate reference we have sacrificed complete consistency of arrangement.

General Index

General Index

General Index

General Index

General Index

General Index

General Index

General Index

General Index

General Index

INDEX OF MODERN AUTHORS

We define as "modern" those authors active since the invention of the printing press. Figures of the earlier period are identified first by the Latin and then by the vernacular version of their names. Our term "author" is used broadly to include as well editors and scholars who may not have written anything. We have tried to catch all the places where an author's name appears but have not traced all those where he or his work is referred to without name; thus, in the immediate context of those contained in this index, the reader may find additional references to the same or another work by that scholar. For other details of organization and abbreviation, *v.* the introduction to the General Index.

Index of Modern Authors

Index of Modern Authors

Index of Modern Authors

Index of Modern Authors

Support for the
LIBRARY OF EARLY CHRISTIANITY
from the following donors is gratefully acknowledged

The Annenberg Foundation
Ave Maria School of Law
Christopher A. Beeley
The Gladys Krieble Delmas Foundation
Mr. and Mrs. Peter Flanigan/New York Community Trust
Herrick Jackson and Polly Jackson/The Connemara Fund
Rev. Richard T. Lawrence
The National Endowment for the Humanities
Mr. and Mrs. Michael Novak
Dr. and Mrs. Paul S. Russell
Mark Ryland
Sacred Heart School of Theology
The Cynthia L. and William E. Simon Foundation
The Strake Foundation

Michael J. Aquilina Jr.
Rev. William R. Deutsch
Rev. Gerard H. Ettlinger, S.J.
Everett Ferguson
Rose A. Frascello
Michael Gaddis
Craig L. Hanson
Rev. Stanley S. Harakas
Walter Harrelson
Daniel and Ann James
Joel D. Kalvesmaki
Adam Kamesar
Paul R. Kuhn
Henry Ciemniecki Lang, Ph.D.
Johan Leemans
Rev. Joseph T. Lienhard, S.J.
Samuel J. Mikolaski
Michael Mintz
Susan E. Myers
Rev. Karen L. Onesti
Rev. Dr. L. G. Patterson
Claudia Rapp
Michael Slusser
Louis Swift
Dr. Karen Jo Torjesen
Efthalia Makris Walsh, Ph.D.
Robert Wilde

ALSO IN THE LIBRARY OF EARLY CHRISTIANITY

JOHN F. PETRUCCIONE,
EDITORIAL DIRECTOR

THEODORET OF CYRUS

The Questions on the Octateuch, vol. 1,
On Genesis and Exodus (2007)

English translation with
introduction and commentary
by Robert C. Hill

THEODORET OF CYRUS

The Questions on the Octateuch, vol. 2,
On Leviticus, Numbers, Deuteronomy, Joshua, Judges, and Ruth (2007)

English translation with
introduction and commentary
by Robert C. Hill